Doctor Mary in Arabia

W9-DES-910

Middle East

Doctor Mary in Arabia

Memoirs by
Mary Bruins Allison, M.D.

EDITED BY SANDRA SHAW

Introduction by Lucie Wood Saunders, Ph.D., and
John Clarke Saunders, M.D.

 UNIVERSITY OF TEXAS PRESS   AUSTIN

Copyright © 1994 by the University of Texas Press
All rights reserved
Printed in the United States of America

First edition, 1994

Requests for permission to reproduce material from this work should be sent to
Permissions, University of Texas Press, Box 7819, Austin, TX 78713-7819.

∞ The paper used in this publication meets the minimum requirements of
American National Standard for Information Sciences—Permanence of Paper
for Printed Library Materials, ANSI z39.48-1984.

Library of Congress Cataloging-in-Publication Data

Allison, Mary Bruins, 1903–
    Doctor Mary in Arabia : memoirs / by Mary Bruins Allison, edited by
Sandra Shaw, introduction by Lucie Wood Saunders and John Clarke
Saunders. — 1st ed.
        p.   cm.
    ISBN 0-292-70454-2. — ISBN 0-292-70456-9 (pbk.)
    1. Allison, Mary Bruins, 1903– .   2. Missionaries, Medical—United
States—Biography.   3. Reformed Church in America—Missions—
Arabian Peninsula.   4. Reformed Church in America—Missions—
India.   5. Missionaries, Medical—Arabian Peninsula—Biography.
6. Missionaries, Medical—India—Biography.   I. Title.
R722.32.A45a3   1994
610.69′5′092—dc20
[B]   93-31393

Table of Contents

Preface

I write these memoirs in my retirement after almost forty years of practicing medicine in the Arabian Mission of the Reformed Church of America. A diary, copies of my letters, photographs, and reports to the Church remind me of events, but my memories are still vivid, or so it seems to me.

Many have undertaken to draw up an account of the things that happened in the Arabian Mission. The missionaries who preceded me (Samuel Zwemer, James Cantine, and Fred Barny) set down the early history. Dr. Paul Harrison wrote two volumes, mostly about medicine in Oman. Dr. Eleanor Calverley and Dorothy Van Ess described life in Arabia. John Van Ess wrote about the Iraqi Arab. Dr. Stanley Mylrea composed his excellent unpublished autobiography. But none of them lived through the astonishing changes that I saw. The journey of my soul was unique. Since I have the time and opportunity, I find quite unexpected pleasure in writing my bit of the history of the human race, and in trying to produce with words a creation that is distinctively my own.

E. B. White wrote, "Only a person who is congenitally self-centered has the effrontery and the stamina to write essays." The same surely applies to anyone writing an autobiography. However, to me it was an unusual and thrilling experience which I had for a life career. Dreams take me back to Arabia repeatedly.

Life is an amazing experience. I've always been surprised to find out what happens next. I've even been surprised by what I do that I didn't really intend to do. Memory is still more wonderful. How can I recollect so distinctly what happened sixty years ago? It's interesting to rethink, analyze, and write about it and wish I could live it over again without the errors. But nothing will ever be the same again, everything has changed, and it is time for me to retire.

What motivated me to choose this career? Growing up in a pastor's home, being part of a missionary church, and having uncles who were physicians sparked the idea that grew almost unconsciously. I don't understand why my two brothers did not feel the same calling. I felt I had been given great blessings, and that my only response to the Giver could be, "Take my life and let it be consecrated Lord to Thee." I wanted to follow the Master, heal the sick, and preach the Gospel which meant so much to me. If I'd been a boy I probably would have followed my father's profession as a minister, but that wasn't considered appropriate when I was young, so I chose the missionary and medical career as the next-highest vocation.

I was proud to be a member of the medical profession, with its great ideals of service to suffering humanity, its miraculous achievements, and its great practitioners. Even more I loved being a part of the Church's mission to Arabia and sharing in its solemn responsibilities. I want to tell of the wonderful people with whom I lived and worked, "the saints who from their labor rest." I hope to show the kindly Arab personalities I came to know; their generosity and hospitality as well as the sweetness and care of my Arab women patients, who took their suffering and sorrows without complaining. Then, I have to confess my own errors and shortcomings, for they were many.

This is the story of an era of great changes, of West meeting East in religion, customs, language, traditions, personalities, technology, and the care of the sick. The church of my fathers had begun a mission venture in Arabia in 1890 and had won the respect and gratitude of the then unknown, poverty-stricken Arab people. I arrived there while Arabia was still poor and saw it change to the richest per capita region in the world due to the discovery of oil. This is the story of Aladdin's lamp all over again, but this time the lamp has been given to a whole population instead of just one man. During the years 1934 to 1975 while I was in the mission field, medicine also made momentous changes which were as exciting in Arabia as they were at home. I just happened to be there to see and report a small part of the change which the Arabs say was the will of God.

The world asks what success the Arabian Mission and I had in promulgating the Gospel to the Muslim Arab. Perhaps an Arab can best say. A young Kuwaiti Muslim, Dr. Abdul Malek K. Al-Tameemi, wrote an unpublished 1977 doctoral thesis titled "The Arabian Mission: A Case Study of Christian Missionary Work in the Arabian Gulf Area." Dr. Al-Tameemi concluded that the mission was a failure because of the many difficulties it faced. The staff was too small, not more than thirty at any one time (and usually many fewer), while the Arabian population totaled almost 10 million. Finances were never sufficient. Other reasons examined to explain the mission's failure were geographic, social, political, and religious. The Muslim religion was firmly entrenched, for it was not only a religion, but also the basic framework of culture and government. Though Abdul Malek does not consider the truth of the Christian message, his thorough study of eighty-seven years of Christian mission is a remarkable tribute, by a Muslim.

It is said that Muslims cannot be converted. The great mission crusades have bypassed the Muslim countries. Truly we knew few Arabs who became Christians, and many who did convert later returned to Islam. The wonder is that there were any converts at all. Our practical age judges success by statistics and commodities. But there are other criteria in the Kingdom of Heaven, where failure is never final. The fact that the Church was there for so long, and is still there, is a triumph. It was not an "impossible dream," for with God all things are possible. Christ said, "All power is given unto me." Perhaps mission is intended to be presence, rather than proselytism—to be a seed planted and waiting to grow.

I loved the land and people of Arabia. In the style of the exiled psalmist, I too say:

> If I forget you O Jerry and Maurie, O Mirium and Lateefa
>   Let my right hand wither
> Let my tongue cleave to the roof of my mouth
>   If I do not remember you, O Mohammad and Musa.

M.B.A.

Introduction

This is the memoir of a remarkable American woman, one of the first women trained in medicine in the United States who chose to use her skills as a missionary doctor in Arabia.

When Dr. Mary Bruins Allison first went to Kuwait in 1934 she arrived in a very different country from that familiar to Americans today. She lived there through its transformation, then saw the beginning of similarly rapid change in Oman. During the forty years that she was a medical missionary, the practice of medicine also was altered profoundly. Here Dr. Allison tells of her experiences as she grew up in the Middle West early in this century, as a physician, and as a participant observer during a period of dramatic change in a part of the world that was unknown to most Americans when she first went there.

Kuwait was a small country with a mud-walled capital city on the shores of the Persian Gulf in 1934. Largely peripheral then to international economic and political concerns, the country declined during the nineteenth century in regional economic importance also. Earlier, Kuwait City had been a major port in the seaborne trade between India and the Middle East. Its shipbuilders were known for their design and craftsmanship, and Kuwaiti boats were capable of sailing as far as China, making Kuwaitis players in world trade. Kuwait also was famous for the pearls its divers brought up from the Persian Gulf. Merchants were the dominant group in the city, but prosperity rested also on the skills of shipbuilders and pearl divers. The Al Sabah dynasty had ruled the country since 1756, though it was nominally part of the Ottoman Empire.

Kuwait had lost its prominence in long distance trade before Dr. Allison arrived. Steamships ended the superiority of the Kuwaiti wooden ships and the economic basis of the country was weakened further during the 1920s by competition from cultured pearls developed in Japan. Deprived of its major resources Kuwait City was declining into a coastal town, isolated by its desert hinterland, dependent on small-scale trade, some pearling, and fishing. Agriculture was minimal because of the lack of rain and fresh water sources. The country could not support a large population, and most people outside the city were nomadic herdsmen who raised camels for subsistence and for sale for the transportation of goods and people. Kuwait's position politically reflected its economic weakness, and its rulers signed a treaty making it a protectorate of the British in 1899, a status it retained until 1961. Major international problems were boundary disputes with Iraq, which led to war in 1913, and in 1961 when independence came, as well as in 1990.

The population of Kuwait was relatively homogeneous during the first part of the century. Its people were Muslim with very few exceptions, and mainly Sunni, though there were some Shi'a from southern Iraq and Iran. Merchant families were the most wealthy, but there was not a wide cultural gap between different sectors of society. There were few public services; thus there was no sewage system in Kuwait City, and no public supply of drinking water, which had to be imported in goatskins and casks from Basrah in Iraq one hundred miles to the north. Neither were there hospitals or clinics, except that of the Arabian Mission of the Reformed Church in America established in 1911, and no secular education system. The predominating diseases during Dr. Allison's early years in the clinic reflected the absence of sanitary engineering; thus there was high infant mortality, trachoma, tuberculosis, and intestinal diseases. Care for the aged and sick was provided within the family.

An American and an Englishman, negotiators for oil concessions, were already in Kuwait City when Dr. Allison arrived, however, and she met them at a party given by one of the small number of foreigners living in Kuwait then. They made a deal with the ruler of Kuwait which gave their respective companies, subsequently partners in the newly established Kuwait Oil Co., exclusive drilling rights in return for an initial payment of $175,000 to the ruler, an annual rental of $35,000 during the years of exploration, and a royalty of $1.10 per long ton (Nyrop et al., 1977:92). The return to Kuwait was altered over the years. The drillers struck oil in 1938, but production was suspended until the end of World War II.

The impact of oil production on Kuwait was extraordinary. Revenues were paid to the rulers, thus the state amassed vast amounts of wealth and invested heavily in public works. The development of a water desalination plant was a priority, as was an adequate sewage system. Within two decades, the government also established a public education system that provided free schooling from kindergarten through university for Kuwaiti citizens and some foreigners, and a health care system which provided comprehensive coverage through a system of well-equipped hospitals and clinics. Kuwait City was partially torn down and rebuilt with international style office buildings, hotels, and restaurants. Oil revenues were redistributed to some extent among Kuwaiti citizens, and the wealth of the ruling family increased.

By the 1960s, the oil boom had brought Kuwaitis the highest per capita income in the world. Kuwait presently has the largest share of known oil reserves, which are expected to last until the end of the first decade of the twenty-second century at the present pumping rate. The finite nature of oil resources led the Kuwaiti government to support diversification through fisheries, irrigation agriculture, and petroleum-related industries, but these businesses remain small compared to oil. Air and sea pollution increased greatly with oil production. Oil also catapulted Kuwait into a new position in world politics, first made clear after the Iraqi invasion in 1990, when Kuwait's importance as an oil producer enabled it to secure immediate support from the United States and Europe.

The foreign population of Kuwait increased dramatically during the oil boom as the government hired large numbers of people to initiate development quickly. In addition to Iranians and Iraqis who were long established workers in Kuwait, Palestinians came and Egyptians as well as Indians; the oil companies brought their own skilled personnel into company communities. Foreign workers remained distinct from Kuwaitis; politically, neither they nor their descendants were allowed to become citizens, except in most unusual circumstances, unless they could prove the arrival of ancestors in Kuwait before 1921. Foreigners were segregated residentially when Kuwait City was rebuilt, but the level of pay continued to make their situations attractive. Foreign professionals designed the water desalination plant and the infrastructure for a modern city, while foreign laborers provided most of the work force. They established the education system and staffed the schools, set up the health care system which they also staffed, and established newspapers. They added different national and religious elements to the population of Kuwait, as Dr. Allison saw in the new congregations in the mission chapel, which came to include Christian Palestinians as well as Americans and Europeans. She also tells of cooperation then estrangement from the recently trained government hospital staff.

Dr. Allison also practiced medicine in other mission clinics during and after her assignments in Kuwait. She was in India during World War II, where she went to be with her English husband, who had been with the oil company in Kuwait. Later, she was at the mission in Qatar briefly and for a longer period in Bahrain. She tells us something also of her observations in these countries, particularly Bahrain, where oil had been discovered earlier than in Kuwait, and in much smaller quantity, with apparently somewhat less disruptive effects on society. Her longest stay outside of Kuwait was in Oman, which she visited briefly in 1949, and she returned there to work in 1971 after her retirement. Health conditions and care in Oman were similar to those in Kuwait when she first went there, except that Oman had many leprosy cases. Oman was at the beginning of a period of accelerated change. An independent country for most of its history, it had been organized into tribes which acknowledged the overarching authority of an elected iman, or religious and political leader. During the eighteenth century, the office was won by an ancestor of the present ruler, and the rulers became sultans, emphasizing political rather than religious authority and succession within their family. In 1970, there was a successful coup d'etat by the sultan's son, who was interested in modernizing the country by detribalizing it, developing a health care system, developing a secular education system, and creating an indigenous professional group which would include women. These changes were funded by oil wealth, though Oman's reserves were much smaller than those of Kuwait, and Dr. Allison comments on some of them as well as on the extraordinary beauty of the varied landscape of Oman, and the people she met.

This book also tells us something about American women's

lives earlier in this century, about Dr. Allison herself, and the perspective from which she saw Arab women of the Gulf states. The outstanding characteristic of her life is her unwavering pursuit of her goal of relieving suffering, thereby manifesting her Christian faith. The daughter of a minister, her understanding of her religion and the conviction of her faith grew with her from early childhood. She went to college in the town where she grew up and lived at home with her stepmother, father, and half-brothers. Later when she went to medical college in Philadelphia, she continued to see members from her denomination occasionally and sometimes the missionaries to Arabia whose books introduced earlier generations of scholars and others to the Gulf region. She never wavered in her commitment to medical missionary work, a life she decided upon when she was very young, and certainly about the choice at the core of her being, which must have conveyed satisfaction in her sometimes lonely life.

Dr. Allison is also an intrepid woman who did not hesitate to go into difficult and thoroughly unfamiliar situations, whether delivering babies in poor homes in Chicago or attending the wives of the Kuwaiti royal family. Resourceful, intelligent, and with a sense of humor, she was able to work effectively in all kinds of situations and tells interesting stories about them. She worked hard most of her life, because she had such large numbers of patients whom she had to treat with very little staff assistance. Like many physicians, she grieved deeply over her mistakes, but the patients lost were rare in comparison to the two hundred or more people she might treat in a day. She sought additional training when she had leaves and consultation at every opportunity. Her un-airconditioned summers in the intense heat of Kuwait must have tried her ability to cope, and one enjoys with her the delight of swimming in the Gulf, the occasional social events in the foreign community, and the celebrations in the homes of wealthier Kuwaitis which gave her opportunities for a closer look at Kuwaiti life.

Dr. Allison's experiences also give us a glimpse of American women of her time and place. Born in 1903, education was available to her and her pursuit of a career was unusual but not extraordinary. Other women of her generation became scholars, teachers, and presidents of women's colleges, finding achievement easier in fields that required specific training than in business. Many, like the wives of the missionaries in Kuwait, pursued active careers that they shared with their husbands. While such women preferred marriage, that was not their primary goal, as it seemed to become for a later generation of college-educated American women. For women of Dr. Allison's generation, education was a privilege that prepared women for specific roles which could not be dropped easily with marriage.

Dr. Allison's career was facilitated by family support. There was never any question about whether she should go to college. Her goal of becoming a physician and medical missionary was encouraged, and money from her relatives enabled her to go to Woman's Medical College in Philadelphia, the goal of many young women of the time. Women of her generation were usually the first or at most second generation of women educated in college. Those from prosperous families were able to go into professional or academic careers, while women from other families went into work that required less post-college training.

Dr. Allison saw Kuwait through the eyes of a physician and an intelligent Christian woman, thus she expresses great sympathy for the pain and suffering of her patients. She was always aware of her differences from them as a physician sent to provide care for those in need, and her empathy with them may have been greatest in sharing their times of pain. She did not force her religion on people, but she was genuinely surprised when those women she felt closest to showed no interest in it. Her convictions did not allow her to see their basic similarity to her in that they also had grown up in a religion which they never questioned. On the other hand the cultural contrast which she saw in Kuwait and elsewhere was of great interest to her, and she was a keen and honest observer whose findings about women have been replicated by students of other Arab societies.

Dr. Allison's accounts of women show how their lives began to change in Kuwait during the oil boom. Her work is unique in giving a longitudinal perspective on their lives from the perspective of a woman observer. She saw poor women mainly in the clinic, but she occasionally visited women from the merchant and royal families. Town women were secluded, i.e., they stayed at home as much as possible; poorer women had to go out but richer women did not, except on occasional visits to other women; nomadic women moved about much more freely. Rich women usually managed large households that might include children, sons' wives, and husbands' mothers as well as servants and even household slaves when Dr. Allison first went to Kuwait. These women spent their lives in groups of other women with whom they competed or cooperated for household goods of all kinds, including a husband's attention if they were co-wives, though the rule was that a husband should treat wives equally. They were not passive personalities. At home, they might control other women and at the clinic they were sometimes demanding and almost aggressive.

The change these women experienced with oil wealth was the opening of the world to them, especially to the women of the royal and wealthy families. With a husband's permission, and accompanied by family, they were able to travel everywhere and they spent lavishly for European clothes to be worn to women's parties and for luxuries of all kinds. Their household lives remained structurally unchanged and their relations with their husbands changed little despite appearances. They might spend summer vacations in Europe or in the mountains in other Arab countries and manage their households from a distance in important matters such as hiring a cook. Their daughters, like the daughters of all Kuwaiti citizens, were being educated. Some daughters of the rich and royal families were being educated in Europe and the United States, but when they returned home, they faced the problem of whether their lives would be enclosed within their families or open to wider social spheres. Dr. Allison notes that some of these younger women had opened boutiques when she last visited Kuwait, some taught at the women's university, and a few were in government ministries.

The oil boom brought other Arab women to Kuwait, especially Palestinians and Egyptians who came as professionals themselves or as the wives of professionals. All differed from the Kuwaitis in that they were not accustomed to seclusion or veiling, though they were like them in being deeply enmeshed in their families and in being circumspect in their behavior with men, so their social groups also were made up of women. Another group of women in Kuwait was made up of nurses from India, some of whom were recruited for the Arabian Mission before the oil boom, and others who came to work in the new hospital because most Arab women did not regard this as appropriate work for them.

Dr. Allison shows diversity among women in pre-oil Kuwait

on the basis of wealth and social position; national origin and religion were differentiating factors later. She also saw diversity in Oman, where national modernization policies proceeded so rapidly that television newscasters were women by the late 1970s. Later studies of women in different Arab societies also show variations in women's work, involvement in the public sector, and seclusion. There is variation in Muslim Arab countries in the extent to which countrywomen work outside the house in paid or unpaid labor in agriculture, as well as variation in the roles of educated women. In Egypt, for example, women work in the modern sector as physicians, engineers, professors, social workers, and artists, but these roles are associated with little or no reduction in familial responsibilities. Elsewhere, in other Muslim societies, there are reports of greater wealth increasing seclusion, especially in rural communities, where it was regarded as prestigious to stay in and be free of work outside. In recent years, women's seclusion and veiling appear to increase with the impact of fundamentalist religious movements. On the other hand, contemporary Arab feminists search for ways for women to define themselves that are not necessarily Western but contribute to the development of a new sense of identity that is forged within fresh interpretations of Islam.

Another important characteristic of Dr. Allison's book is the demonstration she gives of how a religious person acted in her time. Her faith oriented her toward the world, leading her to train herself to help others. While she often reflects on her experiences, her beliefs never led her to turn inward in a search for self-fulfillment; rather they pushed her toward a life of helping others whom she introduces to us.

Dr. Allison's book is also about the practice of medicine during the 1930s and afterwards in communities with limited medical care. Her understanding of her mission reminds us that religion and medicine have been closely intertwined during much of human cultural history. Modern medicine and most religions separate the two, in method and theoretical orientation, but the vocation of medical missionaries recalls the older linkage. A basic orientation in medicine during the first part of this century was that the physician was charged with alleviating disease while doing no harm, a guiding principle that Dr. Allison certainly applied as she delivered babies, and treated people for parasites and infections or burns and wounds. In more recent practice, medicine has tended toward curing the disease process without adequate consideration of the untoward effects the cure may bring. Such an approach might have been less effective in the circumstances of her early practice.

One of the striking features of Dr. Allison's practice was that people were so eager for her help. The large numbers of patients who came daily to the clinic attest to the success of the earlier medical missionaries in relieving distress and teaching the value of medicine. It would be interesting to know whether the desire for medical care was universal among Kuwaitis, but the fact that she treated nomads, townspeople, rich and poor suggests that it was. This would indicate that she was not hampered in her practice by folk cures, though she recalls instances in which ignorance of causes of disease led some patients to misunderstand the treatment process. We do not know whether or not she supplemented medicine with folk cures as she became more familiar with Kuwaiti culture. In ideas about health and disease held in other countries, one must remember that in the 1930s, when Dr. Allison was in medical school, there were many fallacies in popular thinking about disease in the United States. There must have been fallacies in Kuwait as well, and fallacies never end!

Today in the United States, for example, we find the common belief that vitamins reduce the need for food, thus enabling people to stay thin. People do not understand that vitamins only make food metabolism more efficient: therefore both are needed. Dr. Allison realized in her Kuwaiti practices that most important of medical practices everywhere: instruction. In this way, as public health educators in the United States are doing today, she helped people learn more about causation and therapy in general as she and her patients dealt with a particular disease.

When Dr. Allison first went to Kuwait, she was confronted with many victims of infectious diseases. If she had returned in the 1980s, she would have found more patients suffering not from infections, but from organic degenerative diseases. But if she were to return in the 1990s, she would be likely to find bacteria and viruses that have mutated and an era of microbial resistance at hand. Dr. Allison exulted in the benefits of the developing era of antibiotics after beginning her practice without them; but we now see decline and sudden death caused by drug-resistant mutations with the likelihood of hospitals as a source of drug-resistant disease.

During this century, medicine has been transformed by the development of theory and practice at the biochemical and molecular levels. Pre-twentieth-century ideas about medicine had been based on concepts that developed historically, many of them derived from medical practice and theory that had been introduced to Europe by the Arabs. Modern medicine seeks to understand disease process at the levels of biochemical and molecular functioning, a perspective that has revolutionized thinking about disease and health, but one which was not considered in Dr. Allison's period of training. New theory and practice emerging from this perspective have led to the elucidation of diseases which had been treated symptomatically, and even to the understanding that mental disorders such as depression have a biochemical basis. Dr. Allison tells us how fascinating all this was for her when she returned to the university during her leaves.

The twentieth century is marked also by the development of medical technology and the expansion of successful hospital treatment of disease. Post-oil Kuwait reflected this change dramatically. The development of the health care system involved the establishment of a modern hospital with the most sophisticated equipment and a highly trained staff. This, combined with the impact of sanitary engineering, made the incidence of some conditions comparable to or lower than in the United States in 1990. Maternal mortality rates, for example, were reported during the 1980s to be 4 per 100,000 compared to 8 per 100,000 in the United States; mortality of children aged 1 – 4 in Kuwait was 0.7, and 0.4 in the United States (United Nations, 1991:67).

As a medical missionary, Dr. Allison shows how knowledge attains ethical value and human significance when it is applied. She also tells us about Kuwait and the other places she worked as they were and as they changed. Readers meet here a remarkable woman whose life leads us to reflect on our own and whose company it is a pleasure to keep.

LUCIE WOOD SAUNDERS PH.D.
JOHN CLARKE SAUNDERS M.D.
September 21, 1992
Upper Nyack, New York

REFERENCES

Nyrop, Richard, et al. 1977. *Area Handbook for the Persian Gulf States*. Washington, D.C.: U.S. Government Printing Office.

United Nations Department of Economic and Social Affairs. 1991. *The World's Women, 1970–1990*. New York: United Nations.

Timeline of Events

	1929 U.S. Stock market crash Great Depression begins
1932 Internship at Wisconsin General Hospital, Madison, Wisc.	
1933–1934 Arabic study with Calverleys at Hartford Theological School	
1934 Second internship, University of Illinois, Chicago Ill. Arrival in Kuwait	*1934* Oil concession granted to joint U.S./British enterprise, forming Kuwait Oil Co. Ltd.
1937 Marriage to Norman Allison	
1939 Car trip through Europe and Asia Minor to Kuwait	*1939* Hitler invades Poland; World War II begins
1940 Follows husband to India	
	1941 Japan attacks Pearl Harbor and British outposts in Asia; U.S. enters the war
1942 Returns to U.S. Medical practice in New Jersey	*1942* Kuwait wells plugged, drilling suspended for duration of WW II
1943 Rejoins husband in India Decision to divorce	
1943–1945 Work at Dahanu Road Mission Hospital India	
1945 Return to Kuwait medical practice	*1945* End of WW II German surrender Atomic bombs dropped on Japan Japanese surrender
1946 Oil drilling reinitiated, Kuwait First oil exports from Kuwait	
1948 Partition of Palestine	

1948 State of Israel
proclaimed War in
Palestine/Israel

1950–1951 Furlough in U.S.

1950 Shaikh Abdullah as-
Salim begins to lay the
foundations for the
Kuwait welfare system,
including extensive
provision of free medical
care for citizens

1956 Decision to merge men's
and women's hospitals in
Kuwait

1956 Suez Crisis

1957–1958 Furlough

1958 Hospital board formed to
facilitate input from
Kuwaiti citizens and
government
Kuwait City's old walls
bulldozed

1959 Full mission meeting in
Kuwait

1960 Hospital merger
completed

1961 Kuwait terminates
protection agreement
with Great Britain
Kuwaiti independence
declared
Iraq threatens invasion;
Britain sends troops from
Kenya

1964 Medical malpractice
complaint

1964–1965 Furlough in U.S.

1965 Transfer to Bahrain

1967 Kuwait medical mission
closes

1967 Arab-Israeli War. Kuwait
supports Palestinians and
other Arab combatants;
adheres to oil embargo of
U.S. and G.B.

1970 Retires from Bahrain; return to U.S.

1970 His Majesty Sultan Qaboos bin Sa'id takes power in Oman; establishes a domestic development program, including provision for medical care

1971 Sent by Mission Board to Oman

1973 Easter: return visit to Kuwait
Oman government takes over mission hospital

1973 Arab-Israeli War. Kuwait contributes both troops and financial aid to the war effort, and calls for reductions in oil production and price increases to pressure Western supporters of Israel, especially U.S. Kuwait provides major support for Palestinian guerrilla groups. Oil price rise leads to economic boom for oil-exporting economies, particularly in Gulf States.

1974 OPEC oil price increase announced

1975 Leaves Gulf for retirement in Redlands, Calif.

Mary Bruins (age 10), Paul (age 7), and
Richard (age 4), 1913.

Second Reformed Church, Pella, Iowa (Mary's home church).

Mary Bruins Allison, M.D., 1942

Women's Mission Hospital, Kuwait, 1950.

Typical interior of Arab home: hareem and cistern.

Kuwait bazaar, Old Market Place.

Arab children at front of hospital.

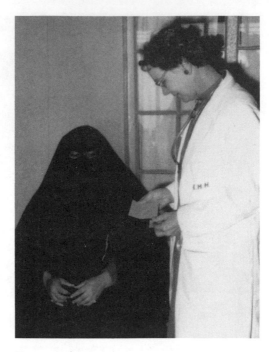

Woman at clinic with Dr. Allison, 1938.

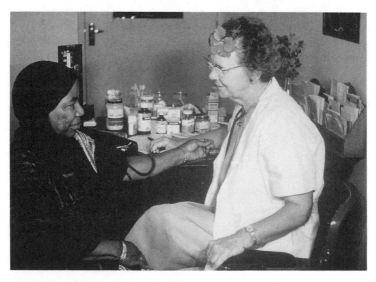

Woman at clinic with Dr. Allison, 1955.

Women's clinic: Dr. Allison, Helper Beebe (center), and Nurse Bhagyamma (right).

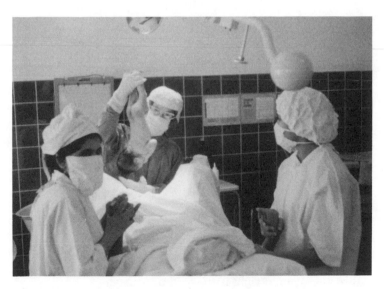

Delivery of a baby, Dr. Allison and Indian nurses.

Baluchi women at Oman Hospital; woman in center is a hospital helper.

Muscat, Oman; at right is the road to Mutrah.

Doctor Mary in Arabia

1. Early Life

It wasn't until I was ten that I was told the story of my real mother.

My parents met while my father was at college in Holland, Michigan. He boarded with my mother's family, the Huizingas. Henry Bruins and Mary Huizinga fell in love and became engaged, but after he graduated my father went off to study for the ministry at Princeton Seminary.

Mary waited for him for seven years. Henry had won a prize for his thesis, which he used to study in Scotland and Germany and to tour Europe by bicycle with a friend. But he was faithful and came back to marry my mother. They moved to Pekin, Illinois, for their first pastorate at the Reformed Church.

Mary wanted to go back home to Holland, Michigan, to have her first baby so that her two brothers could deliver her. Dr. Tom and Dr. John Huizinga had been so successful in practice. After a normal delivery on March 19, 1903, serious infection set in. My mother died ten days after my birth. My father's distraught letters to his sister Hannah reveal his broken heart and tell what happiness had been theirs. I read them over when I was an adult, after I had become a physician.

Aunt Jennie Bruins came to keep house for my father and care for me. In July 1904, after more than a year, my father married Lillian Fastenau, who had been singing in his choir. She was a pretty, dark-haired girl with a lovely soprano voice. Lillian came from the German Missouri Lutheran Church, so my father thought it would be easier for them to start work in a different church. He accepted a call to the Presbyterian Church at Albert Lea, Minnesota.

Lillian Fastenau was a good mother and took very good care of us. It was given to me to have a happy childhood with good and wise parents who loved each other and made a success of parenting. I was the heir of a proud family in a prosperous land at a thrilling time to be alive.

My first conscious memories go back to our home in the town of Albert Lea, Minnesota, about 1907 when I was four years old. Family pictures show me to have been a healthy, attractively dressed child usually with tousled hair. Some show my baby brother Paul and me, sitting in the wide swinging seat on our front porch, in a family group of relatives who came to visit us. We lived in the manse beside the Presbyterian Church where my father was pastor.

I had a variety of toys and a playroom with a wallpaper border of children's playthings. Mother told me that I was a very active child always asking, "Mama, what am I going to do next?" Fortunately, she had been a school teacher and knew how to handle such questions.

I had an early desire to roam. My parents tried tying me to a tree, so I wouldn't be run over. In those days, the fire engine horses were dashed through the streets for exercise, and the tether was the only way to keep me safe. One time, I disobeyed the family rule and crossed the street to play with another child. My father came for me, sternly ordering, "Mary, come home at once." He held my hand as we walked home and I asked, "Papa, are you going to spank me?" The rod was not spared in our rearing.

Once when Grandpa and Grandma Bruins came for a visit, my father gave them a tour of the church building. I followed and was amusing myself running between the pews. They left, thinking that I had gone out, and locked the door. A desperate fright seized me with a feeling of solitude, silence, and forsakenness. I screamed and wept until they missed me and came to rescue and comfort me. It was a foreshadowing of a feeling which would come back again often in my life but has always been relieved so far. I am fortunate to have an optimistic, happy temperament and am very determined. As one of the British ladies in Kuwait later told me, "Mary, you have a sort of a mulish character." I'm sure she was right.

This mulishness showed up early. My father made his pastoral calls on a bicycle and used to take me along, seated on the handlebars. One time we stopped for ice cream. He ordered strawberry for both of us. I declared I wanted chocolate and stubbornly refused to taste the strawberry ice. I still regret my ingratitude. I knew I was wrong. A sense of sin came early and stings still, or I wouldn't have remembered it all these years.

Sometime in 1907 my father accepted a call to be the minister at the First Reformed Church in Milwaukee, Wisconsin. I don't remember moving, but the change in location when I was four reminds me what had happened by that time.

MILWAUKEE CHILDHOOD

The beautiful church building in North Milwaukee, at 1015 Harmon (now Brown) Street had lovely art glass windows. I can still see them in my mind's eye, one a large window of Christ and the Children. Two others I loved were the Boy Christ with the Elders, and another of the Good Shepherd. Tragically, they were all destroyed years later when the church area was taken for a freeway.

As a child, my world was bounded by the church and our neighbors, many of whom were of Dutch descent and members of my father's congregation. We felt free to visit all the neighbors who attended our church. On Sunday afternoons we went calling to eat treats and collect the funnies. Hawkshaw the Detective and the Katzenjammer Kids became our regular Sunday literature.

One neighbor family had four children about our ages. We all soon acquired roller skates and spent Saturdays ranging the territory, zipping down hills and coming home with our long black stockings in tatters. As we grew bolder, we would skate to the downtown library past the Schlitz Brewery. Fortunately for us, traffic was very light in those days.

Some of the neighbors didn't live like us. One stout woman had many children and didn't seem to keep house like our mother. She was delighted to talk to anyone about fascinating things that were never discussed in our family. Saloons and drinking were also common, though my family did not live that life either. Some families went regularly for a pailful of beer at mealtime. The father of a little boy who lived across the street ran a saloon. The son had to take his father's lunch there daily. Once my brother Paul went along with him. He took a long time, and my father finally asked me, "Where is Paul?" Of course I knew, and led Papa to the saloon where the two children were eating pretzels at a table. My father strode in and dragged Paul out by the ear, making plain his disapproval.

Another family, two maiden ladies and a brother, was Roman Catholic. One of the sisters went to early mass every day. The brother occasionally used to get drunk and noisy.

The neighborhood had been Dutch but it was becoming predominantly Jewish. I played with some of the Jewish children, but quite early I felt it was my duty to talk with them about the superiority of our religion.

One day my brother, his friend, and the janitor's son were discussing who owned the church. The janitor's son claimed his father did, because he took care of it. The friend claimed that his father did, because he ran the church before we came. But we knew our father was chief and certainly owned it.

I was sent to kindergarten at the Lloyd Street School when I was four and attended for two years because children had to be six before entering first grade. It was a short walk to school. Across the street from the school there was a shop with the most delectable items: all-day suckers, long black strings of licorice, and toffee apples for a penny apiece. We were given as many pennies per week as we were years old, but that didn't go as far as my desires.

My moral education began early. My father used to keep a box of coins from church offerings on a shelf in his study. He told me it belonged to God. I asked, "How do you get it up to God?" He answered me casually, "We send it to the Board." I had seen builders raising a board on pulleys, which didn't seem a safe way to send money. But of course big people know everything. One evening when my parents were out, I climbed up on a chair, secured a handful of the coins, and hid them behind my bed. My mother found them the next morning while cleaning. That day when I came home from school, my father took me on his lap and reasoned with me about the money. I agreed with his reasoning and there was no punishment. But the Tempter returned. I went to the study again at night, pulled up a chair, and climbed up to the shelf. Then conscience took over. I decided it was wrong and went back to bed, leaving the incriminating chair in place. Next day my father asked, "Mary, did you take some more money?" I protested, "No, I thought about it. I didn't take any more." It seems my father believed me.

Another time, a neighbor asked me to go get a bottle of milk from the store and gave me money. The store had candy. The Tempter suggested that this wasn't God's money and I yielded. When I met the lady, I blandly explained that the heavy bottle slipped out of my hands and broke. I wonder whether she believed me. I was the minister's daughter and was supposed to be honest.

When I was six, I started first grade. We gave Miss Marks, our Jewish first grade teacher, veneration more appropriate to higher beings. Under her tutelage I quickly learned to read. Arithmetic was uninteresting, so I ignored it until one month I had failure in it on my report card. My father cared enough to type out the multiplication tables for me, and from then on I had to recite them to him every evening until I knew them. We had German lessons for a half hour daily. For some reason, I disliked it. My father had to go to the city hall to get a permit to excuse me from that subject. He was an indulgent parent.

From early childhood, my parents taught us a love of books. Before we could read, my mother kept us enthralled by reading aloud from *Alice in Wonderland, Robinson Crusoe,* and the *Swiss Family Robinson.* We had many magazines in our home, like *Ladies Home Journal, Life,* and *National Geographic.* I dug into my father's library as soon as I could read. *Pilgrim's Progress* had such exciting pictures. Later, I tackled the *Confessions of an English Opium Eater, Sartor Resartus,* Lord John's *Beacon Lights of History,* and the series of the *World's Best Poetry.* My father took out library cards for us, so Paul and I used to skate to the public library every Saturday to get a new book for each of us. I loved the Oz stories, the Elsie Dinsmore series, and the Five Little Peppers books.

As pupils, we considered our public school much superior to the Catholic parochial school. We had sewing classes in the fifth and sixth grades and cooking in the seventh and eighth. We usually liked our teachers. One of them drew me aside and asked, "Did you send that valentine addressed to someone who didn't get one?" Sometimes I *was* thoughtful. Some of my artwork received attention when the Milwaukee Art Society offered special classes at the gallery. Our teacher had taken us there by street car to get instruction and practice. I was thrilled to win a prize.

When I was eight, I decided to be a missionary. I had graduated from the primary class in Sunday School. When I went into the "big" department, I felt that I now was mature and should take on responsibility for my life. About that time some real missionaries came to speak in our church. Among them I remember Sam Zwemer clearly, because he wrote my name in Arabic on a card. I treasured that card for years. Anyhow, then and there I told my Sunday School teacher that I was going to be a missionary.

I also decided that religious teaching was great fun. My father drilled us on the catechism, embellishing the Bible stories with fascinating details. I almost wept over the story of poor old Jacob, who declared that his wicked sons would bring his gray hair with sorrow down to the grave.

I began to acquire a deep admiration for the medical profession, too. An active child, I tried acrobatics on the convenient iron rod railing around the church lawn until family friends informed my parents of the inappropriate scene I made in my underwear. Once I fell and sprained my ankle, so Uncle Dick the doctor came over to strap it. He treated my frequent tonsillitis by painting my throat with tincture of iodine. We all came through mumps, measles, and whooping cough without much trouble, either.

PELLA, IOWA, AND ADOLESCENCE

In 1917, Dad accepted the pastorate at the Second Reformed Church in Pella, Iowa. Pella was our hometown from 1917 to 1927. Set in the rich, fertile Corn Belt, it had a population of about 3,500. The community was predominantly Dutch, settled by immigrants from Holland who came in the 1840s during the religious turmoil in the Netherlands. Family names reflected Dutch origin: Van der Lindens, Jaarsma, Gosselink, Scholte, Dykstra, Michmerschuizen, and so forth. The hamlet retained much of the Dutch character in the appearance of the shopfronts, neat houses and gardens, as well as the stern, thrifty, stolid attitude of its people.

On Sundays all business stopped. Social life centered in the

large Reformed Churches, whose Sunday congregations were re-
portedly larger than the town's population. Senior members of
the community usually spoke Dutch, my father's mother tongue
(Mother's was German). But we knew only English and disdained
to learn the old people's language. The ministers, called "Domi-
nees," had great prestige and authority. As preacher's children,
we felt we had an important position to uphold in the community.
It was virtually our extended family, and its concerns were deeply
felt in the manse.

I greatly admired my father. His sermons were optimistic and
stimulating and made a great impression on me. He firmly believed that the world was getting better. The leading men of
the church admired him, too, and became my father's lifelong
friends.

Father's job was strenuous. Besides his Sunday duties at the
adult Sunday School class, the two sermons, and three Christian
Endeavor Societies, he had midweek prayer meetings, teachers'
classes, the evening high school catechism, and three Saturday
catechism classes for children. He was expected to call on all the
homes once a year. He served as chairman of the consistory, and
had no secretary for a church of over two hundred members.

The war was going on most of those years, but it didn't seem
to affect our life. Once I heard my father talking about German
atrocities, and my uncle said the Belgians deserved it for the way
they treated the people in the Congo. But I was glad when the
bells rang announcing the Armistice. Uncle Dick had been a
prisoner of war, and Uncle Karl, an aviator, came home. I was so
thrilled when he kissed me. I went over and over the feeling in
my mind.

The Dutch tradition favored education, so Pella had good
public schools, as well as a parochial Christian school and Central College. We had good teachers in the public school, and good
libraries were available.

I spent four years of my life at Pella High School, but nothing
much seemed to happen. The small high school next door to our
house had only the essential subjects: Latin, algebra, English, science, geometry, economics, chemistry, physics, home economy
for the girls, and woodworking for the boys. I loved my teachers,
especially the men, and spent diligent hours studying and trying
to figure out questions that might stump the teacher. Outside of

class, we had group sings, played basketball, and held declamatory contests.

The government sent a pleasant woman doctor to our school to lecture to the girls about sex and reproduction. We were shown a movie on the terrible effects of syphilis and gonorrhea. When she invited questions, I asked the unanswerable, "When does the human embryo get its soul?" When I was twelve, I noticed some blood in my urine and told Mom. She had neglected to tell me the facts of life before that.

Despite the changes of adolescence, I was still very much a child. I was large, clumsy, with pimples and straight, fine hair (at that time, the girls bobbed their hair and got permanents). I was not popular, because I kept my nose in books. Our classes seemed to be predominantly girls. The boys were shy and backward, so very few girls dated. I had a few girlfriends, but no intimates. My brother Paul and I would fight bitterly over the subject of which sex was preferable and whether women were inferior. On Saturdays, I had to help with the housework; but Paul was allowed to get a job at the bakery, which seemed much more exciting than what I had to do. Also Paul was allowed to drive the car, which my father said was not proper for girls. On Saturday nights there would be band concerts in the town square. On Sundays we were busy at the church.

I kept my dream of becoming a medical missionary. I read the whole Bible and joined the church when I was fourteen. It seemed that my faith grew unconsciously. I don't remember making any decision about it. I had become a Christian due to my heredity and environment and never had any serious doubts. Christianity gave my life deep meaning and a sense of destiny. I believed that the Word of God demanded that one choose some kind of Christian service. It seemed to me that the career of a medical missionary was the highest vocation to which I could aspire, so I took that as my calling.

I was maneuvered a bit to teach the beginner's class in Sunday School. I tried to make the lessons dramatic, until we played Moses in the bullrushes and the boys pretended to pick up the Jewish babies and hurl them into the river a bit too vigorously. Another time, one little girl put her arms around me and said she loved Jesus, too. A week later, she died. I felt glad that I had given her something to take with her.

Don't let this make you think I was too angelic. I was quite
self-centered. I did hate to do the housework with Mother on
Saturdays, and in my arguments with Paul about females' supposed inferiority, I was quite capable of one-upsmanship. When
I won a scholarship to Central College by only a fraction of
a point, I felt it was mean of me because the other girls then
couldn't go.

CENTRAL COLLEGE

The summer after I graduated from high school, there was a
typhoid fever epidemic in Pella. We all got it and were sick all
summer. When I started to college that fall, all my hair came out.
It was very tragic to start college looking like a plucked chicken.
I tried to cover my bald head with ribbons, but feared the effect
on my love life.

Central College at Pella, Iowa, had been started by the Baptist
Church, which gave it to the Reformed Church about 1915.
When I started college in 1922, the college had old buildings
and a small student body of about two hundred. But it also had
a nucleus of earnest, devoted professors who maintained strict
discipline. Though small, Central College had basic, thorough
courses in science, mathematics, history, literature, Bible, philosophy, drama, speech, and athletics. I remember the faculty
there with great affection and respect. In medical school I compared my Central College training to that which others had received, and found it excellent.

A variety of activities brought the students together. There
were daily chapel attendance, volunteer work, YWCA, literary
society, and a senior play; for fun we had receptions, banquets,
parties, picnics, games, and a campus clean-up day. We never
missed dancing, which had been out of the question in the conservative Dutch town of Pella.

I didn't make Glee Club, despite my love of music, but I did
make good grades. When one of the seniors asked me about a
new student in class, I said that he was good—about as good as I.

To be young, inexperienced, and in college was very depressing. Despite my academic success, I worried about my shortcomings in other areas. I won a prize in the oratory contest, but the
judge told me it was only because the others were so poor. I
wasn't any good at tennis; I just couldn't get the racket to make

contact with the ball. I didn't play cards because I couldn't remember numbers. When students gathered to analyze the world's
problems, I would listen spellbound. They overflowed with lofty
expressions and ardent feelings, and I longed to contribute some
equally sparkling remarks. None ever came to my mind, so I sat
silently.

My first ventures into sexuality were confusing and painful. A
shy boy in one of my classes asked me for a date. I accepted
because I felt so sorry for him and hated to say no to anyone who
gave me any attention. But when my mates made fun of the awkward young man, it was too much for me to bear, so I withdrew
my attention and he got the message.

I didn't have much patience for silly romances. My girlfriends
flirted and giggled with boys for hours, while I thought the whole
process was stupid and went home to read books. I did have a
date for the college banquet, but I didn't know what to do and
felt uncomfortable all evening.

I lived at home for the four years of college, spending my evenings studying there alone. My weekends were much as they had
always been. There was housework and cooking to do on Saturdays, and Sundays were filled with sessions at church. I had no
sister and my two brothers ganged up against me. I was jealous
of the dormitory girls who seemed to gain more social maturity
than I did.

Sometimes I was in the depths of despair, but then minor
successes induced feelings that I had unusual talents. With my
nose in books, aiming for high grades with a feeling of holy
calling, I must have been an obnoxious companion. No wonder
that the men I admired didn't ask me for dates. I took refuge in
Tennyson's lines: "More bounteous aspects on me beam, me
mightier transports move and thrill; So keep I fair through faith
and prayer, a virgin's heart in work and will" ("Sir Galahad,"
The Complete Works of Alfred Tennyson [New York: Worthington,
1880], 75).

I quietly nursed my misery with dreams of a future career: "It's
great to be out where the fight is strong; Out where the heaviest
troops belong, And to the fight for God and man." In the midst
of my fits of weeping, Mom would say, "What's the matter with
you anyway?" I dreamed of a glorious future. Would I be a

martyr? Could I stand up to being burned at the stake or sawn asunder?

My dreams were encouraged when a missionary from Arabia, Dr. Paul Harrison, came to speak in our churches. He told anecdotes about his medical work and life in Arabia. He described how the Arabs welcomed the swarms of locusts. The insects were an agreeable protein addition to the diet. They were boiled in great vats. The head and wings were removed to get at the egg case, which tasted something like caviar, he said. With dry, droll humor Dr. Harrison also related his dismay at discovering why his tubercular patients had aimed their sputum at the hospital walls. The patients explained that if they spat on the floor, someone might slip on it and break a leg. Dr. Harrison then told us of a desert trip on which he was faced with treating a man with a strangulated hernia. The helpers boiled up the instruments for the operation and spread them out on a clean sheet in the tent. Immediately, they were covered by flies. Paul figured that flies who survived that heat and sun must have sterile feet, and went on with the operation. It must have been true, for the patient never even had fever and was completely cured.

Aha, I thought. That would be the life for me!

GRADUATION AND MY FIRST JOB

Graduation Day with cap and gown soon came and went. I don't remember a thing about it. The august General Synod of the Reformed Church met in Pella, which I do recall. Because my father had the preeminence of being one of the hosts, I had a chance to meet the church leaders.

My attention turned to my future, and medical school. The first hurdle on my path was money. When I was eighteen, I had received an inheritance of $2,000 as the share of my mother, Mary Huizinga, from her family's estate. My father gave me long instructive talks about investing the money in stocks. Although I needed the funds to go to medical school, he advised me to save it for emergencies. I took his advice and decided to teach high school for a couple of years to earn enough to start medicine.

I took a position as a high school principal at Green River, a small Iowa town about a hundred miles from Pella. I'd just as soon forget that year of my life. I taught algebra, English, general science, physiology, and physics, with girls' athletics after hours. I worked very hard and spent most evenings studying and correcting papers. The freshman class was composed of thirty young devils who had already wrecked other teachers' careers. They were set for the fray and I wasn't. The school board decided I couldn't cope with their problem, notifying me that my services were no longer needed.

The bottom dropped out of my world. I walked the snowy streets in my misery, thinking I might as well commit suicide, but I didn't. Instead, I got a new position teaching the same subjects in the Academy at my old college, which revived my courage.

I lived at the dormitory and made preparations to enter medical school. I chose the Woman's Medical College of Pennsylvania at Philadelphia because many of our women medical missionaries had gone there. I also wanted to avoid the distresses I'd had with men and hoped I would find some real girlfriends. My finances improved. Grandmother Bruins gave me a thousand dollars, as I was her only descendant who wanted a missionary career, and the church board promised to pay my $400 tuition. I also added to my resources by taking a summer job as a waitress at a Michigan lake resort. In the fall, I left for Pennsylvania to begin my medical training.

2. Medical Training

"Hope springs eternal in the human breast," so boldly I ventured to begin the medical course at the Woman's Medical College of Pennsylvania at Philadelphia in August 1928. In those days the college and its hospital were located across the street from a high wall surrounding the Stephen Girard school for orphan boys. I found a room on the third floor of a typical Philadelphia house nearby.

The first morning began with anatomy and our cadavers. They were bodies found in the streets that had been preserved in formaldehyde for two years. If unclaimed, they were given to medical schools. Four of us were assigned to each body. My partners were Bessie Jeong, who was Chinese; Kasui Togasaki, who was Japanese; and Carmen Thomaschetsky, who was Polish.

We lived like vestal virgins, devoting our days to lectures and laboratory work and our evenings to study. Our rooms were cold. We took our meals at cheap restaurants. There were seven of us students in one house. We spent long hours discussing medicine, sex, and religion. Most of the other medical students considered my ideas absurd, an impossible dream. To them, religion was for the birds. They thought it was presumptuous to use our technology to entice people to change their religion: other cultures had developed religion to suit them, we had no right to impose our ideas on them. Most of my colleagues wondered at my faith. I wondered at their lack of it.

In the assembly room stood a large sculptured relief of the ideal woman physician, surrounded by grateful patients and cripples, with the inscription:

Daughter of Science, pioneer, thy tenderness hath banished pain
   Woman and leader in thee blend
Physician, surgeon, student, friend.

It fit *my* ideals, but I seemed to have been born in the wrong generation.

We found it a help to study together to remember the vast mass of material. My friend Bessie was ingenious. She would make up a tale of nerves running under muscles with an erotic tinge which made it funny. We used the old phrases to remember bones and their connections and "On old Olympus, tiny topsy a Finn and German picked some hops" to remember the cranial nerves. Once in a while, we went to hear the Philadelphia orchestra or see a play. On Sundays, I wrote letters and loved to go to hear Dr. Campbell Morgan give his famous Bible lessons.

I was fascinated by my studies. The body is curiously and wonderfully made, whether studied in dissection or microscopically. Each kind of cell can be distinguished and named. Most enthralling to me was the study of embryology, the development of eggs. Parallel blood vessels appeared like magic. Two parallel vessels would unite and begin to beat and behold, a heart. The ectoderm turned in to form a tube which twisted and became the brain, spinal cord, and nervous system. These things were too wonderful for me.

We crammed for exams. With the training at Central and three years of teaching science and mathematics, I coped quite easily. They gave us a medical intelligence examination at entrance. It was no wonder I scored the highest, but afterward my grades were not so brilliant. Professor Mollie Geiss, teaching us Materia Medica with a twinkle in her eye, let us know that medicine demands absolutely correct knowledge. We felt bad when some of us flunked out.

My soul yearned for a real companion. Bessie Jeong and I grew close. She was raised in San Francisco. When her father wanted to marry her to a wealthy Chinese gentleman, she fled to Miss Cameron's Presbyterian home for troubled girls. Miss Cameron arranged for Bessie to attend Leland Stanford University, where Bessie decided to become a medical missionary to China. Bessie's friend, Miss Allis, was a wealthy lady in Philadelphia who had a lovely home. Her father had been the Doctor Allis who invented the Allis forceps. She frequently invited us to Sunday dinners which were a real treat.

At the time of the stock market crash in 1929, letters came from my father, dark with the tragedy that had befallen him. He had inherited a large sum and invested it in stocks, with grand ideas of supporting me as a missionary and giving a large endowment to Central College. He borrowed and bought on margin and lost half of his funds. I shared deeply in his grief and depression and wrote to comfort him. Everybody suffered. My parents eventually found a flat in Milwaukee. When Dad was appointed Executive Secretary for the Council of Churches, his gloom began to lift.

Brother Paul wrote that he was marrying Margaret Munson, which made me feel sad. Our family was breaking up. I came for the wedding. For the rest of the summer, I again worked as a waitress in a Michigan summer resort, making just enough to cover my expenses.

In my junior year the college and hospital moved up to a beautiful new location and building in Germantown. We had to find new lodgings. I had become estranged from my best friend Bessie, who suddenly became strange and refused to talk to me. When we met in the halls, she gazed stonily ahead as if I were nothing. I was deeply distressed. I heard that she was slandering me. We had been partners in Anatomy and had shared the strenuous laboratories of Physiology and Pharmacology, studying together night after night. Now I couldn't talk with her, because she gave me no replies. She was invited to join the medical sorority and live at their house. They didn't invite me. I went through a dark night in my soul. Would I never find a real friend? I thought of the Psalmist's lines, "For it was not an enemy who reproaches me; / Then I could bear it. . . . / But it was you, a man my equal / My companion and my acquaintance. / We took sweet counsel together / And walked to the house of God in the throng" (Ps. 55:12–13). From that time on Bessie and I were not friends.

Two other students and I found an apartment. Bianca Trellis was from a Spanish family in South America and Rose Butler came from Jamaica. Rose's father was English, her mother Portuguese. We enjoyed living together, shopped for and cooked our own food, and studied together evenings. Both of them had boyfriends.

I dated Bill Hawkes, a Philadelphia seminary student. Neither of us had enough money to splurge, but we took long walks in the beautiful Wissahickon Valley and Fairmont Park. Neither of us was ardently in love. When I told Bill that I was definitely committed to a foreign missionary career, we parted, as he had other plans.

Suddenly, a telegram came telling of my father's death. I took the train to Milwaukee. Father had loved to keep his car in perfect running order. One morning adjusting the engine, he had the motor running with the garage doors closed. He was found too late—overcome by carbon monoxide gas. When I saw his body, I took hold of his hand, distressed to find it cold. I would have to look forward to seeing him again only on the other side of life. Friends came with the family from Pella and from our Milwaukee church to lay him away in the Milwaukee cemetery. I trusted he was with the One who is the Alpha and the Omega. I felt I must now carry on his life.

Paul, Margaret, and their baby Barbara were living in Milwaukee and helped Mother. She carried on courageously, took a job as companion to an elderly lady, and studied investments to use the remaining funds as well as possible.

I returned to Philadelphia to continue my studies. Medicine was a stern discipline as well as a fascinating study. I revered the profession of a physician as a supreme privilege, strongly enough to sacrifice my energy to learning it well. In a lecture on mental health, the question was asked, what is the best thing we can do to help other people? The final answer that came up was not to cure the bodily illness but to give an idea of how to live better.

We dug into pathology, medicine, and surgery. My notes read that flea bites were serious in typhoid fever, and later I found out it was phlebitis. There were courses in pediatrics and in obstetrics with demonstrations of difficult deliveries using forceps (done on a manikin). Then we did twenty deliveries at homes. Gynecology had its kind of surgery. The specialities of dermatology, eye diseases, nose and throat troubles, and X-ray were separate courses. But somehow we survived all of the courses and the examinations. Some girls failed. One developed tuberculosis and died.

For my senior year, I got an appointment at the Children's Heart Hospital nearby. It had beautiful grounds with a lake and a lovely old home where the nurses and I lived. The hospital was for children with hearts damaged by rheumatic fever. My part was to be resident, conduct examinations of the children, keep records, and do weekly blood examinations on all the patients. I bought a car for $75.00. I practiced driving in the days when there was no insurance or driver's licenses required and drove, all alone, to Milwaukee. I spent one summer observing at a hospital laboratory, and another summer observing at the Wills Eye Hospital in Philadelphia, because I knew eye disease was something mission doctors had to treat.

We were so very busy, we didn't feel the need of entertainment. Sometimes we took off a weekend and went to Atlantic City to walk the boardwalk. I found some relief from the dry desert of studying the human body in Keswick, New Jersey, a Christian retreat where I found some "pollen for my soul." I accompanied a kind neighbor, who used to come to the hospital on Sunday afternoons to sing hymns for the patients, but there wasn't much relief from the pressure of medical school.

In our senior year we dealt with real patients. On Saturday afternoons we went over to the Pennsylvania Hospital for autopsies. Bianca, Rose, and I would take our sandwiches with us and thought nothing of sitting on the floor of the autopsy room, with the bodies on the table, eating our lunch while waiting for the professor to arrive. We concentrated on our studies and reports and gave little thought to the human beings we saw.

At last, we graduated. The faculty gave us a reception at a garden inn where we entertained them with skits and stunts, mimicking the peculiarities of our professors. We had the dermatologist asking in his sweet way, "Could I see a little more skin, please?" and another professor asking the students what to do when a patient developed acute coreopsis. We really had a lot of fun. After that I sat for the three-day examination for the National Boards of Medical Examinations.

INTERNSHIPS

The year of internship is an important part of the training of a young physician. She is given some responsibilities in examination and treatment under the supervision of a resident. There is a real possibility of serious error, but some risks have to be taken in the creation of a physician. It was strenuous, but I enjoyed it all.

I was accepted as an intern at the Wisconsin General Hospital at Madison, Wisconsin, which paid no salary but was considered to give excellent training. Three of us women interns lived in a small house and took our meals at the hospital dining room. We were to be on call at all hours except when some other interns would take our calls. My mother took a position as housemother at one of the university sororities so we could be together occasionally.

My year was divided into medicine, surgery, children's orthopedics, and pediatrics. Medicine was divided into men's, women's, and the "diabolic service," which meant diabetes and the metabolic diseases. Dr. Middleton was our favorite teacher. He was a great tease and never happier than when he found some lapse in our records and from then on called us by that name. I wrote a diagnosis as "diabetes and rales," so that was my nickname.

The "Camp of Philistines" were the surgeons. In surgery, the operating team would consist of the chief, his assistant, the resident, and their intern, who had the privilege of holding a retractor. I seldom got a chance to suture even the skin. Surgeons were just beginning to try lung surgery, but that and the total breast removals seemed appalling to me. I resolved to be undaunted.

I began to have profuse menstrual flow, which was very embarrassing. Once I even had to leave the operating room. It was a shortcoming of my medical college that they didn't make a pelvic examination of their students. I learned during my second internship that I had a large fibroid uterus. It shows how stupid young doctors can be. I thought my profuse flow was a sign of my good health. I couldn't make my mind up to do the necessary surgery until a year later.

Another failing of the medical college was that we were not taught any method of birth control. Some of the professors and leaders were Roman Catholic and refused to allow it to be mentioned. I had to learn about methods when I came back to the U.S.A. on my first furlough from Kuwait.

The patients and their families began to be real people to me when I came to appreciate their heartbreaking human tragedies. I especially remember the children. One who had been bitten by a skunk died in agony from hydrophobia. Another little boy had leukemia. When he had profuse nasal hemorrhages with clots, he asked me, "Is that my brains coming out?"

Blood transfusion procedures were being worked out in a crude way. I wanted some new clothes so I gave 500 cc of blood and received $25.00.

In orthopedics, the most important thing I learned was how to put plaster of paris on babies with club feet. There were a lot of them in the hospital, and they had to have their casts changed every three weeks as the feet grew and gradually straightened.

I'd had a really sheltered life and was shocked when some of the residents used profanity. One of the nicest and most handsome of them would swear a string of obscenities and then glance at me and say, "Oh excuse me. That embarrasses you, doesn't it?" I wouldn't know what to say. I had told the others that I was planning a missionary career, so they treated me as a very pious person. Of course, I did think my course was superior and so must have been somewhat aloof. It was exciting to associate, dine, and work with men again after years of being mostly with women. However, none of them asked me for dates. It didn't make any difference to me. I was too interested and busy with the hospital work.

Since it was possible that I would be sent to Arabia, Rev. Edwin and Dr. Eleanor Calverley invited me to study Arabic with them. They had been in Kuwait for twenty years and couldn't return for health reasons, so they had settled in Hartford, Connecticut. Rev. Calverley was teaching in the School of Missions there. I had a semester until the next internship, so I went to Hartford. They gave me a room at the Hartford Theological School dormitory. We'd have great discussions in the dining room there. I began to study Arabic speech, writing, and reading, with courses in the history of the Middle East, Islam, and missionary methods. I frequently spent my evenings at the Calverley home, where the famous Dr. Duncan Black MacDonald lived. He had been a celebrity in Middle East studies and had written many books. He helped me with Arabic and enlivened the table conversation with anecdotes of his lifelong associations with the Middle East.

Since my first internship had not included obstetrics, I took a second internship at the University of Illinois in 1934. I arrived in Chicago on a cold, dark January night by train from Hartford.

When I got off the streetcar near the Mitchell St. Maternity Center, the conductor warned me: "Ladies don't walk around this neighborhood." It was in the slums where "the cats go hunting in pairs," as they said, but nothing happened to any of us on the staff as long as I was there. It was an adventure to go out to all kinds of homes in Chicago at any hour by streetcar, to deliver babies in winter. A little later a movie was made of life at the Center.

The Center ran a prenatal clinic which we helped when we were not out at a home. There were six of us interns, two residents, nurses, and medical students, of whom some were hen-medics. When a call came we went out in pairs, a doctor and nurse or medical student, carrying the two maternity bags which were our identification. Our vehicle was always the streetcar, which ran at long intervals in the wee small hours when it was freezing cold and windy.

As soon as we arrived at the home of the woman in labor, we would examine the case and get everything ready for delivery. Then, if there was time, we were supposed to call the Center by phone from some nearby shop, as most of the poor people did not have phones. Sometimes no shops were open. They kept track of us on the bulletin board at the Center. As long as it seemed a normal delivery, we were supposed to stay on the case until the baby arrived in good condition, and then clean up the place, leaving mother and baby in good condition. Most were normal cases which delivered soon, but sometimes labor went on for hours and even days. The family would get impatient and ask, "Doctor, why don't you *do* something?" But we had learned that nature's way was best, so we had to wait. Sometimes sleep overwhelmed me. I found a way of putting chairs together, wrapping in my coat, and getting some sleep. One time I lay down in the bed beside my laboring patient.

In those days, before antibiotics, we were trained to be extremely clean in all techniques and make no vaginal examinations without scrubbing as for surgery. The women had been told to have a pile of clean newspapers and a kettle of hot water ready. The newspapers were put under the pelvis of the woman and changed as soon as soiled. When the case was not making progress, we called the Center, which would send out the "Wrecking Crew," which was a car with one of the residents, equipment for anesthesia, and forceps. If this could not deal with the situation, the mother would be taken to the hospital for Caesarian section.

There are a few cases which I remember. One woman delivered a twelve-pound baby without much trouble. Another had twins, each one weighing eight pounds. One Negro girl was unmarried, her family was unsympathetic. She never let a groan pass her lips. The family refused to keep the baby, so I called to ask whether I should bring the baby back with me for adoption. When Beatrice Tucker, the resident, understood that the baby was black, she said, "No, we can't place black babies." My roommate Dr. Grace Loveland was out on another case and phoned in that the mother had had twenty-four deliveries. We thought there must be some mistake, but Grace said that the older siblings were holding a party downstairs while their mother was delivering her twenty-fifth child. It was strenuous work, but we were young, thrilled to be doctors who were shouldering responsibilities and doing what doctors should be doing.

The next part of the course was at the Lying-in Hospital of the University of Illinois. Dr. Delee, who started the work and wrote the textbook we studied, still had an office on the birthroom floor. He was making movies of the various problems and techniques of obstetrics for students and would lecture to us occasionally. He said doctors shouldn't marry; their lives belonged to their patients. On the birthroom floor, interns were scheduled for twenty-four hours on duty and then twenty-four hours off, to enable us to follow a case to completion. We knew what exhaustion was after twenty-four hours of strain.

A few times on afternoons off, we went to the Chicago World's Fair. The men interns were intrigued by the girl who did the fan dance. Grace and I couldn't understand their fascination since we were all dealing with complete female anatomy every day at the hospital.

It was the era of the Great Depression. We received no salary, only a place to sleep and our meals. My brother, Richard Bruins, had his Ph.D. and a job in the city. He got almost no pay so I would invite him over frequently for a good meal.

I formally applied to the Church to be sent out as a missionary, but because of the Depression the Church had no funds. I received a very good offer from one of the universities, which wanted a woman physician, and began to wonder whether the

Lord really meant me for a missionary. But the women of the Michigan Classis heard of me and offered to raise my salary of sixty dollars a month above their usual contributions. My uncle, Dr. A. Huizinga, offered to pay my travel expenses. So I was officially appointed to work in Kuwait, Arabia.

I spent the summer of 1934 readying my supplies: uniforms, two evening dresses, curtains, bedding, books, and instruments which were packed in two trunks and twelve parcels. There were good-bye visits and the train trip to New York and speeches in some of the churches. The men of the Mission Board met with me and also promised support. My tension was extreme and once I broke in hysterical weeping.

When the final day came, some of the women of the church went with me to the ship. I had a stateroom to myself full of flowers and gifts. The ship was of the American Export line, which combined tourist excursions with freight to the Mediterranean Sea. There was a gorgeous display of glamorous food in the dining room—whole roast piglet, great rib roast, decorated vegetables and fruit with glazed pastries, and an ice-carved swan. My friends stood on the wharf waving and throwing me long strands of confetti which gradually snapped apart as the ship began to move. I was truly cut off from the first part of my life.

3. Early Years in Kuwait

It was a delightful ocean trip with interesting people. We saw Gibraltar and spent days ashore sight-seeing at Palma, Marseilles, Naples, Pompeii, and Alexandria, with a three day trip to Cairo, Haifa, and finally Beirut. There I had a few days to see that beautiful city and take a car up to the mountains to see the Cedars of Lebanon. A car took us across the fertile, wide Baka Valley to Damascus, where I stayed in the hotel and visited the Grand Mosque of St. John the Baptist. It used to be a Roman temple, then a Christian church, and now is a mosque. I also saw the street called Straight where St. Paul lodged, which is still used. To cross the desert, there was a Nairn bus, which took twenty-four hours to reach Baghdad. We stopped at an oasis, the Rutbah wells, where dinner was served.

At Baghdad, our missionaries, John and Margaret Badeau, took me to their home. They had built a two-story house using the lower floor for church meetings and the upstairs for their living space. The neighborhood had changed after they arrived and had become a center for prostitution. The city of Baghdad had none of the romance associated with its history. The buildings were plain mud walls, the streets were dusty, the only bridge was a pontoon of rocking boats. There were very few trees. The museum had interesting things contributed by the archaeologists but was unorganized.

John and Margaret Badeau concerned themselves with the Christians living in Baghdad; this meant the Armenians, Nestorians, and the foreign population. There were a few Muslim inquirers who came for visits. John had a fund of fascinating stories of people and their adventures of living in Iraq. Later, he was transferred to Cairo to head the American University there. He was appointed to be our American ambassador to Egypt and became a trusted friend of King Farook before the king abdicated.

Dr. Harold Storm and his little boy traveled with me on the railroad to Basrah. He was the physician of our mission hospital in Bahrain whose wife had died in her second childbirth in Kuwait. He had announced his engagement to a lady who had been a missionary in China. Harold was one of the doctors who loved to travel and run a clinic for a few months and then move on. Some people felt that Christ's words to the followers whom He sent out to preach meant that when their message was not received, they should shake off the dust from their feet and move on. Most of us did not believe that applied to a mission field. Harold did extensive travel all over Arabia and wrote a book about his trips.

The distance from Baghdad to Basrah was only three hundred miles, but the train took twenty-four hours because it made long stops at villages. So we had bedding rolls and slept on the benches. Waking with the dawn, I was thrilled to see the signpost outside, "Ur Junction," and realized that I was back where Abraham set out.

On my arrival in Basrah, George and Christine Gosselink (old friends from Pella, Iowa, and Central College) met me and took me to their home. The compound was on the sweet-water Ashar Creek, which rose and fell with the tides each day. The compound included two residences, a boys' school with library, a dormitory, a small chapel, and servants' quarters all made beautiful with a garden, trees, and flowers. The school was run by the Rev. John Van Ess and my friend George Gosselink with the help of some local Arab teachers. Its students, from prominent Arab families, later became leaders and were deeply appreciative of the training they received at this first modern school in Basrah.

Another mission school, for girls, had been set up further down the creek. Muslim Arab girls did not usually receive any education beyond the Qur'an school. It was considered dangerous for girls to read and write. Their families arranged marriages for their children when they matured, and then of course they had to stay home. When the wives of the first evangelistic men started to help women, they had to begin with very simple club work, teaching sewing, knitting, and handcrafts. Later the club developed into a primary school with classes for reading, writing, and arithmetic. The girls had to be protected, so their compound had a high wall and guarded gate. The enclosure surrounded a well-built house, a school building, and a lovely garden with date trees.

It was interesting to walk through the narrow streets of the shopping area called the Sook. Since there was plenty of sweet water for irrigation, the shops were full of vegetables and fruit and many kinds of supplies brought by ships. The Arab shops were closed on Fridays, the Jewish shops on Saturdays, and the Christian ones on Sundays. We went for picnics in gondolas out to the huge river—the conjoined Tigris and Euphrates, lined by great date gardens.

After several days, Dr. Mylrea drove up from Kuwait in his Model A Ford to bring me and all my cartons to my new home, a trip of 125 miles. At Safwan, an oasis with a few wells and some struggling date trees, the police carefully examined our passports and visas. The road was a dirt track through a dry, monotonous, empty desert. We came up to a Bedu running alone and offered him a lift. He stood on the running board and told us he had walked 10 miles to buy a new garment and carefully held a tin inside the car filled with some vile-smelling mixture which he said was for his daughter, who had so much trouble with lice.

A NEW LIFE

It was a late September afternoon in 1934 when we came to the top of a row of low hills and saw the blue line of the Persian Gulf. Toward evening we arrived at the Jahra gate of Kuwait City where the guards welcomed Dr. Mylrea. I entered the city and a new life began. It was like being born anew. I knew what ecstasy felt like—to reach the place of my dreams. The streets showed a disregard of any straight lines, running off at odd angles in varying widths. Jinns travel in straight lines, it was believed, so changing directions offered some protection. We drove to the seaside where I was to live.

Nurse Mary Van Pelt, with whom I was to live, and Mrs. Mylrea were serving tea to guests after an afternoon of tennis. Dr. and Mrs. Greenway were introduced. He was an Anglo-Indian physician employed by the British to inspect all foreign shipping. He also ran a small private medical practice. But most impressive was Archie Chisholm, a tall, handsome Englishman with a monocle and British expressions, "now really," "how appalling," and "quite all right." I was thrilled. He was residing in Kuwait trying to get the ruler, Shaikh Ahmad, to sign an oil concession for the British Anglo-Iranian Oil Company. His antagonist was Major Holmes, who was contriving to get it for the American Gulf Oil Company. The ruler hesitated for over a year in deciding which company was making the more favorable offer. The competition was finally solved by forming the Kuwait Oil Company, in which each protagonist had 50 percent interest.

Mary Van's rented two-story house next to the hospital had been built to suit Americans. It had a ten-foot wall with two large wooden gates that had bolts and locally made locks with six-inch-long keys. Within was a barren open court in front and in back, and the rooms. In the space between them was a crooked stairway up to the second floor. The walls were built of sea rock and adobe mud. Inside, the walls were whitewashed; there were twelve-foot-high ceilings and large hanging fans for coolness during the long, hot summers. The ceilings were artistic, of black mangrove logs from Zanzibar which the termites could not spoil. Above the logs were bamboo strips and woven cane matting sealed by a layer of mud. The windows were deep-set, as the walls were two feet thick. Mary had them hung with beautiful heavy-embroidered eight-foot curtains. The cement floor was covered with matting and Persian carpets. One of the rooms was the living room with a fireplace, delightful on cold winter evenings. Mary had good furniture brought from home and from India, too.

The other room was the dining room, with lovely Indian rosewood furniture. Behind it was a pantry where the Persian houseboy, Mahmoud, washed the dishes; there was also a locked storeroom for keeping food.

The kitchen was a separate room in the back courtyard where Melicko, the Persian cook, prepared delicious food (that Mary had taught him to make). There was a kerosene stove and a pressure burner. It had to be pumped by hand and gave a very hot flame.

The upstairs had a wide veranda with a lovely view of the sea. Here, Melicko would bring my breakfast at 6:30 every morning. It was the most beautiful part of the day; the air was still soft with the night's coolness. The sea would be streaked with shades of blue. Men worked in the shipyard in front, laying out and sewing the seams in the huge lateen sails or mending their fish nets. On hot summer nights we slept on the verandas, but I wasn't really comfortable out there because the wind flapped the sheets and blew my hair around.

Mary had prepared one of the two bedrooms for me with some leftover furniture, a desk and a bed to use until mine came by ship. Each room had a bathroom. The bathroom had a small tank of brackish water from the well in our courtyard. Mahmoud kept it filled and brought up pitchers of hot and cold sweet water for baths, which we took in a tin tub. The lavatory was what we called a "thunder-pot"—a commode. To my embarrassment, an old Persian man came to empty the pot at the seafront twice a day.

The morning after my arrival, the group decided I must immediately start Arabic studies. The Reverend Fred Barny offered to give me an hour of class early every day, reading the New Testament in Arabic and then studying Arabic grammar. He and Mrs. Barny were nearing retirement, but his Arabic was meticulous. The school, which Edwin Calverley started for Arab young men, had to be closed for lack of funds during the Depression. So Fred Barny's remaining responsibilities were giving the English and Arabic worship services, visiting the hospital patients, and running the Bible bookshop in the bazaar. He was a good teacher.

It was a privilege to be given the time to delve into the New Testament with the diligence required to understand it in a Semitic language, especially while I lived in a similar culture. The Bible took on new meanings for me. Arabic takes years and tears to acquire, but it is the only entrance into the Arab mind. So the policy of the mission was to require all career missionaries to do two years of study and to pass strict examinations in the language.

The course of study also included the essentials of the Islamic religion. We read part of the Qur'an in Arabic with Apologetics. It would have been better to have native teachers in Arabic or to attend some of the schools in the Middle East where Arabic is taught, but the mission did not have funds for this. So the Rev. Fred Barny and Mrs. Mylrea taught me for about a year and a half. Rev. Barny taught me the reading of the New Testament and then Bess Mylrea gave me a couple of hours every morning reading an Arabic primer, writing, talking, and visiting with Arab girl callers.

We held classes in one of the small rooms at the four corners of the chapel. The Rev. Garret De Jong built the chapel when he and his wife Everdene were missionaries in Kuwait in 1930. Building was a duty we all had to learn. Some friendly British engineers helped by counseling. Friends at home sent $5,000, which paid for this first Christian church in Kuwait.

The chapel stood to the rear of the compound. It was a rectangular one-story building with small rooms at each of the four corners for offices, vestry, or classes. Between the two rooms at the front was a roofed portal with two sturdy cement pillars. A beautiful teak door opened into the sanctuary with a lovely vaulted ceiling and front copping of yellow brick. Ast Ahmed, the skilled Persian mason, had worked out his own original design of crosses in the artistic brickwork.

Garry De Jong told in a letter, years later, how the local carpenter drilled holes by holding the board between his feet and using a drill worked by a bow. He quickly learned how to make the forms for the cement pillars. Garry obtained steel girders and good cement by ship from England. To get an adhesive mud for the roof, Garry obtained a special kind of clay, which they made into a large puddle on the ground. This was kept wet and kneaded with straw by the laborers' bare feet for three weeks. When it was really putrid, it made an excellent waterproof roof—fully a foot deep, with the characteristic Kuwaiti protruding watervents. The outside was finished with stucco. The stucco and the cement pillars were an innovation much admired by the Kuwaitis. The chapel served as a place of worship for the daily morning matins and for Arabic and English services on Sundays.

COMING OUT IN KUWAITI SOCIETY

On Sunday afternoons, everyone at the mission went to a rented house in the middle of town where Yacoob, the colporteur, lived with his wife Esteer and their five children. Yacoob was a survivor of the Armenian massacres in Turkey, hired by the mission to help with the Arabic preaching and to run the small Bible shop in the bazaar. At this meeting we sat on mats in the open courtyard and sang Arabic hymns with the aid of an old organ. The sound attracted passers-by, so men, school boys, and a few women would drop in to listen to the reading and preaching and then unceremoniously drift out. The Word was given. Why were there no takers?

Bess Mylrea took me calling at the homes of her Arab women friends to introduce me to local life. She sent Nasr, our mission's Bedouin messenger who was an artist in the social graces, to inquire if a visit would be acceptable. We walked the empty beaten tracks between windowless clay walls whose heights were equal so no house would overlook the private territory of another. Access to the house was by a large wooden gate with a small door to admit one person at a time. Children playing on the doorstep were expecting us and rushed inside to announce our coming. Inside the gate was a bent passage with a partition concealing the open-air courtyard called the *hareem*, meaning "forbidden." Here the women need not veil, but kept their heads covered with a scarf, ready to cover their faces if one of the men of the household suddenly appeared.

The center of the large, bare court usually had the opening of a cistern to store rainwater. Around it were verandas with many doors and iron-barred windows with wooden shutters. These opened into rooms which provided separate domains for each household in an extended family system sometimes consisting of forty or more members. These would be the elderly head of the house, several brothers with one or more wives, unmarried grown sons and daughters, children, widowed and divorced sisters, orphans, and servants.

Our hostess welcomed us at the door of her room with poise and dignity. If an Arab woman accompanied us, the exchange of ritual greetings was as involved as a litany. The phrases were formal yet poetic and gave a grace to meetings that must ease the strains of the confined hareem life and its rigid traditional code. The women of good class seldom went out of their houses except for formal calls or deaths. In fact, there were no places for them to go. Women did not go to the mosque. All shopping was done by the men, and clubs and schools for women did not exist. Even sickness did not permit exit at any time, because a recent widow was supposed to mourn in her room for four months.

We removed our shoes, leaving them outside the door to inform any man of the house that women visitors were present so he would not enter.

Our hostess' personal room served as her living room, bedroom, and a storage space for her and her children. The furniture consisted of a high, wide four-poster bed with curtains. There was ample space below it for children's bedding rolls, tin trunks, and sometimes dishes. Most of the women still owned one of the ancient heavy wood chests decorated with brass medallions and lines of brass studs standing on its four painted spool-like legs. Here were kept locked the family treasures of jewelry, festal garments, and heirlooms. The room seemed dark, as the window shutters had no glass. The floor was covered with cane or coir mats and crude Persian carpets. There were some shelves in the walls filled with colored tinsel vases but no pictures because custom proclaimed that any likeness of human features would invite idolatry.

We sat down on the long, stuffed pallet along the wall, leaning against the cushions behind. The Arab women neatly folded their legs, but mine had not been so trained and my skimpy Western clothing did not cover me as their flowing clothes did. Our hostess courteously understood and bade me stretch out, but to point the soles of one's feet at others was insulting, so I kept shifting my position and never was comfortable.

The Arab ladies wore wide pants with gold embroidery called *serwall*, which fitted their ankles tightly. Above they wore a dress of some gay color under a gorgeous black mantle that could be draped over the head. A scarf always covered the head and neck. Women loved to display their jewelry, usually a nose ring, necklaces, rings, bracelets, and anklets. All of this should be gold if possible, but silver was acceptable, especially if set with turquoise, which was believed to confer fertility.

The women inferred that I must be Bess' daughter, as she had white hair. One asked me where I had come from and when I answered, "America," she asked whether that was one of the cities in the desert and whether it was as beautiful as Kuwait. "How many children have you?" was a question the women constantly asked me. Conversation centered on the recent unusual rains that caused some houses to collapse and on neighborhood news items: births, deaths, sicknesses, marriages, and pregnancies. In 1935, great interest was aroused by the birth of the "quints" in Canada—a wonder, to be sure, but not rated as highly as if they had all been boys. Sometimes religion was mentioned. One Arab lady said generously, "Your religion is better than ours but what can we do? Islam is the will of God for us." One asked, "Why do you

Christians worship three gods when God is One?" One of them had heard the hymn, "Create in Me a Clean Heart, O God" and asked us to sing it. Bess usually carried our end of the conversation, while I was in despair feeling I would never understand this language.

Our hostess concerned herself with heating the teapot in the brass charcoal brazier. She drew a large round tray with dishes from under her bed. She had thoughtfully prepared everything, a cake baked over a kerosene stove, as they had no ovens, heavy cookies, pistachios, pumpkin seeds, dates, and oranges. The cup of tea would consist of hot goat's milk, very strong tea, and plenty of sugar. It was surprisingly good except for the swarm of flies that accompanied the food. One often landed in the tea. It was hospitable to fill the cups to overflowing so a saucer saved the spill. Our hostess did not eat or drink herself—she kept busy making the event pleasant for us. Finally, she served us a couple of teaspoonfuls of hot, bitter, strong coffee flavored with cardamom seeds from a graceful brass coffee pot. The tiny cups were always held in the right hand, as the left was considered unclean. Custom decreed that we take the cup three times and then shake it to signify that we were satisfied. As a final gesture, one of the women would sprinkle our heads with rose water from brass shakers, then pass around an incense pot containing glowing charcoal and frankincense from Oman. Our hostess showed us how to hold the incense pot under our clothes to carry the fragrance home.

We asked permission to leave with the phrase, "I seek to be cheap," to which the answer was, "you are dear"; and "towa nas," which means, "people are still passing." Our hostess showed us the other parts of the house. There was a rather smelly enclosure for chickens and a couple of goats. I asked to see the kitchen, a small room with a vent high up for smoke and light. Walls and cooking pots were black with years of soot, as the fuel was branches of palm trees and desert thorn bush, both cruel to hands and fingers. The small hearth had cement supports for cooking vessels. Some houses had pressure kerosene stoves. I learned later when treating patients that these stoves could explode and cause tragic burns. What a lot of patient suffering these women had to bear!

We said our farewells with charming phrases, *Fee aman Allah*, and its reply, *Fee aman el kareem;* and *ma' salamah*, which means, "In the keeping of God" and "Go in peace."

Mary and I were invited for dinner to the house of the prime minister, Mullah Salah. His house was near the palace on the east side of Kuwait. Abdulla, the son, greeted us and showed us the men's rooms at the front of the house. Outside, the house consisted only of high walls, blank except a few windows in the men's quarters. The front room was intended for male guests and had curtains, Persian carpets (one of silk was hung on the wall), a radio, and many long mirrors. Behind the men's room was a very large bare, open court called the hareem. About twenty-five rooms opened into this courtyard. It was paved with small cement blocks. In the center was a cistern that held rainwater. The family caught the water by hanging a huge funnel made of sailcloth across the courtyard when it rained.

Each member of the family—grandparents, brothers, their wives and children, unmarried and divorced sisters, children, cousins, and servants—had his or her special place in this extended family of fifty to sixty persons. In the hot weather, the whole household would sleep on the flat roof, which was divided into separate enclosures for men and women.

Abdulla, the prime minister's son, was quite a young man and spoke English very well because he had been a pupil of Rev. Calverley. His wife Bederea was a sweet-faced Arabian beauty. Bederea was to become a very special friend to me as the years passed. But on the day I first met her, I embarrassed myself. I remember that she wore a white satin dress, embroidered in gold, with gold and pearl jewelry. Over it she wore a figured black chiffon thobe. She was so gorgeous that I couldn't help but express my admiration. Alas, it was quite the wrong thing to say. Arab custom demands that when a guest admires an article in the host's home, it should be given. Abdulla ordered Bederea to take off the thobe and give it to me. I was frightfully embarrassed. Mary Van came to the rescue and whispered to Bederea that she give me one of her old ones.

I survived that first faux pas and found there were other astonishing social events to attend. Archie Chisholm, who was trying to get the ruler to give the oil concession to the British, invited us to a typical Arab dinner. We sat on the floor on his Persian

carpets with kerosene lanterns and a glowing charcoal brazier.
His Indian servants served us on low tables. The meal consisted
of a whole roast lamb stuffed with rice, raisins, and nuts, wild
bustard, bowls of vegetable stew, pots of buttermilk, dates, and
oranges. Archie stood up in his formal dinner suit and monocle
to tear the roast to pieces, then filled our plates with roast and
handfuls of hot rice. Afterward the servants brought brass ewers
and basins to wash our hands, as we ate Bedouin style—with the
fingers of the right hand only. Later Archie showed us the pearls
he had bought for a bracelet for his English fiancée, costing fifteen hundred dollars.

The British government maintained its prestige in the Gulf by
sending its navy to make formal calls at the various ports. The
ruler would be invited to the ship and welcomed with a twenty-
one gun salute. When the Royal Navy visited Kuwait, ships had
to anchor quite far out in Kuwait Bay. Sometimes the officers
invited the mission to a dinner on board. We went all the way out
in a launch if the tide was high enough. Otherwise we had to take
a rowboat from the beach out to the launch. One night the tide
was so low that there was only mud, and laborers had to carry us
in a sort of chair. I never thought that mission life included a
reception on a battleship with those naval officers in their trim
white and blue uniforms with gold decorations. After the dinner,
liquors were served. I couldn't resist trying port, which I'd read
about. At this adventurous request, Dr. Mylrea turned and exclaimed, "Why, Mary!"

In March, Mary Van made a birthday picnic for me. We drove
out in the desert, which was covered with a low plant they call
arafitch, which had tiny green leaves with yellow flowers. There
were miles of small yellow daisies, some red flowers, a spike-like
hyacinth, and in the low places hundreds of tiny blue iris. This
spring was very unusual due to the plentiful rains. Near a hill
called Burgon, there was a pool of black pitch which the geologists call seepage—an indication that there is oil below. The
American geologists were riding around and joined us. It was
exciting to talk with some ordinary Americans. They told me they
didn't approve of missionaries. The roads were only tracks, so
part of the time we just rode over the daisies.

News came over the radio that while King Ibn Saud was worshiping during the yearly pilgrimage, three men from Yemen at-

tempted to kill him with daggers. In Arab history, many have been
assassinated at that time of prayer, as they should not be looking around. Ibn Saud's bodyguard saved him and the men were
killed.

KUWAIT CITY

Kuwait occupies a territory about the size of the state of Connecticut. It embraces Kuwait Bay, a salty blue arm of the Gulf
about ten miles wide from north to south, with a fine deepwater
harbor where ocean vessels can anchor to be unloaded by lighters.

Kuwait City in 1935 was a long, narrow settlement extending
about three miles along the south shore of the bay. The mission
property was located on the seafront at the western end of town,
while the ruler's palace was situated on its eastern extremity.
From our house, we could watch the ever-changing blue water
and the pink hills on the opposite side.

The Arab houses were mostly one-story box-like buildings of
sand colored sundried mud and sea rock. The flat roofs had para-
pets often crenelated and pierced with wooden gutters extending
out over the street to carry away rainwater. The outer enclosures
of the houses formed a continuous high, blank wall forming passages for pedestrians and donkeys in between. Few were wide
enough for a small car. The walls had no windows on the street.
The entrance was a single large wooden gate with a small postern
door in it for easy entrance. Inside the gate, a passage led first to
a *divaniya* where men visitors could be entertained and then led
around a corner to the large, bare open courtyard with rooms,
doors, and windows opening into it. This courtyard was the hareem, reserved exclusively for the women of the household.

The seafront had numerous sea walls built of coarse rock extending into the water to form enclosures for the protection of
local ships. Customs yards and government buildings lined the
shore, and two wide streets led downtown. Between the streets
was a large, bare open plaza called the *Safat*. It was usually filled
with Bedouin from the desert, who came to buy and sell sheep,
goats, camels, and desert produce. The two wide streets also
formed the shopping districts. There the streets were partly roofed
for shade with beams and corrugated metal sheets. Each trader
had a separate stall to display his goods, usually cloth, foodstuffs,
spices, perfume, and mechanical items. There was a section of

the market called the *sook el banat,* or "girl's bazaar," reserved for poor women to sit and sell clothing and various odd items.

The other buildings in Kuwait City were the modest, mud-plastered one-story mosques with their slightly higher minarets. From these a muezzin proclaimed the solemn prayer call five times a day. Only men attended the mosques or stood outside in the open in straight lines making their genuflections in unison. Women said their prayers at home.

The landward side of the town was protected by a city wall of dried clay. The wall boasted towers and three city gates with massive wooden doors. These were closed at night and always guarded, so the authorities knew who went out and came in. The desert outside the wall was mostly clay and gravel. Trails and paths outside the city led to some small suburbs and villages down the coast. The estimated population of Kuwait City in 1935 was about 75,000, although no census had ever been taken.

The Arabs assert that the history of Kuwait began about 1710 when a desert tribe came from the south during a drought seeking food and forage for their animals. They had a loose tribal organization with a leading family, the Al Sabah, whose head was called the amir or shaikh (which means "old man" in Arabic). The ruler would sit in the town center every day to judge cases, solve problems, and consult with the other elders.

The Turks laid some claim to the territory, but the famous Shaikh Mubarrak ended the Turkish claim by killing his ruling half-brother who favored the Turks. When Shaikh Mubarrak seized power, he invited the British to become protectors of Kuwait. The British accepted the invitation in 1899, establishing a Political Agent in Kuwait City in 1904 to handle Kuwait's foreign concerns without interfering internally. Our visas and permits to live in Kuwait had to be approved by this office.

When I arrived in 1934, the British Political Agent was Colonel H. R. P. Dickson. Colonel and Mrs. Dickson and their ten-year-old daughter, Zahra, lived in a large two-story house on the seafront. They were most hospitable, inviting the expatriate community to lovely British functions at their home. He loved to tell the tales he gathered from the Bedouin every spring, when the whole family would spend weeks living in a Bedouin tent in the desert. Colonel Dickson wrote two long books about Kuwait, preserving details of Kuwaiti life that otherwise would

have been lost—delightful gossip of the Bedouin, their love stories, intrigues, jealousies, and battles. He had spoken Arabic
from childhood.

Mrs. Dickson was an admirable mate and an accomplished
woman in her own right. She taught herself Arabic, made friends
of the Arab women, painted scenes of their life, and was a generous, charming hostess. She wrote a book about her life in Kuwait, where she stayed on after the Colonel's death in 1959.

The seafront gave evidence of the skill of the Kuwaiti shipbuilders and sailors. From our veranda, I was fascinated to watch
the graceful vessels with their great lateen sails. When boats took
to oars in the shallow water, the men kept in rhythm with a deep
bass chant. Life here seemed romantic and very different from
the American Middle West. I learned about neap tides and spring
tides and never ceased to marvel at the color of the water, always
changing with the time of day, the wind, the tides, and the season.
Alan Villiers was in Kuwait then, writing his book *The Sons of
Sinbad,* about the tough life of actually sailing one of these ships
from Zanzibar to Kuwait.

When I arrived in Kuwait, shipping in the ocean-going booms
and baghalas was the country's main industry. The north wind
consistently blew the ships south when the date crop was ripe in
Basrah, carrying them first to the Persian Gulf ports, then to
Zanzibar and on to Karachi. Seven months later the south winds
carried the ships back home to the Gulf again. They brought rice,
spices, and Japanese cloth from Karachi and mangrove logs from
Zanzibar for the roofs of houses.

One summer from our veranda I watched the building of a
large ship on the seafront before us. The shipyard was fenced
in and guarded day and night because of the superstition that
if a woman jumped over the keel, the ship was doomed. Women
vied to accomplish this feat, for they believed it would guarantee
pregnancy.

The ship's keel was laid first, and the ribs were then fashioned
from natural bends in the limbs of great trees. The men used an
adze and bow drill. The wood had to be imported from India,
as Arabia had none. For months the carpenters banged away at
the crude locally made spikes, which ranged from nine inches to
three feet in length, driving them in with a sort of musical rhyme.

The launching was a festive day. Everything was decked with
the red flags of Kuwait, crowds of men gathered, and drums and
chanting inspired the men to work. Women had to stay at home.
One man took charge of the operation of sliding the huge ships
on boards and wooden rollers. Motion was applied by men turning the arms of two large capstans set on the sea bottom at low
tide. They bent their backs to supply the force that pulled the
ship with ropes. Then, using a barrel-shaped log hanging by a
rope from the deck, they swung it to advance the ship by striking
its supports. Slowly but surely, the ingenious maneuver was successfully executed, and after some hours the ship was low enough
for the incoming tide to lift her. The ships were not painted but
smeared with a rank, putrid fish oil whose odor permeated the
whole town.

MISSION HISTORY

The Rev. Edwin Calverley and his wife Dr. Eleanor Calverley
arrived to begin their mission career in Kuwait in 1912. They
had completed their two years of Arabic language study at Amara,
Iraq. They lived in an Arab house in the middle of town where
she began a medical practice, as she recounts in her book, *My
Arabian Days and Nights.* He started a school for boys who wanted
to learn English. Arab families considered learning the language
of unbelievers a sinful waste of time.

When they went home on their furlough, Dr. Mylrea had a
two-story house built for the Calverleys at the foot of the hill near
his house. When they returned, Edwin managed the building of
a line of rooms with ample verandas in front of his home to provide a women's hospital for Dr. Calverley. Dr. Calverley brought
an Indian girl to help her as a nurse, so some rooms were built
for her between the hospital and the Calverleys' house. This
nurse was very lonely and unhappy. Then Dr. Calverley found
two elderly Persian widows who helped her in the medical work
as untrained workers.

The location of the two hospitals side by side on the seafront
was hygienic. As there was no running water, the seashore and its
high tides provided a facility for cleaning, for excreting, and for
emptying bedpans. Sweet water had to be purchased and delivered in goatskins by donkeys. It was brought by sailing vessels

from the river in Iraq. The ships were stabilized in shipyards, mooring at high tide so that the men and donkeys could come at low tide to fill the goatskins.

The Calverleys served twenty years in Arabia and were greatly respected and beloved for their tact, wisdom, and loving service. In 1930, Edwin developed a neurologic disease from the heat which prevented them from returning.

DR. MYLREA

It was also my privilege to be associated with Dr. Stanley Mylrea and his wife Bess. They were my neighbors and colleagues in mission and medicine during my early days in Kuwait. Bess gave me daily lessons in Arabic and introduced me to her Arab women friends.

Stanley Mylrea, who was fifty-eight years old when I started my career in Kuwait, became a father figure to me. An Englishman, he had gone to Turkey in 1897 to help in the terrible Armenian massacres. He was deeply impressed there with the need for missions. To prepare himself he went to Philadelphia to study medicine, where he met Bessie London who became his wife. Samuel Zwemer invited him to join the Arabian Mission of the Reformed Church of America. In 1907, the Mylreas came by ship to Bahrain to study Arabic and spend five years working in the mission hospital. In 1913, they were appointed to Kuwait.

Stanley Mylrea was a dignified, aristocratic Englishman, proud of the accomplishments of the British Empire. He had an attractive, intelligent face with an air of determination and a vivid flow of speech graced with appropriate Biblical quotations. His fiery temper often caused him embarrassments. But his sincerity and kindness won him many friends.

He loved to tell the stories of his early days in Kuwait. The ruler, Shaikh Mubarrak, and the prominent families, being jealous of their Muslim faith, absolutely rejected the idea of allowing the despised infidel Christians to live in their city. However, the astonishing success of Dr. Bennett in treating the family of the powerful Shaikh Khazal of Mohamerah, Iran, made them reverse their opinion. Dr. Arthur Bennett was the first physician to arrive, making his calls riding on the haunch of a donkey like the Arab boys. He wrote me years later telling that in order to qualify to practice under the Turks who then ruled the area, he had to

travel by horseback across Iraq and Turkey to Istanbul to take a
medical examination in French. He succeeded.

Shaikh Mubarrak (who had expelled the Turks and allied himself with the British) invited the Arabian Mission to come and
live in Kuwait to run a hospital. The shaikh agreed to sell a vacant
area with a hill on the seafront of Kuwait Bay, west of the resi-
dential area. When Dr. Mylrea arrived, he found that the land-
marks laid down by the ruler's men were incorrect. The shaikh
was furious at the criticism of an outsider. Stanley kept making
regular calls on him. After prolonged postponements, Dr. Mylrea
persuaded the shaikh to come and measure it for himself. Finally,
the ruler arrived with a retinue and crowd and approved the
revised landmark. He also made a speech to welcome these foreigners to Kuwait because they came to help the people. In addition, he gave the entire hill as a gift.

The Mylrea house was built on a platform on the hill in back
of the hospital. Like the hospital, it had a line of rooms with deep,
shady verandas facing the sea. The walls were two feet thick with
very high ceilings of mangrove logs which the white ants would
not eat. Above them, cane matting from Iraq and a thick layer of
clay formed the roof. This kept the house surprisingly cool in the
hot summers. Teak doors and windows opening on the veranda
were innovations for Kuwait. The Arab houses had blank walls
on the street with a single door which led to a courtyard where
all the rooms had access. Then Dr. Mylrea planted a row of tam-
arisk trees in the courtyard.

The winter of 1934 was blessed with unusual rains, so in the
spring Dr. Mylrea's hillside was beautiful with daisies. An Arab,
admiring the sight, remarked with some surprise, "It seems God
loves you Christians." This seemed incredible to an orthodox
Muslim.

Stanley enriched our Sunday evening services when he read
the lesson in his classic English tones. After the service, the
Mylreas and Nurse Mary and I always dined together. Both our
houses had good cooks, so the meal was always an event. After
dinner Stanley would read to us from *Winnie the Pooh* or Dickens.
At Christmas, he read selections from *A Christmas Carol* for our
community parties.

Once a week, we reciprocated with a formal dinner. We women
loved to wear our graceful long dresses. Alternately, we were

guests or hosts of His Highness Shaikh Ahmad al Jabir al Sabah, the British community, and officers from the visiting British naval ships. We loved to sit out under the black velvet sky and trace the brilliant starry constellations. Alas, the beautiful stars disappeared in the murk of the oil flares in later years. Perhaps due to the difference in customs or language, we never invited the Arab Christian families or the Indian or Arab hospital helpers to dinner. The British group preserved a class difference.

Stanley felt his lack of surgical training, so refused all but emergency surgical work. He had a tragic experience just before I arrived. Ray De Young, the short-term missionary in Basrah, came to him with infected ingrown toenails. Stanley operated but the young man died of septicemia. There were no antibiotics then.

In 1935, Stanley had an infection in the sole of his foot which he thought was due to a foreign body. He asked me to incise it. Only later did I learn that he was a mild diabetic. I injected novocaine, which was wrong. The infection spread and fever developed. I was in anguish at the terrible prospect of causing his death. The hospital work had to go on, so Nurse Mary saw the male patients and I saw the women with Bess as my interpreter. To my great relief, Stanley recovered slowly. When I suggested he come to his office with crutches, his pride could not endure it. It was humiliation for a doctor to appear incapacitated.

Stanley delighted in retelling the tale of the famous battle Kuwait fought at Jahra in 1920. King Ibn Saud, having founded his empire, longed to annex Kuwait, with its excellent deepwater harbor. His forces began raids on Kuwait's camels, goats, and sheep. Panic united the population to make the tremendous effort of building the city wall on the side not protected by the sea. Efficient organization and the cooperation of thousands was required to build the wall during the hottest summer months. The city wall was made of clay, more than three miles long, twenty feet high, six feet thick, and supplemented by crenellated loopholed towers every two hundred feet. The top of the wall had a concealed platform for riflemen. Three massive wooden gateways were built like fortresses.

The Saudi forces attacked at the small agricultural village of Jahra, eighteen miles west of Kuwait. They would have won if the Kuwaiti forces had not been helped by the arrival of another tribe. The Saudis withdrew with hundreds of wounded. The Kuwaitis brought their 120 casualties to the mission hospital, laid them down on the veranda, and departed. Stanley and his small group of locally trained staff worked continuously for twenty-four hours. All but four of the wounded recovered. The next day, waiting in a crowded coffee shop, Dr. Mylrea was irritable and complained bitterly that the town had let him do all the hard work, showing no appreciation of its heroes or doing anything to help them. Suddenly, he saw a member of the royal family arise silently, with great dignity, and depart. Stanley deplored his impetuous words. Late that night, three men came bringing a bag of a thousand rupees, saying that the town leaders appreciated what the doctor had done. They regretted their omission and offered help with funds and supplies. From that time, the hospital was an accepted part of the community. The Arabs never forgot their gratitude. A second threat from Ibn Saud was averted with the help of the British navy and air force.

Many problems of running a hospital had to be worked out. Stanley brought dhobis (laundrymen) from India and built a place for them to live and beat the sheets on stones. When a huge bill for customs on hospital supplies arrived, Shaikh Mubarrak canceled it and customs were never charged the mission again. Shah Raza, who had some training in pharmacy, was brought from India. A house had to be built for him and his family.

Edwin Calverley and Stanley Mylrea gave daily talks about Christ in the hospital. One of their servants became a Christian. Isa, the cook in the men's hospital, had been much impressed with the Bible stories which were told every morning before starting the clinic. Quite soon after his employment there, he had come to Dr. Mylrea and said he wanted to be a Christian. He was alone with no wife or child. He had some brothers, but they seemed to pay no attention to him. After some teaching, he was baptized and always stayed faithful. The mission gave him a room to live in on the compound. As long as he was well, he worked as the cook and openly witnessed to his faith in Jesus Christ. He was not persecuted in any way except that the Muslims just ignored him—because he was a humble man. When he died of a fever, we buried him behind the church. He was the only true convert that I knew of among the Kuwaitis. Dr. Mylrea had a very nice tombstone made for him telling of his life, but it was broken by some vandals. Another one was made by Garret De Jong and stands behind the church to this day.

It reads:

> Isa son of Ibrahim: The faithful servant of the Messiah
>   Born 1902   Died 1949
> Well done thou good and faithful servant, enter into the
>   joy of thy Lord   Matt. 25:21
> I know whom I have believed   2 Timothy 1:12

Isa had no immediate family to harass him for his apostasy to Islam and remained faithful until his death, when he lamented sadly, "I die alone."

The inpatients had to bring a relative or friend to help them, as there were no nurses. Most of them had food brought from their homes. About 1930, a great smallpox epidemic killed thousands of children. Dr. Mylrea recommended vaccination which the government carried out.

The mission maintained good relations with the ruler by making regular calls at his councils. One time a thief was caught. The punishment for the crime was to have his hand chopped off. Edwin and Stanley went to the ruler to protest this cruel procedure. The shaikh yielded to their petition and we never heard of another such punishment in Kuwait.

Dr. Mylrea's wife Bess had her own adventures. Bess Mylrea was a real partner to her husband. She had a beautiful face and figure and was given the Arabic name Happy. She had had tuberculosis when young and was never very strong, as she had a chronic cough. The Mylreas had no children. Bess' home was always well organized, and she was a gracious hostess to the many visitors. Her command of Arabic was excellent; she taught me for several hours a day. In the afternoons we would go calling together on her many Arab friends.

She also taught some of them English. One book had a story about pigs, which are considered filthy and unclean by Muslims. Bess was embarrassed to read the story and explained that we keep them clean and fit for human food, sometimes even calling children "pigs." Her student agreed, adding that Arabs call people pigs, too, and added naively, "It isn't nearly as insulting as to call someone a Christian."

Bess enjoyed dressmaking and had a dress form in one room. Women peering through the windows on her veranda were sure it was the Christian's idol.

In the early days, Bess helped in the hospital, but when Dr. Eleanor Calverley and Nurse Mary Van Pelt came, she withdrew. She played the organ for all the services and had a piano at home. Sunday mornings she had a Sunday School class for Arab women in her home. I enjoyed listening and learning the Arabic hymns.

Bess found a tumor in her breast in 1939, so the Mylreas went to India for surgery. She died there at Kodaikanal in 1942 after great suffering and was buried there. Stanley retired to India after serving for twenty-eight years in Kuwait. He had received honors from his country—the OBE and the Kaiser-in-Hind medal. He wrote his unpublished memoirs, which I have consulted to verify my story. He came back to visit his friends in Arabia. He was with us at the end of 1951 when he suffered a heart attack and died on January 3, 1952.

At his funeral a member of the royal family gave an eloquent address expressing deep appreciation for Dr. Mylrea's life of devoted service to the people of Kuwait. The nobleman closed, saying, "He was the father of modern Kuwait." We buried Stanley in the Christian cemetery, now part of the Al Ghanum compound. A bronze marker there proclaims, "The son of man came not to be ministered unto but to minister."

LIVING WITH MARY VAN PELT

Before I came to stay in her house, I heard that Nurse Mary Van Pelt had a difficult personality. Mary had been appointed in 1917, studied Arabic in Bahrain, and started to work in Kuwait in 1919.

At first our relations were pleasant. I admired her efficiency. She had made the house comfortable and attractive with her own and some borrowed furniture. She had trained the Iranian cook, Melicko, to prepare good meals. His younger brother, Mahmoud, kept the house clean, served the meals, carried water to our bathrooms, and ran errands, as there was no phone. We had formal dinners for the British guests and even Shaikh Ahmad which were perfectly served. But Mary referred to the house as her home, implying that I was her guest. Of our monthly salaries of sixty dollars, we each paid forty for the household expenses.

Melicko's salary was twenty dollars a month and Mahmoud's, fifteen. Mary kept the keys to the hospital's old Ford car and always did the driving, claiming she was responsible and I was only a student.

Mary had been in the mission seventeen years and was past her youth. She had rather stern features, gray hair always neatly arranged, and an erect, trim figure. She liked to hold on to the conversational ball, going into great detail. After Dr. Esther Barny's three years in the women's work were finished, Dr. Mylrea asked Mary to take charge of the women's and children's work.

Mary spent long morning hours treating patients and came home for lunch looking very weary. After a short siesta, she would go back in the afternoons to arrange supplies and attend to management. All the help she had was Jameela Elias, a young Iraqi Christian woman who had had some medical training in the British hospital in Basrah. Jameela could read and write some English. She and her husband and little son lived in the rooms back of the hospital. Mary would see the patients, write out a prescription for each which they took to the drug room where Jameela dispensed. The other helpers were two older poor Persian widows who had never been to school but helped with the cleaning. Persians were considered second class citizens in Kuwait. The proud Arabs considered nursing a menial position. The work was extremely hard and long. Thirty-seven thousand women and children were treated in 1934 alone.

Mary made it a point to know the important families, so when she heard that one of their slave women, Haseena, was to be given her freedom, she immediately employed her. The woman proved a great help in the medical work, where it was of utmost importance to know the veiled individuals of the prominent families and how to deal with them. Haseena was a small, thin black Ethiopian with fine features, intelligent, courteous, and cooperative. She had a husband and children who needed what she could earn. We were very glad to have her as a helper and friend.

After my first few months, relations between Mary and me became strained. She refused to talk about anything that happened in the hospital. After my morning lessons, I would go to the clinic, but Mary made it quite clear that she did not want me there. She asserted that since I was a physician, I must take charge when I was in the room. Since it seemed to embarrass her,

I stayed out, as I realized she was doing the work to give me time
to learn the language. She had a sharp tongue criticizing my
blunders and absurdities not only at home but in company. Once
I broke down into tears. We had to live very intimately, and most
of the advantages of youth and education were on my side, which
must have been hard for Mary to take.

Mary planned our meals with Melicko, our cook. There was
always fish and rice available, but chicken, squab, mutton, and
beef could be had at times with a few vegetables, oranges, and
dates. Melicko made good bread and cake, and when ice was
available, we had ice cream. He was very earnest about his work.
He stuttered when he wanted to tell us something. He lived on
the opposite end of town, so he had to walk three miles and get
to our house in time to give us our morning tea at 6:30. He had
another long walk to the bazaar to shop daily for fresh food, as
we had no fridge. Then he would walk home again, only to come
back in the evening to serve us dinner at 8 P.M. Dinner was quite
a production, as Mary insisted that we always wear long dresses
even if we were alone.

Table conversation was often strained, but Mary would tell me
stories and interesting items she heard. One was that the Iraqi
army had one regiment of Christians from the ancient Assyrian
Church of North Iraq. The leaders of the Iraqi army called the
Christians into a walled enclosure, telling them to stack their
guns outside, as it was to be a speech, and then massacred the
whole regiment. In 1939, the Rev. Roger Cumberland, a missionary in Mosul, was shot and killed. It was suspected that he knew
too much about the massacres and might tell the outside world.
Another time, some Bedouin came to the bazaar to buy gunpowder. They used to test it by burning a pinch in the palm of their
hands. If good, it was supposed to burn so fast that it didn't hurt.
This time it hurt and the man threw the sparks back into the
barrel, which exploded. Twelve men passing by were hurt and six
died in our hospital. The curious thing was that the men in the
back of the shop, which was a small enclosed space, were not
injured.

Mary had taught Melicko to cook when he was still a boy. His
family were Iranians who still spoke their mother tongue. They
were considered second class citizens, for the Arabs considered
household service degrading. Melicko's salary was small, but

by living with his parents even after his marriage, he saved his money and bought a piece of property at the edge of one of the main streets. The lot had a mud wall and wooden gate inside of which he built rooms for his growing family. His mother loved him so much that she arranged a second wife for him. He told us he didn't like the idea and after a little while, divorced the second bride. Melicko was thrifty and without guile. When he came back from a pilgrimage to Mecca, he described the sacred ceremonies. One of the rites of the Hajj is that every pilgrim should sacrifice an animal to be eaten and shared with the poor. Now that the pilgrims number many thousands, they brought huge herds of sheep and goats from Somaliland. The meat is more than the population can consume, so they have to have great fires to burn the carcasses. The waste of it so distressed Melicko that he expressed his disapproval openly. This shocked the listeners, as Muslims think that anything religious must not be criticized.

I always wanted to try out my Arabic, so while I waited for lunch, I would converse with Mahmoud, our teenage houseboy. He laughed uproariously at some of my pronunciation until I learned that perfectly good Arabic words usually had a sexual meaning, too. One night, I suddenly woke with the feeling there was someone in my room and called out, "Who is there?" Mahmoud answered, "I." I was frightened, ran to Mary's room, and he ran away. I suppose he took my casual chatter as an invitation, because in Arab society, proper women do not talk with men at all. Mahmoud became psychotic with mania. Once, Mary came in and found him stark naked. She called Dr. Mylrea, and he and Melicko took Mahmond home. He had to be confined with a chain and iron ball on his leg at home and gradually recovered. It was the only treatment available. We had to find another boy.

Mary did not take any active part in the evangelistic work, but she was faithful in attending all the worship services. She told me one Arab lady had confided that she and her husband read the Bible together in secret. Mary did good works, too. She made a pet of a very dignified small boy patient Abd el Kader, who had been operated on for intestinal obstruction. The boy stayed in the hospital a long time and would attend worship services with us. Once, she had left him sitting in her car when she was shopping, and other boys dragged him out and beat him saying he was a Christian. Mary also helped a widow by providing tuition for her son so he could attend school.

Despite all our contact with the local community, we still felt a bit isolated from the larger world. When radios became available, Mary and I put our money gifts together and bought one. We could get the BBC news at 9 P.M., but otherwise it didn't work very well. The news always ended with "God Save the King." Mary greatly admired the British, and some people teased us by saying she even stood up when the radio played the British national anthem, but I never saw her do that.

Mary was nicer to men than to women. I think she regretted that she had never married. She revered Dr. Mylrea and called him an empire-builder. She made friends with some of the skippers of British India ships that called at Kuwait every fortnight. She was very kind and thoughtful to them and let them occupy our guest room.

For the first winter, life meant long, quiet hours of study alone in my ivory tower with only the noise of the waves on the beach. It was isolated, but I enjoyed it. Mary said there were forty people living in the house next to us, but I never saw one of them except the man who used to stand on the flat roof at sunset to watch the sunset. The Arabs set their watches at twelve when the sun disappeared and the next day began. Sometimes a sudden, roaring north wind, called the *Shimaal,* would strike the house like a slap in the face. Our windows were crudely made of wood, so Mary showed me how to stuff the cracks with cotton to keep out some of the cold air. We had unusual rains that year, and once I came home to find my ceiling dripping with a pool on my bed. It fell to Mr. Barny to get a new layer of clay put on the roof. On cold evenings it was extremely pleasant to sit and study by the warm fireplace. We had electricity from the city plant only at night, so we did our reading then.

Two afternoons a week we closed the hospitals and drove off to play tennis with the British. A walled court had been made on the east side of town by favor of His Highness Sir Ahmad al Jabir al Sabah, ruler of Kuwait. Beside the court were cement seats covered with Persian carpets for spectators, and boys were provided to pick up the balls. The shaikh came and visited with us and Dr. Mylrea introduced me. He had a distinguished appearance in his gold embroidered cloak and snowy white head scarf with a gold aghal. He had a dignified, friendly manner as he welcomed me, bestowing on me the distinction of an Arabic name, *Wusmeyah* (this referred to the first rains which had just come after the hot summer). Then he went into a side room to play caroms with his friends.

The British were proficient at tennis, but I was in poor form. After the games, one of the families invited us to tea, which was a ceremony. The Dicksons had a tall Pathan factotum, impeccable in a white uniform and tall, starched turban, who with great dignity served tea and watercress sandwiches from bone china cups and plates. I was thrilled.

We got out to explore the city, too. Mary and I went for walks in the market. We used to watch the baker. He used whole wheat flour and let the dough rise in lumps. Then he flattened it on a wooden holder and slapped it on the inside wall of a barrel-shaped clay oven heated by glowing dung. The dough stuck to the hot wall and when it was done, the baker removed it with tongs. It was delicious when hot and fresh.

Mr. Jashanmal, the Indian merchant, had a variety shop. He always sat at the door to keep an eye on everything. Here we could buy toothbrushes, soap, films, some tins of food like rancid butter, etc.

The cloth bazaar was a small separate court, shaded by beams and palm branches, where each merchant had his private stall with beautiful Japanese cloth. But only men were shopping. Women of good class did not shop. But in the covered *sook el banat* the poor women sat, veiled and concealed in black, selling small piles of odds and ends like a few eggs, unshelled peanuts, nails, pins, and old clothes.

In another place, men were sewing quilts with others, fluffing up the matted stuffing of old mattresses. They had an instrument like a harp with one long pliant string on which they would engage some cotton then twang the string, which vibrated and beat up the cotton to its usual sponginess. Later, I had to engage them in the hospital to remake our mattresses.

We passed the exciting spice shop with its tantalizing smells of seeds, roots, coconuts, chilies, whole ginger, garlic, dried limes, tamarind, frankincense, and rose water, all new to my Midwestern American nose.

Rainwater was still standing in a big pool in the center of the marketplace. Men were digging a pit to drain it. Later we heard that they came across a lot of human bones in digging and took them out to the cemetery to bury them. Some people criticized this saying that they were mixing up male and female bones together. How would the people sort themselves out on the judgment day? Some people had been drinking the rainwater standing in pools. Dr. Mylrea advised the ruler that this would cause sickness and suggested that signs be installed around town to warn people. The Shaikh considered this and then remarked that after all only the very poor people would drink that kind of water.

The sight of foreign women walking around with unveiled faces attracted a crowd of small boys consumed with curiosity, who quietly followed us until the shopkeepers drove them away. Some were friendly and talked with Mary. With the unusual rains, some of the clay walls of the houses collapsed. Some people had been killed. As we passed close by one wall, a small boy said, "Don't go near there—that wall is going to fall." Another said, "Let them go. Let the wall fall on the accursed Christians." Some of them made jingles, which is easy to do in Arabic:

> Christians, Christians, they don't pray
> Even chickens are better than they.

The chickens presumably are giving thanks when they raise their heads after a drink. The fact that we Christians did not openly perform the five daily formal prayers with genuflections as the Muslims did was observed and criticized.

We passed the low wall around the barren cemetery where each grave was marked only by a random rough stone. But I noted on one new grave lay a small, worn pair of girl's sandals.

Once I went for a stroll alone wearing a hat with a perky feather. A boy on a donkey met me. He couldn't take his eyes off this sensation as he swung around departing on the donkey and said, "Ma sha Allah," which means, "What hath God willed."

Some large ships were drawn up on the beach beyond our house. Men would hide between them to play games of chance. Gambling, as well as drinking, is strictly forbidden in the Qur'an. So one day the police raided the place and we had ringside seats from our windows. Most were caught immediately, but some swam out in the water. One little Bedouin boy, his long black braids flying, crying "Ya waili, wailo" (woe is me), ran so fast that the police couldn't catch him.

WEDDINGS

In Basrah, Mrs. Van Ess once asked the girls she was teaching, "What do parents most desire for their children?" The answer was immediate and unanimous, "To get us well married!"

In Kuwait, too, the topic of marriage was of absorbing interest to the women. Since custom kept men and women absolutely separate, no courting was possible, and the choice of a mate was done by the parents. In the Middle East, from the time of Abraham, Isaac, and Jacob, cousin marriage was considered happiest and proper. It is a protection for the wife and children, since both sides of the family are concerned in the stability of the union. Also, it keeps the extended family's financial resources under family control. A young man is considered to have a legal claim to marry his cousin on his father's side if he chooses. So marriages are planned from childhood. Since second and multiple wives are allowed in the holy book, the Qur'an, and women slaves and concubines were available, the evils of consanguinity were not very evident.

The Qur'an gives explicit rules for many marriage customs. The giving of a dowry by the man to the woman is laid down as a law from the Almighty. The dowry may be cash, jewelry, or animals among the Bedouin. The dowry presumably is the bride's property, but since she may be very young and inexperienced, her family decides how to use it. Sometimes it has to be used for the wedding expenses. They used to marry the girls very young. One told me she had never menstruated but had one baby after another.

Marriage is a legal ceremony, not a religious one. The mullah, religious teacher, may be present and read from the Qur'an and say prayers, but not always. The rest of the wedding is a social event to display the hospitality and wealth of the bride's family. There is as much elegance as the family can muster in a solemn, dignified style. Usually most of the women of the neighborhood and women friends and relatives are invited. Some gaiety is put into the event by the hiring of a group of black women musicians who entertain with African music, hand clapping, singing, and dancing with drums and lutes.

When friends of Bess Mylrea and Nurse Mary had weddings in their families, they invited the missionary women to the hareem celebration. Um Abdulla Falay invited us to the wedding of her daughter Muneera, who was about twenty years old. Since births were not registered, no one knew exactly how old she was. Muneera had waited a long time, for there wasn't a right cousin available. Finally, arrangements were made with a merchant of the right social class. He had another wife but was said to be good and kind. Besides, it was time for Muneera to be married. The groom sent two hundred rupees (about sixty dollars), which was used to decorate the bridal chamber and rent some gold jewelry for the bridal week.

We arrived in the evening. The street in front of the house gate was full of black-cloaked women trying to get in. The gatekeeper was supposed to admit the invited and keep out the gatecrashers. The poor man couldn't identify the veiled women, so the crowd smothered him. We had to push our way into the open courtyard where about a hundred women were sitting on mats being served with sweet drinks and biscuits.

Um Abdulla took us in to see the bride, who was sitting alone on the floor of a small, dark room saying her prayers. She was wearing a blue silk dress over which was draped a gorgeous, graceful gown of red georgette embroidered with real gold thread and lines of sequins. She had heavy gold jewelry, a headpiece of one-inch gold squares linked together in a block and set with turquoise and cornelian, necklaces, rings, bracelets, a nose ring, pendants on her long black braids, and anklets. She was the picture of Oriental splendor. But it seemed the wedding was for everyone to enjoy except the bride, who is kept in the background and is supposed to appear reluctant to be married. We left her, sorry that she had to stay in seclusion. Um Abdulla then took us to see the bridal chamber. It was one of the best rooms of the house. The couple would occupy it for the first seven days of the marriage, receiving callers. After that, the bride would be taken to her mother-in-law's house, which would then be her home. The room was large, with a high ceiling, newly plastered walls, and was lit with several bare electric bulbs. Seating consisted of the usual cushions along the walls, which were upholstered in blue silk (there were no chairs). A marble-topped table was loaded with glass vases full of paper flowers, while the walls were decked with long mirrors that still had their price tags on them. A large four-poster bed hung with white georgette curtains and pink silk bed coverings occupied a third of the room. A large wooden chest decorated with brass medallions and studs held the bride's treasures. We sat in the courtyard to await the coming of the bridegroom. As in Jesus' story of the ten virgins, he tarried a long time—two hours, in fact. Finally there came a cry, "Here's the bridegroom!" and the young man appeared.

On the wedding day the men of the groom's family attend mosque for the regular evening prayers. After some masculine celebration, they come to the bride's house, where the men of the bride's family welcome them with congratulations. An incense pot wafting fragrant frankincense is passed around. Silver rosewater shakers perfume the guests' clothes. Bitter hot coffee flavored with cardamom is served by male servants. Then all the men depart, and the father of the bride escorts the groom to the bridal chamber, where he awaits his bride. The women bring her, veiled, and present her to the groom. The door is shut on the couple, who supposedly see each other for the first time. Next morning evidence of the bride's virginity is displayed to the family.

Tragedies can happen too. One groom, on discovering the bride was black, deserted her immediately. Usually the outcome is happy, and the bride sits in splendor to receive female visitors for her grand week.

MY FIRST CASE

One morning Shaikh Ahmad, the amir, sent his car and driver to the hospital asking Nurse Mary to treat his royal wife and cousin, who was ill with fever. Mary attended her at the palace called Desmon, which was at the east end of town. After several days when the lady did not improve, the ruler conferred with Dr. Mylrea, requesting that the new lady doctor come and treat his wife. Mary was furious, but she had to go along with me because I couldn't talk yet. I examined the patient in the hareem and diagnosed a pelvic abscess. Then I went back and talked the case over with Dr. Mylrea, saying that surgery was indicated. We would need a table, a little anesthesia, and a good light, and the surgery should be performed in our operating room. Dr. Mylrea informed the shaikh, but he declared that his wife never left the palace, so the operation must be performed there. He consented to the surgery and promised to have anything we needed ready. We prepared everything as we used to "prep the Wrecking Crew" in Chicago. I reviewed the case in my medical books, just like reading over a recipe before baking a cake; I had never seen such a case in all my training.

With everything in the cars, Dr. Mylrea, Nurse Mary, Jameela, Shah Raza, another woman helper, and I drove over. I went with fear and trembling because this was my very first case where I had to make the diagnosis and then carry out the surgery myself, and my patient was the first lady of the land. As an intern I had always had some chief or teacher around to ask for help. But no longer.

The room had been emptied of all its Persian carpets and cushions, and a wooden table was provided. We set up the necessities and put the patient on the table. Shah Raza, the Indian compounder, gave a little chloroform, which was the only anesthesia we had. I scrubbed in a basin, scared to death, with my knees shaking so much that I feared they wouldn't hold me up. Mary was afraid, too, and said, "At least don't cut the bladder." I picked up the knife, plunged it in, and the diagnosis was immediately confirmed as the foul pus poured out. The shaikh came in and said, "What an awful smell." In a month, the lady was completely well. She presented Mary and me with gorgeous pearl rings.

The Arabs have an expression, "Allah Kareem," which means "God is good." He certainly was. My reputation was established, I felt some self-confidence and thanked God.

My involvement in the medical work intensified after that success. Nurse Mary sent for me one day when I was studying, saying I'd better go with her on a home delivery case. We drove over with some of the neighbor women who had come to tell us about the case. They were not relatives, but in cases like this of real trouble, the women will help each other. The poor girl in labor had one room which her husband had rented from the family that lived in the rest of the house. The room was very small and dark, with no furniture except some floor mats, a pressure-cooking stove, some pots, a bedding roll, and a tin trunk. The girl was lying on some sand to avoid soiling her bedding. It was her first baby, and she had been in labor for three days. The pains which propel the fetus had stopped ominously. I knelt on the ground to examine her, heard no fetal heart tones, and found the head impacted so that forceps would have to be used. Mary explained that we would need to take her to the hospital; we couldn't do the operation on the floor. The patient cried that her husband wouldn't let her. I suggested that someone go to the bazaar and find him, explain the situation, and get his permission. She sobbed in her misery, telling us that her husband had gone on a trip to Iran and had told her that if she left the house before he came back, he would divorce her. She had no relatives to help her, this wasn't her country. She wailed, "If you can't help me here, let me die now."

My hand was forced, so we went back to the hospital and prepared the sterile equipment and returned. I tried to think where to lay the patient, as there was no table and forceps have to be applied perpendicular to the buttocks. The only solution was to position her across her doorstep so her feet would be outside, a little lower than her buttocks. I performed the maneuver as I had been taught, in as careful a technique as possible, but it was not sterile. The baby was dead. The mother never let out a cry though she had no anesthesia.

I saw too many women die from infection in those days before antibiotics and hated to make aftercalls only to see that infection had set in. It so happened that Christmas was near and I was invited to go to Basrah, so I used that for an excuse to not make an aftercall. Months later, when I was sitting in the hospital one day, a woman came throwing her black abba over my head. She embraced and kissed me. It was my young patient, who recovered and, when her husband returned, came to thank me. Medicine seemed a thrilling experience at that moment, and I thanked God.

UNDER THE KNIFE

By summer of 1935, I had decided to have a hysterectomy for fibroids in the uterus. Surprisingly, the physicians at Woman's Medical College had failed to examine the pelvis on their own students. I, too, had failed to recognize my menses as abnormal. Just before I left for Arabia my fibroids were diagnosed, and I couldn't make up my mind then about the operation. Dr. Mylrea sent me to Dr. Boyes, a surgeon who ran the mission hospital at Tripoli, Lebanon. The Rev. and Mrs. Dykstra of Muscat, Oman, and I traveled back across the desert again to Beirut. Then I took the local bus to Tripoli, which was thrilling, as the road ran along the edge of the rocky cliffs overlooking the blue Mediterranean. Dr. Boyes performed a successful operation for me, but I had some regret because now I could never have a child. I figured I had something better in a missionary career serving my Lord.

Dr. and Mrs. Boyes had no children of their own and made their hospital their home, gathering up the tragic young people orphaned in the Armenian massacres and finding them places as nurses' helpers and young doctors. It was a happy place. Mrs. Boyes personally supervised the kitchen, feeding everybody. Having a Christian community to help made running this mission hospital quite different from ours in Kuwait. The mission in Lebanon had decided that they would work among the restricted and depressed Christian population, whereas the Arabian Mission aimed to work especially with Muslims.

I met Rev. and Mrs. Freidinger, who invited me to be their guest at their home at Souk El Gharub. It was a lovely, quiet village set with piñon pines at the edge of a mountain high enough to overlook Beirut and the sea. They found an Arabic teacher for me during my recuperation. I discovered the book *The Forty Days on Musa Daugh*, the true story of the siege and rescue of a band of Armenians in the days of the massacres. Their story had been suppressed by the Turkish government.

Mrs. Van Peursom sent me a letter from Bahrain with a request. She and her husband had been part of the mission medical team which was invited by King Abd el Azeez Ibn Saud to come to Riyadh, the capital of Saudi Arabia, to treat the sick. There she had a chance to talk with many of the wives of prominent men. One of the wives was a Lebanese nurse who had agreed to accompany a doctor from Lebanon to open an office in Riyadh. When she arrived, she found it was a trick and she was to be given to an Arab. She fought the swindle, but there was no way for a single woman to escape from the city and no one to help her, so she had to admit defeat and enter the hareem.

Two sisters informed Mrs. Van Peursom that they had been kidnapped from their Christian family in a Lebanese village and taken to Riyadh and married to Arabs. They begged her to send someone to their village and bring them information about their family. So Mrs. Van Peursom asked me to try to find the place. Mr. Freidinger and I drove to the village and found a man who was a cousin of the girls. The mother was living in another village, so the cousin rode with us and explained that the girls were not kidnapped but sold by their mother. She was a widow, people were starving, and life was desperate. The mother had remarried. We found her at home and told the tale. She listened stoically with no show of emotion, seeming hardly to be interested. Was she trying to cover up her guilt, or had she wiped the memory from her mind? I couldn't have brought pictures of the girls because pictures of women are forbidden in Muslim society. She gave us coffee and wrote a letter for her daughters. We took her picture and went home. I don't know whether the letters ever reached the wives.

Before returning to Kuwait, I spent a week at a conference in a Christian mountain retreat called Dhour esh Schweir. The water was not tested, so I caught amoebic dysentery. I returned to Dr. Boyes, who was beginning to use the new drug Vioform, which cured me.

HOME

By the end of the summer I had spent all my money except just enough to travel back to Kuwait. I counted it twice a day, but one day it disappeared. Mrs. Freidinger said the cleaning woman had come that day, so she talked to her. The woman admitted she had taken it, but she was desperate because her son was in prison and not being fed. She returned the money, so I started my trip back. Kuwait now seemed like home to me, and I was glad to get back.

Kuwait was not only picturesque in its austere beauty. I began to find it intensely interesting and felt admiration and even affection for its way of living. People had an innate poise and dignity of bearing. Life had a feeling of timelessness and peace, with utter indifference to human hurry and effort. Even the sounds were natural: donkeys braying, dogs barking, roosters crowing, and cats fighting. There were very few cars.

The little group of Christians living in Kuwait celebrated Christmas with enthusiasm. Colonel and Violet Dickson gave an English Christmas party at their home with crackers that we popped to find paper hats and horns, and plum pudding baked with tiny silver favors inside, all served in the British tradition. Afterward, Dr. Mylrea read selections from Dickens' *Christmas Carol* as we sat around a warm fire.

The mission invited all the English-speaking group to a carol sing in the chapel followed by an elaborate tea. We women spent a lot of time making sandwiches, cookies, and sweets. Another day, we all helped with a party and tea for the families of the hospital staff and the Arab Christians. All their children were invited and given a gaily wrapped gift from the guild boxes. On Christmas Day, important Arab men and some women would come to call at our houses, as Christ is mentioned in the Qur'an as born of the Virgin Mary.

Holiday calls were important in Arab society. They had a planned strategy. The first day, one end of town stayed home to receive visitors, and on the second day the opposite side stayed home. Usually the calls were short; Arab coffee and sweets were served. The Arab men would call only on the men of the mission, so Nurse Mary and I were left out except for a few friends. The custom is still repeated now with as many as a hundred or two hundred Arab men coming to salute the remaining missionaries. At the Muslim holidays the mission returned the courtesy. Our men called on most of the men of the royal family and other important houses. We women called on the women of the houses to find them graciously receiving us in their best rooms and dressed in their elaborate gold-embroidered clothes. It was a pleasant occasion which knit the town together.

Business was bad during those years. The Saudi government had put an embargo on importing Kuwaiti goods, so the men took to smuggling large quantities of sugar and tea into the surrounding countries. Col. Dickson told of some sailors, shipwrecked and washed up on the Iranian shore, who were imprisoned for illegal entry. When some of their goods washed up later, they were punished for smuggling. One man told me how he was putting gold in the cylinders of a small car hoping to get it into India. Another man swallowed twenty gold coins, but when they didn't pass, he had to come to our doctors for surgery.

The Japanese had begun to make cultured pearls, so there was no longer enough profit for the great Kuwaiti pearling fleets that used to go out every year. One time five men went out on a small private dive and happened to find an extraordinarily large, lustrous, white pearl. It was so unusual that Shaikh Ahmad paid almost twelve thousand dollars for it. About this time the Shaikh was invited to the royal court in London to celebrate the

King's twenty-fifth anniversary. Dr. Mylrea asked Shaikh Ahmad whether he was going to give the pearl of great price to the king. He said no, he was going to show it to him. I heard that his devoted bodyguard went with him, keeping the pearl in his mouth for safety. The great pearl is said to be in the royal safe in Kuwait, but no one I know has ever seen it.

MISTAKE

In spite of the joyousness of my first Christmas in Kuwait, our community had suffered greatly that year (1935). It has been said that "in the world, ye shall have tribulation," and mission hospitals are no exception. Disaster struck when Shah Raza, the Indian compounder, gave the wrong drug to a small boy who died in convulsions. The druggist had dissolved cocaine in a bottle, intending to put it into an eye-drop dispenser, but the stopper stuck, so Shah Raza set it aside. He forgot to change bottles. When he received an order for a drug for the little boy, he made the error of dispensing the cocaine solution instead. The child drank it and went out to play. As soon as Shah Raza noticed his mistake, he rushed to inform Dr. Mylrea. They called the boy in from the playground and started treatment, but it was too late. The boy expired. Heartsick, they summoned the boy's waiting mother and revealed the catastrophe. Immediately she broke into wild, harrowing screams. She tore her hair and clothes, shouting, "Christians are killing Muslim children!" She swore she would have Shah Raza's life. Everything stopped. Men carried away the limp body. Then, ominously, everyone disappeared from the hospital.

Dr. Mylrea drove over to call on the ruler to inform him of the disaster. The chief magistrate, Shaikh Abdullah Jaber, came over to investigate the affair. The next day the police came with an order to arrest the compounder. Shah Raza said good-bye to his wife and children and limped (since he was lame) to the car carrying his bedding roll. He was imprisoned with an indictment of first-degree murder.

The situation was complex. Shah Raza was an Indian Christian convert from Islam who was willing to talk about Christ to the Arab Muslims. This had offended them. A week before the accident, he and his little girls had been on the beach. The girls were playing with this same boy, when the boy ducked one of the girls and Shah Raza spanked him. He ran screaming to his mother that a Christian had beaten him. She concluded that the poison had been given to her child in revenge. The stricken family were also Persians, an inflammable foreign Shiite minority in an orthodox Sunni Arab nation.

Shah Raza had an Indian British passport, so was due to be tried and defended by the British Political Agent in Kuwait. The agent, Colonel De Gaury, was not friendly to the American mission. Upon investigation he found there was some question about exactly where Shah Raza was born. He declared the passport of doubtful validity and refused to help. The problem would have to go back to the Indian government, which would take a long time. If the passport was invalid Shah Raza would be considered a subject of the Shaikh of Kuwait and be tried under Muslim law. This law reads that the injured family have a right to demand a life for a life. On the other hand, they can receive blood money as compensation. This is a device worked out by the Bedouin tribes to prevent bloody feuds which might last for generations.

The affair was further complicated by three groups of antagonistic personalities: contentious leaders of the Iranian faction, hostile to the Christians and to the Sunni government; a group of wealthy, powerful Arabs from Iraq who seemed to enjoy causing political strife; and the British government representatives, who disliked having Americans in prominent positions in Arab societies.

For a few days very few patients came to the hospital. Eventually they came back because they had no place else to go. Nurse Mary took Shah Raza's place as pharmacist. I offered to help run the women's clinic with Bess Mylrea as translator. Crowds gathered in town and marched around the hospital yelling that Christians were killing Muslims. Shah Raza's wife, who lived in a little house in the back of the compound with her six children, was frantic with worry.

Bess and I talked it over and thought it might help if we would call on the bereaved mother to express our sympathy. This family had been friends of the doctor for a long time. The child's father had been sick, and Dr. Mylrea called on him at home nearly every day until he died. A brother had been treated for tuberculosis and because the family was poor, all care was given free. So we agreed to try to call. Dr. Mylrea walked with us to the door. Bess and I went into the women's quarters. The mother was sitting in the center of a large group of silent black-draped women in the open courtyard. She was tearing her hair, her clothes were rent, and she threw dust about. She shouted continually until her voice was in shreds, "An eye for an eye, a tooth for a tooth, and a life for a life." The hostility was palpable. Bess tried to talk but it was useless. So after a while, we arose and left.

Dr. Mylrea and I went to call on Shah Raza in prison. They had put him in an upper room instead of the foul, dank dungeons below. Prisoners were not fed, so his wife sent meals daily by a servant. He was disconsolate. I felt like weeping, too. He had worked thirty years without an error and one small mistake had such tragic consequences. Members of the Shiite sect sat outside under his window cursing him all night so he couldn't sleep.

Dr. and Mrs. Mylrea were stunned, weighed down with grief and worry. I was studying the Psalms in Arabic and marveled how they fit. "My sorrow is continually before me. I am bowed down and brought very low. All day long I go about mourning. I am utterly crushed. My friends and neighbors avoid me. They stand far away because of my troubles." (Ps. 38, selected verses). Days, weeks, and months went by. The ruler refused to communicate with Dr. Mylrea.

Finally, the case came to court. The veiled mother stood up and demanded Shah Raza's life. A witness said he saw the druggist forcing the boy to drink. Since the witness was obviously almost blind, his story did not even look true. We offered blood money, but the mother scornfully refused. No decision was made. The ruler probably was afraid of the vociferous Iranian minority, so Shah Raza stayed in prison. This went on for almost seven months. At last the ruler sent word that the hospital was to pay the family blood money over twice the usual amount. Shah Raza must leave town.

At last the tension was over. We escorted him and his family sadly to the launch to get the ship to India. He went back a broken man. He told us later that he was never able to get work as a compounder again. The town seemed to forget the incident, and the hospitals soon were overflowing with patients once more.

4. *A Real Doctor*

The new year began with difficulties at home and increased pressure at work. In January of 1936, my Aunt Jennie Bruins arrived. She had been making a trip around the world and came up from Bombay by the British India ships which carried cargo, passengers, and mail, to stay with me for a month. She never approved of my missionary career but could understand it. There definitely was tension between Nurse Mary and Aunt Jen and me. Mary made sharp criticism and disparaging remarks. However, Aunt Jen and I would walk across the empty lots back of the mission to visit Joan Scott of the Kuwait Oil Company and found her a relief from the hostility in our house.

Since the medical work had lost a trained helper in Shah Raza, the station decided that I should continue to run the clinic for women and children. There was no chance of finding and bringing another trained helper from India in the near future, so I took on significant responsibility sooner than I had expected to. Dr. Mylrea ran the men's work and Nurse Mary acted as pharmacist and storekeeper for both hospitals. Mr. Barny continued to give me an Arabic lesson in the afternoons, as I had not completed the required two years of language study. My progress had been nothing but passing.

The social custom of Arabia at that time decreed that the life of men and women be rigidly segregated, except in intimate family life. Men and women meeting in the street did not greet. In fact, they acted as if they weren't even interested in each other. When a man had to talk about a woman, he used an expression which meant, "Excuse me for mentioning it." It meant that the subject was disreputable like dogs or donkeys. So the men's and women's hospitals were separated, though they stood side-by-side on the seafront.

The women's hospital consisted of a one story line of rooms, a consultation room, a treatment and drug room with five bare rooms with wooden beds for inpatients, and a scrub and operating room. There were wide, shady verandas on the two long sides, with wooden screens to conceal patients. All the windows were very small and high, which made the rooms dark. The consultation room had a table for the doctor, a few chairs, a couple of benches, a sink with running salty water, a screened examination table, and a ceiling fan. The seafront served as bathroom and toilet.

Bess Mylrea sat beside me in the consultation room as interpreter, but even so, the first few months were a blur of confusion and desperation to me. I had been forgetting medicine in applying my mind to learning Arabic. I still couldn't understand most of what was said to me. The local women considered a person who couldn't comprehend Arabic to be stupid. They had never tried to learn a foreign language. But after repeating the same questions in Arabic a hundred times a morning, I began to catch on.

All of a sudden, the troubles of hundreds of strange women and children had been thrown on my shoulders. I was stiff and tense with anxiety. The tragic accident of Shah Raza was fresh in my mind. It was the feeling of being all alone in the responsibility that was agony. During my internship, there were always other interns, residents, and the chief to give me a clue when I didn't know what to do. Sympathetic nurses often made tactful and helpful suggestions when I faced a dilemma. But now I began to doubt myself. Nurse Mary wasn't much help. She would fix her cold, blue eyes on me and say, "You are a responsible physician and quite competent to handle all situations," and walk away.

I was under a terrible strain of not knowing whether anything would succeed. For medical practice at home in the U.S., my training had been adequate, but now I was transplanted into an entirely different setting. The cardinal law of medical treatment is, "First, do no harm." But sometimes I could not be sure that I had fulfilled that charge. The pressure of our work was intense. There were more patients than could be properly treated—130 to 200 patients, five mornings a week. I tried some surgery beyond my training. Some people died who should not have died. They have gone to our Father, but I have to live with the accusing memory.

I was not protected from stupid mistakes and colossal blunders by virtue of being a missionary. I had some triumphs; still, failure was bitter. I could only gain experience through trial and error. I had put my hand to the plow and could not look back. I felt I was needed, asked forgiveness of God, and continued my work.

A crowd of patients gathered early every morning on the benches or the mats on the veranda. Draped in their heavy black abbas and closely veiled, the women gossiped with each other and tried to control their crying babies and lively children. Nearly all had walked a mile or more and were in a hurry to get treatment and return home before the heat of the noonday sun. Their pathetic confidence in me, that I could do something to help, made me feel humble. They had no place else to go.

My predecessors had worked out a system of handing out tin tops of different colors to the women, in the order in which they arrived. This kept some order. Each one had a numbered card with her name which corresponded to the record cards on my desk. It was important to keep records, but there was no helper who knew numbers, so I had to look up each one myself. Many patients lost their cards or brought cards of someone else in the family. I would admit five women to the office to be seen in turns and ask what the trouble was. Then I would stamp the date, write down the chief complaint, sometimes make a quick examination, and write out some drug to be obtained in the treatment room. As the clinics ran from sixty to two hundred in those early years, that was all the time I could give each one. I felt that some of them had come to the hospital just to get out of their homes and see other people.

My only trained helper was Mrs. Jameela Elias. She was a young Iraqi woman of the Roman Catholic group in Basrah. She had some training at the British military hospital there and had been working in our hospital for three years. Her husband and small son, Edwaar, lived in the rooms back of the hospital. She shouldered the strenuous drudgery of the treatment room, giving the medicines, instructing the patients how to take them, making injections, and carrying out simple treatments or telling the elderly Persian women helpers what to do. I had to rely on Jameela's help a great deal, but it was embarrassing when I had to go to ask her what kind of treatment was expected and available for various complaints.

That was before the days of sulfa and antibiotics. Patients had to bring their own bottles. We gave them medicine enough for three days. Jameela would dilute the concentrated solutions of cough mixtures, solutions of potassium iodide, iron, quinine, and strychnine, and diarrhea mixtures. The patients brought match boxes for ointments like zinc oxide, ammoniated mercury, yellow oxide of mercury, etc. We had few pills, aspirin and calomel came as powders. So in the afternoons, Jameela had to weigh out the powders and have the helpers divide them and fold them into paper squares. She treated the trachomatous eyes by inverting the upper lid and painting the conjunctiva with a dilute solution of silver nitrate. Dressings for ulcers and draining abscesses had to be changed. And then there were the numerous injections. People were firmly convinced that injections were much more efficacious than oral drugs. It meant keeping water boiling to sterilize the syringes and needles for injections of vitamins, bismuth salts, milk, emetine, and Neosalvarsan. Jameela worked very hard—usually cheerfully, but sometimes understandably irritated and weary.

We had very few inpatients. They had to bring their own bedding, as all we had was the locally made bare wood bedsteads. Patients also had to bring someone from their family to stay with them and take care of them, emptying bedpans in the sea. Food had to be brought from their homes. The only nursing care we could give was to take temperatures and dress wounds. Jameela helped me with hospital deliveries, which came at any time of the day or night. Usually, I was asked to do the deliveries at homes.

The agreement with the ruler was that we would treat his family at home. But sometimes the royal car would arrive during a large clinic and I would have to take the medical bag, leave the patients, and go off on a call which might take a couple of hours.

During that first year I worked, Jameela's husband developed a septic sore throat. In spite of using all I had, he died. Since he was Christian we buried him in the space behind the church and the back wall of the compound. She continued to work for us. We paid her out of what we took in and thought it was a fair salary, but looking back and learning how difficult it was to get helpers, we should have paid her more.

Mission policy was that the medical work had to be self-supporting aside from the salaries of mission personnel. Buildings and equipment were gifts from friends in the home churches. So I had to ask the patients to pay for their drugs. The women rarely had cash, as by custom they did no shopping. This was the men's duty. All of the women declared they were very poor and couldn't pay. It was easier to collect payment at the men's clinic, so I didn't turn away the women who really needed treatment. Some of the women would say, "Send the bill to my husband." They assumed that everybody knew who they were, but the women all looked alike to me. And to make matters even more confusing for me, wives did not take their husband's name but kept their own (Fatima bint [daughter of] Abdulla, for example). Some of the women would tell me that it was my duty to treat them free of charge, as I was a Christian and would burn in hell unless I helped Muslims. Gradually Dr. Mylrea taught me how to keep accounts, write out the bills in correct Arabic style, itemize and price each item, and then send the bills with our messenger, Nasr, to find the husband's shop or office in the bazaar. I began to know the names of some of the important houses: Jena'e, Bhebehani, Saadoon, Jusaar, Sidhan, Ma'arafi, Mutairi, Gharabeli, and the El Ghanum. If I collected small coins worth about five dollars a day, I thought I was doing well, and could pay Jameela and the other helpers.

CASES IN THE EARLY YEARS

One main complaint was sore eyes due mostly to trachoma, which was easy to diagnose. Another was "chebd" (meaning liver). The patients located it in the mid-abdomen. I never discovered exactly what it meant. The British had a feeling they called "liverish," but Americans didn't seem to get it. I soon learned that roundworms were endemic. I gave a dose of castor oil and then prescribed three days of ten drops of oil of chenopodium daily. One small girl told me she passed a hundred roundworms. She laid them in piles of ten each on the flat roofs which the people used for defecation and came up with ten piles.

The variety and number of complaints encompassed the whole book of medicine. There was pain in the knees and back, diarrhea, toothache (there was no dentist in Kuwait), abscess, skin infection, cough often due to prevalent tuberculosis, fevers of unknown origin, malnourished and sick babies, and all the troubles of pregnancy and sterility. One favorite symptom was "galb" (meaning palpitation of heart). Many had rates of 120 per minute, for which I never found the cause. In the early days we did not see appendicitis or diphtheria. I wonder why. Later when Kuwait began to import our foods it became fairly common. There was practically no malaria because there was no sweet water for breeding mosquitoes. Diagnosis was difficult. We had no X-ray or laboratory. When I wished to make a physical examination of a patient, some demurred, saying that a doctor surely knew everything so why bother.

The heat was a burden. Once on a house call, I wondered why I couldn't shake the thermometer down to normal and then realized the *room* temperature was 110 degrees. To cool off when the clinics were finished, the Mylreas and Nurse Mary and I would put on our suits and get into the car to go for a swim on the sandy beach outside the city wall. That was pure joy. We would return for lunch. Then as was the Arab custom, we slept away the hottest hours of the afternoon. We got up and went to work a second time until sunset.

Some of the incidents which stand out in my memory record what Kuwait was like before oil and picture what missionary life was.

One afternoon, three women dressed and veiled in elegant black were brought in by their black manservant, who related the complaints of each in turn. A physician was considered to have some sort of magical insight. The women resented questioning and felt an examination was too much trouble.

Another day, the first three delivery cases who came to the hospital were difficult. The mothers came too late and all had dead babies. The prevalent opinion was that God had ordained that women should bear children; He would see that the process was carried out according to His will without interference by doctors. In fact, it was presumptuous to interfere.

Usually when labor pains began at home, the women would retreat to one of the small back rooms of their house to avoid making a mess in the living rooms. She reclined on a bed of sand

with some older woman sitting with her. There were no real midwives. If the case delivered normally, the woman cut the cord of
the baby and dressed it in black swaddling clothes. She straightened the legs and bound them and the arms into a compact
bundle tied up with long strips like a little mummy. Then they
would pack the mother's vagina with bits of rock salt for several
days. This was done to heal wounds and shrink the parts back to
their former size. However, this treatment dehydrated the vaginal
tissues and often reduced the cervix to a hard core. At a following
delivery, the cervix would not dilate to allow the baby to be born
and the mother would die.

Other things could go wrong, so God evidently intended
people to learn how to help. I found forceps were a wonderful
help. A Caesarian section was usually out of the question, but I
found if I was very slow and patient, forceps could deliver most
of the babies. The women would wait two or three days, sometimes, before coming to the hospital and even then had to get the
permission of their husbands. Several times, it was too late to
help. Once, I was called to a case in a home and arrived just in
time to deliver a baby arriving breech. Quickly, without washing
my hands, I made the correct twist and delivered a live baby.

I had just begun working in the clinic when an appalling case
of human suffering appeared. A stern-faced Arab dragged in his
wife. The helpers laid her on a bed and called me. The woman
lay silently gasping for breath, her throat cut in a gaping wound,
her chest open with a stab wound exposing the throbbing heart.
Her tortured eyes sought mine as I realized, in anguish, my im-
potence. In sad silence, she died after agonizing for a couple of
hours. The Arab helpers in the men's hospital joined in the discussion of the justice of the case. The man suspected his wife of
the crime of adultery. According to the custom, it was said to be
his right or even his duty to execute judgment even to the punishment of death on her. No legal penalty was imposed on him
for this act. He was to be honored for showing courage in de-
fending the law of Islam, by which this crime deserved death. In
wrath, the man had first cut her throat but missed the great blood
vessels. Then he stabbed her chest but only opened the heart cavity. She had lain in the house in that condition three days and on
the fourth, his anger cooled. Perhaps he felt remorse for his ter-

rible vengeance and brought her to the hospital. The men helpers felt that he was justified. The women were silent. It strengthened my resolve to serve the women who suffered this injustice.

The Muslim belief is that all that happens is the will of God, and that the right attitude to Him is to mention Him in every sentence. They used the sacred name so frequently that it seemed like swearing. To say, "hurry up," the expression is *Yallah*, "O God." To express wonder it is, "what has God willed." Excuse me is, "I ask forgiveness of God"; good-bye is, "In the keeping of God"; the reply to any remark is *Al hamdallah*, "the praise be to God." Any future proposition is always prefaced by *In shah Allah*, "if God wills." When I directed patients how to take their medicine, the invariable answer was, "If God wills"—so whatever the outcome, the safe retreat was that God willed it. However, the rule could not be depended on to cover all medical errors, as the case of Shah Raza showed.

The Arabic language lent itself to other picturesque expressions. The women loved to use the diminutive like the Scotch with its "wee hoose" and called their children little chicks. Men made speeches with such thunderous blasts that the listeners sometimes admitted they didn't understand what was meant.

TRACHOMA

Sore eyes were a major affliction to the Kuwaiti population. The smallpox epidemic in 1930 had caused much blindness. Trachoma was endemic. It began as inflammation in children, and when burned out, caused scars in the lining of the upper lids. When these scars shrank, they turned the lids inward, causing the lashes to brush the cornea. This was agony and eventually destroyed vision. People tried to pull out the irritating hairs with tweezers, but they grew back quickly.

Dr. Wells Thoms, our mission doctor in Muscat, visited Kuwait and taught me the lid-graft operation, which pushed the lashes away from the eyeball. With local anesthesia, the upper eyelid was everted and a slit was cut just behind the lashes. The incision was kept open by suturing the lid to a bandage around the forehead. Then from the inverted lower lip, a sliver of mucous membrane was lifted, cleaned, and then laid in the incision opened in the upper eyelid. The sutures were left holding the lid open and the eye was dressed with yellow oxide of mercury ointment. I took a couple of sutures in the lower lip if I took two slivers from it. The patient went home, waited for two days, and then came back to remove the sutures and replace the upper lid. It was a very successful operation because the blood supply to the lid was so good. The graft nearly always took, so the lashes would be pushed away from the eyeball. Once some men from one of the British ships came to watch the operation and remarked that it was a very ladylike procedure.

Dr. Calverley left behind a set of eye instruments, so I tried cataract surgery. The first two cases were tragic. The patients lost what little vision they had. Then came Bebe, slowly groping along the veranda trying to find her way. Her eyes had no infection, so I dared to try again. For once, it was a smashing success. She was poor and had no family, so she offered to work in the hospital the rest of her life. She was sweet-tempered and always willing to do the meanest task. We got glasses for her, and from then on her name was Bebe, the Wearer of Glasses. Most women refused to wear spectacles.

THE SUMMER'S HEAT

It was hot in the city, but dry, so the heat was more tolerable than on ships in the bay where the air was also extremely humid. In those days, the ships had no air-conditioning. Many men died from heat stroke and are buried in Kuwait's cemetery. In my second summer, Dr. Paul Harrison substituted for Dr. Mylrea, who went home on furlough. One night, the sailors brought us an officer from a freighter who was overcome by the heat and not expected to live. I had just read a medical journal article about the discovery that people working in the heat needed increased salt intake. Paul had not read it and doubted its efficacy. I determined to try it, but we had no parenteral fluids. I found some big bottles, rubber stoppers with holes, rubber and glass tubing, needles, and adapters, made them fit, and boiled the lot to sterilize it. Our still provided distilled water. We weighed out the salt needed, boiled it, and ran in about 2,000 cc's intravenously. Nothing happened. Paul decided the man's heart was getting irregular, said he would sit with the patient, and advised Jameela and me to get some sleep. Next morning, I came over early and was thrilled to see the officer sitting up and asking for food. I'll never forget that happy feeling. He complained because they hadn't left him any clothes or his dentures. His shipmates thought he was finished. The man went away on another ship, but we never heard from him again.

At the end of the summer, the sad babies whose mothers did not have enough milk fell victim to an epidemic of diarrhea and dehydration. Bottles and milk powder were no solution, as the people had not the slightest idea of preventing bacterial contamination. I recommended letting the babies nurse the goat directly, but that idea didn't seem appropriate to their mothers. The idea of giving a boiled egg met the objection, "But he doesn't eat. He only nurses." One baby died because the family kept the formula nice and warm in a thermos where bacteria grew very well. The town women had learned to give babies a small dose of opium for diarrhea and to quiet crying. The effect of this home remedy was evident when the child lay white, quiet, with pinpoint pupils. An injection of caffeine helped, but later we had nalorphine, which woke them up in a minute. We were at fault once when the clinic mistakenly gave tincture of opium instead of paregoric. Fortunately, the babies were brought back in time to save them. Bedouin babies, newborn, came in with tetanus and rigor because the Bedu tied the cord with a thread pulled from the edge of a woman's abba, which dragged over sheep and goat's dung. Sometimes the mother developed tetanus from infection at childbirth. We tried to save them, but to our sorrow most of them died. The women who had no help in deliveries were often so badly torn in the bladder that urine leaked. The tear would not heal. They smelled so bad their families couldn't stand to have them in the tent. Once while I was trying to repair such a tear, where the surgical field was at the bottom of a deep hole, the electricity went off and I had to finish with a flashlight. But some of them recovered.

A Bedouin came bringing his wife on a donkey and said he had walked twenty days. He shouted as is the Bedouin custom, "Are you sure you have good medicine?" I assured him that most people were cured. He paid about sixty cents and I gave him the best we had. One Bedouin woman came from a long distance with one enormous breast. I was puzzled what it could be. She seemed well otherwise, and it wasn't painful, so I tried an exploratory aspiration and drew pure milk. Finally, I tried a trocar, and we evacuated a hundred ounces of good milk. I wanted to give it to some of our sick babies, but the woman refused. It seems if a woman gives her milk to another's child, it is the same as adoption.

Among the clinic patients there was a definite class structure. Most of them were Arabs who had a rigid social ladder. The women of the ruling family demanded medical house calls. The aristocratic women of the merchant and shipping class would not wait their turns at the clinic, but expected to be seen immediately. The Persian helpers understood this requirement and informed me which were VIP's and must be admitted right away. It didn't seem fair to me, so I charged them an extra fee. The poorer women usually did not complain and showed an attitude of respect. This respect extended even to the concubine of the ruler, who was a very pleasant, dignified black woman and the mother of his royal sons. The clinics were so large that some people had to wait a long time. When they grew impatient, they shouted, pushed, and kicked the office door. I couldn't blame them.

A large number of patients were Iranian. I did not learn their language so had to have an Iranian woman for interpreter. They seemed to have a freer life than the Arab women, and some were willing to be helpers in the hospital. No Arab woman would do that work. It was considered a servile, low prestige position. Two elderly Iranian women, Khanum and Haji, helped us for over five years. They couldn't read or write or speak good Arabic, but they helped Jameela give drugs and do some treatments. We couldn't have done without them. I was grateful for them. In the evenings, Haseena, a freed slave from the Sagaar house, would stay in the hospital. She knew the important houses and the correct attitudes. When patients came at night, she would call me and help out.

An unsatisfying aspect of the clinic was the lack of continuity. After treating a child, we often didn't see the mother for a month. Sometimes the child died. When I asked what happened, the mother would reply, "It was the will of God" and try to smile to show she was submissive to the Almighty and then break down in sobs in bitter grief.

A doctor was supposed to be able to fix anything that went wrong with the living body. One patient with tuberculosis said, "You can cure me if you want to." I had to specialize in omnipotence, but when confronted with an aching tooth or a face swollen with a dental abscess my courage failed. Dr. Mylrea had trained one of the Iranian men helpers to extract teeth, so I went over to learn from him. He took the dental forceps, grasped the tooth low to the root, and rocked it until it loosened, not heeding the cruel pain or groans. I tried it myself, but to my horror the jaw-bone seemed to come out with the molar. It turned out to be a sequestrum, a loose bit of bone which had to be removed anyway.

EXPECTATIONS AND DISAPPOINTMENTS

Just outside the Jahra city gate was the encampment of a Bedu tribe called the Sulaibi ("cross"), who did odd jobs and were despised. At the holidays, the women would let down their hair and dance openly with their men, which the town women never would do. One girl of the tribe came with her mother to deliver her baby. She couldn't take the baby because she wasn't married, so we kept the cute little girl several months. By that time the oil company brought some families, and one of them helped us and wanted to adopt it. Dr. Mylrea and I and the family went to Shaikh Abdullah Jaber, the chief magistrate, who remarked how well the child was cared for and gave his written permission for adoption. They took her back to Arkansas and I heard of her no more.

In spite of the seclusion and veiling of women, Satan did seem to appear and girls would come to the clinic asking to be relieved of an unwanted pregnancy. It was considered the duty of a brother or father to wipe out the sin by killing the girl. I knew that happened, so I regretted having to refuse. But I promised if they came for delivery, we would keep it a secret and find a mother for the baby, and they could go home immediately. One woman with sterility asked for a baby left with us. She promised to bring it back for care, but I lost contact for a year. When she returned I asked about the child. She told me the child was well. "It turned out to be black so we are making it our servant," she said. The stern treatment of girls suspected of fornication may have been to avoid the suspicion of incest which one girl told me did exist.

One time when Miriam was my Iranian translator and I spent too long talking with a girl in trouble, she exclaimed, "She is a sinner. Let her bear her punishment." I remonstrated, "We all have sinned." She answered, "But I haven't done any great sins."

Sins are classified in degrees of guilt. The greatest sin is to worship anyone except God as Christians do.

Once the wife of one of the government officials whispered in
my ear and asked me to come and help her daughter. I drove with
her to the so-called "bad area" of silent streets where no children
played around the doors. We entered a door into a small, neat
courtyard and then into a bare, clean room furnished with only a
low cot. Here her daughter, a very young girl, was unsuccessfully
laboring to deliver a baby. Clearly, the girl was unmarried and
taken to the area of secrets where no one talked. We brought the
girl to the hospital and delivered the live baby with forceps. Over
my protests, the mother called a taxi and took both of the patients
home immediately. The next day the girl's father sent for me to
treat his daughter at home, which I did. There was no baby in
the house and nothing was said about the diagnosis. I suspect the
mother decided the baby couldn't live and found some way for it
to die. As long as there was no talk, there was no penalty. I felt
this father knew and loved his daughter.

Other problems relating to fertility were not simple, either.
There was Nadia, who had been married at the age of twelve and
had become a great help to her mother-in-law, Khadija. Nadia
was greatly loved. Years went by, but she didn't have menses or
become pregnant. Finally the mother-in-law brought her to the
hospital, where it was found that she lacked female organs. Society dictated that a marriage must be fruitful, so after a while,
Khadija found a second wife for her son. Nadia accepted the
situation without resentment and became a sister to her partner's
wife. When the second wife produced children, Nadia helped her
and graciously cared for them as if they were her own.

The women seemed to prefer polygamy to divorce. Divorce
meant that they would have to go back to their father's or a
brother's home. The women usually married again. Polygamy is
a harder situation than monogamy, but it has some advantages.
However, it could be a source of great bitterness.

The women were always under the fear of being divorced. The
Qur'an permits a man to divorce his wife by saying the words,
"You are divorced" three times, and the marriage is finished.
The woman then must return to her father's or brother's home
for protection. She may marry again after four months, but the

children belong to the husband who fathered them, although he did not always take them away from her immediately. The women felt that if they were pregnant, they were less likely to be divorced, so they were not interested in family planning. They kept on having many pregnancies even though many children died.

One woman became paralyzed from her waist down after a home delivery and was admitted to the hospital. The carpenter sawed a round hole in the wooden bed and we cut a mattress to fit with a bucket below. It was a distressing case. She lived a couple of months and died. All we could do was to keep her clean. A relative took care of the starving baby.

Amoebiasis must have been common. I remember draining a liver abscess with a trocar and getting the typical chocolate pus.

Cases of food poisoning were called "malhoos." The word meant licked. They were certain that the common house lizards had licked the food. One native treatment for food poisoning was cautery, which was used so often on little babies that the abdominal burns needed as much treatment as the diarrhea and vomiting. The women told me how they heated a long nail in the fire and then touched the baby's abdomen with it. They felt they had to do something.

The head scarfs were so tightly wound that I usually did not ask the patients to remove them. If I did, often especially in the Bedouin, the lice were thick and sometimes the scalp inflamed. One woman did not want to remove her face veil. When I insisted I was embarrassed. She was veiling closely to hide a ghastly harelip. I didn't dare tackle that kind of repair. Another woman came with a swollen, bruised scalp. She had been beaten by her husband. The Qur'an tells men to beat their wives for disobedience.

In 1937, we received the first sulfa, called Prontosil. It was a red fluid in ampuls for injection. What a miracle it was. The year before, I had treated a case of extensive skin disease of both hands and arms. It took a month to heal with wet compresses. With Prontosil, it cleared in a week. When the fee was the same the second time, the woman objected vigorously, claiming we should charge less because she recovered so much faster this time around.

The only time reckoned by my patients seemed to be the "now." The past was finished. The future was the will of God, which no one could know. There were no records of births or deaths. It was impossible to make appointments. The day ended at sunset, when watches were set at twelve o'clock, as in the parable of the laborers hired at the eleventh hour. After sunset it was the next day. This arrangement could be confusing when one was invited to an Arab evening function. Friday was the Muslim day of worship but not necessarily a day of rest. Days had a rhythm governed by the five times of prayer. The first prayer came at dawn, then noon, then "asr," when the sun had gone three-fourths of its way across the sky, then sunset, and two hours after sunset. Months were lunar, which made their year about ten days shorter than ours. This caused Ramadan, the month of fasting, to come sometimes in winter and sometimes in summer, when abstaining from water could be serious. Muslim years were dated from the flight of Mohammad from Mecca to Medina (the hegira), so the year 1981 A.D. is 1400 AH, for example.

Numbers were ignored. When I'd ask a woman how many children she had, she would count on her fingers, "First Miriam, then Mohammed, Abdulla, Ayisha, and Abd el Karim." Children were individuals, not numbers; about half of them died. Bederea insisted she'd had seventeen, with eight living. Bedouin women frequently reported twelve births, with one, two, or none living.

The dead were buried the same day if possible, and buried without coffins. The body was washed, wrapped in a cloth, and laid in the grave facing Mecca. A mullah would pronounce the words to remind the spirit what to say to the angel of death. The grave was closed, marked only by a crude stone, and then abandoned, since the spirit had departed. Walking through the cemetery once, I saw a new grave where a little pair of women's sandals had been tenderly laid. Someone's heart ached.

Climatic conditions in Kuwait were perfect for the overproduction of flies. They sat in lines around the babies' eyes. They crawled behind my glasses. They swam in the tea we were offered. Paul Harrison says he watched one of them trying to swim against the current of his sweat as it poured. Screen doors were no help. The flies waited for them to open and swarmed in. When we put screens on the patients' rooms, people poked holes in them to throw out the garbage.

When locusts swarmed, the Bedouin would catch them in bags, dry them, and boil them for food. These locusts were large, three inches long. The Bedouins would pull off the head and wings and eat the eggcase. I found them tasty, rather like fish roe. Once Bess told her servant to watch her garden while she went off, but when she returned, she found the locusts had eaten everything. The servant protested, "You told me to watch it, and I did."

The women brought their laundry when they came to the hospital. The seashore, after all, provided the facilities. They used a white powder, pounded the clothes, and laid them on the rocks to dry while they came to the clinic for medicine. Well-organized housewives they were.

Surgery and maternity cases demanded sterilization of instruments and dressings. In the afternoons, Jameela and I heated up the old barrel-shaped sterilizer with the kerosene pressure stove. We boiled the instruments and gloves in water and scrubbed in a basin, as we had no running sweet water and had to wear wet rubber gloves.

At the end of the year, we were required to send a report of our work to the Board. According to the 1937 report, we saw an average of 122 people every day. The treatment was necessarily inadequate. I specialized in omnipotence and learned my trade at the expense of the poor.

What was I doing about my mission to tell about Jesus Christ? Bess, and later other wives, gave a short talk and prayer on the veranda before starting the daily clinic. Once I sat on the floor with a Bedouin woman and tried to tell the story. Later, I heard her ask the helpers, "What was that doctor talking about?" I'd visit the inpatients and try to read from the gospels, but their rooms were always full and noisy with crying babies, children, and visitors, so I had to hope that actions would speak louder than words.

Our mission's message to the Muslims was to teach that we as Christians believe that Jesus Christ is One with God. The Qur'an states that Jesus is a prophet but denies that He is the Son of God and it denies His crucifixion. Christians believe that when Jesus Christ was crucified, He as God took the punishment for our sins upon Himself, so that he can give us forgiveness of our sins. In His resurrection Jesus Christ gave us eternal life with God.

Each morning in the clinic we would begin by telling stories of the life of Christ, teaching His parables, telling about His crucifixion and resurrection and then saying a prayer for the day's work.

5. Medicine and Marriage

While I was devoting my days to medical work, I lived my spare time on a different level. The coming of the oil company to Kuwait brought those exciting young bachelors. Since there was no feminine competition, I received all their attention as the belle of the KOC. I had no previous experience in this capacity. When Norman Allison determinedly pressed his suit, I was in a quandary. I had committed my life to what I thought was the service of the Lord. The Church had entrusted me with its mission. The women of Michigan had sacrificed to send me. The women and children of Kuwait needed a woman physician. The mission of Christ had not yet borne fruit there. Had I put my hand to the plow, only to fall back and be unworthy of the Kingdom? Yet there was this forlorn longing for a mate. Marriage is ordained by God but was it for me? "It is not good that man should be alone," the Bible said. The rules of the mission were that when a woman member marries outside of the group, her appointment by the church board ends. It seemed unfair that a woman cannot expect, as a man can, both a career and marriage. For a woman it is very difficult. Some mission wives devoted themselves to their homes and children, but they were considered missionaries.

Mary Van had hoped for marriage in vain, so she thought she was doing me a favor by inviting Norman to dinner often. Mary had a sharp, critical tongue, so our home was not harmonious. It was comforting to feel a manly arm around my shoulder. Norman was a Christian, a son of a Scottish minister, but he did not feel the same call to full-time service that I did. He had gotten a high school education and then trained on ships as a marine engineer and traveled all over the world. He was tall, blue-eyed, strong, nice looking, and courteous. I told him I could not bear children and thought that would end my problem. But he declared he loved me for myself alone, pleading on his knees. He agreed I could keep on working as a doctor while married to him. His work as the engineer for the Kuwait Oil Company might keep him there or might not. Even though he worked in Kuwait, he was far away. The first well drilled was at Bahra, across the bay. We could see their lights at night, but Norman had to drive fifty miles to come every Friday and other times.

"If thy eye be single, thy whole body shall be full of light." When I found myself falling in love with Norman, my eye was no longer single. I struggled with the awful problem of how to reconcile the conflict between love for an individual and my duty to God. Clearly these two loves did not run on the same track. My thoughts whirled in turmoil. I was never at peace. The struggle raged like a tempest. It was sheer agony. I prayed to be delivered.

> Master, the tempest is raging, the billows are tossing high
> Carest Thou not that we perish, How canst Thou lie asleep
> When each moment the danger is threatening, a grave in the
>   angry deep.
>   Mary A. Baker, "Peace! Be still!"
>   from *Hymns of Praise*, no. 2 [Chicago: Hope, 1925]

Was it adultery to allow anything to divide me from what I thought the Lord wanted me to do? "Lead me not into temptation. Deliver me from evil." Was I trying to serve two masters? I vacillated; sometimes I was friendly and sometimes I told Norman to leave. I suppose I seemed to be playing a game of being hard to get. It went on for a year. The other missionaries did not comment. They seemed to think that I had to make the decision on my own and didn't want to interfere. Could I live single all my life? The appalling chaos in my mind went on like an unending nightmare. Without marriage, can one be a truly human being? Is celibacy a desire to escape from the work and pain of living with and loving another human being? Saints should not have close friendships or exclusive loves. To follow Christ and love all people means death. I loved living. The strain of the clash was getting to be unbearable. So one evening I gave Norman my promise to marry him. I felt if I could just end this indecisive battle I could put my mind and ability to working it out somehow.

So we were engaged but I wasn't ever at peace with myself. I still and always had my doubts. My mother disapproved but sent me a wedding dress. The Board was shocked. In my church in the U.S. one lady declared that now that I was getting married they need not pray for me anymore at the Sunday service.

Mary Van was thrilled and arranged the wedding in the mission chapel. So we were married on June 14, 1937, and went up to Baghdad for a week on honeymoon. Was I Eve who beheld the goodly fruit and stretched forth her hand and took and ate of it? Things were never the same again. Christ said that if anyone would follow Him, he must hate his own family. I didn't have the moral strength to do that. We found a house on the seafront near the hospital. The oil company furnished a good Indian cook so I could continue working in the hospital as before, but Norman could never understand or quite agree to my sense of duty. Yet we were in love. Most of the time I was happy and tried to put other thoughts out of my mind. I was so busy I almost stopped writing letters.

Mary Van Pelt went home soon thereafter and did not return to Arabia. Norman and I moved into the house next to the men's hospital where Mary and I had lived. I didn't conform to conventional bride's behavior when I had to get up nights to deliver babies. The oil company people had Fridays for their day off, so we went to parties and picnics in the desert and on the beaches. Once we invited Shaikh Ahmad to a dinner party at our home, for which we were reproved by the oil company office. Rulers were to be entertained only by the officials.

SCOTLAND TO KUWAIT, OVERLAND — 1939

My mother came and spent the winter with us. In the spring Norman had his vacation and we flew to his home in Scotland, stopping in Athens and Budapest to see the sights. Norman's mother invited us to stay with her in her apartment in Paisley, Scotland. Her maid reported that she found some lice on my pillow. I had always referred to my patients as ladies, but now Norman pointed out that evidently that wasn't the case. It was so cold that I always cuddled up to the fireplaces until Norman had the tailor make some clothes of that lovely Scotch wool. My mother came, too, for a week, and we got acquainted with the Allison family. Norman bought a car and we traveled all over

Scotland, Loch Lomond, the Isle of Arran, up to John-o-Groats, and down to Edinburgh. It was lovely, but I kept wanting to get back to Kuwait. I took a refresher medical course, and we visited factories and industries that Norman was interested in.

My cousin John Bruins and his family were in Prague on the U.S. consular service and invited us to come and visit them. We planned to go to Prague and then drive to Istanbul and maybe Kuwait. The automobile club planned the trip for us, so we ferried over to the Hoek of Holland. The international situation had become serious, but we hoped it would subside so we could continue our trip. We drove over the incredible autobahns of Germany, which were empty of traffic. In the end we couldn't get to Prague because Hitler's armies surrounded Czechoslovakia, but we stopped to see Vienna and Budapest, where Norman's brother, Gordon, was working. We drove on through Romania, which reminded me of Wisconsin because the frost was on the pumpkins and the fodder was in the shocks. We passed old churches, ruined monasteries, and quaint old villages where bullocks dragged produce and children in wooden shoes stood out to stare at us. We didn't have time to stop and explore. We had to hurry, as we had only a month to reach Kuwait, so we crossed the mountain pass in the south of Romania at midnight. I was really frightened. It was so dark and the road so steep and poor, but we reached Istanbul at last. We spent a few days seeing the ancient city, its mosques, St. Sophia, the sultan's palace, and the seraglio, where we gasped in wonder at the bowls full of emeralds, the masses of diamonds, pearls, jewelry, china, and clocks.

The information was that if it didn't rain, the roads in Turkey would be passable. It hadn't rained, so we ventured to ferry the car to the Asian side and spent the night at a hotel in Brusa. It began to rain. We had crossed the Rubicon and now would have to put up with whatever weather turned up. The road the next day reminded me of Iowa mud. It poured rain, but we reached Afyon, the town named after opium, and found a hotel. Next morning, the sun was shining and the top of the mountain nearby was covered with dazzling white snow with wind blowing a veil across its face. We felt encouraged and set out again.

The roads were full of holes. They crossed ditches where there was no bridge, so we usually had to drive beside the road. We came to Konya, which St. Paul called Iconium when he preached

Christ there. The present-day city seemed entirely Muslim with
many mosques and only men to be seen on the streets. We found
a hotel which consisted of one large room above a restaurant. The
room held eight beds, one for each patron. At supper, we talked
to a traveling engineer who knew English and told us that in the
next town, Eregeli, we should visit the manager of the cotton
spinning factory because he was so kind to tourists. By that time,
we had hit so many boulders and bumps that the brakes on the
underbelly of the car had been completely wiped off, and we had
to drive very slowly in order to stop.

At Eregeli, we asked for the spinning factory and found it. At
the office, a very pleasant man made us welcome. Norman explained that he was an engineer who was very much interested in
cotton spinning and hoped to see the place. I had heard of the
unspeakable Turk, but this man was not that at all. We explained
the sad state of our car, evident from its coating of mud. The
Turk said his driver could take care of it and the driver drove it
away. Then our host showed us his guest rooms and said we
should use them. He and his wife would have dinner with us
later. How good it felt to clean up in hot water! At the dinner,
his wife couldn't speak English but he did. I thanked him for
his magnificent hospitality and asked him why he took unknown
travelers in so generously. He told us how he had been sent to
England and Germany to learn cloth making and how kind the
people he met there were to him. He resolved that whenever he
could he would try to repay their goodwill. The next morning he
gave us a guided tour of the factory. When we were about to set
off again, he said that our planned route crossed a river in flood,
but that he would send his driver with us to show us another road
in the hills. The driver could come back by train. The driver
came up with our car—washed, clean, filled with gasoline. Its
brakes worked very well! The man had performed miracles. He
took us along a small road in the hills, and we set him down where
he could get the train. From then on, the term "the unspeakable
Turk" had a new and different meaning for me.

The next feature was the Cilician Gates of the Taurus Mountains, with a famous pass where armies had crossed. We reached
it at the end of the day, so we couldn't see the scenery. Also, it
started to pour rain again, but we went on. Finally, the mud became so deep that we had to stop. There was a Turkish military

truck stuck in front of us and another behind. We spent the night sleeping in the car. Next morning the Turkish soldiers helped to dig us out. I took some pictures of us which I don't like to have my friends see because we were so covered with mud.

I had hoped we could stop at Tarsus, where St. Paul grew up, but it was out of the way. When we came to the corner of the sea where Syria joins Turkey, there were no roads and no fences, so we drove over the dried-up rose fields where they make attar of roses, navigating with a little compass. Ruins of old forts and castles stood along the way. We passed a pitiful group of Armenians carrying all their worldly possessions, fleeing from their homes in the province of Alexandretta, which had been taken from Syria and given to Turkey. Another car of tourists, young Englishmen driving to India to work in the civil service there, caught up with us. There were no towns nearby so we slept in the car again. Next morning we cooked our breakfast and decided to travel with the Englishmen for a while. It was wonderful to find a nice hotel at Aleppo and clean up. We visited the mission school and then drove through Lebanon, passing Hama and its huge hundred-foot-high water wheel, raising water with a mighty creak for irrigation. Damascus was lovely. From there we traversed the desert to Baghdad. From then on there was no more mud, just deep dust to plow through. We stopped at Amara to have tea with the mission and reached Basrah at sunset. My college friends, the Gosselinks, took us in and we reached Kuwait the next day. Ours was the first car that had made the trip. The customs officials agreed that since Norman and I had served the city, they would not charge us customs!

BACK TO WORK!

It was easy for me to slip back into medical work again, since the oil company gave us a house next door to the mission hospital. That was a very happy year. I loved the work and was very busy. Norman and I were in love. We had a good cook provided by the oil company and gave dinners in the open courtyard. Our associates in the oil company spent their evenings in the club playing darts and cards, drinking, or just talking. That was harmless enough, but boring to me.

Unfortunately, the oil well drilled north of the bay proved to be a dry hole. Norman told me the company was thinking of sending him elsewhere. It was an unbearable thought to me. So I went to an old friend to talk the situation over. Of course, word got to Norman that I had discussed his business with others and he was furious. That was our first real battle and I wept. I loved Norman, but I felt that my God-given talent which I had to use was for the medical work in Kuwait. Norman complained that I was a selfish person and that I cared more for my career than I did for him. Life was difficult during this period of uncertainty.

A NEW HOSPITAL, A NEW NURSE

An American family, the Bacenstos, left a legacy of twelve thousand dollars to build a new women's hospital in Kuwait. So plans were drawn up, and we rented a nearby house with a courtyard to treat patients in during the hospital construction. The temporary hospital had crude, clay-floored rooms opening into the courtyard. We divided the rooms up for an office, treatment room, and patient rooms.

The old hospital was eventually demolished, and the new building began under Rev. Barny's direction. The evangelistic missionaries usually got stuck with the construction jobs because the doctors were too busy. Rev. Barny borrowed a cement mixer from the oil company to make building blocks. The Arab women sat down to watch this wonder and came in to tell us of this marvelous machine. "It eats, and then it vomits!" they exclaimed.

Rev. Pennings eventually replaced the Barnys and oversaw the completion of the building. Our new hospital was beautiful, with verandas, ample windows, two stories, plenty of rooms, a graceful stairway in the center, and tiled floors. Friends gave us money for new hospital equipment.

We planned a formal opening and invited Shaikh Ahmad to cut the ribbon. He did it very graciously, announcing that he was dedicating this building to the glory of God and the service of man. Then Dr. Mylrea gave him a guided tour of the offices, operating room, delivery room, and patients' rooms with the new beds and brightly colored bedspreads. Shortly after that, the crown prince of Arabia came to visit our ruler. Our men went to pay their respects and invited the prince to come and have tea at our new hospital. When the Saudi prince accepted, we splurged and decorated the hospital with our Persian carpets, all our linens, and real china. We planned to serve the royal party ourselves.

But His Highness sent word that he trusted there would be no women present when he came. So we had to hide in one of the upstairs rooms to peek at the function and let the servants pour tea. Later, we heard that the prince criticized Kuwait because he said too many women could be seen on the streets. The Saudis seem to feel that it is their duty to uphold the traditions of Islam.

It was a pleasure to work in the new building, but we soon found problems. The flat roof was cement. Under the hot summer sun it cracked, so when it rained, rain poured into the rooms. The oil company kindly tarred the roof; then the next summer, it was the tar that dripped down into the rooms.

The new building was popular. Maternity cases and inpatients increased, so we had to find another helper like Jameela. I traveled up to Basrah on that errand, renting a seat in the local taxi. The Van Esses and Gosselinks directed me to some Arab Christian families. I called on them. Application for help from girls had to be made to their fathers. I presented my plea in my best Arabic on the grounds of Christian need in mission service, offering a good salary and promise of providing good living conditions. The fathers were adamant. They stonily refused to consider allowing their daughters to be persuaded. After several attempts, I gave up and took the train to Baghdad to stay with Elda and Bern Hakken, our missionaries. Bern knew of an Egyptian girl in Hilleh, so he drove me there. As the town was near the ruins of ancient Babylon, we stopped to look and sat down to eat our lunch at the Ishtar Gate, with its wonderfully preserved colorful tiles of fanciful animals. We laughed and talked about how the Babylonian guards would have driven us out three thousand years ago.

At Hilleh, we found Labeeba, who was a nice-looking Egyptian girl about twenty-two years old. She told me her story; some I learned later. She and her sister belonged to a Muslim family and had been sent to a Christian mission school in their village for education. They were so impressed by the Christian story and lives of their teachers that they became Christians. When they announced it to their family, they were horrified. The family imprisoned the girls behind bolted and barred doors and windows. In the evenings, the men of the family—uncles, cousins, grandparents—held nightly sessions until midnight, putting the girls in the center of a circle. They used every avenue of persuasion to entice the girls to change their minds and shouted threats of dire punishment if they didn't. Amazingly, the girls put their trust in Christ. One night when the guard and dogs were asleep, they unlocked the gate and escaped and went to the mission in Cairo. The girls found a refuge there, worked in the mission hospital, and learned English. The government and their family traced them. Since the family was unable to change the girls' minds, they were given the ultimatum; stay in the hospital and never go out on the street.

Two women missionaries from another church who wanted to start work in Iraq heard of the Egyptian girls and asked Labeeba to go with them. They all settled in Hilleh. After some years, the American women became ill and had to return to the U.S.A., leaving Labeeba behind to continue mission work. Labeeba was sort of an orphan. She lived with an Arab Christian family, but the husband was becoming offensive with his attentions, so she was anxious to leave. She accepted my offer of work in Kuwait immediately, and we made preparations to return to Kuwait. Sometimes, as in this case, the Lord surprises me with miracles.

There was one near-embarrassment when we went through the immigration office on the Kuwaiti border. Labeeba's passport said that her name was Fatima bint Mohammad, because the Egyptian government refused to change the name of a Muslim to a Christian one. We had to hope that gossip would not reveal her background.

Jameela welcomed Labeeba and they lived together. We built another room for her in back of the hospital. But she was lonesome without any friends or relatives nearby. I felt I should spend time with the helpers and wanted to invite them to my home, but Norman wouldn't have it—I had to spend my evenings with him. Labeeba did not have real nurse's training, but she knew English, had some education, and could read, so she was a great help. When I was transferred to Bahrain, she left the hospital and I lost track of her. May God bless her and Jameela, for we were very close in those days of hard work.

CASES

One day, I was called to attend an older lady of one of the aristocratic houses. She had fallen, and from the unnatural crepitus in her upper leg, I was certain it was a fracture. She could only be treated in the hospital, but she insisted that it wasn't a fracture, and she didn't want to come to the hospital. Finally, she gave in and they brought her with a splint by car. We had no orthopedic equipment, so I studied the sketch in the surgery book and explained it to the carpenter. Between the two of us we assembled the splint, pulleys, ropes, and weights and set them up on one of our new beds. We put the whole apparatus out on the veranda where our aristocratic patient could get the breezes in private. She was quite comfortable but the next day she was weeping—she said she couldn't say her prayers. That problem was solved by turning her bed around to face Mecca. We had no X-ray, so I had no idea what kind of a fracture it was. The woman stayed with us three months; then, fearing the worst, we let her stand and walk. To my amazement, the bone seemed to have mended. The old lady sang my praises for years afterward. Truly, *Allah kareem*, God was good to me.

Another time, our Iranian carpenter asked me to come to his home to help his daughter, who was in labor with her first baby. She had been in labor three days and had gone into convulsions that were terrible to see. The patient had bitten her tongue so her face was swollen and bloody. The women of the family refused to consider taking her to the hospital, although the men were willing. That day we had just finished a clinic of 205 patients and were dead tired, but still we collected the whole staff and all our equipment and proceeded to the house. The carpenter produced a table so the baby could be delivered by forceps. The child was barely alive. I gave everything we had to the unconscious mother. Next morning, when I arrived, blood was streaming over the doorstep from the body of the sacrificed sheep. The mother lived a few more hours and died. I went back depressed by yet another failure. Those toxemias can only be avoided with good prenatal care.

Another pregnant girl came to the clinic with hypertension indicating toxemia. I advised her to stay home and rest and I would make house calls. After I had come a couple of times, the family sent word that I should not come again. It made the patient nervous. I found out later that she delivered normally at home. There's nothing definite in the medical business.

A pregnant woman who stayed in the hospital was edematous over her whole body—one of the signs of toxemia—but her blood pressure was normal. The mystery was solved after giving her worm medicine. When she evacuated a bedpanful of worms, the swelling went away. Well, I kept learning. One can be allergic to intestinal worms, too.

Ramadan is the month of fasting. As the Muslim year is ten days shorter than ours, Ramadan can fall in winter or summer. If it comes in summer, it really means suffering, for the fast is not only from food but also from water (in addition to smoking and sex). The fasting begins before sunrise every day for a month and lasts until sunset. Then night becomes the time for feasting and visiting. People are supposed to stay up all night—and just to make sure they do, men come around with drums to keep them awake. Everyone wants to work half-days and then sleep in the afternoons, including the essential hospital helpers. All the government offices and the post office and schools close at noon. With the lack of sleep and water, and the temperature soaring to 120 degrees, people are irritable. Running the hospital can become very difficult during Ramadan. The day clinics were usually small because people felt that having an injection would be breaking their fast. Thus many of them wanted to come at night instead. Some had problems related to the religious observance, for the nightly feasting on a starving stomach could cause ruptures.

But the fast is an important religious duty commanded in the Qur'an. Lulua, a very sweet, beautiful woman, came to me in Ramathon (the month of fasting) pregnant, still nursing a baby, and fasting. I protested, "Lulua, you are not well enough to be fasting now." She replied, "But I fear God."

At the end of Ramadan there were five holidays when everybody wore new clothes. Our men would call on the ruler and other important men. We women called on the royal first lady and then the other wives of the shaikhs. It was a formal call and gave us a chance to visit them. They served sweet drinks and coffee and passed around rose water and the fragrant incense pot.

AYISHA, AND MY OTHER PATIENTS

I first met Ayisha (not her real name), a friend for many years, as a young girl at a tea at her mother's home. She was not beautiful nor did she have an attractive personality. What I admired was her stubborn determination never to be discouraged. She insisted on being the center of attention through loud incessant talking about trivial matters. Her father had been an educated man who had traveled, and Ayisha prided herself on that fact. Her family married her to a prominent wealthy man. One day she came to me and whispered that she wanted to talk privately, so I arranged it. She told me she had brought me her partner wife, who had a cough. Ayisha wanted me to see the partner wife and write a note to the husband that the other woman had tuberculosis, adding, "Then he'll divorce her." She was certain, after I said I couldn't do that, that I just didn't want to help her.

Another night, Ayisha's husband called me to treat her at their home by sending a car and driver. It was midnight, but it was evident that no one was sleeping. About a dozen women were fluttering and whispering, with Ayisha in the center—agitated, shouting, frenzied. Her clothes and hair were in disarray. In these cases, I found it was no use asking what had happened, for either the family didn't want to tell or didn't know, or they figured that a jinn or spirit had possessed the person. I had no good drugs in those days, only bromides and luminol, which were not effective in a hurry, so I gave an injection of a quarter grain of morphine and waited a half hour. To my surprise it seemed to have no effect whatsoever. I had to do something, so I gave a second injection which did quiet her. Ayisha had given birth to four girls, which was counted an inadequacy in her union with the sayyid. So she was divorced. There couldn't have been much peace wherever she was, for she was no meek, languishing hareem creature, but a forceful personality.

The husband was a friend of the mission, a pleasant, generous man. He was especially fond of women and always had his allowed quota of four wives. He divorced them from time to time and none of them ever resented or complained of him; I knew several of them. When he died, we heard he had left thirty-seven children.

He let Ayisha keep the four little girls with her until the family found a new husband for her. This one was a tall, cheerful Bedouin who lived in town. Some time later, the pair came into my office, each carrying a baby. Ayisha had twin boys. The husband was glowing with pride, as she had produced only girls from the sayyid, but she gave birth to twin boys when he took over. She needed help feeding them, but I didn't see her for some years.

This husband divorced her, too. The family found another husband and Ayisha kept on having children.

Forty years later, I returned to Kuwait for a visit and Ayisha invited me to her home. It was very agreeable to be remembered with such effusive compliments. Ayisha had a new house with servants and children and grandchildren always with her. She introduced me to her sons, who had been educated in America and were very friendly. We sat down to a table laden with food, and she sent me back with her son and filled my arms with gifts. She told me she had had seventeen children, about half of whom survived. Now she was the head of the household, still the same loud, determined character.

In one of the neighboring houses, there lived two young unmarried girls whom I used to visit. One evening they called me to come over. I found them in great mental distress, relating the story of being out in the desert in a car and seeing several jinns—"little people of the earth," as they are called. Jinns are described several times in the Qur'an, so they figure as real persons. The girls described their black faces, hideous bodies, and screeching, threatening voices. "We began to die," one said in dead earnest, trembling with agitation. My own reaction was that this was a childish tale of goblins, but in the state that they were in, I couldn't pass it off. They had called me in as a doctor, and they believed that a doctor should be able to treat all human ills. I hadn't had any training in psychotherapy, and any that helped Americans wouldn't fit with the myths that possessed these people. I had no effective drugs, either, but the whole household was watching me. I had to do something. The one thing that impressed them was the hypodermic injection. People felt cheated if I didn't give one on a house call. The only effective one I had was morphine, and I used that. At least I was showing that I would do something. The girls were relieved and I heard no more about it. Perhaps just the gesture of a friendly human being can be therapy, or as Jesus said, "according to your faith, so be it unto you." I'm sure most of my treatments helped only because the people believed in the mystique that surrounds the name of doctor.

Another time, being called to a home, I found the patient was a young black slave girl. She was hysterical and bound with an iron ball and chain on her ankle. As usual, the family could not account for her state. The master of the house had come back from a trip to Bombay and she became possessed. Again, I had to resort to morphine, which quieted her. I never found out anything more about it. This discontinuity of cases was very unsatisfactory to me. I hardly ever knew the final outcome of any treatment.

When inpatients with fevers and infections became comatose or irrational, the families usually insisted on taking them home, saying that this kind of trouble couldn't be treated by our medicines. Some years later when we had drugs to treat tuberculosis, a young woman with tuberculous meningitis was taken home. I offered to come and give the treatment at home or to let the mullah come and read over the patient in the hospital. Evidently that wasn't acceptable to the family. I made a few calls at the home and found the patient lying on the floor with the mullah (religious teacher) sitting beside her and reading from the Qur'an. She died soon after.

Tuberculosis was rampant in all its forms—in the lungs, glands, bones, and meninges. All we had to give was cod liver oil, cough mixtures, and vitamins. I tried some surgery to remove neck glands, to curet carious bones, and to amputate useless legs. But nothing helped. On one housecall, a young girl had cough with profuse bleeding and emaciation. I decided she had not long to live and gave her an injection of morphine. She asked me to come again and wanted that "sweet blessed needle," which I gave her. I never heard of her again. How wonderful it was, years later, to have Streptomycin and drugs to treat this disease. I remember the joy I felt treating a little girl, the only child of an old man. She had tuberculous meningitis and stayed with us long enough for a cure.

Anything could turn up at the clinic, so it was a continual adventure. Abscesses and infections of the hands and fingers were common, because the women broke up the sharp branches of palm trees, brought by ship from Basrah and used as fuel for cooking. Women who came down to the beach to wash their clothes were attacked by the sting ray hiding in the sand. Some were stung by scorpions or stepped on needles at home. Injections of novocaine helped some, but imagine trying to find a needle imbedded in a foot without an X-ray. I tried, but usually had to give up. During my internship, I had learned how to straighten club feet with plaster-of-paris boots. Many children were brought in who had drunk kerosene. The women would keep it in any kind of bottle, and the babies often mistook it for water. Usually the child did not drink enough to do any damage.

Parents had learned the value of vaccination for smallpox, but it was difficult to get good vaccine. Once, I went up to Basrah with a widemouth thermos and brought the vaccine back packed in ice. I have a letter telling of our peak morning. There were 250 patients, but a lot of them had come for vaccination. Vaccination was not yet universal. I refused to admit one child with hemorrhagic smallpox because it would endanger too many lives and there was no treatment.

SPRING

In the spring the Kuwaiti desert was beautiful with green plants, tiny yellow daisies for miles, and patches of blue iris in the low places. The town Arabs loved to take their families out to live in tents for a few days during the spring. The Dicksons invited Norman and me for a day with some of their Bedu friends. Col. Dickson related their story. The wife had produced only daughters, so the husband was considering adding another wife. She had bounced back with the retort that if he did, she would take the sheep and goats which had been her dowry and return to her father's house. So the subject was dropped. In the meantime a cousin from Iraq dropped in with the intention of marrying a daughter. The parents did not like this man but could not deny him his right to marry his cousin. They informed him that he must prove his worth by serving them for a while by drawing water for the flocks and hunting for fuel. He brought his mother and set up a tent to settle down. They would wait each other out to see who would wear out first. Some other Bedouin men were talking. Col. Dickson, laughing, translated for us. They were asking whether they could marry women as big and strong as Mrs. Dickson and me, because they said we could work so hard.

The oil company requested us to move out to their settlement at Magwa, fifteen miles from Kuwait, to live in the double Nissen hut. We made it into a pretty home. I had a taxi to take me to Kuwait each day. Dr. and Beth Thoms took the place of the Mylreas and the Pennings replaced the Barnys. The hospital income increased, so we agreed that I should get a salary equal to what a single missionary was earning.

And then there was the issue of my marriage. Marriage should be a sweet silence, but neither Norman nor I knew the game. Norman had no sisters, had attended a boys' high school, went into engineering, and then went to sea. My own thinking had always centered around missions and medicine, so we didn't have a lot in common. At home, we had a good Indian cook, furnished by the oil company, and a houseboy to do the other work. I'd give orders for the day and then get home by five to keep Norman company. Norman wanted to listen to the radio and news from Europe—we heard of Hitler invading Poland, though it all seemed so far away. I'd try to talk, but Norman would lapse into silence. He said he was very busy but never wanted to talk about his work, so I didn't know what he did. He didn't approve of my American way of using my knife and fork. He wondered why I didn't get his bath water drawn and arrange things for his bath. Evidently that was what British wives did. I claimed that we Americans were bathed when we were children, but when we grew up, we were proud to manage that for ourselves. At one dinner we attended, Norman drank too much and got sick. Next morning he chided me, saying that wives were supposed to prevent their husbands from drinking too much. Norman wanted me to help serve alcohol at our house, too, which made me embarrassed.

Is marriage ever a perfectly happy state? At first Norman wanted me to teach him Arabic, but that didn't work out. Sometimes, we'd get into arguments which ended with me angry and Norman silent. He never objected to my working, but I could feel that he was unhappy about it. He said, "Why don't you take up writing?" and complained wistfully, "You care more for your career than you do for me. You're quite selfish." Sometimes Norman didn't want to drive to Kuwait for church on Sunday evenings and I'd break down into tears. Did either of us know each other? I really loved him, enough to do almost anything except give up my calling to the medical mission.

WITH NORMAN IN INDIA

When news of the war became serious in 1940, Norman decided he ought to join the British Indian Navy. We packed up everything. He went to Bombay and I moved into one of the hospital's large upstairs rooms.

At the hospital, we began having trouble getting drugs. A long-overdue order from England didn't arrive. The Indian and Iraqi drug firms refused to send us anything. A friend of mine from the Woman's Medical College in Pennsylvania, Dr. Ruth Crouse, offered to come out and take my place.

I was due for a vacation so took the British India Lines ship and went to spend three months with Norman in Bombay. He seemed to be glad I came, but I didn't know what to do with my time. I rode the streetcars, saw people sleeping on sidewalks and cows meandering among the traffic, and walked around Crawford Market. The market was a large complex of sheds where all sorts of foodstuffs, fruits, vegetables, meat, and flowers were for sale. In desperation one day, I walked into the Parsee Tata Hospital and introduced myself to some doctors in the eye department. I asked permission to stand around with the students in their clinics. But I was still terribly restless and longed to go back to Kuwait for a few months to help Ruth get started at the hospital and learn a little more Arabic. Norman did not object, so I took the ship and went back to Kuwait, feeling sad. He looked so handsome in his naval uniform.

Three months later I returned to India. Norman had been transferred to Simla, up in the mountains above New Delhi. I took the train there. Norman said, "Take the first class, it's air-conditioned." They "air-conditioned" the train by putting a tub of ice in the passenger compartment! Simla was a lovely Indian town where the British set up their government offices for summertime. There were no cars. Whenever we went anyplace, we took a rickshaw drawn by one or two laborers. That didn't appeal to me. Norman suggested that I work in the naval code and cypher office as many of the other wives did. They paid us a small salary. It was most interesting to find out how numbers could hide words. They also had an x-machine. When a word was typed on it, only numbers came out.

I was determined to see the Taj Mahal while I was in India, but Norman couldn't get time off to go with me. So early one morning I went by myself to the railroad station and bought a ticket for Agra. I was told that the train would be a half hour late.

When the train came along, I sat down in a second-class compartment and read a book for the three hours the trip should take. Three hours later, when the train stopped, I asked a conductor when we would arrive at Agra. "This is not the train to Agra. This is the train to Bombay," he said. "There will be a train later in the afternoon when you can go back to Delhi," he added. So I got off and wandered around in some rice paddies, then ate my sandwich and banana under the shade of an old Mogul tomb. After lunch I walked around the town through a farmer's market where I was followed by dozens of curious little boys. All of a sudden a voice in English asked, "Madam, shall I show you around?" My benefactor turned out to be the Indian clerk of the company that quarried the beautiful red and white stone for the magnificent secretariat and government buildings in New Delhi. He offered to show me the quarries, but it was too far. We went instead to see the maharajah's elephants and visited some boy students who were having class on a rooftop. We had tea at the railroad station. He offered to pray for me for a month if I would give him a rupee, which I did. I took the train back to Delhi and squirmed sheepishly to tell Norman where I'd been.

Some days later, I took the right train to Agra. I spent the day at the Taj Mahal walking around the beautiful white marble tomb of a woman who knew how to be a real wife to her husband. The gardens, fountains, dark cypress trees and reflecting pools, mosque, and palace where Shah Jehan spent his last days were lovely. I came back with pictures of both places.

Norman and I had two rooms in a pretty tourist hotel that served good meals. Norman was affectionate and looked stunning in his handsome naval uniform. We enjoyed sex. We'd walk home from the office together and stop to purchase items (which I always had to carry). Norman said officers weren't supposed to carry anything in their hands. We were invited to cocktails and went on picnics in the mountains. I should have been very happy, but I was not. I had a lot of free time. I walked alone through the fascinating Indian bazaar and up into the mountains where there was a temple to the monkey god. There were hundreds of monkeys and a priest who fed them. I sat down alone and wept bitterly for hours. "Why art thou cast down, O my soul? And why art thou disquieted in me?" There was no way now to go back to Kuwait unless Norman died. I despised myself. What a horrible creature I was. I put on a smiling face. I didn't want Norman to feel hurt. We never did get to talking together about the deep things of life. Did Norman ever realize how I felt? Or was this just the discipline of learning to live with and love one another? Was it the relation I felt I had with God that kept us apart?

When the weather cooled, the whole British community moved down to New Delhi. We moved, too, and lived there in another grand hotel. We rented bicycles and rode around to see the sights of Mogul palaces and tombs. Once at a busy street corner I collided with a cow and her calf while a traffic policeman looked on. To keep busy, I did hire a teacher to learn Urdu, which was easy for me because it had so many Arabic words. I visited the Anglican mission hospital, St. Stephens, and offered to help in their clinic. They needed a doctor to be on duty at night, so I left Norman's bed a couple of nights a week. Other nights, I'd take sleeping pills to forget my grief. Was marriage a sham and delusion?

Meanwhile, the war grew in intensity. We listened to the BBC news. I got some news through the code and cypher messages, though Norman knew more through his office. The Japanese were steadily advancing; Singapore fell. Our world was collapsing. Norman told me that the British government would not fight for India. If the Japanese wanted to take it, they could just walk in. Norman would have to leave with the British Navy, in any event.

Then one Sunday morning came the news of Pearl Harbor. Norman knew of an American ship, the *President Harrison*, which was passing by India and picking up Americans to take them home. He wanted me to pack up for Bombay and sail home on the ship, because he thought he wouldn't be staying in India much longer. So I regretfully packed up and took the train to Bombay, saying good-bye to Norman.

6. The War Years

The passenger ship *President Harrison* had picked up stray Americans from all over Asian ports. We were a mixture of oil men, businesspeople, writers, and missionaries. The ship was blacked-out at night and zigzagged its way to Durban, where we spent three days touring the city. Most nights we sat on the top deck singing songs, telling our life histories, and having a wonderful time. Anchored at Trinidad, we saw the disasters of war firsthand in disabled ships with gaping torpedo holes. Trinidad was a lovely island with a fascinating botanical garden. When we reached New York safely in April, we heard the false news that our own ship had been sunk! Somehow I escaped the terrible suffering of the rest of the world. *Allah kareem.*

As Norman could not send me any money, I found summer work with a wealthy group from Philadelphia's main line. They had cottages and a lodge in Maine and wanted a resident physician. They offered my mother and me room and board. We dined on steak and lobster daily.

A Dr. Johnson, a pediatrician in Englewood, New Jersey, wanted to join the army and was looking for a missionary to run his office while he was gone. He thought that the war would last just a few months. My mother and I came to live in his lovely home and I took over his practice. For the first time in my life, I began to earn good money. I inherited a secretary, a car, and an organized daily program of medical practice. An hour of telephone calls from worried mothers would begin at 8:00 A.M. I would visit several schools to examine sick children, then make a stop at the hospital to do physical examinations of newborns. Office patients began to come in at 1 P.M. We allowed twenty minutcs for each child. I made house calls at odd times in the morning and most evenings. To get around I had to really study the street maps of New Jersey. It was hard work to travel at night. On one house call, I found one little girl unconscious with a stiff neck, indicating meningitis, and decided this needed expert attention. I tried to take the mother and child to the medical center in New York in my car, but the pouring rain stopped us. We got a taxi and delivered the child safely to the center, where the specialists saved her from death. I continued to find the practice of medicine thrilling.

My brother Paul, his wife Margaret, and their four little girls were living in Douglaston, Long Island, on the opposite end of New York from me. Paul was teaching chemical engineering at Brooklyn Polytechnic. I drove over often for weekends. Margaret had pelvic surgery. I came and observed that she was normal, but six months later she was found to have an inoperable ovarian cancer. My mother went over to keep house. Margaret was only thirty-five and happy with her home and children, but she slowly wasted away. Death came in six months. I still have a feeling of guilt. Why didn't I do more to help her? Paul thought we ought not to tell Margaret that she had cancer, but I'm sure she knew it. I think we could have helped if we had talked over the future together.

From time to time, another girl physician and I shared our evenings. She regarded my missionary aims as ridiculous. When I asked her what solution she had for the world's problems, she confided that though she didn't speak openly to many people, she considered the only hope for the world was Communism and forcible division of the available wealth and power. I was aghast to discover that people who seemed so like myself could have such contrary ideas.

DIVORCE

Norman stayed in the naval office in India, as the Japanese did not come and take it. I poured out my days in letters to him, loving him more when he was at a distance and didn't interfere with my work. But suddenly he wrote that he wanted a divorce to marry someone else. He said our marriage had not been a success, so it was better to terminate it. The letter brought me heartbroken agony. It cut so deep that I could not weep. Through a mission board, I found I could get a place in a mission hospital in India, so I made plans to go and gave up my New Jersey practice. For some months beforehand, I lived with Paul's orphaned family and my mother and took a course in tropical medicine. I thoroughly studied malaria and the love life of intestinal worms. For a while, I couldn't get a passport to leave the country. The State Department said that five hundred ships a month were being sunk in the Caribbean Sea. Finally, I obtained passage on a British ship and again we zigzagged back to Bombay.

I stayed with Norman a week. He claimed I cared more for my career than for him and that I was completely selfish. It is true that a physician's life can take up one's full time, especially if one regards it as a God-given talent. This encounter in my life was an illustration of what Jesus said, that He had not come to give peace on earth but rather division. Norman left India and went back to work in the oil field in Iran. I took the train and went to work with the Church of the Brethren, who had a hospital at Dahanu Road, seventy-five miles north of Bombay. I met Norman in Basrah again two years later. He seemed a perfect stranger to me by then. I agreed to help him get a divorce by writing that I refused to live with him. I think I made an error in marrying him, because I knew in a way that we were not spiritual mates. Somehow, without intending to, I became a eunuch for the sake of the Kingdom of Heaven and decided I would not marry again. My marriage was a sad and tragic episode, but I learned something from it that I couldn't have learned in any other way.

Would I never find a real friend? Every close friendship had sadly broken up. The question of my guilt in consenting to the divorce dug into my soul. I had never thought I would come to this predicament. My thoughts went over and over the problem. Jesus said that divorce was due to our hardness of heart. Male and female were created to become one, which naturally should last for life. My heart was too hard to consider forcing myself to live with Norman when he plainly didn't want me. Christ allowed divorce in just one exception—adultery. And adultery can be spiritual as well as physical. In our case, we never became one spiritually—in our idea of what was most important in life—so our oneness was shattered, if it ever existed at all. As a result we

couldn't live together. Anyhow, that's the way *I* figured it out.
Since there was wrong on both our parts, we would have to rely
on the Cross for forgiveness. I think remarriage would have been
acceptable, but I reasoned that for a woman physician, marriage
would always be difficult. Medicine was so demanding, and it
would not be wise for me after one failure. Anyhow, I devoted
myself to missionary medical work again and never was sorry or
lonesome.

THE DAHANU ROAD MISSION HOSPITAL (INDIA)

Nurse Hazel Messer and I lived in an open two-story mission
bungalow in the middle of a large green compound. There was a
large home for the Indian girl nurses, a two-story hospital with
wide verandas, a separate clinic building, a small chapel, and lines
of rooms for the staff and patients' families, including Doctor
Peter's family. The American doctor, Barbara Nicky, had gone
home. The group worked harmoniously and Hazel and I liked
each other. We had an Indian cook who gave us mostly a vege-
tarian diet with Indian curries and lots of peanuts and bananas.
The house was open and did not need screens, as there were no
flies. But there were mosquitoes at night, so we slept under nets.

The area was mostly agricultural. Farmers raising rice and
dhal—the pealike protein food. The town extended to the sea a
couple of miles from the hospital. There the fishermen caught
the long transparent fish which they dried on clotheslines and
called Bombay Duck. A large group of Parsees had rose and fruit
gardens. They sent the produce to Bombay's market by the early
morning train. We would take the nurses for a walk in the Parsee
gardens on Sunday afternoons and so made friends with many of
the Parsees. They had one great problem—the large bats called
flying foxes. The bats came at night and ate the fruit when they
couldn't be seen or shot. Then they would spend their days hanging on the trees in the Hindu lands where the Hindus would not
allow any killing. Whenever there was a holiday, the Parsees would
send us buckets and buckets of roses.

I started to learn Marathi from one of the Indian helpers. She
would sit beside me in the clinic to translate and help me. The
main medical problem was malaria with subsequent anemia, because the people did not eat meat or eggs. There was no blood
available for transfusions, so the pregnant women suffered most.

I begged one woman to drink an eggnog which I made myself. She agreed, but the very idea was so nauseating to her that she promptly vomited it.

One night a little boy unconscious from cerebral malaria was brought to me. The treatment is an intravenous injection of quinine. I filled the syringe from an ampul of solution of quinine and started to give it. The child suddenly died. I learned too late that the drug must be diluted in a thousand cc of saline and given slowly. This is a grief that doctors have to live with.

Nurse Hazel Messer was a cheerful soul about my age. She had come from a farm in Ohio. Hazel carried the burden of running the forty-bed hospital, teaching and directing twenty nurses. She did it very well. Our salaries were very small—less than I got in Kuwait.

Every morning, the staff gathered in the hospital for devotions. Then Hazel, Dr. Peter, the Indian physician, and I made rounds. The upper floor was mainly maternity. The lower floor held all other kinds of cases. There were two large wards with a few private rooms. Because the patients came long distances to the hospital, their families would accompany them. The families were given a room in the lines where they could live and cook. Each caste had to have its separate food. Dr. Peter and I made rounds on the families, too, to tell them when the patient could go home and to make the very small charges for the care. The nurses were taught midwifery, as well as nursing, so I took only the abnormal cases. Dr. Peter asked me how Americans managed to pay for heating our houses. He could afford very little kerosene for cooking. Most of the fuel was dried cow dung. Some Hindu women kept water buffalos and came delivering the milk. They wore gaily colored clothes, carrying as many as three shining brass pots on their heads. The Hindu women looked so much better than the black-clothed Arab women. We had a bathroom in the hospital with a septic tank, but most of the people used a nearby field. We had to be careful where we walked.

Dr. Peter was about my age and had been educated in India. He had never traveled abroad. Neither of us had much training in surgery, so we avoided it as much as possible. We ran the clinic in the morning and afternoon. The patients had to bring their own bottles for medicine. One man who had brought his own bottle complained to Tarak, the sweet-tempered compounder, that the bottle was dirty just as Tarak was filling it for him. Tarak, who tried to please everybody, poured the drug into a beaker, washed the bottle and put the medicine back in it. So everyone was satisfied.

There were several dramatic cases. Early January first, they brought in a small boy, about three years old, who was gasping for breath and turning blue. I was alone. Something had to be done quickly. I grabbed the unsterile knife from the shelf, laid the child on the table with his head hanging over the edge and with no anesthesia, cut his throat to open the trachea. He was immediately relieved. I held it open until Hazel could find a tracheostomy tube, which fit and kept the trachea open. That was about the bravest thing I ever did. I was real proud of myself. But what caused the obstruction? I couldn't solve that problem. A week later, I went with the patient and his mother to the Tata Hospital in Bombay, where they specialize in cancer, and turned him over to them. After some time, they found that the cause was a congenital cyst near the trachea which happened to swell and suddenly became large enough to obstruct the trachea. They were able to remove the cyst.

Another case threw me into the depths of despair. An Indian woman came for delivery in beginning labor with the fetus coming breech. She had low fever, weak pains, but complained bitterly of the pain in her back. I gave morphine to give her some relief, as the case was not progressing. After a couple of hours, the nurses called me back. She was in terrible distress, bleeding vaginally and vomiting blood, screaming with pain, but the baby was still not coming. I was baffled and couldn't think what could cause this. I couldn't think of a thing to do. How I wished for someone to consult. Within an hour she died undelivered. The dark clouds descended on me. I felt I had no right to act as a physician. It was a bitter experience. After a week we found out from neighbors what the real diagnosis was. The family was hiding a case of smallpox. If the government found out about a case of smallpox, they would send an officer to vaccinate the whole family and quarantine the house. The Hindus feel that vaccination will displease the goddess of smallpox, so they reject it. My patient had been in the first stage of one of the virulent forms of smallpox before there is any skin eruption. Then I remembered that one of the symptoms is an agonizing backache. The fact that she was in labor had nothing to do with her death. She couldn't have been saved.

The Hindus do not circumcise the boy babies as the Muslims do. As a result, the boys have much penile inflammation. I wonder how the Semites learned that this operation is a healthy procedure. There was the case of the baby girl born with an imperforate anus, which fortunately could be opened through the vagina.

MONSOON

After a hot, oppressive spring, the monsoon rains suddenly began on June fifteenth. How wonderful to see the world abruptly don a green color! Even our emotions changed. The rain poured like an open faucet over our house. Our leather shoes and suitcase turned green, and the dhobis (washmen) at the hospital couldn't get the sheets dry.

During the monsoon, a British military plane crashed in the country about thirty miles from us. The air force men came to "do the necessary" (as the Indians say). They stopped at our house and we found rooms for them. They had a grim task in the dank humidity, dark, unceasing rain, and sticky mud to find the plane and the broken, decomposing bodies and bury them. The villagers helped recover hundreds of sacks of mail. The searchers came back in the evenings wet, muddy, and quiet. The airmen gave us their cartons of K-rations, so we concocted some wonderful dishes and tried to cheer them up.

Tales of rich and powerful rulers reached our ears, though we didn't move in those circles. The maharajah of a nearby princely state had been to Europe and came back to his palace bringing a gorgeous French lady who was to teach him how to play bridge. The royal mother of the maharajah took a violent dislike to the foreigner and plotted to get rid of her. The French lady was in the habit of taking an early morning walk around the racetrack. So the rani hired a couple of thugs to kill her there. It might have been a quiet palace affair except that the British ambassador and his English wife happened to be guests at the palace just then. The English lady also happened to take an early morning walk on the racetrack. The thugs got the wrong lady. So it became a serious political situation. However, the ambassador had to agree to hush up the matter. The British officer who told me the story said he saw the rani once, playing cards at a club in Bombay. He said she had a face like a meat chopper.

One of the British members of the Indian civil service spent an evening with us telling tales of the English letters written by their Indian employees.

One clerk wrote asking for a raise in salary and concluded, saying, "Fancy yourself, my dear sir, trying to support three adults and six adultresses."

Another said that he was considering another job and was in a quandary, writing, "I am sitting on the horns of a dilemma and my god, is it uncomfortable!"

One quotation was, "My life is like a rolling stone, flitting from tree to tree and gathering no moss."

In one of the Indian medical journals, I read the report of the treatment of an eye case. The author concluded his account of the treatment by saying, "Then we lost her sight."

Bedbugs tormented our patients, who couldn't sleep from their bites. The sheets would get speckled with blood. Finally, we obtained our first DDT and Hazel delightedly started spraying. The enemy came out, tried to climb the walls, staggered as if drunk, and gave up. We were delighted.

In the monsoon, snakes appeared. Dr. Peter and Tarak killed an eight foot cobra near their house. A Russell's viper slithered across our front walk. The neighbor's little girl, who brought us buffalo milk every morning, reached up to a shelf, was bitten, and died in a few minutes.

The rains lasted just three months and abruptly ceased. Then cholera began. We saw some cases in the homes. If we got to them early enough, we gave 1,000 cc of saline intravenously and saved them. We had no vaccine but kept our hands clean. The disease probably was transmitted through the well water. One patient with cholera arrived at the hospital about 1 P.M. and was told the clinic would open at three. He waited and died. Somehow my failures stand out in my memory more than any successes.

The life of the people was dull and monotonous. The Warli tribe made a fermented drink from the toddy palm. They would have a social gathering of men, women, and children, warming up the toddy in earthen jars over a fire. It made for a gay night.

The tribe's people would pass our house late at night, singing and laughing.

The Church of the Brethren had a custom which afforded some drama. Once a month, there would be a love feast in the little chapel. We sat on the floor on mats to eat curry and rice on a banana leaf. After that, we all went outside for the foot-washing ceremony. Each of us washed someone else's feet and had ours washed and dried. Returning to the chapel, we had communion. Hazel would use raisins to make the fruit of the vine and chapattis for bread. The Christian group had about thirty members, with a leader who had some training and could preach. A Marathi Christian poet had put the whole Christ event in hymns with music that the people loved. They started to sing them. Hazel and I stayed until eleven and went to bed, but the Indian group sang the songs until the sun came up.

Daulot and Rustom were a Parsee couple whom I came to love. During the monsoon, Rustom sent word that he had stepped on an iron nail while working in the water in his gardens. It was pouring rain; there was a river in flood between the hospital and his house. But I set out and walked across the railroad trestle bridge over the raging river. I treated his cut and gave him tetanus antitoxin. They were very grateful and seemed to think I'd done something very courageous. But everything I do seems to go wrong somehow. Rustom was allergic to horse serum and broke into such hives that he had to be brought to the hospital for treatment for my treatment. Fortunately, he survived.

One day Hazel had business in the town of Dahanu. The two bullocks that drew our cart both had diarrhea. The driver sat on the bar between them, hitting them with a heavy stick, twisting their tails and tickling their soft underbellies with his foot. We sat in the two-wheeled cart with a cloth sunshade and a mattress about a yard square so we had to fold under our legs. It was three miles to the village and took forty-five minutes. I tried to think we were better off than most of the rest of the traffic, who were walking. We passed a toddy shop where the Indians drink any time of day. Some customers were reeling along the road. We passed the smelly place where they were drying the fish on clotheslines to make Bombay Duck. Some little boys ran after us so fast that their dhoties fell off, but they didn't seem to mind it. We had to go to an old fort, where the officials took a long time to sign a permit. Indian officials take the business of signing their names very seriously—perhaps they hope for a bribe.

A man hanged himself on a tree near the clinic. As it is against the law for anyone to touch such a body until the police arrive, the staff had to leave the poor fellow hanging there while we had afternoon clinic. Of course, everybody came out to look at the sight. Nobody knew him or why he did it. By evening the police came and took down the corpse.

We had three rare and unusual cases in obstetrics. The first had placenta previa, in which the placenta is lower than the fetus and comes first. She bled so much that she died. We had no blood. Another was a case that tried to deliver at home without success. After I felt inside, I found she had a hydrocephalic fetus. For this, the head has to be ruptured and after fluid flows out, the delivery is easy. The head was as big as a football. The third case was a woman who was crippled with osteomalacia, a disease in which the bones get soft and bend and twist due to some lack in the diet. She couldn't deliver normally at all. Dr. Peter and I decided we must do a Caesarian section. It was late at night, and we had no lights except kerosene lanterns so had to put it off until morning. I had never done a section by myself and tried to sleep but kept dreaming about the operation. When we finally got to it and prayed for help, I tried to act nonchalantly to encourage the others, but I didn't feel that way. But we went to work, took the knife, and before long took out a live, screaming, baby boy. The mother made a good recovery, too. My head was in the clouds.

That night, I got up to go to the bathroom, which was across the veranda covered with a thin blue cotton rug. There seemed to be a fold in it. I got a torch and saw it was a snake about twenty inches long. Hazel kept canes handy all over the house, and I seized mine and beat the poor little thing. Hazel came out and said it was probably a krait—very poisonous, but it was dead. Hazel thought it might have a wife around somewhere.

In the rainy season we had many cats and dogs taking refuge in the hospital. I decided we had to get rid of them. With the men's help we threw gunny sacks over their heads and held them while I gave an injection of strychnine. It seems rather horrible, but what else can be done?

One of my letters from Dahanu, dated April 17, 1945, is interesting enough to quote—with a few corrections.

Dear family,

As the *Bombay Times* puts it, the weather conditions are rapidly deteriorating. The temperature is almost a hundred and very humid. I feel dopey. The trees have lost their leaves, but some are breaking into blossom with bright green leaves. One has the most awful perfume like bad halitosis and is nauseating.

The handsome young rajah of Jawahar state came to call driving his cream-colored Buick. He told us about his new palace and invited us to come and spend a day there. He sent a station wagon, as some other missionaries, Mrs. Ebey and Miss Schwartz, were here. Naturally an obstetrical case came in just as we were ready to go, but we persuaded Dr. Peter to take it.

The trip was only forty miles, but the road was poor, the hills were steep, the dust was red. Between our sweat and dust, we quickly turned completely red. We drove east across many dry river beds and up into the hills of the western ghats. One of the hills was shaped like a cone, very steep with a temple at the top. It is called Mahalaxmi after Laxmi, the goddess of wealth—a very popular deity. Once a year they have a large pilgrimage here. A priest brings down sacred fire and lights a great sacrifice. Hazel said she observed it once. They had a band which burst into music as the fire appeared, playing "Yes, We Have No Bananas."

We stopped at a distillery where they make a kind of whiskey from the berries of a tree. The Warlis make toddy from the palm, but the Parsees go in for the distilled stuff, which does a lot of damage. We walked around the large well and distilling vats.

Our first glimpse of the palace was like a scene from Hollywood. A big flag flew in front to show that the rajah was at home. The grand entrance was draped with purple for some holiday. The entrance was being landscaped and terraced. The building was gray granite with battlements, towers, and cupolas on all the corners. Some parts were three stories and some two. Over the entrance was a model of Ganesh, the elephant god—the family patron. The rajah and rani were at the front door and led us to two guest rooms to clean up. Did we need it? We were red dust all over. There was a wonderful bathroom with tub, seat, and bowl. I wanted to take a bath but Hazel stopped me because the rajah sent a servant saying that drinks were ready.

The rooms were large—the furniture was ordinary but the best they could get in wartime. The rajah and rani were dressed in formal Indian style. She was lovely and slim in a green silk sari and shining gold ornaments. The children came in—a boy of eight and two little girls who were cute in bright colors and gold anklets of bells which tinkled as they walked. They have an Anglo-Indian nursemaid. They took us all over the palace. Half of the upstairs is his, the other is hers and the children's. It had a wonderful view, being at the edge of a ridge and looking over the bare hills beyond.

At the table, there were four servants. First, there was soup and salad, then a magnificent vegetable curry, as they are Hindu. There were ten different side dishes, chutneys, and many kinds of bread made from various grains with interesting flavors. We ended with mango fool, which I think cannot be beat.

In the afternoon, the rajah offered us a drive through his town. We went in his Packard. They say he has fourteen cars. It was a rule that when he drove through the town, everybody must come out and bow. I felt embarrassed to see the crowds come out and bow low before our car with the rajah and rani. The little brown children toddled out naked and tried to imitate their elders. There were three women who did not bow. They were untouchables—sweepers. They had to turn their backs to the car. I suppose even their looks would offend his honor.

He told us how his parents had died when he was nine years old. A Scotch-Irish lady offered to bring him up with her own boys. So he grew up partly in England and went to school there. When he told us about his ancestors who came from Rajputana to conquer these people and boasted that that was how he had the right to rule, I looked quickly into his face to see if he was laughing, because I thought that was a first-rate joke. But he was very serious, which made it funnier to me.

He drove us to the old Indian palace which was built by his father. It was an old Indian style of carved wood and painted in brilliant colors. He keeps his offices here and has big pictures of his family and friends on the walls. When we drove through the gate, suddenly there was a terrific racket. He said those were the drums they always beat when he comes. Coming back through the town again, the people came out to bow, all except two loose donkeys who got in the way. Like animals, they kept in front of the car for a long way. Hazel was giggling on the back seat because the donkeys seemed to be the only ones who had some self-respect and sense of proportion.

At the palace, some men had caught a little wild pig and didn't know what to do with it. If they let it loose, a tiger would get it. No one there would eat pork. I said we ate pork, at which the rajah just laughed. We took some pictures and went home.

I happened to meet a physician in Bombay who told me about a disease prevalent in India which wasn't known in Europe— Tropical eosinophilia. He did me a great favor, for I began to see cases. The patients had asthma and a terrifically high blood eosinophilia count of 30,000 to 40,000 per cc. He also told me the effective treatment—three or four intravenous doses of the drug we were using for syphilis, Neosalvarsan. So I treated men, women, and children with it. The results were so gratifying that I felt on top of the world. In the medical library in Bombay, I read that the condition was probably caused by a mite that lives in stored grain.

Since we couldn't buy meat in Dahanu, Hazel or I would sometimes take a day off and go to Bombay on the morning train to go shopping at Crawford Market. There were always a bunch of small boys at the entrance to carry things in big baskets. If you didn't take one, the rest would annoy you. The Hindu boys wouldn't carry meat and the Muslim boys wouldn't carry pork. A convenient train went back in the evening. I asked an English gentleman if I could sit in his compartment for the two hours. "Yes," he said, "What part of the Middle West are you from and what mission do you belong to?" I thought quickly and asked him what part of Scotland he was from and whether he went to New College in Edinburgh. In our conversation, I found out that he was an English missionary who had married an American missionary woman from the Middle West. Hazel and I would often walk down to see the evening train stop at Dahanu. As it was the main track to Delhi and the northwest frontier, important people would frequently be passengers who were willing to chat.

There was some leprosy. A woman came and threw herself at my feet. This was most embarrassing to me. She was begging treatment because she had no feeling in her feet and the rats gnawed her at night. There was also a case of lacerations by a tiger. For the first time, I tried skin grafting. We didn't have the right knives, so I picked up bits of skin with a needle and shaved them off and transplanted the dots. It was gratifying to find that most took well.

Pinworms were endemic. I caught them too. The only drug we had was gentian violet, which made me nauseated.

The Church of the Brethren had been working in this part of India for about thirty years when I arrived. They had another hospital at Bulsar about a hundred miles north of Dahanu. But most of their missionaries moved around in the tribal villages where people who had no caste lived. They rode bicycles and lived in sheds built for cattle. I spent a couple of days with one of the ladies, sleeping in a bedding bag. It was very unpretentious humble work. They visited and taught as the opportunity came. They told me they had over thirty thousand baptized Christians. Some people criticized these lay missionaries for baptizing before the people had been thoroughly prepared. There was not much resistance to persuading the people. It was a great contrast to our work in Arabia, where the resistance is so staunch and our results so meager.

ASKED BACK

I had spent two years at the mission hospital at Dahanu when Rose and Jerry Nykerk wrote to me from Kuwait. They asked me to come back to the hospital and bring two Indian nurses with me. Rose and Jerry were worn out. They had no help running the only medical work in Kuwait during the war years. I decided to return when Dr. Nicky came back to the Dahanu hospital. It would be difficult to find nurses willing to go with me. I took the train to Dr. Scudder's hospital in Vellore and spoke to the nurses but found no takers. I took my bedding roll and traveled by train to various mission hospitals. Some girls wanted to come but their parents wouldn't let them. Finally at Nellore, I found Bhagyamma, an older nurse who had lost her job and was willing to try something new. I could offer the girls a much higher salary than they received in India. Bhagyamma agreed to meet me in Bombay when all the arrangements were made. Back at Dahanu, Indira Waghmare, one of our nurses, offered to go with me. I was very grateful to her. I regretfully said good-bye, because I did love the people at Dahanu. The Parsees came bringing twelve leis of roses, which filled our train compartment with fragrance. I felt real sorry to leave all my friends there.

At Bombay, we stayed with the Blickenstaffs. They kept a double apartment for missionaries who had to stay a few days. The two nurses and I took taxis to go to the numerous offices for visas, passport signatures, health certificates, and Indian government permits for the Indians to leave. There were endless restrictions on travel. It took us three days to complete the paperwork before we could get on the British-India ship going up the Gulf. I started teaching the nurses Arabic. One night, during a storm, a passing vessel wired asking for a doctor. I didn't want to go, as the waves were high, but thought, "This is my duty." So Indira and I went down the ladder and with some sailors got into a lifeboat and went to another ship. The sailor seemed to have appendicitis. I was too afraid to attempt surgery in that situation. Since they had penicillin, I recommended that. We went back over the tossing waves again. I was relieved to hear later that the man recovered without surgery.

The historical office at my medical college asked some questions of its graduates. What is your philosophy and how did you cope? I don't have a philosophy, only a faith which never let me down. I believe that the Christ-event with His love and power is the only hope for the world. I believe that God intends me to work and to think clearly about my duty. I believe that the truth and the right will somehow conquer—that the best is yet to come. As Dag Hammarskjold wrote, "In our era, the road to holiness lies through the world of action." I know these ideas cannot be proved by what we call science or reasoning. They lie in the realms beyond logic.

I had longed for a warm human companion but found only disappointment. I would no longer seek that but use my talents to help others. I'd make full use of the advantages of being single. Perhaps God would use me. I had the gift of health so that "my cup of joyous energy overflows" even in my retirement. I felt sorry for my patients and really cared for them as well as wanting to heal their sicknesses. I felt humble to find that people trusted me. I found wonderful hospital helpers among Arabs, Persians, and Indians, and friends in the British community and a family in the mission. "God setteth the solitary in families."

There are shortcomings in my thinking. I always felt a feminine inferiority and thought that most other people were wiser and stronger than I. "I said I will be wise but it was far from me," said the wise Solomon. In my practice there was much inexperienced fumbling and colossal errors. The triumphs are mostly forgotten, the errors I have to live with in sickening remorse. My soul cleaveth to the dust. I never became very close to any of the Muslims. When I tried to talk about deep things they became silent. Perhaps this kind of talking demands more time and thinking than any of us were willing to do.

The aim of all the missions was not to proselytize but to share in love with all the best we have to give—graciously, tactfully, and honestly. To refrain from giving is to not care about others, which is evil. My main regret is the many things I left undone or failed to do.

7. Kuwait Practice Renewed, 1945

I decided to return to Kuwait because it seemed like home and I had no other place where I wanted to live. Dr. Nicky had returned to her hospital at Dahanu. Rose and Dr. Jerry Nykerk asked me to return. A friend of mine from the Woman's Medical College, Dr. Ruth Crouse, was working in my place for five years in Kuwait but returned home to be married. She had been very well liked. Living in Kuwait was no sacrifice to me. It was an incredibly great privilege.

But when I got back, everything was different. As I wrote to my family in 1945:

> Kuwait is an astonishing picture of a poverty-stricken medieval town coping with the disrupting bonanza of the discovery of a great oil field in its back yard. The town has gone from kerosene lanterns to neon lights in one year. The traffic problems are bewildering with over four thousand cars and trucks. But all this means very little to the average Arab woman, who still stays at home or goes on furtive trips outside draped in black trailing garments, fearful of everything.

The Kuwaiti government asked the mission to find an American doctor to take charge of their medical work. Dr. Potter, the secretary of the Arabian Mission, was to find someone suitable. He announced that finding a doctor for the Kuwaitis to hire was not mission business, but he put an advertisement in the *American Medical Journal*. Only a poorly qualified Armenian physician applied and was accepted. He turned out to be so unprepared that he was soon discharged. The Kuwaitis never asked the mission officially for anything again. We lost a great opportunity.

Shaikh Fehed and his wife, Bederea, asked me to take charge of the women's medical work for the government, but I didn't feel capable of the administration and didn't want to leave the mission work. Shaikha Bederea took over the management of the Amiri Hospital herself and did it very well. With the increased demand for medical services both the government and mission patient loads increased quickly.

NEW FACES

The boom brought new demands from every quarter. The Kuwait Oil Company capped all its wells and just maintained an office during the war. Afterwards, they came back and started drilling. At first, they had no doctor so asked us to take care of their staff. It helped financially. Later, they started a small hospital near ours. I was very grateful for their surgeon, who helped me with some cases. I gave my blood for a case of a ruptured ectopic pregnancy. The girl died before we could do anything. The Indian helpers, being ignorant, inadvertently poured my blood down the sink. O dear! The mission welcomed me, but there were some new faces and some of my friends had gone. Mary Van Pelt had gone home and decided not to return. The Mylreas had retired in Kodaikanal in south India where Bess died. The Barnys had retired, too.

Dr. Maurice and Eleanor Heusinkveld with their two little boys were additions to the mission. They were studying Arabic and living in the two story house built for the Calverleys. Dr. Gerald Nykerk was in charge of both hospitals. Rose helped with the clerical work and was mother to their children, Nancy, David, and Laila. Jerry was sweet-tempered, a beloved physician. Rose was vivacious and had the ability to talk with good humor all the time. Since I lacked that talent, I was glad someone else could keep the conversational ball rolling. Sometimes her remarks were rather sharp. Maurice was a distant relative of mine, a huge man, tall and heavy. He tried to be kind, but he wasn't easy to like. He refused to deviate from what he considered correct. I was described by the oil men as "pure as the drifted snow until she drifted." Eleanor was slight, slender, graceful—an angelic blond.

Yacoob Shemmas and Esteer had five children. He was the Assyrian colporteur. The three boys went into some business, but Aylie, who was about sixteen, helped run the women's hospital. She had no regular education but was intelligent, knew English, and could read and write. It caused some distress when three of us came to displace her. Jerry solved the problem when the women patients became so numerous that some of them went to the men's side. He decided that he needed Aylie to help over there. The younger sister Farida started to work giving out drugs on the women's side. Farida and I worked together for many years and were always congenial. Jameela and Labeeba had left and I was never able to trace them.

The hospital building, which was new in 1938, was in a sad state by 1945. The flat cement roof had cracked so the rains and water marks made all the ceilings of the upper floor stained. The walls and floors were black with soot from cooking fires. The toilet pits were full. The salt water well pump was broken. It had been impossible to get supplies during the war years. As soon as we could get any, we started to clean up the place. Jerry had men stretch cloth over the roof and put tar over it. It kept out the rain, but during the next summer, the tar oozed through the ceilings. We hired masons to scrape the walls and paint them with all we could get—whitewash with glue in it so it wouldn't wipe off. We had to find some poor Persian laborers who were willing to get down into the pits in the bathrooms and haul up the vile, stinking mess with buckets and ropes to empty it in the sea. I felt embarrassed to have human beings do that hard work, but I paid them high wages. The electric wiring had to be redone. We got ceiling fans as soon as possible. John Buckley, the oil company's marine engineer, generously offered to help. He fixed the pump and made himself useful in many ways. Two elderly Persian women did odd jobs and cleaning, and Haseena, the ex-slave, was still with us. We soon had to take on more older Persian women helpers. None of the Arab women were willing to work in the hospital, nor were any young girls allowed to learn to be nurses. At that time it was considered a servile occupation. The beautiful teak doors were scraped and rubbed with rancid shark liver oil, just as the Arab sailors rubbed their teak ships. We polished and replaced the brass sign saying that the hospital was in memory of Mrs. Kate Van Santvoord Olcott. She was a wealthy woman of New York who had given her entire fortune to the Arabian Mission. A man came and fluffed up the cotton mattresses with his harp-like instrument and remade them. It took three days for some men to break down a wall and put in a new door between the two operating rooms. It was so strongly built. It was a lot of fun to see the hospital improve.

Bhagyamma Avelili, the senior nurse, and Indira Waghmare, the recent graduate, moved into the same house with me. It was the place I had lived with Mary Van. The two nurses had one bedroom and I had the other. Living with the two Indian nurses made interesting company but had its strains. Melicko was our cook and we had a small Iranian boy to do the cleaning. The nurses said the American food was tasteless, so we had curry and rice twice a week. We could buy cans of American roast pork for about thirty cents. During the war, the U.S.A. sent shipments of it to our Russian allies through Iran, where it was pilfered. When the Muslims found it was pork, they couldn't eat it. I was invited to dinners with Europeans, but the nurses were not. When I returned the hospitality and had the Indian girls sit at the table with the Europeans, it was awkward. They ate in absolute silence. I spent some hours trying to explain the problem of putting two civilizations together to make excuses for why I couldn't invite them, but there was resentment. I took them swimming, but that was something foreign to them. One night, we went swimming when the fluorescence was brilliant. Every motion of our bodies was luminescent like fairyland. Even our swimming suits glowed a long time.

Haider was a bright young Iranian boy who had worked in our mission homes. He learned English and our ways of living and thinking. When he joined the hospital staff, he quickly showed organizational abilities. Later, we obtained an X-ray machine and sent Haider to India to learn to run it and read the plates. He gradually became invaluable, but he was quite capable of telling us what the Islamic morals of any situation were. He remained a determined Muslim.

NEW CASES

At the hospital, our cases were as varied as ever. One time the oil company surgeon came over to our hospital to help me remove a large parotid tumor from a woman's face. It was a cold winter day, so I had a kerosene heater to warm the operating room. One of the nurses started to give the patient open drop ether. When the patient was unconscious, the nurse accidentally knocked the large bottle of ether on the floor where it broke. In a flash the whole floor was aflame. *Allah kareem,* the next second, it was over. Nothing more caught fire. We caught our breath, looked at each other, carried out the heater, and went on with the operation. It was successful. God was forgiving.

A little Bedouin girl was brought in with large tuberculous neck glands. Her family begged me to remove them. I hesitated because it was a difficult and dangerous operation. But I accused myself of being cowardly and lazy. I began the surgery with some local anesthesia and promptly got into trouble, as the glands lay right on top of the big blood vessels. I removed some and closed the wound. We put her back to bed, but that night she died. It was a very low time for me. I have heard of other doctors who when confronted with such a situation have committed suicide. I couldn't think that would do any good for anyone.

There was a case of a healthy baby boy born with a fat, heavy tail. It looked so dreadful that the mother refused to take the boy home. I wondered whether it could be amputated. With a little local anesthesia, I made a cautious incision. At first I encountered nothing but fat. So, encouraged, I went deeper. To my horror I came upon intestines. *Al hamdallah* (praise be to God), they were empty. By the time the child was five days old, they should have had food residue. So I followed them up and found they were not connected with anything. It must have been one of those cases where parts of an incomplete second fetus are retained in the other body. The intestines could be safely removed, so I amputated the whole tail, sutured the skin, and the baby looked quite normal. The mother accepted her child. They went home where I hope they lived happily ever after.

One pregnant woman who had been bleeding at home for twenty days was brought in. I scolded, "Why didn't you bring her in before?" They blandly answered, "It wasn't time for her to deliver yet." She had a placenta previa, in which the afterbirth comes before the baby. The mother loses all her own blood and usually dies. Fortunately we had a couple of boxes of blood plasma given by the Red Cross after the war. So we did a Caesarian section and saved that one.

One mother delivered triplets who were small but healthy and could live if they were fed correctly. So I suggested that she take one home with her and leave the others with us for a while.

She had been having marital difficulties and thought if she could present the partner with three babies, she might win him back. So she took all three and we never heard from her again.

Nurse Indira went out for a home delivery and delivered two very small fetuses. The women of the family confessed that something had passed before Indira arrived. She looked around and found two more small dead fetuses, so we could claim a case of quadruplets, though all were dead. The women tried to conceal it, because they felt it was a disgrace for babies to be born in litters like cats or dogs.

A little Bedouin girl who had fractured her arm was brought in. Her grandmother, thinking she knew how to treat such cases, had plastered the arm with dung and tied it up tight with ropes. The arm was gangrenous. We had to amputate it. The government's medical service was starting up, so I told her that sometimes they could make something to help her. I, like the grandmother, sometimes rushed in to help and did only damage.

The Western techniques that were quickly entering Kuwait brought tragedies as well as benefits. One night I was called to the hospital. They said it was a burn case. The lady, draped in black as usual, was helped out of the car and led down the hall by a man. I led them to a bed and raised her clothes. She was completely and deeply 100 percent burned. I asked what had happened. They said she was cleaning clothes for the household in gasoline. Nothing could be done. She died in a couple of hours.

Because of the crowds of patients, I had to delegate drug dispensing authority to the Indian nurses. When penicillin became plentiful, the people considered it the ultimate cure for anything and demanded it by name. One visitor to an inpatient asked Bhagyamma for an injection of penicillin, saying she always got one when she didn't feel well. The nurse complied. The woman fell down and died. She had had enough injections to sensitize her. It does happen everywhere. I had to explain and try to console the family and Bhagyamma. This family took it very well. It seems I remember mostly tragedies; those who got well, I forget.

Friday was the Muslim day of worship. The men went to the mosque for a sermon. It was not especially a day of rest. The oil company, wanting to please the Arabs, took Thursday and Friday for their weekly days off. Most of them weren't Christians anyhow. On Good Friday, we had a short service in our chapel for about ten people. Later that day the oil people had a tennis match back of our compound. Rose and Jerry went over to play. Maurie Heusinkveld thought that was highly sacrilegious and told them so. Rose always had a reply and a hot temper. Sparks began to fly. I was neutral on the subject of days.

The oil company brought a lot of Indian clerical staff and their families, who used to come to our hospital. One sent his wife with the note, "The bearer is my wife. She is in the family way. I want this thing stopped both now and forevermore." Another Indian couple presented themselves, with the wife having scabies. I gave them directions on how to use the benzyl benzoate liquid. She was to take off all her clothes and rub herself all over with the fluid for three days, and then she could take a bath and put on clean clothes. He looked aghast, "You mean she has to go naked for three days?"

In the yearly report to the Board sent in December 1947, the outpatients numbered 26,825. We saw them for four hours in the mornings, averaging 108 per day, but some days there were over 200. We kept records as well as we could. Inpatients were 465, surgery mostly minor but 25 majors, obstetrics 120 cases with 42 abnormal, eye surgery 140 lids with 2 cataracts. The people had more money and paid well, so we could hire more helpers. I found a young boy, Yusuf, who could read numbers, so he gave out the patients' record cards. He had a chair and table in the waiting room. He complained that the women were smothering him, so we had the carpenter build a fence around him. People now came in taxis. They would park their cars in front of my office windows and run their radios, gossip, or tune up their cars. It was so noisy I couldn't hear. So we built a fence there, too. After some years, we got an air-conditioner. The helpers usually did good work. They hadn't got to striking but would tell me, "This isn't my work," when they didn't like some job.

As had been the case before the oil boom, the inpatients had to bring some of their family, because the Indian nurses were too busy to give bedside nursing. They were trained midwives, too, so they could take over most of the normal cases. The patients had to bring their own food, too, as we didn't have a cook or kitchen. We couldn't have a ward because each family demanded a room to themselves. I sometimes thought that even cleanliness was too much of a luxury for a mission what with the dust, open halls, and high winds. Everything gradually became dust-color.

The hospitals also ran their own finances. I always had trouble with numbers but tried to keep the accounts and dutifully send out written bills every month. One time, things became so messed up that I was three thousand rupees short. John Buckley brought over Mr. Archer, the oil company accountant, and for a couple of nights we went over accounts. John claimed Archie went into nervous prostration over the mess, but we did figure it out so the numbers of outgo and income matched. The women's hospital paid all its expenses. After a while, we even began to make a profit.

At the end of every year, the missionaries from each station—Amara, Basrah, Kuwait, Bahrain, and Oman—left their work to helpers and gathered together for a conference. Each kind of work had to have a written report of the year's work. Finances were gone over by a committee for accuracy and suitability. We were limited by rules as to how much could be spent. We were always sure that the maintenance department did some finagling, but they were so useful that we passed it up. The stations that had a balance, which were usually the hospitals in Kuwait, were trimmed of their leftover funds, which were given to the poor stations who had a deficit. We also gathered together for inspiration, fellowship, and fun. One of the problems I brought up was to build a good nurses' home for Kuwait. A building committee would try to draw plans, but we couldn't agree.

In 1947, Jay Kapenga came to live in Kuwait. He lived in the old Shah Raza house and improved it. He took his meals with the Indian nurses and me. He liked maintenance work, so he built a wall for the hospital courtyard and some small kitchens where the patients could cook. He repaired the line of rooms back of the hospital so the nurses could have a house of their own. Then he repaired the seawall in front of the hospital, as it was washing away.

Two new American nurses arrived, Louise Essenberg and Joan Olthof. They came on a short-term plan so didn't study Arabic. My mother came out for the winter, too. All of them were very helpful in running the household and managing supplies and the storeroom.

We started each morning clinic with a short talk to the gathered women with their children and babies. About half of them were Persians who didn't understand Arabic. My Arabic had become rusty, but I tried giving the talks anyhow. Some things got across. Once, I told Jesus' story of the man who said to his son, "Go and work in the vineyard." The son said, "Yes, sir," but didn't go. Another son said, "No, sir," to his father, but afterward he went and worked. So I asked the women which son did his father's will. To my surprise, the patients answered with one accord, "The son who said yes to his father." Thinking my Arabic was not clear, I repeated the story. The women reiterated that the son who honored his father's face did the more important thing, and how he acted was not significant. Another time I told the story of Christ washing the disciples' feet and how he told us we should do the same. So I had a basin of water and towel ready and got down on my knees and started to wash one lady's feet. The patients, like the Apostle Peter, were terribly embarrassed. Usually the women made no comment, but one or two told me they thought my stories interesting.

I collected many of Elsie Anna Wood's pictures of the Bible stories. She had painted them from actual scenes in Palestine, so the people looked like Arabs instead of the European artists' productions. I had them framed with a verse in Arabic for explanation and put one in each room. About 1948, some Christian families of the Assyrian Church came from northern Iraq. Among them was Sitt Sara, who became our Bible woman and was very acceptable. I noticed that when I took part in the talks, it calmed me for the morning fray. Once we showed the movie of the life of Christ, which made quite an impression. One Bedu observed after it, "So that was the way it was." I had a picture of the crucifixion in the hall. Many stopped to study it, but no one made any comment.

Mr. Southwell, one of the directors of the KOC, was at our house one day and told my mother and me that the company had just acquired a plane to bring supplies and men. I was due a vacation in the summer of 1947, so he offered the two of us a place on the plane on its flight back to London. It was beautiful. We spent an afternoon at Malta seeing the town and spent a night there. Next morning, flying at 4 A.M., the pilot invited us to the cockpit to watch a glorious dawn over the snowy Alps. John Buckley asked his mother to give us hospitality in London, which we

greatly appreciated. Later, his aunt invited us to be her guests at
Morgan Porth in Cornwall. It was a lovely vacation.

NEW PROBLEMS

In the great human adventure of crossing cultural boundaries
inter-religious animosity was bound to surface. For me it happened this way. When the Kuwaiti government began its own
medical work with physicians from various countries, a Kuwait
Medical Society was organized. Our hospital cooperated and took
our turn to invite the society to meet in our buildings and discuss
selected topics. I didn't have any good case to present, and so I
decided to read from a paper I had been working on on the position of women as dictated by the verses about women in the
Qur'an. During my reading I could sense the chilly reception of
my topic. I perceived that most of the new doctors were Egyptians. I did not realize the seriousness of my mistake at first, but
it soon became apparent.

The ruler, the amir, had employed an Egyptian secretary, Izzat
Ja'fer. Some of my talk was promptly reported to the secretary.
So Izzat took it upon himself to defend the faith. He sent the
mission a harsh, pejorative letter saying that my criticism of
women's position in Islam was insulting: it was a naked exposition
of hostility to the religion revealed by God; it was a blasphemous
attack on the local culture. He demanded that I immediately hand
over my paper to the authorities and apologize.

I had few friends to consult in my time of need. At that time,
Jerry and Rose Nykerk had been requested by King Ibn Saud
to work in Saudi Arabia, and Dr. Lewis Scudder and his wife
Dorothy had taken over the men's hospital. Also, the Heusinkvelds went to Bahrain. The Rev. Garret De Jong and Everdene
had returned for the evangelistic position and the house on the
compound.

I was sunk in the slough of despair. The darkness of a starless
night surrounded me. Like the psalmist, "Because of my foolish-
ness, I am troubled; I am bowed down greatly. I go mourning all
the day long" (Ps. 38:5). The ruler was very ill with a heart attack,
and Dr. Scudder was attending him. We guessed that he would
not be bothered just then. But it was a serious situation. Therefore, Garry De Jong helped me. We decided it would be best to
write an apology and hope the affair would subside. We wrote

that the paper was intended as a sociological study and analysis of the position of woman in a Muslim culture. It was hoped that it would lead to a mutual understanding of two different ways of life and had no aim of offending Muslim sensibilities. I wrote that I apologized for any implied criticism of the Muslim religion. At that time, I was asked to go to Qatar for four months. Shaikh Ahmad died of a heart attack, and Izzat Ja'fer lost his job and returned to Egypt. In the political turmoil of choosing a new ruler my small cultural error was forgotten.

FOUR MONTHS AT QATAR, 1948

At the annual mission meeting, a request was received from the ruler of Qatar to start a hospital in his capital city of Doha. We didn't really have enough doctors but considered it such a wonderful opportunity that we felt we should try in the hope that it might work out. To start, each of the doctors was to spend some months there with an Indian nurse or two. In the year that Shaikh Ahmad of Kuwait died (1948), it was my turn to go to Qatar. That January, I traveled by ship to Bahrain and by launch to the peninsula of Qatar. I left the Kuwait women's work to Dr. Scudder and the nurses.

The shaikh provided an Arab-style house on the seafront. It had a beautiful view but was mostly a walled square, enclosing a large, empty courtyard with two-storied rooms around the edges. We used the downstairs rooms for a clinic and patients and the upstairs rooms for the male and female Indian nurses, the cook, and myself. It was not well built. The cold sea winds blew through cracks in the windows. The bathroom was far away and had poor facilities. It was too cold to take a bath. I got itchy scabies, for which we had no drug.

The ruler's house nearby was in a similar style. I went to call on him several times, but the big room where he sat was usually full of men, so I didn't feel comfortable. So I called on his hareem instead. A prominent family, the Shehadis (not the real name), had three sons who were shrewd politicians and acted as managers for the shaikh. I had to work under their supervision. Their sister, Sara, demanded that I come over and visit with her daily. She had no husband. She was large, the pompous dictator of the family hareem. She shouted her orders. In Arab society, a sister has more power over her brothers than wives do.

Sara expected me to entertain her with the news of the outside world, but I had a hard time thinking up topics. I took her a *National Geographic* magazine with pictures of the archaeological digs in Iraq. Among other things, I said that the Iraqis used to worship the moon. That caused a furious, vehement denial. Arab peoples never worshiped the moon, Sara said. She had never been to school and had no idea of history. Oh dear, I always seem to say the wrong thing.

I don't remember any cases in Qatar except one boy with tetanus who we pulled through. The ruler sent over his servant with a note, "Abdullah my servant is sick. Cure him." One of the younger wives in Sara's hareem lost a baby girl and was grieving. She whispered to me, "Please come to my room and read me comforting words from your book." I was very glad to do that.

Toward the end of my four months, one of the local merchants took the nurses and me for a drive to some of the local settlements where there were wells. Some minor shaikhs had built walls, rooms, and small gardens around the wells. The village women welcomed us as if we were the most delightful guests. They were gorgeously dressed with real gold jewelry. Everywhere they compelled us to sit on the floor with them and pressed food and drink on us. They let me take a lot of pictures, which unfortunately were lost in the mail.

There was one English lady, the wife of an oil company manager. I used to visit her often and told her the story of my medical faux pas in Kuwait. A few days after that, I was due to leave and expected the Shehadi men to send the car. Nothing came. I went to Sara's house, but the door was locked and no one answered. I was getting desperate and asked another merchant to send me a car. He told me that the family had been informed that I made speeches against the religion and therefore would do no more favors for me. That malicious gossip could only have come from the English woman. The English personnel were often jealous of the Americans and some curried favor with the Arabs to enhance their own position.

I was so glad to get back to Kuwait. Qatar didn't seem friendly. Perhaps I missed the companionship of the other missionaries. Later, we had to give up the medical work in Qatar because the Nykerks developed pulmonary tuberculosis and had to go home. They had been requested by King Ibn Saud to work in a Saudi town where they treated a lot of that disease and also had a cook with the condition. Losing another doctor spread the work too thin. It didn't work to employ Indians to run a mission hospital.

CHANGES AND OBSTETRICS IN KUWAIT

By this time, Kuwait was exciting. It had become a real boom town. The war was over. The modern world burst on the city and no one was ready for it. There was a feeling of whoopee!, ta-ra-ra-boom-de-lay! Shopkeepers were cheerful, their shelves piled full with cloth from Japan and canned foods from all over. Laborers from Iran crowded the narrow streets, walking with brisk steps, carrying heavy loads and calling "balak, balak" (watch out). Drillers were finding more oil, tankers began carrying it away, and money increased. Ships brought supplies. At one time, we counted forty-two freighters sitting out in Kuwait Bay. They couldn't be unloaded because there weren't enough launches. A Dutch engineer, Mr. Van Dee, was brought to dredge out the bay. They built a small pier, but the big ships couldn't come near land.

The men of the ruling family, who all had the title of shaikh, divided up responsibility for the various departments of government among them. Shaikh Fehed had some years of education in Beirut and was the only one with any modern education, so he was put in charge of the medical work. A hospital was started on the seafront at the east end of town. They built it like the big Arab houses—a large courtyard with rooms around the empty center. They asked Dr. Nykerk to come over and see it and tell them which rooms should be for operating and which for patients and clinic rooms. After it was finished, they thought they ought to have running water and some sort of sewerage, so they had to tear it up a bit. They tried to get an American doctor, but none responded to their search except an Armenian. He came and sat in an office, drew up grand plans, but the situation was beyond his capacity so they discharged him. They obtained an English doctor who made the best of the situation. They brought doctors from Egypt and India, with nurses from England, Palestine, Egypt, and India.

They also brought a town planner from England. A question came up about who owned the large city center where the Bedouin came to sell their animals and where the town's celebrations were held. Shaikh Fehed said he owned it, so they paid him a million dollars, which satisfied him. Schools for boys and girls were planned on a cost-plus basis. Things got rather out of hand that way but buildings did get built. Four thousand teachers from Egypt were brought to teach, and Egyptian leader Nasser became the ideal hero of Islam. Kuwait's narrow streets were choked with cars. The planner drew maps of new ring roads and a green belt outside the old city walls. A seawater distillation plant was started that used the gas which came off from the oil wells, making it economical. There was so much gas that it had to be burned in huge flares. They lit up the night sky so, that we couldn't see the stars anymore. The English drillers told us that they were burning up enough gas every day to heat London for a year.

We heard that a German firm had been hired to start a sewerage system. They hired a lot of laborers and began digging. The story went that they collected thirty thousand dollars from the bank and took it with them and flew off in a plane. Whether all this tantalizing gossip was exactly true or not, I don't know. Some things were visible. Of course there was no newspaper, but this was the chit-chat that went the rounds.

Returning to the women's hospital in Kuwait was like jumping on a car going sixty miles per hour. The clinics were larger, with more patients willing to stay in the hospital, more baby cases, more money to count at the end of the day, and a crucial need to hire and train more helpers. Young Arabs when they launch into the modern world have boundless self-assurance and are masters of positive thinking. Boumona came of the Assyrian Christian group and asked for a place in the hospital. I asked, "Have you learned anything about working in the clinic?" She answered, "Yes, I know everything. Just teach me how to give injections."

Shaikh Fehed was the half brother of the ruler, but because his mother was a black concubine, his rating was a little lower than the sons of the Arab wives. So he went to prep school at the American University in Beirut when he was young, which improved his prestige. He fell in love with his half sister Lulua, who was a widow, and married her. Later, he married a young cousin, Bederea. Shaikh Fehed was always very friendly and appreciative of the mission. He frequently invited us to his homes and always asked me to sit at his right hand, the honored place, and introduced me to his guests in impressive phrases which naturally went to my head, where they weren't crowded. He asked me to take charge of the women's work in the government hospital. I declined because I knew I couldn't handle that kind of management and didn't want to leave the mission. His young wife Bederea took over that job, had an office in the hospital, and managed very well.

The mission hospital was open all day to patients, visitors, families of patients, casual strollers, and animals. We had an occasional dog, lots of cats, and big sea rats. The cats offered the rats no fight, they just sat down and watched them. But at night we locked the doors. We had a night watchman, Abu Abbas, but being a man he couldn't sit in the women's hospital, so we made him a little booth beside the door. He was to call me if a patient came at night. We didn't have enough nurses or staff to have a woman helper on duty at night.

In the clinic, I'd been seeing Nureeya, the sweet young wife of a city official. She was getting very heavy with her first pregnancy and told me she was fasting, as it was Ramadan. I was trying to give her some prenatal care, which most women regarded as superfluous. I protested, "Nureeya, you cannot fast now, you need lots of fluids and milk all day long." She answered, "The word of God does not excuse pregnant women from fasting. I fear God." I asked, "Will you come to the hospital for the delivery?" She answered, "I don't know. It shall be as my husband says. He thinks that it is the will of God that babies be born without outside help." "Nureeya, you know sometimes there is trouble." She sighed, "Then if that is the will of God for me, I must bear it." "Nureeya, if you come to the hospital, I will be ready to help you any time." She concluded with, "In shah Allah" (If God wills).

Abu Abbas came banging on our house gate at 2 A.M. I heard him but turned over thinking, "Oh, no!" He was right to persist and kept on banging. "What is it?" "Walada" (baby case). I thought I might as well get fully dressed. It happened in winter when the temperature can be forty with a cold north wind and a chill factor which must make it thirty-two. So I ran over to the hospital to get it over with. The family was waiting in the car. It was Nureeya and her husband. I unlocked the gate. Nureeya's husband and mother helped her walk in and down the hall. Next, we had to figure out how to get the heavy girl up the stairs. There was no elevator. Fortunately, the stairs were built wide for this situation. She could still walk, so rather heartlessly we all helped, pushing and pulling her up to the obstetrical room. Finally we got her on the table. A brief rectal exam told me this was going to need forceps. I sent over for Nurse Indira to come and help.

Nureeya had been in labor for two days at home. The baby's head was stuck in the midpelvis, and the mother's contractions were beginning to weaken. Oh, dear. I remembered what the chief of staff at the University of Wisconsin warned me. "Don't think, because you have six months in obstetrics, that you're a specialist." This kind of case would properly have had a Caesarian section earlier in the labor. Now it was too late for that. Anyhow, it would have been dangerous and not my line. Fortunately, we had good light and a table with stirrups to hold the mother's heavy legs comfortably.

Indira and I cleaned her up and got out the pack of sterilized dressings and instruments we always kept ready. I started scrubbing my hands up to the elbows just as we were taught in Chicago. But here it meant ten minutes in cold water in a basin. Indira boiled up the rubber gloves. I wished I could give Nureeya something for pain, but it was too dangerous. In the early days, I had given a mother a little chloroform. The mother's heart had stopped. We couldn't get it started. I reached in and delivered a live baby from the dead mother but resolved never again to use it. Ether wasn't much help. Morphine goes right into the bloodstream and to the baby, who gets too sleepy to breathe as fast as he must. I used some local novocaine in the perineum, but it didn't help much.

I came to admire the Arab women. They were heroic and took what most American women wouldn't stand for. They felt this suffering was the will of God. It was sin to complain or ask relief.

When everything was ready and the patient was draped, further examination confirmed my worst fears. The waters were gone, the mouth of the uterus was wide open, the fetal heart tones were good, the head was presenting, but it was lying crossways in the midpelvis. It would have to be turned around in order to come down. Yes, I'd had plenty of practice doing this on the manikin. You put the forceps on the baby's head, turn it a little, and readjust the forceps. The baby slowly turns. But in this case it didn't. It just stuck. I'd never seen a situation just like this in Chicago. I wished Delee was here to show me what to do. If it isn't done right, the forceps either damages the baby's eye or tears the mother. What should I do? It wouldn't turn. The best I could do is to apply the forceps somewhere in between and start pulling down. It might hurt the baby's face but it could be alive. If I pulled gently, maybe the head would mold and give a bit. Nureeya let out a groan and called on her Lord, "Ya Rubbi," and I prayed and pulled gently. I let up, loosened the forceps, and then pulled again. I got down on my knees to get the right angle for delivery. "Not strength but art" was the motto in Chicago. I took plenty of time. The clock marked an hour. But slowly there was change. The head began to turn, as it must for the baby to be born. Hurrah, it was moving! I made the incision to widen the outlet. The novocaine helped. "Now push, Nureeya, you can do it." She helped then and the head was born. The rest of the body came easily. The baby's left face had some cuts and bruises, but he didn't breathe. Quick, Indira, give me the stiff catheter. How glad I was that they taught me in Chicago to get the tube down the throat with a forefinger, push it into the trachea, and give the baby his first breath of air and press his chest to expel it. Gradually, he started breathing on his own. *Al hamdallah* (Praise the Lord).

Next, the afterbirth must come. Usually it comes easily but sometimes it is adherent. Then you have to go up after it and scrape it off so high that you'd think you were reaching the heart. The next danger is the terrible post-partum hemorrhage, but an injection of ergot intravenously usually stops it. I know I did everything a little wrong. But, *Allah kareem*, I felt the awe and wonder that never goes stale that He allowed me to be part of the miracle of helping a new life into the world. The only thing left to do was to suture the incision I made. "In my heart there rings a melody."

We had a trolley to take the mother out through the cold, windy halls to her room. The local custom was for the mother to get a vacation of forty days after delivery called the *arbaeeya*. If possible she goes back to her mother and is relieved of household duties.

Every day was an adventure. One day just as the clinic was finished, a woman rushed in imploring me to come quickly to the house—something had gone wrong with a delivery. I grabbed the bag and a sterile bundle and jumped into the car which brought her. The driver wanted to show me he knew English and said, "This is the palace." It sure wasn't, but in Arabic, every consonant must have its vowel. He meant place.

The patient was half sitting against the wall with the fat little body born but the head stuck inside. The baby cannot breathe and dies in five minutes. There was no time to wash. I was on my knees in double quick time, twisted the slippery body around to deliver the arms and then turned the body so the head came out in the smallest diameter. I learned that maneuver at Chicago. The head popped out and the baby took a breath and screamed. That was my fastest delivery. For once, I came in the nick of time.

We weren't always so lucky. We had an Indian lady doctor who had to deliver a breech case that came in at the last minute, too. The mother's bowel movements contaminated everything. Neither one of us thought of it, but the cord got contaminated and the baby developed tetanus and died a week later. Too late I learned that we can have tetanus bacilli in our stools.

By 1950, more mothers were coming to the hospital for deliveries. I didn't like to spend the time it took for home deliveries, but sometimes I gave in to some important women. So Ayisha sent her servant at night. It always happened at night when the situation was not in keeping with my feelings. It was one of those hot nights when sleep flees anyway, so I did my duty. They took me upstairs. Ayisha had an upper room with a wide open veranda where she had her mat. I had plenty of youthful ardor, limber knees, and confidence in my ability to handle the case. She had a kerosene lantern. After an examination, I sat down to wait for nature to do most of the job.

I went downstairs once to a kind of privy. Its walls were shiny black. I thought how odd. I'd never seen walls painted black in an Arab house. When I could see in the dark, the walls were not painted, but solid with black, healthy cockroaches. The climate in Arabia seems to be ideal, they have no enemies and grow to full three-inch size. The men were sleeping on mats in the courtyard. One of them was blind. He was pulling out his watch. To my surprise, he snapped open the spring face and with a delicate touch felt the hands.

Long hours dragged by waiting and watching the fetal heart tones and the descent of the head. Finally the baby was born normally. The woman servant brought a basin of water, bathed it, and wrapped it in swaddling clothes because it was the custom. She straightened out the wee legs and arms, binding them tightly with a long black cloth, and tied the bundle with a long bandage.

The stars were still brilliant in the enormous sky. With the first glimmer of dawn, the prayer call floated from the minaret. "O may I never face a dawn with all the awe and wonder gone." It seemed more thrilling after a night of watching through the darkness for a baby to be born. Kuwait awoke and stirred. The men wended their way solemnly to the mosque. The women at home washed, wound their heads with their long black scarves, spread their prayer rugs toward Mecca, moved their lips in devotion. Their faces reflected their peace with God. They had fulfilled a duty. It was well with their souls. I was the one out of harmony watching them. The dawn called for a sweet hour of prayer. The new mother didn't say prayers, because she was unclean. Another day on an aftercall, I brought my camera and wanted to take a picture to remember that night. Ayisha let me picture the scene with the baby but not herself.

Early one Sunday morning when she knew I would be at home, Amina came to visit me on our wide upstairs veranda overlooking the blue seafront. Under her abba was Wusmeyah, named after me and almost six months old.

"How are you and all your family, Amina? What is on your mind this morning?"

"I've been wishing you would read to me from your book like Mrs. Mylrea used to do. I liked the part, 'Let not your heart be troubled.' Now that she's gone we don't have a Sunday morning class."

I put the story of the two men who went to prayers into local language. "A mullah and a beggar went to the mosque and prayed. The mullah went up in front and prayed, 'Ya Allah, I thank You that You have made me a good Muslim, better than other men. I give all the alms that are required, I always pray at the regular five times a day, and I fast more than necessary.' The poor man at the back of the mosque said, 'Ya Allah, I am a sinner. Have mercy on me.' Amina, shall I tell this story for the women before clinic some day? Do you think they would agree that the second poor man had the better prayer?

"Amina, I want to thank you for the tea at your house. The lady I brought with me was the wife of one of the oil men. She was so glad to see an Arab house and meet your family and neighbors. Were the women displeased because I offered to read from the gospel? Some of them got up and walked away, some were talking with each other and Dalal kept muttering 'La illah illa Allah wa Mohammad rasool Allah,'" [The Muslim Creed: "No God but God and Mohammad is the prophet of God"].

"No, they weren't angry, but they didn't understand. They liked to have you read. My mother appreciated it."

"Thank you, Amina, you teach me a lot. My tongue is still heavy. Where is your husband working now?"

"He's working for the oil company in the desert and gets thirty rupees a month, but we can hardly live on that."

"How do you manage to live? How many are there in your house?"

"There are my three boys and two girls, the old man and woman, myself and Wusmeyah, but she is still nursing. My husband eats at the oil company camp. There are eight of us at home. For breakfast, we buy bread for four annas. [There are sixteen annas to the rupee, which was worth about thirty-seven cents.] We have sixteen flat rounds of bread [the size of a small pie]."

"What do you have for lunch?"

"The same thing—just bread."

"And what for dinner at night?"

"Rice and peas with some butter and sometimes fish. Meat is too expensive for us."

"Why don't you keep a goat for milk for the children?"

"It costs too much to buy the alfalfa."

"But the goats get something to eat when they go out to the desert every day with the shepherd."

"That isn't enough to eat. We have to buy green stuff for them."

"Amina, do you own your own house?"

"No, we rent it for two and a half rupees a month."

"What about other things like clothes?"

"That's just it," sighed Amina, "The girls are growing up crying for new dresses and we can't buy any. It would be so nice if you would give me just a little of that nice white cloth you have for dresses for Wusmeyah. See, I dress her in white like English babies instead of black, and she wears diapers."

"How many babies have you had, Amina?"

"Sixteen, but only eight are alive now."

OMAN, 1949

Muscat station wired us for help in the summer of 1949. Dr. Thoms was at home on a furlough, the Indian doctor had deserted, the hospitals were empty, the Kapengas were alone, and the baby Peter was sick. "Please send us one of your doctors," they pleaded. The Nykerks and I considered the situation and decided it would be easier if I went. The short term nurses Joan Olthof and Louise Essenberg could run the women's clinic.

So I took the British India ship down the Gulf to Oman. The wet, steamy heat made the trip miserable. The officers helped us to drag our mattresses out on the deck to sleep at night. A man teacher from Palestine and I went ashore at Dubai to think about something else. The ruler was sitting in the bazaar judging the people like Moses. We were invited to dine at an Arab house, where we sat at the foot of one of the wind towers. It was delightfully cool. They asked me to see a sick lady who I guessed had malaria, so I wrote out a prescription for atebrin. Heaven help the sick whose diagnoses I guessed.

After many stops, we reached what has been called the "comic opera port" of Muscat. With its two picturesque Portuguese forts, the seafront was a crescent surrounded by mountains that come down to the water: cubical buildings along the seafront, high mountains in the far distance. We went ashore in little boats. Sweat trickled down inside our clothes, the stones and pavement were slippery and slimy. The customs officers went through everything.

Jay and Midge Kapenga were living in Mutrah, the twin city of Muscat. They occupied the large upstairs of the mission house next to the hospital. We lived on the wide, lofty, screened verandas. They generously took me in as part of their family. Baby Peter sat listlessly in his pen, pale and flaccid from fever and diarrhea. Midge in her fretfulness said, "I'm so tired of being pregnant." I tried all the drugs available. In my worry, I tried to escape into books and came across an appropriate sentence in Cooper's *The Last of the Mohicans.* The hero was rescuing the fair females and exclaimed to them, "Manifest no dismay lest you invite that which you appear to anticipate."

The medical magazines had articles about the new drug Streptomycin. I thought that might help, so I wired to Bahrain station

bought some, went out to the airport, and found a private plane
with a lone pilot. Ed asked if he would take the drug to Oman.
"Yes," the pilot said, "Where's Oman?" Ed wired us that the
plane would drop the drug at 4 P.M. The three of us waited at the
tiny runway. Midge had some old flour, so we wrote out in large
letters on the ground, "Thank you," and filled the letters in with
flour. Promptly the tiny plane circled, then thrilled us by coming
straight toward us and releasing a package which opened a golden
parachute and landed at our feet. The plane waved its wings and
was off. The incident was not unnoticed by the authorities, for
the police were promptly at our door. We gave them the parcel
and explained. The reason for the flight was graciously accepted
and they returned the drug. Peter soon returned to normal.

The twin towns of Muscat and Mutrah were surrounded by
low, bare mountains which cut off any breezes. The bare rocks
radiated heat down at night until it was hot even in the darkness.
It was a terrible land. The natives deserted the cities as much as
possible in the summer. Those who had to stay were thin and
looked miserable in ragged, dirty clothes, wet and smelly, covered with prickly heat and large, raw ulcers of the arms and legs.
Many were blind. The mosquitoes were bad, so there was lots of
malaria.

The hospital had drugs, and workers trained by Wells Thoms,
so I started to sit and see patients. I had to take a small towel to
wipe the sweat and then would wring it out several times. There
were so many Baluchis, whose language I didn't know, that I had
to have a helper. Khair en Nisa (beautiful of women) lived across
the street from us in the large district of datestick huts. She was
a widow and had become a Christian. As she was poor, she took
in roomers, some of them men, and she had the unfortunate experience of becoming pregnant. It resulted in a nice little girl,
Miriam. The situation was condemned by the rest of the Christian community, but Khair en Nisa said the birth was something
like that of the baby Jesus. To keep my mind off my misery, I gave
Miriam lessons in reading the Arabic Bible every morning.

The staple foods were dates and fish. The dead and dried fish
remnants along the seafront gave the town a distinctive odor. The
bazaar in Mutrah was a narrow passage covered with palm logs
and branches. A part of the city was separated and walled off

from the rest of the town. A separate people lived there called the Khojas. They were Indian merchants who originally came from Hyderabad, India, it was said. I was called to some of the houses and walked the narrow passages to glance into indescribably dirty rooms or patios where women sat and swung in wide, hanging seats.

I remember a few cases. A man came from the interior mountain valley bringing his two wives, accusing them both of sterility and being unbearable. He wanted them both to be treated. Rather absent-mindedly, I admitted them one morning. Later it occurred to me that there are always two sides to that situation, so I declared that he would have to be examined first. This concept had never occurred to his masculine mind. When I had to tell him that apparently he was the one who couldn't have children with multiple wives, he left disgusted.

One of the young men on the staff had a cough. I knew nothing about running the X-ray machine, but with the help of one of the staff, I was surprised to get it to work. Once a week, Jay took me over to the women's hospital in Mutrah where the Indian nurse Mary had been serving the local women for thirty-two years. With the help of the staff, some records were kept and show that in those four months, we treated 9,000 outpatients, made 41 house calls, had 45 inpatients, did 25 X-ray exams, and performed 110 minor surgery operations and 5 obstetrical deliveries.

I thought I ought to call on the ruler, Sultan Saeed bin Taimur, so sent him a request to call. He sat in the government building in Mutrah. After thinking it over for three weeks, he invited me to come. I had a hat and went over really proper. The long downstairs hall was lined with his Bedouin guards. He graciously visited with me in his upstairs reception room. Both of us spoke English. He was dressed in splendid robes of state and a gorgeously wound turban. He offered me the Omani sweet, helwa, made of rice, honey, cardamom, and almonds. It is a brown, sticky gelatinous substance which is eaten with the fingers. When you get used to it, it is delicious.

It was gratifying to meet with the group of twelve baptized Christians. The small chapel was usually full on Sundays. Either Jay or one of the local men would preach.

I love to remember the good times. We drove out to the sandy beaches walled in by rocky cliffs and went swimming. In the clear depths the tropical fish swam in joyous colors of scarlet, blue, and gold patterned in designs that no artist could have invented. Jay took me and some boys for a trip up the coastal plain to Birka. It was about sixty miles but took about four hours because the road was so poor—just tracks in the sand or mud. This plain extends up north of Mutrah for more than a hundred miles. It varies in width from five to ten miles between the sea and the mountains. The mountains catch the rain which keeps the wells full enough for irrigation. So the area is green and lush with gardens, date trees, and villages. The whole area is called the Batinah.

It was an adventure. Where the mountains came down to the sea, Jay and the boys let some of the air out of the tires, and we drove through the sandy bottom of the sea at low tide. We had to time our return for the next low tide. Arriving at the village of Birka, where all lived in datestick huts, we were received at the house and enclosure owned by the mission. There was an Arab family living in it. They welcomed us as if we were the most delightful sight they had seen for days. I watched while the wife went surreptitiously to her locked tin trunk and got out a bag of rice to cook for us. I knew they usually ate only dates and fish, which they could get locally. The gardens were green and refreshing, much more attractive than in the cities. We had another bumpy trip back that evening.

In October, we went back together to Bahrain by ship for the annual meeting. By that time the charm and enchantment of Oman had entered my soul.

RUNNING THE SHOW IN KUWAIT

Practicing medicine in a foreign country was an adventure, but running a foreign hospital was another kind of challenge altogether. At that time the men's and women's work were separate. Dr. Maurice Heusinkveld had just finished his Arabic studies and was in charge of the men's hospital. I had no one to help in the women's hospital except the two Indian nurses and some volunteer oil company wives.

The women's work was expanding. We desperately needed more nurses. Indira and Bhagyamma had finished their two-year contract and were due to go home on vacations. How could I spare them? Our income was good. We could afford to hire more nurses and pay them higher salaries than they could get in India.

Bhagyamma offered to search for new nurses in the Indian mission hospitals, because no Kuwaiti girls were willing to become nurses. I was sure Bhagyamma's mature persuasion would be more effective than mine.

The only travel was by British India ships, which took two weeks to reach Bombay. Bhagyamma traveled alone on the second class in the train to Madras, near her home. Then with her bedding roll, she rode the rattling small trains to several mission hospitals in south India until she found two young graduate girl nurses who were willing to come. Astonishingly, their parents agreed to let them go.

The real bottleneck was to obtain passports for the girls. The Indian government employs plenty of civil servants and tries its best to give them all something to do. So they specialize in forms to be filled out on every possible subject. The windows, cupboards, and shelves in the official offices are filled with stacks of yellow, dusty, crumbling sheets of paper tied together and inhabited by silverfish, white ants, and spiders. The windowsills are so full that they obscure any light. When the right office is finally located, the official is invariably gone for tea or else on a trip to find a husband for a daughter, which takes several days. Only that one individual can sign the papers.

Bhagyamma's first trip was to the office of emigration in Madras to get instructions for passport applications. First the girls had to get certificates of good character from the hospitals where the girls had trained. Second, the girls had to go back to the villages where they were born for birth certificates. Third, they had to get vouchers of promissory notes from landowners in their villages saying the landowners would be responsible for paying for return tickets if the employers in the foreign country refused to return the girls. Finally, there had to be confirmation of vaccination and inoculation signed by an authorized medical officer with official stamps. The slightest error invalidated the whole paper, so sometimes the girls had to make several trips back to their villages by bullock cart. I gave Bhagyamma permission "to make skillful use of the mammon of unrighteousness," if necessary. The process took months.

When all the weird tangle of red tape was executed and the legal contracts with the nurses were signed and sealed, I could go to the Kuwaiti government office and get an NOC—no objection certificate—permitting them to get a visa. So finally I could send them the money to buy their tickets on the BI ships. "Lead on, O King eternal."

Meanwhile back in Kuwait, I wrestled with the question, Where were we going to house these nurses? At the last general mission meeting, I had been prepared to do battle on the subject of building a proper nurses' home. But the others had torpedoed my idea by haggling over the cost. I came home to size up the situation. On the principle that nothing is impossible, I cast about in my mind for a solution. There were the rooms in the back of the compound where Shah Raza's family had lived—three rooms, a bath, and kitchen. They were built of crude coral rock dug up from the seashore. They were cemented and usable. So the idea germinated, sprouted, and grew to flower as I entertained the idea of being an architect.

I measured out the land with my yardstick and drew sketches for a single room for each nurse, bathrooms, a storeroom, a little courtyard, and a room for a male cook which would have to open outside. We needed a cesspit, stairs up to the roof for sleeping up there, windows, cupboard, shelves, and doors. It was rather fun. Then I called for Ast Ahmed, the Persian mason, and together we figured out the cost and came up with the figure of Rs 10,000 ($5,000). We could raise that sum from our increasing income at the women's hospital.

The station took council together at my behest and agreed to the project if I stuck to the price. They found it easier to let me do something I was determined about than to dissuade me. Missionaries tend to have the defects of their virtues.

By the time all that maneuvering was accomplished, summer was upon us and the rest of the station went off on their three-month vacations. Not daunted, I took time by the forelock and called Ast Ahmed to bring laborers. I plunged into my building career.

The men of the men's hospital, idle because the man doctor was away, squatted around the enterprise to supervise. Ast Ahmed laid out the sticks and strings for the new rooms. The men cockily shouted, "Why did you make the rooms so small? You've got lots of land. Why don't you make them larger?" I had to admit to myself that they were right. I quavered with the restlessness of indecision. Would it be wrong to go against the agreement with the station? No one was there to say to me, "Nay." I had to act on the spur of the moment. Any change had to be from the group up. So recklessly, I ordered Ast Ahmed to lengthen the cords and strengthen the stakes and make at least one room twice as large. Then I went off to run the hospital.

Sober thinking came later when I had time for it. It was going to cost more now. The large room would need a steel girder to support the roof. The solution—there was one steel girder left over from the building of the women's hospital because it had a bend in its middle. I consulted John Buckley, the friendly engineer at the oil company. He thought the crooked could be made straight and did it.

I knew the oil company had a stockpile of doors and windows, so I called on the general manager and explained my need. He was most gracious and said, "Just send your man with a lorry and we'll give you all you want."

Every morning we'd start the day by inspecting the fascinating progress. The walls rose and windows, door frames, and pipes went in. Those were golden days even though the sun was in charge. I was boss with no one to breathe cold criticism down my neck. Ast Ahmed was a dutiful hero, correcting my errors and supplying the details I hadn't thought of. He kept expenses low so we finished up with the amount we had first figured.

At the end of the summer the pavilion was finished and paid for except for the final touches. We prepared the place then with loving care. We made new curtains, bought iron beds, and scrounged for furniture.

We lovingly helped with our own hands to prepare rooms for the new nurses. We had heated discussions over whether Indians should have squat toilets or our kind and ended up by making two bathrooms with one of each. Cane mats went on the floors and new curtains were hung.

When the rest of the station came back, I avoided drawing their attention to the change of plans as if it were something indecent. No one criticized very much. The whole affair had taken a lot of time. I asked myself, "What has all this to do with preaching the Gospel?"

Finally the ship came in and we went down to the *gomerick* (customs pier) to meet them. Bhagyamma produced her trophies. It was her finest hour. They were such tiny girls. How could they do the hard work of nursing? But Simony Thomas and K. Rukmani proved worth their weight in diamonds. They stayed with us many years, faithfully and lovingly giving testimony to the Christian faith of the members of the Church of the Mar Thoma of south India.

My career as an executive reached a pinnacle as the number of nurses increased to ten. It was a source of wonder to me. I was grateful to them but sometimes felt I was their servant.

The girls spread a good reputation for the hospital, so after that it was easier to get more nurses. They then traveled in style— by plane. Fortunately we had room for them all in the rebuilt house in the back of the compound. Later Dr. Lewis and Dorothy Scudder came to take charge of the men's work. Dorothy was an executive nurse and took charge of both hospitals' staffs and relieved me.

Sometimes we had romantic interludes. Kanthirahj was courted by the male nurse Thilagam. Their marriage was a great success. Sosamma married Swamidoss. They later emigrated to the U.S.A., earned American degrees, and lived a success story. He became a hospital administrator in the U.S.A. Suendra tried to smuggle gold into India on her return and was caught by the customs and lost it all. Saramma George fell in love with a Hindu clerk employed elsewhere. I tried to head off Cupid but found it couldn't be done. She married him. Most of the girls stayed with us many years.

We'd ask the nurses when they went home on vacations whether they would marry. They always maintained that they didn't know. The Indian custom was for the parents to find an appropriate partner. The girls usually followed the custom. There was very little divorce. It seemed odd to me to marry a stranger, spend an intimate month with him, and then leave him and come back to work alone in another country. If there was a baby, they would take it back and leave it with the grandparents. Well, that was a fact of life with our Indian staff.

Indira Waghmare had been with us almost four years when one day the other nurses called me from my office to say that something had happened to her. I hurried over to the treatment room. She was hysterical, screaming strange words, tearing her hair, and pulling off her clothes. The Indian nurses always wore white voile saris which they kept immaculate. They looked like white candles. I was shocked to see how black she looked. She refused to swallow any sedative. We had to use force to get her to her room. I realized that I knew nothing about mental disease. It seemed that an evil spirit had taken possession of mild, sweet Indira. I brought her over to sleep with me at night, but neither of us slept. I locked her in her room the next day, but she broke the windows and almost cut her neck.

Desperate, I went over to the government hospital to ask if they had a psychiatrist. They had one who had taken an Arab house with rooms opening into a courtyard and only one door opening to the outside. About thirty men were kept in it as in a prison. There were no nurses. At night, he just locked up the place and left it. The psychiatrist came over to see Indira and agreed she needed to be kept in such a place and given treatment. I wondered how I could get her over there. When I tried to get her in the car she fought like a wild cat. Four of the nurses had to hold her on the ground while I gave an injection of sodium amytal. The Palestinian doctor said he had one room that could be locked like a cell where he could put Indira, but we would have to bring someone to stay with her at night. Bebe, one of our Persian helpers, said she would stay with her. So every evening I drove Bebe over to the house where the two of them slept on bedding rolls.

The doctor started insulin treatment. Enough was given to almost put the patient in shock and then glucose was given by a stomach tube. It was a kind of shock treatment, but it seemed to help. Indira became quieter.

Then Bhagyamma told me what had happened while I was gone on my three months' vacation that summer. A young Hindu employed in a shop had been courting Indira. They went for long walks on the seashore evenings. He couldn't marry her, as he was engaged to some girl in India. Tragically, Indira had broken under the strain. Then I remembered that Indira had asked to go home earlier, and I had talked her out of it because I had not had a vacation for two years. I felt guilty myself but asked Bhagyamma why Indira hadn't told me about her difficulty.

Indira gradually improved and the doctor let her come back to us. He advised me to send her home, however. She stayed with us a while working with me in the office. She was very quiet and wouldn't talk about the affair, so I arranged for another nurse to travel home with her by plane. She never wrote to me. I heard that she seemed to recover eventually and went back to nursing in the hospital in Poona.

As the work increased, we had to find Indian doctors to help. By that time there were apartments to rent in the neighborhood. I remember two lady doctors from south India whose native language was Malayalam, Dr. Mathen and Dr. Lilly. They were both good doctors, but we had some differences. They wanted to do more surgery, but I felt I couldn't teach them and they had not enough experience, so we rubbed each other a bit. At the same time Dr. Nawgiri, a young bachelor from north India, started working in the men's hospital. I didn't notice anything, but the two Indian doctors both admired him. Dr. Mathen had recently become Christian, but her Hinduism was still near the surface. She told me she was sure that Rev. De Jong was pocketing the offering at the church services. She was suspicious of Dr. Scudder. He was a very friendly person and when he was talking with any of us would demonstrate his affection by putting his arm on our shoulders.

Dr. Mathen was tall and beautiful, but Dr. Nawgiri chose Dr. Lilly. They had children who followed them in medicine. After our hospital was closed by the Church, they went into private practice in Kuwait and were very successful. Dr. Mathen left us for a position in Saudi Arabia.

I knew in a general way that hospitals have to be kept clean. Just how it was done hadn't occurred to me until I was in charge of one. When I suggested the job to the nurses, they let me know that nurses are not cleaners. It was not the recognized standard of social behavior for Arab ladies to work outside of their homes. However, the Persians, called "ajemi" (foreigners), were lower in the social scale and would accept cleaning work. They all looked the same to me. Once I put a Persian patient in the room with an Arab. The Arab lady complained bitterly, "She smells bad." We hired a few Persian widows who were willing to clean, but their idea of cleanliness was somewhat lacking.

Um Abbas, Makeeya, and Sharaban mopped the floors, washed the windows, cleaned the bottles, carried water, changed the beds, washed the diapers and bloody clothes, took bribes, stole cloth, and made themselves useful. We had some Indian dhobis (laundrymen) for the whole mission. They had aristocratic features like English statesmen but lived and worked in one room.

They beat the clothes on a cement slab and economized on water because it was expensive. They refused to wash diapers or bloody clothes, as their castes forbade that.

So I made a good, hard try at cleanliness, but I wasn't the executive type. The helpers began telling me what their jobs were. I pleaded for help with my cousin Madeline Holmes in Michigan, who to my surprise gave up her teaching and came out to join our missionary band.

Once I took a patient over to the men's operating room for a procedure because they had an air-conditioner. Next morning, I went over to check on the room and found her soiled sheets lying on the floor. I reprimanded the men assistants, "Why haven't you cleaned up the place?" They stoutly maintained, "We clean up men's blood but not women's." These encounters call for comprehensive collision insurance.

Bebe came from Basrah, blind from cataracts. I gave her a room and considered trying another operation. The ones I did before had been failures. Did I dare to cut into another eye, incise the cornea, remove a bit of the iris, and jostle the lens out through the incision? I watched her grope around the room for a glass of water and decided I must try. The instruments were available. So I wound up my courage. But would Bebe trust me enough to relax, so that she wouldn't squeeze her eye when the jelly might be extruded? *Allah kareem.* It was a triumph. Later, I did the other eye and Bebe could see. We got glasses for her. Bebe was so happy, she offered to work in the hospital. She was divorced, without any family. I had no better or sweeter helper for many years. It was my highest pinnacle of success.

I watched poor Medina, who wasn't cleaning the floors well, and found she was almost blind. The doctors at the government hospital found she had a brain tumor. They offered to send her to London for surgery, but she was too afraid. Heartlessly I had to discharge her.

Begum drank a swig out of the bottle of TR. Belladonna—no one knew why. True to the proverb, she turned "red as a beet, dry as a bone, and mad as a march hare." So I discharged her. Nothing ever was normal in our hospital.

Khaireeya came begging for work. She had just been divorced and had four little children. I reasoned that if I gave her a small backhouse room, I'd have somebody to clean up the worst messes.

I tried to employ women who seemed to be sterile, but as soon as they learned to work, somehow the atmosphere helped them to get pregnant.

Makeeya took care of a baby boy whose mother, a relative, had died in the hospital. The boy got into a bad state of repair, so she sold him for about a dollar.

Miriam was my Persian office helper, as I couldn't speak Persian and there were many Iranian patients. If only she knew numbers, she would be able to get out the record cards, which took a lot of my time. So I tried to teach her numbers. I thought it would be so easy. Miriam's mind could not comprehend the fact that she could learn any writing. I tried several times and had to give it up. She married Yusuf, a relative who worked in the men's hospital, and had a pretty little girl. They were so happy and came to church together on Sundays. When I was gone on furlough, the child developed a toxic sore throat and died. Miriam and Yusuf never came to church again.

Fatheeya was a Palestinian nurse who came asking for work. She told me a story about being discharged from the government hospital because of skin eruption of the hands. I needed help so badly that I believed her and took her on and gave her a room. She was useful because she knew Arabic, but I soon found she was quite incompetent and discharged her. She came into my room when I was alone at my desk and pleaded to be retained. I refused and turned my back on her. I had not guessed that she was a mental case. She seized my hair and twisted me down to the floor. I struggled and it might have been serious had not Madeline come into the room just at that moment and pulled her off my back.

When people began coming to Kuwait for the high salaries, a mother brought Somaya to us. She was of an Anglo-Indian family, a bright, attractive teenager who wanted to learn nursing. The government hospital had refused to take her because when she had a physical examination, it was found that she was an undeveloped male. Somaya was dumbfounded. She'd been a student in a girls' boarding school where it was never noted that she wasn't like all other girls. The Kuwaiti doctors operated to remove the undeveloped testes, but she wanted to be a girl and couldn't think of herself as male. We agreed to take her. She could live at home and get some training, although we couldn't give a real nursing course. I never realized before what hidden tragedies there can be in some apparently normal persons. She had enough testosterone to make her energetic, ambitious, and a very good helper. Her grief was that she didn't have breasts, so she wore artificial ones. In later years, I heard she had male admirers but couldn't bring herself to tell her sad tale and had to reject them.

In the spring, I'd take the Persians out for a picnic in the desert when it was green. I gave strict orders that they might not bring their children, but they always did. So we ended up with a whole army.

SLAVES

There were still household slaves in 1950. One aristocratic Arab lady brought a new slave girl to the clinic and asked me to examine her. I began to think one might be a good investment for myself, so I asked what her price had been. Without thinking, she told me the amount of $5,000 in rupees. It was a bit too steep for me. On examination I found she was pregnant, which disgusted the mistress. A slave woman pregnant by the men of the house becomes a concubine. Her child had the same status as the legitimate children of the house.

Some of the concubines who were patients told how the chief wife always appointed the concubine for the night for the head of the house. The bedroom of important guests, too, was furnished likewise for men.

The practice was declining under British influence. The British Agency proclaimed that any slave coming to the Agency and placing his or her hand on the flagpole could be officially given freedom. The Arabs, too, had an arrangement whereby a slave could sit and beg in the street. People wanting to do a good deed would give alms until the slave could buy freedom. Garret De Jong remembered that there was still a slave market when he came in 1926. Haseena, who worked for the hospital many years, was given her freedom by the Sagar family. She had a husband and children, but when the hospital closed, the Sagar family took her back and gave her a home in her old age.

One inpatient brought a small slave girl to attend her. I happened to be passing her door when the husband whacked the child with a heavy hand. My temperament is usually calm, cool,

and collected, but at rare intervals it seems to flare up with spontaneous combustion. A spasm of sudden, hot wrath enveloped
me, and I turned and smote him a sharp wallop. He stood dumbfounded at behavior so out of the ordinary. I don't know whether
he or I was more astonished at such an inappropriate reaction. I
was really embarrassed at such behavior of a missionary and doctor. I hope by my confession to mitigate my guilt.

The problem of being a missionary in Kuwait was that nobody
understood me. I had to live on so many different levels. The
different levels didn't understand each other. Even the missionaries weren't always friendly to each other. The Indian staff were
antagonistic to our Americanisms. To the Persian staff, we were
the masters and they the servants. The patients considered the
doctors magicians who could cure everything if they wanted to.
The Arab Christians, who came when the money increased, were
sure we also had come to make money. The Arabs thought we
were in the pay of the American government to overthrow their
religion and culture. The British and American diplomatic and
oil company people couldn't understand our Christian calling or
else thought it ridiculous. I always had to be careful what I said.

As Kuwait grew, we began to see a wider range of people in
the clinic—British wives and simple Bedouin, women of the royal
family and poor Persians, young matrons wearing the latest in European clothes under their abbas, women from Dubai complete
with batula (face mask) and trousers, Indians, Pakistanis, Egyptians, Palestinians, Catholics, Protestants, Muslims, and Hindus.
Divine Providence drew us together. They came asking for help,
but so often I misunderstood what they needed or wanted. Lord,
you commanded us to love them, but I hadn't the capacity.

TO U.S.A. ON FURLOUGH, 1950

In 1950 I went home on furlough, leaving an Indian lady doctor
to run the women's hospital. Up to then I did not have status as a
missionary but paid myself a salary, equal to what the missionaries were receiving, from the medical income. I did not receive a
salary because the Mission Board had a rule that women missionaries who married outside of the mission no longer were paid by
the Church. They reinstated me in 1950.

My brother Paul was living in a beautiful large house in Douglaston on Long Island, New York. He had married Bess after

Margaret died. She came from Tuscaloosa, Alabama. She brought her own little girl to add to Paul's four girls. My mother and I were their guests for a while.

The Gulf Oil office informed me that Shaikh Fehed was in New York and had invited me to a dinner at one of the grand hotels. They invited my mother and the Calverleys and said they would arrange for a room to stay the night. I was thrilled and started to tell Paul and Bess about Shaikh Fehed and how hospitable he had been to the mission. I said how much fun it would be to entertain him at their home. Then I suddenly added, "Of course, he is black." A chilly silence descended and Bess with Southern dignity remarked, "You can bring him here if you like but I will not receive him." Suddenly I realized that a great gulf had opened between us. So I quickly asserted, "I'll tell him that I haven't any home in which to entertain him. Mom and I will take him out to see some sights in New York instead." So I bought a new evening gown, and we had a magnificent dinner with Shaikh Fehed in great style, with the officials of the oil company and speeches and delicious food.

The next day we went out in his car with a driver. I suggested that we go to see the Bronx Zoo and Botanical Garden. The shaikh attracted attention in his flowing, brown Arab cloak, white scarf, and gold head ropes. On the way back we stopped at the Washington Cathedral for a tour. Back at the hotel, Shaikh Fehed insisted that we must have dinner with him. He went up to his room on the twentieth floor while Mom and I used the powder room. When he came down he had several men and a very nicely dressed lady with him. I'd been reading in the newspapers how New York takes care of guests with special police women and naively assumed this was one. We went to a prestigious Armenian restaurant for a rice and lamb dinner. The lady told us about her little boy and apartment. She was intelligent and likeable. Then the shaikh insisted we must take in a performance at Radio City. When we reached the place, they said there were no more seats. The lady talked to the ushers and then there were seats.

Paul and Bess gave me a room for a couple of months while I took a refresher course at the Polyclinic. I would ride the Long Island Railroad and the subway into town. Then I took a course in Arabic at New York University. After the evening class, I'd walk over to Dr. Sam Zwemer's apartment on Fifth Avenue for a visit and another lesson in Arabic. I was invited to his eighty-fourth birthday party, too. The next year he died. The Bosches came to New York that spring, so the three of us took another course in Arabic with a Jewish professor.

They asked me to do some speaking in the churches about missions in Arabia. I visited my cousin Madeline in Grand Rapids. She was alone and teaching. I talked up Arabia, which must have fascinated her, for after a year she came to join me in Kuwait as a full missionary to be housekeeper for the hospital.

Then I returned to Kuwait. I sailed on the *Staatendam* from New York, visited the Buckleys in London, and then flew the rest of the way back to Kuwait.

KUWAIT BUILDS, 1951

I was certain the Lord wanted me back in Kuwait. All of a sudden I found myself back there in September 1951. Nothing had changed very much yet. They were building a long, curved, modern three-story building just inside the Jahra city gate. The city wall built of mud was in a bad state of repair since the rains had washed down its upper edge. The young bloods were anxious to remove it, but one of the royal family was sentimental about it. When he died suddenly of cancer, they had the bulldozers out quick and easily knocked it down. Though my mind was taken up with other matters, I was startled to see new roads, houses, and suburbs appearing outside the old walls, of which only the city gates were retained. Homes were designed by Egyptian architects who let their imaginations run wild. Some looked like planes ready to take off. Most had a variety of hues, indicating the starved sense of color in a desert people. One owned by a man with artistic flair had pictures painted on its walls. The houses all had walls around them with artistic metalwork gates. A Lebanese ironworking firm had settled in Kuwait, manufacturing stunning creations. When they put a sign over their shop, "Forgery," people began to take pictures. Life was exciting. Change was in the air.

Some of the oil company people were living in an Arab house in town. They wanted a cistern for sweet water in their courtyard, so they ordered the local mason to make one. With his laborers, he had the hole dug to an appropriate size and lined it with cement. Then to the British residents' surprise, they put all the excavated dirt back in again and packed it down firmly, leveled it off, and proceeded to lay a thick slab of cement over it, leaving an opening in its center. When the top cement was set firmly, the laborers began to dig out the dirt again until it was empty and lo and behold the tank was ready as soon as they put a wooden cover over the manhole. It showed real native ingenuity—something like the way I sew dresses.

Another friend was staying at an Arab home observing the unsophisticated procedure of adding a room to the house. The family decided where to locate it and called in the mason and drew the lines for the dimensions. After the cement floor was poured and the walls of cement blocks were going up, they had a consultation as to where the door should be. When the walls were up they suddenly decided to have some windows and told the mason to knock a couple of holes. After the roof of mangrove poles was laid, they had the carpenter come and measure the holes and make wooden windows and a frame and door. When it was nicely plastered white, they called the rug dealer to bring Persian carpets and spread them out on the floor in layers until they found one the right size. Then everything was just the way they wanted it.

The city had a British electrical engineer hired to plan the new wiring. He used to come to church regularly so told us some of his adventures. One household was using so much electricity that he went over and called on them. He found the owner wanted to have a nice, cool courtyard, so had installed twelve air-conditioners in the open courtyard.

The building mania struck me, too. There were verandas at various places around the hospital, so I decided they could just be walled in and serve for an examination room and other uses. Some people had given me gifts at home, so I used some money to buy aluminum awnings for the upstairs patients' rooms, which were so hot in the afternoon sun. Yacoob the carpenter duly put them in place. The next week, we had one of the regular Shimaals (fierce north winds). It promptly blew them all down in a crumpled mass. It was rather sad.

The hospital roof still leaked whenever it rained. The oil company kindly installed a new kind of roofing—layers of tar paper with a sheet of aluminum inside. It helped for a while and then gave in to the rain. I decided we must have a gabled roof with frames for corrugated sheets of aluminum. Our income was good, but I had to get mission permission to spend so much money. It proved to be the final solution. The upstairs rooms were cooler and the rain stayed out.

The gifts from home were enough to buy an incubator that arrived just in time for a pair of tiny twins. They both had to go in it. A few days later, I noticed one sucking the other's nose—it was just the right shape and size.

A friend gave us two large kerosene heaters, which we installed in the waiting room and offices. It really was cold there in winter. They had to have chimneys, so we had to have a stove pipe sticking out, which looked a little odd. But they didn't have the bad smell of small portable kerosene heaters. They worked if I gave them tender, watchful care. Then, like most machines in Kuwait, they just gave up the ghost. The local people used charcoal braziers. Their houses were never airtight. But an Indian servant at the British Agency was on duty one night and left his wife and two little children snug and warm beside a glowing charcoal brazier. When he came home the three were dead of carbon monoxide poisoning—the room was airtight. It was the saddest funeral held in our church.

When I was home on furlough, some wise men gave me a diagram of how to build a septic tank. I'd had lectures about them when I was learning the rudiments of my profession but didn't pay attention because I thought it wouldn't ever concern me. But the pits under the toilets were filling up again. I acquainted the resourceful Ast Ahmed with the diagrams and engineering problem. He didn't know any more than I did. But his laborers dug out a hole in the courtyard eight feet deep, ten feet long, and five feet wide and lined it with cement blocks. I came and sat down on the edge to help get the baffles at just the right heights and distances. It was an ingenious invention. The Lord had created just the right organisms to digest the noxious material and turn it into gas and water, if it had enough fresh air. So there had to be a vent, inlet pipes with the right gradient, and an outlet pipe for what was called the effluent water, which was to run down to the sea. Ast Ahmed and I were real proud of ourselves when it worked. Well, it did for a couple of years. By that time the city had tankers with pumps to aspirate the sludge.

As soon as we put the finishing touches on the septic tank, Dr.

Maurie Heusinkveld started to improve the men's hospital. There was standing pipe on the roof that wasn't doing anything useful, so Maurie was telling a man up there to take it down. The man just gave it a little shove. The heavy pipe fell smack on Maurie's head and then bounced off onto Haider's head. They called me. Maurie was a big man, but they got him on the operating table. He was confused and fighting while I sutured the scalp wound over his bare skull. He was stuporous and I was plenty worried thinking of brain hemorrhage, but *Al hamdallah* ("the praise be to God"), they both recovered.

One night, I heard a great commotion in the streets outside my house because of a partial eclipse of the moon. Crowds of men and boys beat drums and shouted the creed, "There is no god except Allah and Mohammad is His prophet." The superstition was that an evil spirit was trying to swallow the moon. If people help the force of goodness by confessions of faith, it would drive away the evil spirit. It worked, too.

CARS AND SCHOOLS

When the Bedouin deserted their donkeys and camels to yield to the seduction of motor cars, their driving was furious. The intoxication of the auto was seemingly irresistible, but the Arabs still took the automobile with an air of nonchalance. In 1940, the crown prince of Saudi Arabia visited Kuwait, arriving in a stream of cars with banners flying. His drivers savored the exquisite delirium of bearing the royal presence and apparently felt immune to the restrictions that restrain lesser breeds. Obsessed with power, one driver struck two children in a fatal accident. The prince announced gravely, "Verily, these have committed suicide."

In the ancient rules of desert ritual, when one man meets another the proper greetings must be performed. Incredibly, there was some attempt to carry out the ancient etiquette by applying this ceremony to motor traffic. When two drivers met at an intersection, each had to immediately take stock, determine which had the higher status, and allow the more prestigious to go first. If both estimates agreed, accidents could be avoided. If not, there were often-fatal accidents. In these cases, blood money was paid depending on the importance of the victim: highest for men, less for women, and least for outsiders and servants. But quite soon the city made laws such as we have in the West about right of

way. Kuwaiti lawmakers ruled that damages for accidentally killing anybody would be the same for all.

Meanwhile back at the hospital, I needed help with eye surgery. The government had brought in a Palestinian ophthalmologist who was very generous in coming and operating in our hospital. Sadly I heard he had drunk methyl alcohol because he
couldn't get whiskey in bone-dry Kuwait. He became blind and
died, leaving a wife and eight children. I can't understand how
such a brilliant mind as his could yield to such a witless desire.
I mourned for him.

One summer night, I was favored with an invitation to an evening party given by the ladies of Shaikh Abdullah Jaber's palace.
It was an Arabian Night's dream. The night was cool by the seaside and a dreamy moon rode high. I was led into the large cloistered court paved with white marble tiles, enclosed by a white
marble balustrade. Garlands of fairy lights lit the scene and the
fountain splashed water on one side. The royal ladies were ap-
pareled in formal evening gowns embroidered with pearls said to
have come from Paris, their dark hair delightfully dressed with
fragrant jasmine flowers. Magnificent gold jewelry and flashing
gorgeous gems bedecked their necks, arms, and feet. The atmosphere breathed perfume. Guests reclined on embroidered silk
cushions and mats covered with linen sheets. Persian carpets covered the floor. We were served fruit drinks and Lebanese baklava
made of honey, cream, and nuts. Gorgeously dressed women servants provided rhythmic drum music for other girls who sang and
danced. There wasn't a single man to enjoy all this beauty. It was
a scene from a Maxwell Parrish painting. Later in the evening
there were fireworks, presumably put on by men. The guests carried on conversations which I couldn't follow. I just sat and absorbed the vision of delight. It looked so good, but I had an idea
there was grief underneath from what I heard of their lives. The
women didn't look really happy. I thought to myself, I'd choose
to go back to the hospital gladly the next morning.

Hunting has always been a great sport with the Bedouin. Traditionally they used hawks, which they trained and treated like
pets. Men would walk in the bazaars and even into the cinemas
in later years with a hooded hawk on their wrists. When we were
invited to a shaikh's home, we would see as many as six or seven
hooded, silent hawks, each perched on his stool stuck in the

ground and with his special keeper. They were very expensive. On one of the ships a passenger was taking a dozen hawks all sitting dumbly on a long pole, presumably to sell in Kuwait. At certain times of the year, the men went out hunting for *hubari*, which were bustards. Friends often brought us one for a gift. They were delicious. The Bedouin also hunted for gazelle and once presented a live one to us. They were perfectly beautiful animals with graceful bodies, slender legs, and melting, sad large eyes. I didn't know what to do with the tragic creature. It was meant to be free, and it couldn't live alone if I took it out to the desert again. The thought of killing such a wonderful creature horrified me. One man told me how groups went out to the desert in fast cars and rounded up herds of forty gazelle at once. They would shoot them all. There aren't any gazelles left in Kuwait now.

Boys set clever traps and nets to catch the lovely migrating birds, which came down exhausted. They would twist a wing, push a feather through its nostril, tie a string on one leg and give it to younger children for an animated toy. In the hospital, it distressed me, so I always took the tortured bird away and put an end to its suffering.

Along the seafront road the seafaring men still spread out their heavy white sail cloth. They sat on the ground and sewed pieces by hand to make the large lateen sails. Other places, men sat mending their nets for fishing. Others would make use of the time by sitting and spinning. They had a bag of wool and twisted it into thread by twirling fibers through a spinning top. I wondered how many of them would become Peters, Jameses, and Johns if we could only call them as the Master did.

More and more ships came into Kuwait Bay, bringing the world's goods. Once I counted forty-two ships in the harbor. They had to wait for launches to unload. It often was a long wait, which made the demurrage fees high.

Changes were taking place in many other areas of life, too. Until this time, all schools in Kuwait had been segregated. After the Second World War, when Kuwait became prosperous, the government built many school buildings on a cost-plus basis in order to get them up quickly. Kuwait brought over a thousand Egyptian teachers, some of whom were women. They usually came with their brothers or husbands and lived in rooms in the school buildings. The girls' schools were very popular, but the conservative element didn't approve of the innovation of female education. We began to hear whispers. One girl of a good family was pregnant, then it was two or three, and the story finally grew to ten or twelve girls having been ravished in the schools. At the end of the term the Egyptian teachers flew home and the gossip collapsed. The next year, the girls' school invited us to their final program. Only women were to be the audience. Some girls objected to being on the stage, as they knew they would be looked over as bridal candidates for sons. They put on a play of the crusader days, with Saladin sending his personal physician to treat the sick King Richard.

Despite the initial discomfort, attractive modern schools appeared and soon were filled. In 1935, soon after I arrived in Kuwait, in the whole country there were only three schools, with 50 teachers for only 600 pupils. By 1952 the government was supporting twenty-four schools, sixteen for boys and eight for girls; the number of students had grown to 11,000, and they had 600 teachers.

The real growth came in the years 1952–1956, for by 1956 there were sixty-four schools (thirty-eight for boys and twenty-six for girls). Total student enrollment had reached 25,000, of which fully a third were girls. Fourteen hundred teachers staffed the new schools.

The total school budget was $19,000,000. Two-thirds of this money was allotted for operating expenses and the other third went toward building costs. Kuwait had come a long way from 1920, when the first government teacher was fired because he taught that the world was round. My friend, an Egyptian school teacher, told me about some of the schools' problems. Women teachers were still required to veil, which the Egyptians hated.

About 1938, a census had been proposed for Kuwait, which enraged many Kuwaitis. I remember that one morning in 1938, walking the streets near the mission compound, I had heard the roar of men's angry voices at a meeting protesting the census. They didn't want to give anyone the right to come to their houses and inquire about their women or about sons who might be drafted for military service. This long-delayed census finally was taken in February of 1957, and the government could begin to plan for its growing population of school-age children.

Schools began to require birth certificates, so the women came to the hospital asking for them. I had tried to record the names of the mothers in a book, but some records were lost while I was away in the U.S. and in India during the war. The women had no idea of the year or date their children were born, so it was difficult to reconstruct the events. Also, some women felt such a great need for secrecy that they had not given their true names at the time we delivered them of their children. They had no family names, so it was next to impossible to track down the births. The women had such a lofty idea of my perception that one woman brought her three little girls to ask me to tell her how old they were. Since I couldn't give records to many, I asked the government what could be done. The officials said that if neighbors or relatives would testify about a child, the information would at least identify the person. No death certificates were required as yet.

The Suez crisis in 1956 stirred violent feelings, and there were fiery Arabic radio broadcasts from Egypt. General Nasser's pictures were pasted everywhere. Shops put up signs, "No admission to British or French." Some boys threw onions at my car when I happened to drive through the *sook*. A bomb in Ahmedi—the oil company's field—set an oil well afire. The famous Texan fire fighter, Red Adair, came and put it out. The ruler's private Bedouin police prevented further trouble. It soon quieted and was forgotten.

The cemetery was a large, bare, depressing patch of ground strewn with crude stones to mark graves. It occupied an area near the center of the business district. No one liked the looks of the place. The town solved the problem by getting a *fetwah* (religious ordinance) from Egypt (which was regarded as the seat of authority of the Muslim world). This *fetwah* stated that a cemetery that had not been used for years could be covered with a yard of sod and used as a garden. This was done and the place was converted into a cool, green, breathing garden next to the business area which everyone could enjoy.

KUWAITI WOMEN'S LIVES AND HEALTH IN THE 1950S

Amina, daughter of Sayyid Amr, had been introduced to the mission through Eleanor Calverley, Bess Mylrea, and Ev De Jong, and finally I knew her. Her early pictures show an attractive young face with a high forehead and a pleasant expression. She was about average height and build. Her straight black hair was always covered with a dark scarf. She loved to carry on long, gossipy conversations which I could follow slowly.

Her husband, Mohammad Akeel, was some sort of a merchant who I hardly knew. I never saw them together. Amina's main complaint was her partner wife, her husband's cousin. The partner was the elder and head of the house. It was very irritating to Amina, who used to deplore, "Why, I have to even beg her for a box of matches, she's so stingy." The two wives lived in houses with adjoining courtyards on the important street that led from the bazaar to the royal palace.

Amina's father, Sayyid Amr, was Turkish and came by ship from Izmir. Judging by the respectful way everyone spoke of him, I gathered that he had an impressive personality, was intelligent, spoke several languages, and immediately assumed an important social position. He had passed away by the time I came, but his children always boasted of being his offspring. When he and his family disembarked at Kuwait, Mohammad Akeel watched them arrive. Amina was about thirteen, and he immediately asked for her in marriage, as his first wife was barren.

When Amina had her babies, I helped deliver some of them at home. I have a picture of her with the three little ones. I did not see her often. I was too busy. The other mission ladies used to see her more often. Amina had nine children, three girls and six boys. One baby died.

Kadareeya, the oldest girl, married a young Iranian businessman. He took Kadareeya along with him on trips to Europe and America, where she did not wear a veil. Once she came to visit us and Ev remarked, "You and your husband live just like us now." Kadareeya answered abruptly, "No, not at all." Then she said no more, nor did we dare ask any more.

Mohammad Zaman, the oldest son, had some education in Kuwait and then went to England to study. Zaman was accustomed to being the head man in Kuwait and soon found he had no position in an English boy's school. He got drunk in a tavern and beat up another man and was sent home in disgrace. I happened to call on Amina at that time and found her in despair. Zaman was sitting alone in an upper room, refusing to eat or to talk with anyone. His suitcase full of bloody clothes arrived with him. Amina begged me to pray with her, so we knelt and prayed in Arabic. It seemed to console Amina. Zaman did not recover from his depression for a whole year. He never did make a full return to himself. He never married.

Abdulla, the second son, went to the University of Michigan. Once I happened to wait with him at the house. He was reading *Das Kapital* in English and remarked to me, "You wouldn't approve of these books at all." I said that I'd never read them. He came back another year with an American wife, Mary Jane. I heard that Kadareeya told her that if she wanted to go to church on Sundays, it would be all right with them. But Mary Jane had replied that she never went to church. She seemed to make a good adjustment to Kuwait, with a good marriage and some daughters she sent to the U.S.A. for education as nurses. For lack of a religion, she took up horoscopy as a specialist.

Amina told me once how she and many other Kuwaiti ladies had been talking about the unveiling in Iran. They got together and signed a letter to Shaikh Abdullah, asking him to order Kuwaiti women to unveil as the shah had. Shaikh Abdullah replied that it was beyond his ability to try to set the styles for ladies.

On a visit some years later, Amina came to call. Her husband had died, her rival was gone, and she was head of the house now. It was a new modern one in a new neighborhood and evidently well to do. With Dotty Scudder, we sat down for a long talk about all the gossip in town. It seemed strange to me with all the female exclusion that the women seemed to know a lot of what went on in other households. She pressed a gold and pearl bracelet and turquoise ring on me. I felt very grateful for her friendship. She ended telling of her family—"yet I always fear hell fire." Again I offered her a Bible, but she did not respond.

For the sake of completeness, Amina's daughters were Kadareeya, Nur Jahan, Kamala, and the sons: Zaman, Abdulla, Abd el Wahab, Abd el Azeez, and Farook. She lamented that all their family records had been given to the museum there and lost.

Adultery seemed to be the great sin in Islam. Naturally, women took the punishment. It was supposedly a point of honor for the brother or father of the girl to put her to death, even if there was only a suspicion. I heard that one girl was shot while still in her bed in the government hospital. In spite of veils, abbas, and seclusion, unwanted pregnancies occurred. The women often came to me asking for help. I felt it was wrong to try to abort the fetus. Certainly it was dangerous, as the women were usually past the safe time, and it would be condemned by the local moral opinion. At the same time I didn't feel good about refusing to help and sending the girl out to possible death. So I absolved my conscience by offering to deliver the baby when the time came, helping her to go home immediately. Then I offered to find a home for the baby. So I had a baby to care for from time to time.

There were always cases of sterility who seemed to learn when we had a spare baby and come asking for it. One woman who worked for Mr. Dickson took three children and was a good mother. But a verse in the Qur'an says that adopted sons are not real sons. So these children are always referred to as bastards and are not given girls of the family in marriage. One of these boys went insane when the time came that he matured and couldn't get a wife.

Another woman took a little girl around the time that I was going home to the U.S.A. I did not see her for a few years. When she came to clinic, I asked about the child. She said that it turned out to be black so they were raising her as a slave. My letters mention about ten such cases.

A woman of the Sulaibi tribe, considered low-class Bedouin, came in and left her baby girl. We took care of her for a couple of months. The prostitutes were doing a big business because many men were coming to work in town as the oil boom increased wages. One of the prostitutes offered me forty rupees for the baby and when I refused, she volunteered to throw a boy baby into the bargain. A family of the oil company announced that they would help care for the child and then decided to adopt her. Dr. Mylrea, the couple, and I went to Shaikh Abdullah Jaber, who was really the chief magistrate, and asked his permission to adopt. He was very kind and wrote out official permission. The family finally went back to Arkansas, taking the baby. I did not hear from them again.

A baby boy whose mother had been killed was left with us in 1953. Then a couple of months later an Indian clerk brought a woman from Dubai who delivered a very tiny baby girl. We kept them both in a room and named them Daud and Hadeeya. I read how they were giving baby pigs aureomycin at home to prevent infections, so I protected the tiny one that way. They caught all the infections going in the hospital but survived. We became very attached to them. Gradually we acquired five babies. I sent a letter to the government asking for permission to take the orphans to Bahrain, as our mission had an orphanage there. The government wrote in answer that we were to deliver all such orphans to them. With a heavy heart, I finally brought them over. Daud wept so pitifully that I decided I must try something. So when a wife of a policeman asked me for the boy, I told her I would help her if she would take the girl as well as the boy. I went to Shaikh Saad, in charge of the police, and asked him to help give the children a home. He did, so I could keep in touch with them.

One baby was born when one of the ladies of the royal house happened to be in the hospital. She went right to the mother and asked for the child. The mother consented. The servants of the lady carried it out to her car. That baby would become a slave. I couldn't do a thing to prevent it.

I heard that the government hospital was raising many such children. They would not allow adoption, because the children might be made servants. The government announced they would care for them so they would become nurses and policemen for the state. Once a British doctor came to visit. As she was a pediatrician, she asked to see the orphanage. I asked her if I could accompany her. An Arab house near the hospital had been set up as an orphanage. The babies were all in cribs like animals in a zoo. Everything was very neat and clean. There were Egyptian nurses and helpers taking care of them. The older children sat on chairs in a circle in the courtyard and sang a song for us about how thankful they were to the state of Kuwait. There were no toys or even balls apparent.

There was a Palestinian girl brought to Kuwait by a Christian family. She had a nice baby boy. Marne Akins, the wife of Jim, who was American consul, was helping us in the hospital. She wanted to adopt the boy. Jim tried to get permission but by that time the religious leaders were against it. Jim had to get a directive from Jordan's government that a Jordanian girl could give her baby to anyone she wished. So that baby, at least, was given a good home.

Our mission orphanage in Bahrain had about twelve children. It was very difficult to find someone who could care for these children. Madeline Holmes left our hospital and went down to take care of them for several years. We hoped that they would become Christians, but the children had such social difficulties that some of them became violently antagonistic to Christianity.

One Sunday morning in Bahrain, Rose Nykerk went into the women's room and noticed a pile of dirty clothes lying on the floor. She called the men who were cleaning and asked why they had not removed the mess. The mess moved and cried. It was a newborn baby still attached to its placenta. The nurses took care of it and put it in the nursery. Of course the news spread around the compound in a few minutes.

The Rev. Raymond Weiss and Dorothy had two daughters and had been praying for more children, but none were given. When Ray heard of this gift of a baby boy, he declared that this was the answer to their prayers. He promptly walked over and without asking anyone, took the baby home. Dr. Al Pennings was the Chief Medical Officer for the mission hospital and thought he should have been consulted. The Weiss family took the baby to their hearts. Ray had him in his arms on many occasions. The next year they decided to take a position at Northwestern College, Iowa, and took Baby David with them. They adopted another baby boy to be a brother for David. He has developed into an attractive American boy.

I quite agree with the Muslim ethics that having children outside of marriage is a sin. The sin is against the child who never has what every child needs—a father and a mother. Trying to raise orphans is a poor substitute. The fact that the Weiss child was brought to and left at the mission hospital was an expression of trust and appreciation, for they could have left it at the government hospital, where it would have been well cared for.

I suspected some patients had syphilis, but with no laboratory I wasn't sure. Dr. Storm had worked out a mixture of bismuth and glycerine to inject to treat it. It was safe and easy to give. The patients always considered an injection better than oral medicines. I heard of bejel, which was a nonvenereal form of syphilis among the Bedouin in the upper reaches of the Tigris and Euphrates. I saw some Bedouin children with the typical mouth ulcers. None of them stayed long enough to be helped.

One girl often came in with agonizing headaches. Only after we had a laboratory did I learn that she had syphilis. Then I read about the fever treatment for cephalic syphilis. An intravenous injection of typhoid vaccine was given to produce a modest fever and then a second injection was given to bring the fever up to 105. This did seem to help. After the war, penicillin began to be used. It became so popular that our patients came in asking for an injection of "benecillin" (as they would say it). I heard of one man who gave himself a penicillin injection every day.

Some Bedouin brought a four-year-old girl who had fallen off a donkey and broken her leg. As she had lived in the desert tents, she had never been in a building or seen a white face before. She was terrified, shouting, "The Englaiz are murdering me!" I put her fractured leg in suspension traction, just as I learned at Wisconsin General Hospital. She screamed all night, which kept the Persian women consoling themselves with their water pipes. In the morning, I rolled her bed out in the open hall where the wind and dust had free rein. There, with a new dress and doll from the guild boxes, she was content to stay until she was well.

"Why are you leaning over your bed that way?" asked Indira of an inpatient. She answered, "The helpers told me to stand this way for an injection but I've been here a long time."

My first hysterectomy was on a Bedouin lady who had had a complete uterine prolapse for years. I read it up carefully in the book and asked Dr. Mylrea to stand beside me. I felt I've gotta do this. So I did it under spinal anesthesia. The layers did peel back just as the book said, and staying close to the uterine muscle, I eliminated the error of cutting other vital structures. But I was afraid of surgery. Maurie Huesinkveld flatly refused to even try any surgery. He said he didn't have the training and so it wouldn't be right. I tended to rush in where angels fear to tread.

We had a pale listless little girl with a large spleen. There was no malaria in Kuwait because there was no sweet water to breed mosquitoes. I couldn't make a diagnosis so I brought her to Dr. Allen Mersh, the surgeon at the oil company hospital. He thought perhaps removing the spleen would help, which he did, but she didn't improve. It wasn't until a few years later that I found the whole family had large spleens. Later on Dr. Corine Overkamp found there was a fair amount of inherited blood dycrasias as thalassemia and sickle cell disease in the Gulf. Dr. Overkamp was the latest addition to our mission physicians. She specialized in Internal Medicine, so was a great help to them.

The mission policy was that we got a three-month vacation every alternate summer. The other summer we worked straight through. But mothers of children at the Kodaikanal mission school in southern India could go every summer. This was because it took so long and was so expensive to travel by ship to India.

Kuwait is a terrible land in the long, hot summer. The sun really works at the job; "There is nothing hid from the heat thereof," and "the elements melt with fervent heat." Even the nights were misery. When it didn't cool off, we tried to sleep on the roof, but the winds blew the bedding and the moon stared down on us. We caught up with a two- or three-hour nap after lunch. I would stretch out under the ceiling fan on a floor mat under a wet sheet. I enjoyed reading books like *Gone with the Wind* and Tolstoy's *War and Peace* at that hour of the day. It was quite a peaceful time, as everybody who could went away and no visitors came.

Before we had air-conditioners, I had to keep the office windows open with the ceiling fan on. The hospital made a convenient place for taxi drivers to park their cars. While they waited for the patients, the drivers discussed (in the vigorous and positive way men have of expressing their opinions), tuned up their cars, and played their radios loudly with brutal insensitivity to my patients and me. I felt grumpy and nettled. I gravely informed them of my difficulty, but of course I was only a woman.

I could usually start the clinic with vim and vigor, but by ten o'clock, I'd feel myself drooping and deteriorating. The drug firms were generous with all kinds of samples, among them the new one, amphetamine. As a true daughter of science, I tried the samples out on myself and found that five grains of that drug gave me the exhilaration I needed. It even made me happy. Later on I found that a couple of salt pills would do as well. So it must have been a mild heat prostration.

The native people did not seem to suffer much from the heat, but they would watch for the appearance of Canopus, the Dog Star, which they called Suhail. When it could be seen at night, it meant the end of the furious heat. Babies suffered from it. When I found a temperature of 108, I'd move with unbelievable rapidity and carry the baby, clothes and all, to the faucet to drench it and then hold it under the ceiling fan—often to the distress of the mother. The temperature would always come down fast. At the end of the summer, the babies always suffered an epidemic of diarrheas with dehydration. We didn't have good enough equipment nor enough help to give intravenous fluids. At first, I weighed out the salt and sterilized distilled water, with the bother of finding bottles and tubes and connections to give sub-cutaneous fluids to the babies. It was hard on the babies, but I think it saved a lot of them. The nurses could give five or six infusions at the same time.

But what did I care about such trifles—I was terrifically popular. In fact, I sometimes thought it would be nice to be lonesome. I caught some of the infections. Pinworms were disgusting. It was awful to feel the little worms crawling in and out of you. I had scabies, too. That was in the winter in Qatar when it was too cold to take a bath and we didn't have good drugs. One Indian wife had scabies with terrible itching. By that time I had benzyl ben-zoate, which was very effective.

There was a fair amount of abnormal obstetrics, because many women tried to deliver at home. Only when things went wrong would they come in for help. Vesicular mole, for example, is said to be five to fifteen times more prevalent in Asia and Africa than in the West. In these unusual pregnancies the fetus is lost and the placenta becomes a mass of grape-like vesicles. These cases bleed a little and the uterus is at least the size of a five-month pregnancy. As soon as I knew the diagnosis from the passage of some vesicles, I started the operation of curetting out the con-tents of the uterus with an instrument like a small hoe. There seemed to be buckets and buckets of the vesicles. I was scared that I might be rupturing the uterus. But finally they stopped coming, and I gave intravenous ergotrate to make the uterus clamp down and stop bleeding. The patients made uneventful recover-ies, though there was some danger of developing a malignant kind of cancer.

From the records, there must have been over a thousand D and C's (dilation and curettage) for incomplete miscarriages. I don't think the women tried to abort themselves. Since we had no blood for transfusion, I decided the best treatment for any mod-erate bleeding was to remove the products of conception imme-diately. In later years, young doctors who came out for a short time criticized me severely for this. But I still think that at that time it saved the health and maybe the lives of many women.

With so many lost fetuses, my theology questioned, "What does God do about these lives?"

163

Kuwait
Practice
Renewed,
1945

I did a D and C on one bleeding case and removed placental bits. About three months later she came back with an abdominal tumor which I had not noted at the surgery. I asked Dr. Allen Mersh, the surgeon at the oil company hospital, to operate, and I assisted. On incision, we found it was a living five-month abdominal pregnancy. Allen was Roman Catholic and hesitated a long time before he removed the fetus, leaving the placenta to be absorbed. I was always being surprised.

A Bedu woman came from a long distance. She had been bleeding for a long time, so the smell was putrid. I removed the foul mass in the office without anesthesia. She was deeply grateful and asked me with wonder in her voice, "How is it that you are willing to do this dirty stinking task for me?"

One lady went into shock with hemorrhage after the delivery of her baby and placenta. Desperately I persuaded the men of her family to give blood and she came out of shock. What I failed to do was to make a vaginal examination, or I would have found the cause and maybe corrected it. The entire uterus had inverted, which I didn't notice until the next day. Then Dr. Bosch and I operated and tried to evert it, but the muscle had clamped down too tight. He had to bisect the entire organ and suture it back in its correct shape. She recovered, but I strictly charged her that when she became pregnant again, she must come for prenatal care and delivery. As the custom was, she didn't come back until one night when I watched in disbelief as she precipitated an anencephalic monster with a small, soft head. I didn't see her again. She probably went on to deliver many more babies normally. If I keep on, maybe I'll learn obstetrics.

For cases of placenta previa, when the labor starts with bleeding because the placenta is planted too low in the uterus, I tried inserting an inflatable rubber bag to dilate the cervix (the opening of the uterus). Once on examining the mother, I was certain the placenta lay completely across the opening. These cases suddenly have a torrential blood loss, and delivery from below is impossible. I warned her that she must have a Caesarian section or she would die. She laughed at me; she'd had many babies and thought she knew all about the process. In deadly earnest, I tried to explain why she was bleeding and said I would not take care of her without that operation; otherwise, she would have to go to the government hospital. Her family took her over to the government hospital. I heard later that she died that afternoon.

There was a case of a woman whose uterus ruptured before she arrived at the hospital. Jerry and I operated but she died.

I remember a terrifying case of abruptio placentae. In these cases the placenta loses its attachment to the uterus during labor. There was very little bleeding. The uterus went into a tetanic spasm with such pain that the patient developed shock. The uterus was firm without relaxing as in normal labor and was very tender. I remembered that in these cases the blood loses its fibrinogen and will not clot, which I confirmed by drawing blood. It was almost certain the fetus could not live, so I decided that the best thing to do would be to operate to remove the entire uterus, then tie off the big blood vessels so that there could be no more bleeding. Jerry Nykerk agreed and helped. The case demanded quick action. We gave spinal anesthesia. Jerry encouraged me to take the responsibility, so I grasped the scalpel—the urgency of the situation helped me to forget my diffidence. It was easy to find the three sets of large blood vessels and tie them off so that the sutures would not slip and then just lift out the entire uterus without opening it. The patient made a surprisingly good recovery. I could hear Beethoven's Ninth Symphony.

In one case the fetus had a hydrocephalic head. The diagnosis was apparent from the feel of the widely separated bones of the skull. The head was so large that it could not be delivered. These cases were mentioned in our books, but I'd never seen one. The treatment was to use a kind of spear to puncture the scalp and collapse the head so it could be grasped and delivered. At the same time, the small amount of brain tissue usual in these cases should be destroyed. It was an appalling procedure, but it was the only way to help the mother. It would have been improper to do a Caesarian section for such an abnormal fetus. At the same time it was exciting. But this time, when the fetus was delivered, I found I had not destroyed the brain centers for breathing. The monster gasped hoarsely for almost an hour, to my agony.

During the war, the oil company asked our hospital to care for the wives. One sweet, elderly lady with white hair came to me because her abdomen was swelling. Surprisingly, although she had no previous babies she was pregnant and went on to have a normal child. Another British wife had a normal delivery of a little girl, but when I turned the baby over to adjust the cord dressing, my hand fell into a large, soft mass in the back. It was a meningocoele—a hernia of the nerves of the spinal cord. It was not possible to send the baby home, as there was no transport. Even now these cases are rarely helped. The mother could not bring herself to care for the baby, so we kept it in the hospital for three months until it died.

Because there was no prenatal care, there were occasional cases of eclampsia—the terrible convulsions of toxic pregnancy. I used the injection of magnesium sulfate and delivered the mothers with forceps as soon as possible. Not many of them lived.

Somehow some of the home deliveries developed tetanus. I gave all the sedatives we had—chloral hydrate and phenobarbs— and put a tube down for feeding, but I lost all those cases. In Bahrain, after the government hospitals were well established, I took one case to the government hospital, where they could give artificial breathing through a tracheostomy. For a month they put a nurse on constant bedside attendance. That one was saved.

My admiration for the women grew, for they endured pain without anesthesia in patience and without complaints, usually in silence or calling "O my Lord." They felt that any complaint was rebellion against God. God willed all things and since the pain came from Him, it must simply be accepted. When their babies died as many did in the early days, they felt they must try to smile and say, "It is the will of God." Often they tried to smile and then would break down in sobs. Sometimes they would weep when the baby turned out to be a girl.

The most pitiful cases were the women with torn bladders, from difficult deliveries in the desert where they had no help. The partition between the bladder and the vaginal wall is so thin and has such a slender blood supply that it doesn't heal well. Added to the problem is the constant flow of urine over the laceration. The technical name for the condition is vesicle-vaginal fistula. These women begin to smell so bad that their families cannot stand to even have them in the tents in the open desert. The reek of the repulsive odor is penetrating. I could tell it as soon as they entered the room. Their sad eyes showed their deep, tragic woe. I felt I had to do something.

In the early days I tried to repair them myself and leaped into the fray. If it was a small opening, the tissues could be undermined and moved enough to close the hole. The problem was that the suture material had to be fine enough and yet strong enough to hold for at least a week. The difficulty was that the operation had to be done at the bottom of a small, dark hole. It was hard to find needles that were fine enough, curved and strong enough to put in the stitches. Once during the operation the electricity went off. I had to finish it by having a helper hold a flashlight. Some of the cases did seem to heal.

When the oil company surgeon Dr. Allen Mersh came, I consulted him for some of the cases with large, extensive fistulas. He decided to transplant the ureters into the lower bowel. I watched his excellent technique and assisted. They did heal. The treatment solves the problem temporarily, but the bowel being full of infective stool, infection travels up the ureter to infect the kidneys. However, it did give these tragic cases relief.

Cases of Rh-negative blood seem to be rare in Asia and Africa. The medical profession was just beginning to learn about it when I was in medical school. I learned about it in the *Journal of the American Medical Association.* I remember only one case of an edematous fetus that might have been caused by it.

There were other abnormal babies. One had three eyes in a queer head. Fortunately it was born dead. Another had an abdominal wall that was only a thin membrane, part of the umbilical cord. There wasn't enough tissue to suture it closed. So that baby died, too.

One case had a prolapsed cord. In these cases when the head comes down, it cuts off the blood in the cord, which is the baby's lifeline. I called to Jerry for help. He gave a little anesthesia and encouraged me to do an internal version. I put my right arm up the vagina to push up the baby's head and then alongside it up into the top of the uterus. It felt like a cavernous depth while I tried desperately to feel for and grasp one little foot and turn the body around from the inside with a hand on the outside. It seemed as if I'd never get it, but slowly it did turn. I did find the other leg coming down when the hip descended and the body came down. The soft body protected the cord so the blood could continue to keep the baby's oxygen supply intact. Everything ended just right. The praise be to God. As the Arabs say, "Al hamdallah."

Before antibiotics, puerperal sepsis was the main cause of maternal death all over the world. So in medical school we were taught to avoid vaginal examinations as much as possible and do rectal instead. The fetal sagittal suture was the main feature to find and the occipital suture gave a clue as to which way the head had to turn to be born. My diagnosis improved but sometimes there were mistakes.

My main problem was the cases where the fetal head was stuck in the pelvis and the sagittal suture lay transversely and refused to turn to lie perpendicularly as it has to to be delivered. This is called a midplane arrest. We were taught on the manikin and a plastic head how to apply the forceps and turn the head. It seemed quite easy to use the forceps on the manikin, but it was quite different in a living mother—as I learned. The uterine muscle usually pushes the head down to turn, but when the muscle gets tired, it gives up and stops pushing. So labor stands still. Forceps were invented to help in this situation. Some doctors have used Pituitin, a drug which stimulates the uterine muscle, but we were warned against using it in labor, as the uterus may rupture, so I didn't use it.

The forceps can be applied to fit either the baby's head or the pelvis. I had to decide which and applied them in an in-between position. Then employing the maxim "Not by strength but by art," I pulled down very gently—sometimes from down on my knees—and took my time bringing the head down to where the maternal bones would turn it around naturally. Sometimes, I took more than an hour to do this. The baby's face took the brunt of the process, with bruises and cuts; but I am happy to say that only once did one eye receive damage. Once the head was delivered, it nearly always was easy to deliver the soft body. I always wondered how those conjoined twins could possibly be delivered.

Sometimes the placenta would be retained, and I'd go up to scrape it out of the top of the inside of the uterus. It's surprising how far up I had to go—it seemed I had to go almost up to the lower ribs—my arm above my elbow.

One normal case had been delivered and put to bed when the nurses called me saying she was having great pain. On examination, I found she had a large perineal hematoma. Some artery in the perineum had ruptured and was bleeding into the tissues, which were blue and swollen. I had to take her back to the table to open the tumor and try to find the bleeding vessel to tie it off. She had lost a lot of blood. Her father offered to give; and his blood type matched and he gave, but he was such a small man that I didn't dare take much. She recovered.

When severely abnormal babies were born, the question arose as to what to do with them. They could survive with special care for a lifetime. This is a human dilemma. I chose to neglect them and they died. My conscience still judges me guilty.

There were quite a few cases of club feet brought in for treatment. I had learned in children's orthopedics to apply the plaster of Paris and bend the soft bones to their correct shape. At Wisconsin, there was an orderly who had been doing them for a long time. He taught me how to do it. The Kuwaiti families thought the babies were suffering so from the plaster shoe that sometimes they would take them off. The cases which I could follow did well, but I never could follow the cases for a long enough time to get the satisfaction of seeing a good result.

In the very early years, during a delivery I had the nurse give a little chloroform to one mother. Her heart stopped. I went on and delivered a live baby. These things came with startling suddenness. I ended with a sense of failure, defeat, and fault. Should I punish myself somehow? Should I give up? Would the women be better off without me? No, I must go on, but know that I am only mediocre.

In the later years, during a minor operation with intravenous anesthesia, the patient stopped breathing. I did mouth-to-mouth breathing for quite a long time. To my relief, she started breathing again. When she came to, she knew she had been through a crisis.

It was strange that in the early days we never seemed to get cases of appendicitis. After the oil development and increased consumption of foreign foods, they began to appear at about the same rate as in the U.S.A. One acute case used to arrive regularly when Lew and I were on duty at 11 P.M.—just when my energy was at its lowest.

Once Lew Scudder and I operated and removed a large hydatid cyst from a man's liver. He and another doctor operated one night on a little child for intestinal obstruction and found it was caused by at least 250 roundworms. Lew and I operated on several cases of cancer of the breast. They were horrible because of the huge mass of tissue which had to be removed and the terrible bleeding. In the long run it didn't do any good. They all went on to die later. Quite a number of women with masses in the breast refused surgery even in the very early stage because they refused to lose the breast. There was one mastoid abscess I tried to operate on. She recovered, but I don't know that she was finally cured.

I tried my hand at abdominal hernias and found them quite easy—suturing with the "vest over pants" technique in the fascia. The problem was always anesthesia. I tried spinal, intravenous, or had one of the other doctors give open drop ether.

Hemorrhoidectomy was the common operation for which I used a low spinal injection. When my mother was visiting me in Kuwait, she was bleeding from them. I had the nerve to operate on her. I wonder now at my self-confidence.

There was a case of squamous cell carcinoma of the eye socket. I curetted it and thought I got it all because it was small. I was wrong. They brought in another case of a young woman who had cancer of the face for a long time. Most of her face was a foul cavity. The family couldn't stand the smell anymore. She had one eye left. I offered to put a stomach tube down to give her fluids and food, but she pulled it out. Her family deserted her and she died alone.

I put plaster on a leg with a fracture of the middle of the tibia and fibula (that was before we had X-rays). Six weeks later, I removed the plaster and was sick to see the leg was still waving in the wind. But after another six weeks it did unite.

A little boy was rushed into the hospital gasping and blue. I ran for a knife, unsterile though it was, and cut his throat. The trachea was compressed and pulled back so tight against the vertebrae from his efforts to breathe that I had difficulty grasping it with my fingers to incise it. As soon as it was open, he could breathe through it and revived. I put in a tracheotomy tube and he was comfortable. But the next day when I tried to remove the tube he still couldn't breathe. So I took him to the government hospital, where the throat specialist took a pumpkin seed out of his larynx. Then his mother remembered that a neighbor child had been feeding him pumpkin seeds. It wasn't brilliant of me not to think of pushing up a tube from below, but his parents were pathetically grateful.

The Kuwaiti women wore black abbas which hung from their heads to the ground. The Bedouin's abbas were of heavy black goat's hair; the town women's of lighter material. They wore a black chiffon veil called a *milfah* to completely cover their faces. A black scarf was wrapped around their heads and fastened with a silver or gold pin made in the shape of a hand. This scarf covered their hair and necks. Sometimes they had long, black, thick braids with blue beads for a tassel. Some of the women wore nose rings, but their ears were covered up. A dress called a *nefnoof* served as a foundation—red was the favorite color for the nefnoof. Over that was put a garment of thin material decorated with sequins. It was usually black, very wide so it could be draped over the head and long enough so it trailed behind as the women walked. One of them said it was long to wipe out their footsteps so the jinns couldn't follow them. Their jewelry was silver set with turquoise and carnelian. Women used a black substance for eye shadow and made designs on the palms of their hands and on their bare feet with henna. Sandals and long trousers, tight and embroidered at the ankles, completed the costume.

Later, when the country had become more wealthy, Kuwaiti women felt that only gold was proper for their fine jewelry. Once, I gave each of our hospital helpers a jeweled silver filigree pin from Kashmir. I asked one of them later why she never wore it. She answered, "Well, it was just silver, so I gave it to the children."

The Arabs felt that a person's body should be completely clothed. I had a copy of a famous Madonna painting hanging in my office. No one seemed to notice it, so I asked a patient, "Do you like the picture of the mother and baby?" She glanced at it disapprovingly and replied, "The baby isn't dressed." That was enough to condemn the picture in her sight. On the other hand, veiled women would sit on the ground where men were passing, exposing their breasts without embarrassment to nurse their babies. Babies did not wear diapers. Whenever the baby leaked, the mother would support it between her ankles for the function. The little girls wore ragged-edged dresses without hems. The women said it was to protect them from the jinns, also called the little people of the earth. They would not "possess" a poor, ragged child.

THE MORNING CLINIC

Work began every morning with a report from the nurses and helpers and then rounds on the inpatients. Someone would give the Bible talk to the gathered outpatients, and then I'd sit in the office with an Iranian translator and see everyone in turn. There were so many patients at each clinic that we would admit five women with their children at one time. I'd see one at a time on the chair beside the desk. I had to look at them quickly, ask what the trouble was, look over their past record, and decide what I might guess the diagnosis to be. Then I had to decide what sort of treatment might help (or at least satisfy) the patient, assess the price, and ask the woman if she could pay for it or, if she could not, how we might collect the bill. The clinic was a glorified pharmacy. It worked out to about five minutes for each patient. If they didn't look very sick, I just treated the symptoms—aspirin was my sheet anchor. Then I'd take a little more time for the really sick ones. I felt I had to give everyone something.

I figured the noisy babies were not too sick—it was the quiet ones I had to examine. The cases ran the whole gamut—diarrhea, vomiting, sore eyes, fever, cough, running ears, cautery burns, malnutrition, skin diseases, and the exotic cases, like "the rat took a bite out of the baby's hip," for example. One baby was brought with a meningocoele with a red string tied around it. I told the family I couldn't help, they would have to take it home. Once a mother came in to ask me, "Is my baby a girl?" It was newborn. I found it had testicles in a divided scrotum. The family were embarrassed. "What shall we do? We've told the whole neighborhood it was a girl." I really had no idea what to say to them. Fortunately, there was very little polio, and I didn't see any diphtheria. The vast majority of our cases were more mundane: parents asked us to pierce the ears of their babies, which I objected to.

The women's complaints were principally: low backache, pain in the knees, toothache, sore eyes, tachycardia, abdominal distress, large ulcers of the legs, abscesses, fingernail infections, skin diseases, cough and fever, much tuberculosis, diarrhea, needles in feet, and sterility, for which I sometimes did a tubal insufflation. There was little request for birth control, because the women were afraid of divorce if they didn't keep on bearing children. Women would often say that their disease was from Allah, but I contradicted them, declaring, "No, all disease is from Satan." There were many cases of cracked nipples, breast abscesses, lesions of the vulva, and discharges.

A twelve-year-old girl came to me weeping and complaining of backache. I found she was badly bruised and asked if she'd been beaten. Weeping, she sobbed, "Yes, by my uncle. My father wants me to go to school, but they said that if I go to school, I can't marry their sons."

A small boy was brought by his mother. "What's the matter with him?" I asked. "He fell in the sea yesterday and was nearly drowned, so I think he had better have a dose of medicine," she explained.

I often wondered, "Why do they keep coming in such numbers?" I knew the drugs we had were not very efficacious or even correct. I guessed that lots of women came because it was a good excuse to get out of houses where they were confined and get to see other people. Their attendance wasn't due to our good medical practice, though maybe my charming personality cheered some up. Galen said, "He cures most successfully in whom the people have the greatest confidence." Christ said, "According to your faith, you are healed." The great secret of medical practice is that most illnesses get better by themselves.

The true challenge to me as a doctor was the wide array of disease I encountered. Even so, people were in better health in some ways in those early days, because there was little obesity, no malaria, no vitamin deficiency, no appendicitis, no alcoholism, and no cigarettes. People led a healthier life by default.

The men's hospital had its drama, too. A little boy came with a mouth that looked like a buttonhole. He had chewed gunpowder which exploded. In another strange incident, a drunken Indian clerk had slipped a ring on his penis. When he woke, it was gangrenous and had to be amputated. Lew Scudder was kept busy most afternoons with hernia operations, at which I sometimes helped.

Acute cases could come at any hour. One night a father brought his little son, about six years old. The child was as white as a sheet of paper. They brought his urine, which was as black as ink. The father was willing to give blood, so I matched them by the method of combining father's serum with son's red blood cells and vice versa. Since they matched I gave the boy his father's blood, and he responded favorably immediately. But I couldn't figure it out. Otherwise, the boy was quite well. About a year later, the same thing happened and they went to the government hospital. The doctors there taught me. It was a case of a congenital lack of the enzyme glucose six phosphate dehydrogenase. The boy had eaten a big meal of the broad beans which I didn't know were also called fava beans. These beans contain a toxic substance which normal people can detoxify. But certain people lacking that enzyme are not protected. The toxin dissolves their red blood cells and the dissolved iron turns the urine black. The doctors at the government hospital were nearly all Egyptians who knew their beans. So after that the boy avoided the beans. And I kept on learning.

Some Christian families drifted down to Kuwait from the ancient Assyrian Church of northern Iraq, where there had been massacres during the First World War. Yacoob and Esteer Shemmas were paid by the mission. He helped with the Arabic preaching and managed the Bible shop in the bazaar. They had five children. The two girls worked with us in the hospital. The three sons picked up English and had some education in the local schools. They married girls from the original community and soon flourished in business. Saeed, with his wife Basima, became Kuwait's first ambassador to several foreign countries. But somehow we failed to convey to the Christians our sense of mission and the idea that they had some responsibility for it, too. One of them asked me whether my family in America was so poor that I came to Kuwait to make a living. When I charged these prosperous families for medical treatment as we did everybody else, they were quite indignant. They felt that a Christian hospital should treat Christians free. I was perplexed at their lack of understanding.

Habeeb, the son of Yacoob, had a wife, Kameel. In great distress she brought me her newborn son, Assama, with extreme and irregular tachycardia of sudden onset. I was at a loss to know how to treat it. I'd never even heard of such a case. How I longed for a consultant. I pored over my books, distraught with anxiety, and tried to figure out the dose of digitalis for tiny babies and carefully measured out the drops. What a relief to find the next day that his heart had become normal. Thank God!

Other families came, too, to work with us at the hospital. Sulaiman became our pharmacist. When his wife Lamia had her first baby, she suddenly ran high temperatures. I tried the new drug sulfanilamide on her without benefit. We had no lab, but suddenly it occurred to me that she probably had a latent malaria, and so it was. The delivery had stirred it up.

The related family of Bin Yamin came. He collected hospital bills for us. And the widow Sitt Sara with her son and daughter moved to Kuwait. She became a wise and faithful Bible teacher in the women's hospital. But the Arab Christian group never mixed socially with the Muslims. There was always a barrier between the two groups.

One Sunday afternoon, a young girl was brought in unconscious with Cheyne-Stokes breathing. I found no indications of the cause and did a spinal tap, which was negative. I wracked my brains but nothing came up. She died that night. I slunk off with the mute anguish of failure. Do other doctors have these feelings, too? If so, no one ever confessed to it in medical school.

There were so many babies with fever, vomiting, and diarrhea. One poor woman stayed for days with her baby until it died. I was so anxious to know why the baby had died that I persuaded the mother to let me do a postmortem. I promised I would not charge her any bill for the care. That autopsy procedure was just not done, but she permitted it. I found the liver was full of pinhead-size abscesses.

One woman patient seemed quite well, but she could pass no urine. I couldn't believe it for a couple of days, but it was so. I transferred her to the government hospital, but she died, too.

One night a man brought in his girlfriend with a chest fracture. He told me he had stamped on her chest in a fit of anger. She could hardly breathe. I remembered that chest injuries need special care but couldn't remember what to do. She survived the night, so the next morning, I transferred her to the government hospital, where she later died.

Shaikh Fehed asked me to see his wife Lulua (who was also his cousin). She had a large breast abscess which she was sure was cancer. I assured her it wasn't, and that she should come to the hospital for surgery. The shaikh insisted there must be two doctors present, so Dr. Mylrea and I drained and packed the abscess. This woman was so grateful that she gave me a lovely pearl ring, and Shaikh Fehed also paid a generous fee, even though the royal family did not usually pay for treatments.

In the summer I was somewhat alone when the male doctor went on vacation. A man came in with a sudden abdominal pain. His abdomen was as hard as a board. (Why do the worst cases come at night?) The Indian doctor and I decided on immediate surgery and found a ruptured gastric ulcer. I was surprised how easy it was to suture shut. I could feel that surgery might be thrilling. It was Ramadan, the month of fasting. After the day's fast from fluid and food, the first few bits of food had ruptured his ulcer. He recovered quickly. Most cases did get well, in fact, but I forget them and remember mostly the tragedies.

An Indian wife delivered her baby normally in the hospital, but a day later I found the baby too sleepy and scarcely breathing. I couldn't make a diagnosis. The Indian nurses had to tell me. The wife was a nurse in India and couldn't come to join her husband in Kuwait until after his first year there. In her husband's absence somehow she had become pregnant. She knew how to use sedatives and had tried to get rid of the embarrassing baby. It recovered, but a week later the Hindu husband called me to the house. This time the mother had given enough sedative and the baby was dead. What should I have done? I said nothing. They buried it in the Hindu cemetery.

They brought an apparently healthy little boy with only the complaint that he couldn't swallow. I guessed on polio but couldn't think of anything to do. I went for lunch and when I came back, he was dead.

I was called to the house of a pregnant lady with difficult breathing and gave her what I had in my bag. I came back after an hour and she was gone. I live in a world of sin and misery.

A man brought his wife with what I was sure was a femoral thrombosis (a large blood clot in the big artery to the leg). Did I dare attempt surgery on such a large blood vessel? I was afraid to try it. I kept her in bed and quiet. God was good. Somehow auxiliary vessels supplied the leg and she recovered.

Sometimes I went to call on beautiful gracious Bederea, the

wife of Abdulla Mullah Salah, the young prime minister. She was heavy with pregnancy. We were sitting on the mats talking when he came in, sat down in an easy chair, and began talking with me. Bederea rose immediately on his entrance to courteously serve us tidbits and restlessly move around. I could see that she felt she could not sit down in her husband's presence, and my being there was embarrassing. I made my excuses to leave as soon as possible. I was astonished at his callousness.

Some years later, I heard that one of her little boys had died. The local custom at such a time of sorrow is for relatives and friends to go and call. This visiting at the time of bereavement is called a *taziah* (comforting). We often went to these and found the room filled with women, most of whom sit silently for hours. It was a very beautiful, thoughtful courtesy. Anyway, that day at the taziah I learned that the child had developed a toxic sore throat, and Abdulla insisted that they take the child to the government hospital, where he died. Bederea, in black mourning clothes, lay face down on a pallet, her body shaken with sobs. After sitting a while with the other women we came over to embrace her. Her face was so swollen with weeping that I could not recognize her. I wondered, is that what death means when one has no risen Savior?

The government hospital brought in a young Parsee ophthalmologist whom I consulted about some eye cases. He was most cooperative and came over to our hospital to help. He operated on some cases of glaucoma at which I assisted him. So I invited him for dinner and had waffles made on a kerosene stove at the table. He enjoyed them so much that he went and bought himself an electric waffle maker to make them himself. The next morning he rushed into my clinic showing me the recipe, which called for shortening. "Now whatever is that?" To my sorrow he left the government hospital after a year. When I asked him why, he said, "Everything there is dog-eat-dog." The Egyptian doctors were in charge and weren't fair to the Indian doctors. He complained that there was so much bribery and corruption that he couldn't stand it.

Tales reached us about an Arab who had ordered a gold brick to be delivered to his house. The messenger brought it during the afternoon nap time. The man sent his servant to tell the messenger to just leave it on the doorstep, which he did. They said no one touched it. One Arab told me how he smuggled gold into India—he bought a small car and put the gold inside the cylinders. Another man swallowed twenty gold pieces before leaving for India, but they didn't pass as planned. He came back to Kuwait, where Jerry Nykerk operated to remove them from his stomach and kept one of them for a fee.

KUWAIT WOMEN'S MEDICAL REPORT TO THE BOARD — OCTOBER 1954

Looking backward over the past year's work seems like the string of a million small things—none of great importance, very few dramatic, still less clothed with religious dignity, fulfilling the daily round of duty done in Christ's name and hoping that somehow it is His way of proclaiming the gospel of the Kingdom. This year seemed longer in that I had no vacation, no days free of the responsibility of a hospital full of sick folk, the hospital manager (Mrs. Scudder) away on her three-month vacation, all new Indian nurses arriving at different times, only one Arabic-speaking helper to manage communications, and a third of the Persian helpers away on their vacations.

The statistics show an ever increasing amount of work. A total of 26,000 clinic patients averaging 104 per clinic day were seen, with 109 outcalls. The inpatients are increasing from 188 in 1940, 465 in 1947, 756 in 1953, to 915 in 1954. Baby cases increased from 140 in 1949 to 236 this year. Major and minor surgery cases were 175, with eye operations 44.

The outstanding events of the year were the companionship of my mother, Mrs. Lillian Bruins, who came to share our life and work during the winter months. In November 1953, Nurse Indira fell ill of the mental disease as told on a previous page. In December 1953, I fell down the stairs and broke my left ankle. The oil company doctor took care of it and gave me a walking caliper, so I could get around in the hospital quite soon. The secretarial work was heavy, with business letters to the government and in trying to get nurses from India. During the summer, the nurses' home was built.

Summer, when the days were longest and hottest, was the busiest time of the year. So one of the nurses and I would make rounds before the 7 A.M. chapel prayers. Dirty water would be

dripping from the upper verandas, children's little deposits surrounded the entrance, the families would be eating their break-
fasts and cooking the fish for lunch over smoky oil stoves in their
rooms, and the toilets . . . ! We'd visit our three darling orphans
and the three tiny prematures—two of whom started life at two
and a half pounds but are flourishing on aureomycin and vitamin B12.

Some dilemmas met on rounds:

"Doctor, I must go home today. What is my bill? What medicine should I take? What should I eat? When should I come
again?"

"Doctor, the mason is here and wants to see you about those
walls."

"Doctor, there's a dirty bedpan in the hall. No one will clean
it. It's not my work."

"Doctor, the painter has come. Which rooms should he whitewash today?"

"Doctor, the relatives of the patient that died last night have
come and want to talk with you."

"Doctor, they have just brought in a woman in labor and she's
bleeding. Can you come right away?"

"Doctor, Sharaban didn't come to work today. Who is going to
clean her rooms?"

After opening the clinic with a Bible story and prayer by one
of the mission wives, I'd start seeing patients in the office.

"They compassed me about like bees." Ps. 118:12

Twelve women push their way in immediately. It takes real
force to keep out more. Everyone talks at once:

"Doctor, my heart beats too fast."

"Doctor, my back aches, and my knees and head hurt, and I
have a pain in my stomach. I didn't sleep last night. I'm beginning to die."

"Doctor, the baby has fever and diarrhea. What should I feed
him?"

"Doctor, my partner-wife has two babies and I haven't any.
Can you help?"

"Doctor, an Indian lady has come. She can't talk, so her husband must come, too. Shall I tell the others to cover their faces
so he can come in?" I usually do not admit men to the office, as
the women are in purdah.

"Doctor, I've been bleeding for two days. No, I can't stay for an operation, I've five little seeds at home. I must go home now. Just give me a needle."

"Doctor, the plumber has come and wants to know how you want that pipe fixed."

"Doctor, there is a Palestinian lady come. She doesn't want to wait with the Kuwaiti women. She'll be angry if you don't see her right away. She'll pay extra. Her husband is in the government."

The babies are crying. The cars are honking around the corner. The taxi drivers have parked their cars in the shade just outside the open windows, turning on their radios while they wait. Some naughty little boys try to look in the windows.

"Doctor, the trucks didn't bring any water today. The women are asking for drinking water. What shall I do?"

"Doctor, there isn't any more of this kind of medicine. What else shall I give her?"

"Doctor, the carpenter wants to see you about that cupboard."

"Doctor, this woman is very sick and wants to stay in the hospital. All the rooms are full. Where shall we put her?"

"Doctor, last night a bug entered my ear and went into my brain. Can you take it out?"

"Doctor, I have a pain here. I want an X-ray."

"Doctor, the room you gave my mother isn't good enough. We must have an upper room."

One of the nurses comes in. "Doctor, the helper won't do what I tell her. She shouts at me in front of the patients."

"Doctor, the helper in charge of the salt water pump forgot to turn it off. The water is pouring through the roof."

"Doctor, I don't want plaster on my broken arm. I just want some oil to rub on it."

"Doctor, the oil stove in the operating room blew up. Everything is black."

Trying to listen to complaints in three or four languages, making spot examinations and snap diagnoses, writing out an order for drugs or treatments, assessing the income of the patients, recording the charges in the records, teaching mothers how to make formulas, and telling them when to come back is an overwhelming job. It's impossible, but I take a whack at it all. We finish the last patient by twelve or one. Then the afternoon operations must be planned: what instruments, what time, what nurse to scrub, which nurse to circulate, what anesthesia, all has to be decided. Sometimes then we all go for a swim if the tide is right.

Along with the Arab custom, we have two or three hours' rest during the hot part of the day. But it means that one has to get up and go to work twice a day and keep at it until sunset. Twice a week, I try to teach the new Indian nurses basic hospital Arabic. On Sundays, I try to teach them about Islam. In the afternoon come the crowds of visitors, fifty to sixty of them, bringing all the children, and a nice, big watermelon for a picnic in the patient's rooms. The seeds go over the floor and the rinds—out of the window.

At the end of the mission accounts, October 1954, the women's hospital had taken in over Rs 210,000 ($42,000) and after paying expenses had a balance of Rs 55,000 ($11,000). It was used partly to build the nurses' rooms.

At the mission general meeting the balance of funds in the Kuwait hospitals was given to the Amara, Iraq, and Oman hospitals because they had large deficits. We protested the action because our equipment was wearing out and will cost more to replace.

My cousin Madeline Holmes was most helpful. She took charge of the staff of twenty-five people. They would argue over salaries paid in silver rupees, which they usually couldn't even count. She helped with the endless accounts, pension funds, Indians' accounts, paying for supplies, sorting the money paid in cash, with the hard physical work of carrying thirty-five pounds of silver to the bank every month. She took charge of the sewing and mending and trying to find solutions of what to do for babies' diapers, which disappeared so fast.

That year, visitors began to come from all over the world. Some were interested in the mission. It was our pleasure to show them the hospital and give them some entertainment.

The evangelists maintained Sunday services. In the morning, they held an Arabic preaching meeting, which a few of the staff attended. In the afternoon, they held an Arabic service in the hospital where we sang the Arabic hymns and had a short talk for some inpatients. In the evening was the English service patterned to suit the British residents. It resembled the Anglican liturgy.

The evangelists took the Bible talks for the clinics. When Mrs. Van Ess came from Basrah, she talked on how the creed has changed to "There is no god but the rupee." The evangelists also called on the inpatients.

They were in charge of the Bible shop in the bazaar where Yacoob sat without keeping it clean and neat. Once the government ordered it closed, but some of the businessmen declared they wanted it kept open and so it was.

The evangelists put on the movie of the life of Christ, which was very popular so had to be shown eight times to large crowds. At Christmastime they had to get the government censor to approve a movie of the Christmas story. The censors disapproved mentioning Israel, so the wise men appear before King Herod and don't say anything.

I sent for large copies of the Elsie Anna Wood pictures of the Bible stories, which she recently painted from real characters in Palestine. A man wrote out the appropriate verses in beautiful Arabic for each one. Then they were framed and one or two hung in each room. The pictures of Christ before Pilate and the crucifixion were hung in the hall. People would often stop long studying them, but no one made any remarks.

The mountain stands exactly where it stood
    The shadows that it casts are just as deep
And while I wait to see it disappear
    Becomes the more appalling year by year.
But we work on
    The triumph may be almost at our door
Or just around the corner on its way.
                            (Author unknown)

8. Questions of Mission

A QUESTION OF MISSION

By 1953, it was becoming evident that the line of rooms constituting the men's hospital was no longer suitable for our needs, so at station meetings we began to plan a new building. The Arab men had also been complaining that it was not proper that the women's hospital building should be better than the one for men.

Some animosity had developed between the evangelistic and medical missionaries in Kuwait, especially between the Rev. Garret De Jong and the Scudders. This difficulty was inevitable, because the evangelistic workers received scant attention when they talked or called in the hospital. The doctors, on the other hand, enjoyed overwhelming prestige and popularity. So there was some bitterness, and cruel words were spoken.

The padres felt that medical mission work should be reconsidered and perhaps curtailed. They maintained that since the doctor was the attracting and responsible person that she/he should do the evangelism in the hospitals. The evangelists also argued that the increasing amount of medical work called for more personnel and buildings at the expense of the evangelistic work. And evangelism was, after all, the real reason for the mission. They also complained that the medical work was purely philanthropic and not making any mission impact; that the random broadcast of the Word by clinic talks, pictures, and tracts was not effective in building a church; and that medicine practiced by a doctor who treated more than a hundred patients a day was not good medicine. They felt the medical mission dispensed an impersonal, assembly-line type of treatment, and many patients who were not really ill were taking up too much time. It was felt that we outsiders competed unjustly with the newly developing local government hospitals; that it was questionable whether it was right to push religion on sick people whose resistance is low and who are helpless victims requiring our charity, and that Christ didn't keep on trying to cure everybody—in fact He sometimes just went away. The padres felt that the medical work should serve the Church rather than the Church (or at least the Church's money) serve the medical work. In fact this was the new face of the old conflict in Christian service between words and deeds. Some workers felt that other ventures should be studied. We could emphasize staff training or set up a children's hospital, a home for cripples, or a tuberculosis hospital. It was thought that these kinds of projects would provide extensive enough contact to effectively tell our mission.

The question was whether a missionary doing good deeds could effectively communicate our Good News. Good works were also done by many Muslims, as well as by Communists. We were not presenting our lives as examples, and we had to admit we were far from perfect in many ways.

On the other hand, the Christ commanded the work of healing to the same degree that He commanded preaching. Medical work was the only kind of mission work acceptable to the Arabs. It was our only opportunity to get acquainted, to get anyone to hear our message, and to win friends. We needed to get acquainted in order to understand Muslim thinking, as well as to explain our message. Medical work did not require increasing financial support from the American church. It was paying its own way. Medical work, by its nature, could not be curtailed as the mission schools could be, for it is not morally right for a physician to refuse to attend a sick person who comes for help. The medical work gave an opportunity for local Christians to help their Muslim neighbors and present the Gospel. The Christian religion was not pushed on any patient. Any other kind of work that was being suggested would be much more expensive than running a general hospital and need more highly trained personnel.

We didn't resolve all these questions, but in 1954, we contracted a local firm (the Suhail Co., managed by Abdulla Ali Reza) to build the new men's hospital. A British firm was employed to do the work.

In November of that year we had a formal cornerstone-laying. Mrs. Dorothy Scudder arranged a dinner for invited guests on the tennis court with tables, chairs, Persian carpets, and decorations.

Two hundred and fifty friends of the mission, both Arab and expatriate, came and donated $8,000 in gifts. Shaikh Fehed gave a generous gift and promised more. The Arabs dislike putting a promise in writing. Unfortunately, he died before giving more.

While the hospital was being built, the city bought the property where we single women lived, so we had to plan a new home. We drew up plans which seemed very expensive. The Suhail Co. made a favorable bid because they had the equipment and men on the spot. We figured we could meet the cost from the amount offered by the home church if we could also use the increased income we were making at the women's hospital. We had to ask the mission for permission to do this, but it was given.

We decided to place the house on the compound in back of the hill where the Mylrea-Scudder house was—between the church and the nurses' home. It was to be two stories with a large reception room and office downstairs, three bedrooms with three baths upstairs, and a flat roof for sleeping in summer. Behind the house were to be three single story rooms for a kitchen, servants' room, and storeroom. Both buildings turned out to be very satisfactory.

In October 1955, we had the spectacular dedication of the men's hospital. Dorothy Scudder was an ideal manager, so everything was spick-and-span clean and shined up to the last faucet. The ruler, His Highness Shaikh Abdullah al Salim al Sabah K.C.M.G., C.I.C., and many other important people came for the formal opening of the Mylrea Memorial Hospital. Charles S. G. Mylrea, M.D., O.B.E., for whom the hospital was named, had served in Kuwait twenty-eight years and died in Kuwait in 1952. The place was decorated with banners, Persian carpets, and armchairs. Speeches were made. Yacoob prayed for the hospital and for the ruler, at the mention of whose name the Arabs clapped. After the ceremony the guests were given an escorted tour of the building. The Kuwait Oil Company provided a munificent tea on the tennis court for all the guests, with generous food and decorations.

So the Mylrea Memorial Hospital was launched. It had a fifty-one-bed capacity, with fifteen wards containing three or four beds each, and two private rooms. There were two doctor's consulting rooms with a large central waiting room between. Two well-equipped operating rooms were joined by a sterilizing room. An up-to-date laboratory serviced the hospital. There were also

X-ray and basal metabolic machines. The working rooms were air-conditioned and furnished with hot and cold running fresh water. The staff was three doctors, trained nurses, and a laboratory and X-ray technician. The cost of the building was more than 2 million rupees ($400,000.00), raised partly from gifts by Kuwaitis, the oil company, and friends, and partly from the American church.

By 1955 the Arabian Mission had six stations. The three in Iraq were a girls' high school in Baghdad, a hospital compound in Amara, and two schools in Basrah, one for boys and one for girls. The three Persian Gulf stations were hospitals and schools at Kuwait, Bahrain, and Oman.

KUWAIT HOSTS THE ANNUAL MISSION MEETING, 1955

The whole mission tried to hold a meeting each year to gain inspiration, deepen fellowship, and conduct essential mission business. In October 1955, Kuwait station was host to the Annual Meeting. We had room for the sixty guests (including children) in the new men's hospital building and our new house. Fortunately, we also had enough cooks for the two-week session.

Written reports were read from each department of each station. We divided into committees to present accounts, which had to be reviewed twice for accuracy and suitability. Other committees met on evangelism, education, personnel, communications, and planning. Questions were raised and discussed with conflict and ardent zeal. At the final session, Rev. Hakken led a prayer saying, "We thank God that we are finished with business and everyone is more or less agreed on points of difference."

I was assigned the program for the fun night, so I came up with the idea of writing out the introductions of missionary speakers as if we were at an Iowa mission fest. Some of the ministers read them off, to great effect and general hilarity.

We held the fun night in the courtyard of our house, on our veranda "stage." All of us were so busy I had to call on our in-laws in the American consulate and oil company to put on a couple of skits. One skit showed the MacBuck family leaving on furlough. The stage was set with a confusion of suitcases, cartons, BOAC bags, clothes, a Persian carpet, and various excited children.

Mr. Mac stands at the door saying good-bye to visitors outside, and Mrs. Mac is sorting things and making lists and printing names and addresses on the cartons as air freight, unaccompanied baggage, wanted on board, B.I. freight.

Khamis, the cook, comes in asking for a chitti—a note of recommendation, so he can get another job. Mrs. Mac hunts for a piece of paper and hurriedly writes the note. The cook says, "Jasim the houseboy wants one, too, and Ahmed whom you fired last year has come asking for a chit, too." The very correct Roman Catholic priest comes in to say good-bye as Mrs. Mac is washing up the last dishes and pots to be stored in the go-down until they return next year.

Dorothy Scudder rushes in with several parcels and letters. "Will you please mail this letter to Allen and Hanbury in London. Call Dakins by phone and tell them we haven't heard that they shipped the last drugs. Take these broken operating instruments to a repair shop in London to be returned as soon as possible. This envelope is for the Board rooms in New York and this roll of film for Miss Paige."

Haider comes in to check on tickets, health certificates, passports, permits to leave Kuwait, and tries to weigh the suitcases, which burst open when lifted.

An Arab woman friend comes in carrying a tray covered with a cloth. "I wanted to send a box of dates, and helwa, and a cake to take with you."

Mary Allison rushes in in a blood-stained uniform and dumps her bag on the floor to find a gold coin. "Please take this with you and give it to my mother. When you go through customs, you can just say it is personal property."

It is time for the plane, so Mrs. Mac lays the rest of the stuff on a sheet and ties it up by the corners. They all rush off.

Then the telephone rings with news that the plane will be delayed two days for a dust storm.

SHIRLEY AND THE SHAIKH

Shaikh Fehed was the half-brother of the ruler, Shaikh Abdullah; but his mother had been a black concubine, which definitely showed in his African features. He was about normal height and size. In his bearing, he revealed some of the arrogance of the royal family, but aside from that he was friendly and loved a joke. He had attended prep school at the American University in Beirut, where he conceived a great admiration for Americans.

A white woman from Georgia was provided to him for a wife. With her he had a daughter Lateefa. But he fell in love with his cousin Shaikha Lulua, who was a widow. They eventually married and were very happy, but her only pregnancy ended sadly when the baby was born dead. Since he hoped for children, he asked for another young cousin, Bederea, who was pure Arab. They married and she proved fruitful, so children began to fill the house. Shaikh Fehed received a generous share of the money now coming to Kuwait, as did all the members of the royal Al Sabah family. He provided a palatial private house for each of his wives.

Shaikh Fehed often invited us to the seashore house in Dimna suburb, where Bederea and he lived. "Dimna" meant ruins or manure, so they changed its name to Salmaniya. When the De Jongs and I were about to go on furlough, he asked us to find some woman teacher who would live with his growing family and teach them English and American manners.

It so happened that through various friends in Philadelphia, both of us met an excellent candidate, named Shirley Stephens. She was about thirty years old and had been a successful grade school teacher. She lived in a modest home with her parents. Her father was an engineer and her mother was not well. Shirley had long thought of a missionary career but felt her parents needed her. She decided that one year in service in Kuwait would be a mission and an adventure like Anna and the King of Siam.

So, in 1952, Shirley arrived in Kuwait. Ev De Jong drew up a contract for her in which the shaikh promised the same salary as Shirley would have had in Philadelphia and guaranteed her a private apartment and her Sundays off, to be spent with us at the mission. So she moved over to Shaikha Bederea's house, which was a line of rooms with a large, paved courtyard alongside the seashore.

Shirley was of normal height and size—inconspicuous in her clothes and hair, which she kept short and loose. But when she began to talk, one forgot her modest appearance in the flow of her lively conversation. She was vivacious, a happy soul who managed to hold the attention of any group with her good-humored stories. She adapted herself with a cheerful air to any situation and soon was a friend to the whole household comprising many women, servants, and children. In teaching she kept the situation firmly in her own hands.

School started promptly each morning. Shirley knew no Arabic and the household knew no English, but that did not dismay Shirley. She sat on the floor with the family, ate their food, and began to understand their thinking. She started every school morning with a reading from the Bible for her three pupils: Lulua, about eight years old; Ali, six; and Amina, about four. Soon Shaikha Bederea was asking for lessons, too. Family life was harmonious, but because the promised private apartment did not materialize, Shirley's life had to be communal, and it was a challenge—the bathroom situation being the most difficult for her. During the week Shirley lived in a cloistered situation, but she spent every Sunday with us at the mission. She told stories of her life until we felt we knew much more about Arab thinking than we would have otherwise.

Shirley stayed and taught for two years and then decided that she ought to go back to her work in Philadelphia. By the time she left, Bederea and the children had a good command of English and needed to be attending regular school for fellowship.

In the summer of 1954 the whole family flew to the U.S.A. with a couple of servants. Shirley found a summer camp through her church, so they put the children in camp and the rest of the family toured America with Shirley. At the end of the trip the shaikh so trusted Shirley that he asked her to put the children in a private school in the United States and supervise their lives. There was a Deaconness School for girls nearby, but Ali had to live with Shirley's family, where he had regular duties of making his bed, helping with meals, and washing the dishes. Once Shirley found the girls liberally dusting themselves with talcum to look lighter. Every Sunday, Shirley took all the children with her to Sunday School and church.

Shaikha Bederea had six children (some of whom I delivered) when her husband suddenly died of a heart attack. The pair had taken charge of the government hospital when it started, so Bederea was obviously quite capable of managing her own affairs. At Shaikh Fehed's death, the royal family demanded that his children must come and live in Kuwait. They had almost forgotten their native language. Ali must take his father's place. Bederea hired a Lebanese to live with Ali. He did not turn out to be a good influence. The girls tried the Kuwaiti girls' school but were unhappy, so they went to a girls' school in Lebanon and later to schools in Switzerland.

Shaikha Bederea and the girls visited Shirley and considered buying a house in Philadelphia. A lawyer told her that it would be possible, but her children could not inherit much, according to the law of foreigners holding property. So she proposed that Shirley should be the legal owner of a large house in a lovely neighborhood and Bederea would provide the funds and pay for needed repairs and all the furnishings. So Shirley and her parents moved into the gracious three-story house in north Philadelphia. Her Arab family felt they had a home there, too.

Lulua, who had majored in foreign language, was offered the position of organizing the foreign language programs for the Kuwait radio. The royal family was growing very large and split into two factions. A member of the opposite faction got control of the radio station and ordered Lulua to submit her programs to him for approval. Lulua couldn't take that and resigned.

The girls continued to live in part of their mother's home, receiving a stipend from the oil income to the state of Kuwait. They decided they didn't want to marry and went into business, opened a shop, traveled abroad on buying trips, and hired clerks and other employees to face the public. After a tumultuous youth, Ali settled down, married, and had children.

Shirley continued to visit the family in Kuwait. Shaikha Bederea and the girls took fabulous trips and vacations in the summer. When Shirley's parents died and Shirley decided to retire from teaching, Bederea declared the house was hers.

KUWAIT INTERNATIONALIZES

Air travel proliferated in the 1950s, and Kuwait with its prominence attracted many world travelers. Our mission spent a lot of time meeting and waiting for planes and giving tours of the mission work and city. Even the Bishop of Jerusalem came for a visit.

The Calverleys, who had been missionaries in Kuwait from 1910 to 1930, were spending a year in Cairo. Edwin was lecturing at the American University and Eleanor was writing her book, *My Arabian Days and Nights*. Shaikh Fehed met them there and invited them to be his guests in Kuwait. Shaikha Bederea, his wife, organized a lavish reception with a hundred guests; the prominent Al Ghanim family also received the missionary couple most graciously. Eleanor and I made the rounds visiting some of her old friends and patients.

Medicine was progressing. The Kuwaiti government brought the great English ophthalmic physician Dr. Duke-Elder to advise and lecture the medical staff. Some American physicians and surgeons of our Church came and performed specialized operations for some of our patients. The Arabian Gulf Medical Society was formed and had several large conventions in Kuwait, Bahrain, and Beirut. The Kuwaiti doctors showed a curious X-ray of a woman patient who apparently had two stomachs. After a while they explained that the Bedouin woman hadn't liked the taste of the barium, so she poured it into a goatskin bag she was wearing.

Trouble began in Palestine as the Israelis poured in. *Time* magazine arrived in Kuwait missing the pages that told about the situation there.

In December 1954 we had an unusual eighteen-day rain. The mud houses collapsed—20,000 were ruined. Refugees slept and cooked in the new school buildings, mosques, and hospitals. Cesspits along the streets caved in and smelled bad. I was called out twice on cases of women electrocuted by the 220-volt current. One woman came to the hospital with every hair on her head burned off.

To encourage reconstruction, the city bought up most of the ruined property, paid high sums in compensation or gave new land, and persuaded people to build in the new suburbs. The city brought an English town planner to rebuild the city. Our old rented house was bought by the government for a boulevard, so we moved into a new house. The mission paid for most of it, but it was not quite enough. We made up the difference with money earned in the women's hospital, and my cousin Ramona Anderson gave me a thousand dollars as a gift.

The city brought a Mr. Van Dee from Holland to dredge out Kuwait Bay so ships could come to jetties, but his Dutch methods didn't succeed. Later an American firm, Bechtel, was successful.

The dizzy spiral of rents and costs whirled upward. Madeline's and my salaries were a hundred dollars a month. Food cost us forty-eight dollars a month. We bought a kerosene refrigerator, which helped, but I spent a lot of time down on my knees trying to keep that gummy kerosene burner lit.

The Arabs courteously set about learning some English—with amusing results. When officers from visiting naval ships called, we were invited to receptions for them. Once at the American consulate, a delicious whole fish was served. An officer asked one of the Arab guests, "What kind of a fish is it?" The Arab gave its Arabic name and added, "It's a good one but not the very best."

Shaikh Abdullah used to study an encyclopedia to increase his knowledge. When an English lord came to visit, the ruler observed, "I've been reading about English titles and learned there are five classes of lords. Which one do you belong to?" The lord answered, "The least and the smallest, sir." The shaikh responded congenially, "Yes, I thought so."

All of a sudden there were new roads, streets, districts, suburbs with new names, stop signs, a university, a technical school, hospitals, and an enlarged electric power and water distillation plant. New houses were no longer built with the traditional open courtyard. They had walls, but the house inside the walls was compact and at least two-story. Egyptian architects let their imaginations run wild with fantastic structures in brilliant colors. The new neighborhoods had been well-planned, with schools for boys and for girls, clinics, police stations, shopping areas, water stations for the truckers who delivered to the homes, electricity, telephones, and mosques—some of which were beautiful. The planners set aside areas for industry and for residences. Kuwait City changed so quickly that I began to get lost driving to patients' houses. Landscapers planted trees—mostly a sort of mesquite—which had to be watered frequently by tankers. An experimental garden began to produce flowers. We marveled at a hydroponics experiment which produced eighty tons of tomatoes in one summer.

The Roman Catholic Church persuaded the ruler that since the Protestant Church had land, the Catholics should be granted some, too. So land was ceded and construction began on a very large church to serve the growing Catholic population, which included thousands of Indian Catholics that had come to work in Kuwait. The Church hired an Armenian architect to put on the vast roof. One day I heard a huge crash. The roof had failed.

Fortunately, it had happened on a weekday, because on Sundays they had congregations of 750 people. The Kuwait Oil Company generously offered to put on a reliable roof free of charge.

Our Rev. Garret De Jong invited a group of seventy-five Christian leaders to a meeting in an attempt to form a united Christian Protestant Church. But the group broke up into different sects. Most of them used our mission church chapel for their meetings. To meet the demand for space, the small chapel had been enlarged to twice its original size and a large parish hall had been added, with a kitchen and classrooms.

The sale of alcohol was forbidden in Kuwait, because drinking liquor is forbidden in the Qur'an; according to Sura 2:219, "Intoxicants are a great sin," and Sura 5:90, "Intoxicants are an uncleanness . . . the devil's work; so shun it." However, the British Agency served drinks and many non-Muslims worked in Kuwait, so the government allowed some people to use liquor if they could prove they were Christians. Crowds of Middle Eastern and Indian workers began coming to the mission asking for statements that they were Christians. We had never seen most of these people before, and certainly not in church. Naturally no certificates were given. Mission policy was, no intoxicants served.

In the swirl of cultures, religions, and governments, the mission was inevitably drawn into problems. The wife of a Lebanese worker went back home to Lebanon and married another man by having her friends swear that her first husband was dead. Then she had the nerve to come back to Kuwait with the new husband! The first husband sued the wife in Muslim court and she was imprisoned. The Kuwaiti government finally solved the problem by sending all three back to Lebanon.

The outside world invaded Kuwait's markets. In one memorable incident, some transistor radios appeared inside stuffed dogs. Muslims were scandalized, because local radio programs featured the reading of the Qur'an. The novelty dog radios were promptly removed from shop shelves.

Many of the Kuwaitis suddenly seemed to become very wealthy. I wondered how it was happening, only to discover that Kuwaiti law required any foreign firm coming to do business to have a Kuwaiti silent partner. The silent partner need do no work but must receive 50 percent of the profit. I happened to get acquainted with Sultan Ajeel, a black businessman who was very friendly. I dared to ask him what his business was, and he told me he was a contractor. I asked him if he could send me a carpenter and a mason for some work in the hospital. The next day, he sent one of each and said there would be no bill for their work. Sultan Ajeel turned out to be my Aladdin's genie. As long as I was in Kuwait, he sent me a dozen roses every Christmas.

RAMADAN AND CLINICS, 1954

As usual, Ramadan was a great problem for the hospital. The local helpers felt they ought to have a half day off as the rest of the town did. But the daily work had to go on. At the morning clinics we had to treat gravely sick patients, children, and menstruating women (who do not fast). It was a moot question as to whether an injection broke one's Ramadan fast. Other sick people would only come at night, in order to observe their fast—so we had to run a night clinic, too. During the month of Ramadan in daytime no drinks were served at the new airport and shops were forbidden to sell cooked foods. The young men rebelled against these restrictions. Late in the afternoon, the beach outside the city wall where we went swimming would be lined with cars. The cars would disappear at sunset when the fast ended, leaving the beach littered with empty cans of Dutch beer.

Five days of celebration mark the end of Ramadan. The mission men called on the rulers and other prominent men, while we women made formal calls on the women. Everdene De Jong had become very well acquainted with the women of the royal family and worked out a family tree for them. It had been done for the men by Col. H. R. P. Dickson in his book. Ev showed it to the women of the royal Sabah family and to our surprise, they were very angry and upset about it. They felt that a woman's duty to her family was for her to be unknown to the outside world.

After Ramadan, we were swamped with all the women and children who had saved up their troubles for the past month. Some days, clinics ran up to two hundred patients. I tried to cope but of course it was impossible. The doctor pair had left us for better-paying jobs, and we were hard-pressed to get everything done. Sometimes this led to bad hiring decisions.

A young Iranian claimed he was a graduate of a German medical college whose records had been lost during the war, and Lew Scudder hired him. The man was giving very peculiar doses, so we became suspicious. He had said that he specialized in ophthalmology. I asked him to come over to examine one of my eye cases and handed him a tonometer. From the way he tried to use it, I knew he was no physician and Lew fired him. This fellow did belong to a family of physicians in Iran but had never studied medicine himself.

On December 22, 1954, something a little out of the ordinary happened. Five baby cases came in all at once with toxemia and convulsions. We managed to save them all, but I decided the last one needed a Caesarian section. We had just gotten the mess cleaned up and laid ourselves down to sleep when one of the wives of the oil company men came in with a miscarriage and I had to do a dilation and curettage. Then the same week, just as I was dressed and ready to go to a party at the oil company, three obstetrical cases came in: a breech delivery, twins, and a difficult forceps. I lost one baby. It took until dawn when the roosters began to crow, the donkeys began to bray, and the prayer call rang out.

I felt elated with success when a case of vesicular vaginal fistula healed after a repair. New drugs kept appearing and folic acid tablets cured a spectacular case of sprue.

My cousin Madeline Holmes was asked by the Bahrain mission to take charge of the orphanage there. She consented, as the Board was sending us a new nurse, Miss TeBina Boomgaarden, who lived and worked with me for three years. A new Indian, Dr. Anna Cherian, came to share the work in the women's hospital. New Indian nurses arrived by plane. We all proved to be congenial and the hospital improved.

The Board sent Ruth Young out to live with us and study Arabic. Somehow she couldn't adjust to the culture shock and developed delusions. The secretary had to send her home. It seems impossible to predict which personalities can adjust.

On some house calls, the women would express pity that I had no husband and no children. An Egyptian clerk commented, "We feel sorry for you Christian women. In our religion, we honor women and give them liberty from work so they can stay at home." How impossible it is to understand another culture. I had been feeling sorry for *their* women!

I have been given an optimistic, sanguine temperament, good health, and a dogged persistence. I believe that it is the eternal purpose of the Almighty that what He did in Christ should be proclaimed to all people. I know other people can believe impossible things. To me the evidence is that this is not impossible and that my part in the reconciliation of all things in heaven and on earth is to take some part in telling the story.

I found the study of medicine and Arabic fascinating even though I was a mediocre student. The life of a people so very different from Americans was most interesting. I had a need to be needed. So when I began to treat patients and found that most of the time my care was rewarded, I was thrilled. My understanding of their concerns and cares grew. I came to feel I was a part of them. I cared so much that when it came time to pack up and go home for a furlough, I didn't want to go. Also, I was always very busy.

I understood that there was a great historical gulf between Christianity and Islam, because Islam came six hundred years after Christ to a land which was supposedly Christian. To establish itself it had to make the worship of God a denial of Christ and His crucifixion and put Mohammad in Christ's place. As a result there is a formidable tangle of misconception, alienation, and confusion in both thinking and language. The situation is bedeviled by Western relationships which maintain a conspiracy of silence about our Lord.

When John Van Ess was asked how many converts there were, he answered, "God only knows." Measurements and counting belong to this world. The eternal has other dimensions.

Some have quoted the words Christ used when He sent out His disciples for a short local mission: "Whoever does not receive you . . . shake off the dust of your sandals and depart" (Matt. 10:14). But this cannot apply to whole peoples. The great commission has no such limitations. The people of Arabia have received, welcomed, and listened to the Word. They have given evidence that they want our schools, hospitals, bookshops, and Church to stay with them. The Word must be given in an acceptable form or it cannot grow anywhere. Preaching is unacceptable in Muslim lands, but godly lives speak louder than words. And after all, Christ did not promise success to His followers. He promised a cross.

The lives of some Muslims who became Christians have been written in books. Dr. William McElwee Miller wrote *Ten Muslims Who Became Christians.* Dr. Saeed of Iran is well-known, and Mark Hanna wrote about seven Muslims making their greatest discovery. Paul Harrison wrote of his experiences in a book, *The Arab at Home.* Many humble listeners have told missionaries that they believed in Christ.

I have known a number of converts personally. Isa, the cook at our men's hospital in Kuwait, has been mentioned as a convert. Labeeba Naamen, our nurse from Egypt, is written about above. I met Bishop Hassan Dehqani while visiting in Isfahan. His book *My Life* tells of his Muslim boyhood and how he became a Christian and later an Anglican bishop, against fierce opposition.

Daud Rahbar was a professor of Muslim literature at Ankara University in Turkey. He had earned his doctorate with his thesis, "The God of the Qur'an Is a Just God." At a conference of Christian workers in Jerusalem, Kenneth Cragg asked him to speak. Under Kenneth's sweet influence Daud read the Bible for the first time, believed, and asked for baptism. Kenneth recommended that he wait until his wife and daughters could join him. In Turkey, his entire family found an American chaplain who baptized them all. He resigned his position and took a professorship in America.

A young man came to the Scudders saying he was a Christian who belonged to one of the prominent families in Kuwait. He asked that they not inform the family. He was given a job and room at the men's hospital and came to church. He did well in his work but one time when he had charge of money, both he and the money disappeared.

Some Palestinians working in Kuwait came to Garry De Jong and asked for baptism secretly. Garry refused, explaining that it would have no meaning that way.

At the Bahrain mission hospital, there were many leftover babies, so they started an orphanage. Um Miriam, a poor widow with three children, was hired to take care of these babies as well as her own. She became a Christian, along with her three children—Miriam, Abood, and Joseph Haider. They remained faithful Christians. Their children also decided to be Christians.

The children raised in the orphanage had a difficult childhood. They were not accepted by the community. Some of the boys turned violently against the mission, but many of the others became Christians. Some emigrated to the U.S.A.

There was a tall, muscular Arab who worked at the jetty in Bahrain. He developed leprosy and was treated at the mission, where he became a Christian. He went to work for the Evangelistic Alliance Mission in Abu Dhabi but was very lonely. Arab men have the custom of spending the long evening hours visiting with other men in the men's part of houses. Visitors like this, who spend long hours night after night, were not appreciated by the mission families. Mahmood visited the other mission stations asking them to help him find a wife. Although his leprosy was arrested, his distorted features were too much of an obstacle.

In Muscat and Mutrah, the little community of Christians grew steadily. I joined them in 1971 but didn't get to know them very well. Saeed Nasr had come to the hospital from a village because he had leprosy. He could read, and when he read and understood the Bible, he asked for baptism and has remained a faithful Christian. Khadar es Soon was the leader. Musa, the Baluchi nurse, was a Christian and showed it in his faithful service to the leprous and tubercular patients. On Sundays, he would preach the Good News to them with zeal. But when the hospitals were given to the government, they were given well-paying positions. Most of the men soon ceased to attend church. Was it the deceitfulness of riches that changed their minds?

Lateefa's parents were Christians, but they married her to a Muslim, which divided her loyalties. She continued to help teaching in the mission school. Miriam married a series of Muslim husbands but kept up some connection with the believers. Awash had a Muslim husband. She acquired a good position in the government intelligence department. I heard that she definitely became a Muslim.

After my retirement in California, I heard Bilkis Shaikha speak. She was a wealthy Pakistani woman who after a bitter divorce read the Bible and with the help of missionaries became a Christian. She tried to continue living in her home, but her relatives cast her out. Because of threats to her life, she decided to come to California to live and wrote her book, *I Dared to Call Him Father*.

In the list of Muslims I have known who became Christians, I must include the little group in Aden. On a trip there, I attended the Keith Falconer and Red Sea missions, and the Danish Church. The leader of the local church was a humble man who sold fish. I have not heard from the group since the Communists took Aden and the missionaries had to leave.

When I came home once on a furlough my small niece Cynthia asked, "How do you convert people?" Of course only God's Spirit converts people. I have seen it work in Muslims. Because there are so few converts some missionaries have become discouraged. Even the Church questions whether the work should be continued. Isaiah 55:11 says, "So shall My word be. . . . It shall not return to Me void / But it shall accomplish what I please." In view of the fact that the Western world is so involved in Arabia in business, defense, politics, and education, the religious basis of our society should be represented there too.

The Church might hope that the ancient Christian churches in Arabia would bear witness, but they are so isolated by social barriers and their history of persecution that they have been ineffective. So outsiders are a more powerful witness. Because of centuries of strife and misunderstanding between Christendom and Islam, the job requires great patience and sacrifice. The Muslim feels like St. Thomas, "Unless I see the print of the nails in his hands, I will not believe." (John 20:25). The actual presence of our church is necessary to make Christ visible, intelligible, and desirable. Christian radio cannot do that. So I am not discouraged.

Another question comes up. If those who believe are saved, are the unbelievers lost eternally? My conclusion is that that is something the Lord only knows. All I know is my duty to take some part in proclaiming the Word.

ANOTHER QUESTION OF MISSION: AIR-CONDITIONERS

The Board of Foreign Missions in New York, which was in charge of the Arabian Mission, was composed mostly of senior clergy. Many of them had no idea of the rapid changes occurring in the outside world. Air-conditioners were rapidly being introduced in Kuwait and had become a matter of course. At the general mission session, we recommended that ACs be purchased and installed in our hospitals, nurses' quarters, and homes. As it meant a large expenditure of funds, we asked for Board approval.

They sent us a disapproving letter written by the treasurer, the Rev. Henry Bovenkerk. It provoked me to write a passionate reply. From a copy of my letter, I can infer the questions the Board had raised.

They seem to have asserted that we were making missions so expensive that we were pricing ourselves out of the market. Other missions in other countries nearer the Equator than we would be entitled to have ACs also. Being a missionary meant that we voluntarily assumed suffering and we ought to get on with it; we were asking for luxuries when we should be living like the natives. The Board also asked what percentage of the local people had ACs and would the ACs be used for remedial or preventive purposes.

I wrote a four-page, typewritten, furious reply. Our hospitals were earning enough income to pay for the ACs. The government of Kuwait was giving us electric power free. Several missionaries had ACs in their homes as gifts. Kuwait's weather was hotter and the heat lasted longer than in other mission fields. India had a cool, wet monsoon in its summer. There were many graves of British officers who died here of heat stroke. Our medical work was hardest and lasted longer hours in the hot summer, with temperatures around 115 daily for three months. We had to do a great deal of desk work—accounts, reports, and letters—with no secretary as the Board members have. Our night nurses couldn't sleep in the day because of the extreme heat. We wanted to live like the natives, who now were demanding ACs at home, business, and hospitals. Asking what percentage of Arabs had ACs was an impossible question. There were no such records. To try and decide whether a patient needed an AC as remedial or preventive was impossible. To say that missionaries should suffer was not Christian.

I ended by saying that if our church couldn't support the mission in this changing world, why didn't we ask another church to join us and make it a united mission.

Well, we got the ACs.

Some years later back in New York, I asked about Heinie Bovenkerk, the Board's treasurer who had written that letter. He had changed, too. His house in New Jersey was completely air-conditioned.

MISSION 1955 – 1956

The November 1955 medical report lists the staff of the women's hospital as consisting of: Dr. Anna Cherian; six Indian Christian nurses; three untrained girls (Farida, the daughter of Yacoob the Assyrian colporteur; Kulwanth, a Sikh; and Wadda Rizk, an Armenian); thirteen local women helpers; and one night watchman. The hired doctors were now getting higher salaries than we earned as missionaries, but we could afford to pay them from hospital income and were very grateful for their help.

In 1956, the Scudders and I decided to merge our two hospitals. Dorothy, an efficient manager, took over the management, finances, and accounting for drugs, which relieved me greatly. She was a perfectionist, though, which could be irritating to me because I was a pragmatist and was satisfied if the place just ran.

I had tried to keep the women's hospital a *hareem* (forbidden to men), but men persisted in invading the place to wait for their wives or to call on relatives. They would sit on the benches reserved for the women. I resorted to calling the men imperialists (*istamaroon*) who took what belonged to others. Their only reaction was amusement.

In 1956, we acquired an ambulance and started a medical library.

At the great religious holiday, many animals are sacrificed and the meat given away. I would always receive some, too, but there was just too much meat to be used. In the fierce, hot weather, much spoiled and the surfeiting people crowded the hospital. I was calling at one wealthy house where they had sacrificed forty sheep. The women asked me why this sacrifice took place. It gave me a good opportunity to tell the story of Christ, the one perfect sacrifice for sin.

There was a certain monotony to my life. Day after day the same crowds, same diseases, same miseries, the same personal discomforts, the constant sweat, the constant struggle to make myself understood in a foreign language, and the sense of guilt I got so often when I left the hospital and joined parties at the oil company.

THE BOARD REASSESSES THE MISSIONS

While I had been on furlough in 1957–1958, the Board for
the Christian World Mission of the Reformed Church of America appointed a medical survey team to make an extensive study
of the Arabian Mission's medical work. First, a study committee
was formed of staff, doctors, and nurses in New York to go over
all the mission data, minutes, and reports. The committee then
wrote a paper for the survey team, which went out to the field to
examine the local situation. The survey team presented a very
complete report of its observations in the Gulf.

The Arabian Mission's seven hospitals employed more than
half of all mission personnel. There were four principal centers
for this work: a general hospital in Amara, Iraq; the men's and
women's hospitals in Kuwait; men's and women's hospitals in
Bahrain; and in Oman, one hospital in the city of Muscat and
another in Mutrah.

The survey team studied the proper role of the medical work,
its evangelistic effectiveness, efficiency, staffing, financial condition, building and equipment needs, and service. The paper bore
witness to the complexity of our task in the face of the sweeping
changes that were taking place due to the development of oil resources in the region.

The report stated that the hospitals produced definite evangelistic results, both directly and indirectly. But the constant shortage of people and money was responsible for our failure to take
advantage of those doors that were open to us. The Arab governments had begun to establish welfare states and provide medical
facilities for their own people. Yet the mission hospitals still had
a role to play in the face of the overwhelming need, personnel
and material shortage, and lack of motivation to serve which so
often caused the official government programs to fail.

The team recommended that each hospital establish a local
board of managers, drawn partly from the mission and partly
from the community. It was hoped that this arrangement would
draw the whole community into some understanding of and responsibility for the hospitals, so that the local community would
assume some authority over them. The survey team advised the
hospitals in each area to consolidate, to make one waiting room
for both sexes, to improve the record system and statistical re-

porting, and train substitutes for vacationing or off-duty staff. Any surplus income should go to the Field Income Account and be used for the entire mission. A pension system should be set up for hospital employees. A few more air-conditioners needed to be installed. Much more good advice was included.

Amara hospital in Iraq had forty-two beds, two doctors, and no nurses. It served an area of very poor people, 75 percent of whom paid little or nothing. It was recommended that a nurses' training school be started there. This hospital served the Marsh Arabs, who are a distinctly separate group. A motor launch was required to reach them and was recommended.

In Kuwait, the Mylrea Memorial Hospital had an excellent new building with fifty beds and two doctors. The Olcott Memorial Hospital had one American doctor and two Indian women doctors. The staff had an evangelist, Indian nurses, an X-ray technician, laboratory technician, pharmacist, business manager, maintenance man, storekeeper, clerical helpers, but no housekeepers. Staff quarters were insufficient. Here, the survey team recommended that the medical staff try to maintain closer relations with the local Arab Christian community.

The Bahrain station had a shabby men's hospital (fifty years old) and a fairly good women's hospital with forty beds; two mission doctors and two Indian doctors with Indian nurses were on the staff. The only bedside care provided was simple family nursing. Many patients came from Saudi Arabia, Oman, Iran, and Dubai. Plans should be drawn up for a new men's hospital and a clinic building. Since the municipality had been generous in the past, it was hoped that they would contribute to the new building. A nurses' training program should be started.

In Oman, the twin seaside cities of Muscat and Mutrah were three miles apart. Our two hospitals there served a population of at least half a million extremely poor people. Except for some small clinics in the mountain villages, the mission hospitals took care of all the sick, injured, emergency, surgery, blind, tubercular, and endemic malarial patients. The twenty-two-bed Muscat hospital took care of mostly maternity cases, with a nurse midwife but no doctor. The general hospital in Mutrah had fifty beds, another building for tuberculosis patients with nine beds, and a building for leprosy patients with fourteen beds. But none of these hospitals refused patients. When there weren't enough beds, patients were put on the floor, in the courtyard, or their families put up tents for them. Mutrah had two mission doctors and one Indian doctor. There was no business manager. The staff collected whatever was paid. There were no qualified nurses, only local men who had been taught to do certain procedures.

The team suggested that the Oman hospitals acquire more staff, omit the tours into the mountain villages, train more practical nurses, limit visiting hours, start a kitchen to provide food for part of the patients, and provide bed linen and gowns, at least for the surgical and maternity cases. The hospital sorely needed a refrigerator and a washing machine. All this was necessary, it was true, but the mission did not have more personnel to send. The sultan refused permission to bring in more trained Indian staff.

APPLYING THE BOARD'S SUGGESTIONS

On returning to Kuwait in October 1958, I found the hospital running very well. By this time there were two Indian women doctors, two mission nurses, an Indian nurse supervisor, and a thirty-two-person staff including ten Indian nurses, sixteen local women, and six men helpers. When the Scudders arrived we consolidated the accounting and management duties (under Dorothy Scudder) and began to furnish food for some of the patients. The income was good and I had helpers to keep records and accounts, collect bills, and schedule nurses. We needed more office space and fortunately had a large veranda in the front which we converted into more offices.

We followed the survey team's advice and formed a hospital board. The board had plenty of work trying to make up wage scales for the hospital staff with regular raises and pensions, and comply with all the rules. Our great problem was the lack of Arabic-speaking trained staff. The government brought trained nurses from Lebanon and Egypt but paid them higher salaries than we could afford. It would not work, either, to have two levels of pay for the same qualifications.

A whole assortment of problems remained to be solved. We didn't follow the Board's suggestion about combining the men's and women's waiting rooms, but we did want to deal with the problem of men coming into the women's hospital at any time. I visited a government clinic once and noted that they had a man with a gun squatting at the door of the women's clinic to keep men out, so we considered that approach. The hospital needed complete new electric wiring, new plumbing, and for the first time, we had hot running water. Then there was the problem of the staff's personal needs. We had to rent rooms in the neighborhood for the married staff. Dr. Lilly delivered her first baby, so we gave her a month off.

Although one nurse was transferred to Oman and Dr. Lilly had a month off, we managed. With more assistance the situation wasn't so desperate. The clinics became less of a strain, and we divided the night work more equitably.

It was hard for me to come back to earth after my hiatus. My mind was full of world traveling, meeting people, speechmaking, and refresher medical courses, which weren't much help in our kinds of emergencies.

And emergencies did pop up suddenly. In one week, we had more than our share. There was a case of ruptured ectopic pregnancy. In this condition, the fetus grows in the tube instead of the uterus. The pregnancy often ruptures and starts to bleed internally. Next was a ruptured tubal abscess with peritonitis. Then the next night was a case of intussusception, in which the bowel invaginates itself. If these cases are caught early, the bowel can be pulled out and straightened. This one was caught too late, so the bowel was gangrenous and had to be excised. It needs a special stitch to suture the ends together. I knew that stitch once upon a time, but my brain holds only so much. But when duty said I must, I did the best I could. To my intense relief, the patient survived.

Another woman was in labor at 5 A.M. when suddenly her uterus ruptured and she went into profound shock. Desperately, I called for Dr. Al Pennings to come and help. We had to do something quick. There was no time to sterilize instruments. A nurse got them out for us, we dipped them in a bowl of lysol, opened the abdomen, and found the fetus, placenta, and ruptured uterus in a pool of blood. I decided to excise the whole lot and tried to collect her blood to transfuse it back. She lived until noon.

Shaikha Bederea, wife of Shaikh Fehed, was due to have another baby. The ladies of the oil company held a shower for her and gave her a gaily decorated crib. (She never would put the baby in it, feeling it had some evil influence.) Bederea insisted that I come to her home for the birth. So Nurse Bhagyamma and

I spent two days and a night with her and finally delivered her in the old-fashioned way—with all of us on the floor. Thus Huda, her last baby, arrived. Shaikh Fehed gave me a beautiful blue Pontiac car in gratitude. At that time, he was quite prosperous and was building a new palace in Salimeya suburb that had a wall of Italian marble and a large stained glass window with a scene of a diver under the sea.

Life didn't stay monotonous for long. In came a little boy carried by his father. He had stepped on a broken Pepsi bottle and cut his foot so deeply that the tendons were severed. I remembered one lesson from way back of how to suture tendons together but hadn't ever used it. Al Pennings came over and gave him some ether, using a cardboard cone covered with gauze and dropping the ether on it. I did find the tendons and hoped I got the right ones together. I put the foot in plaster. I could hardly believe it; it healed.

I was called to the top floor of one of the new apartment buildings to find a young girl almost exsanguinated from a miscarriage. The men carried her out keeping her head low. When we reached the very small elevator, I stood her on her head. We got her to the car and drove her to the hospital for the D and C which fortunately saved her life.

IRAQ'S THREAT; KUWAIT'S GROWTH

Great changes were taking place in Kuwait. By December 1958, the city walls were demolished by bulldozers. Their destruction had been fiercely opposed by one of the shaikhs, until he died of cancer. The walls were only sundried adobe, so they could probably have been breached by water-pistols at any time. But to honor the walls' historic significance, the three grand city gates were restored and made the center of traffic circles.

Another of the shaikhs consulted physicians in London and was advised to have a colostomy. He disdainfully rejected this procedure, considering it would make him unclean. He consulted a doctor in Lebanon who treated him and assured him he was cured. But he died later from the cancer.

There was great unrest in Iraq, Kuwait's neighbor to the north. The Suez crisis in 1956 had upset the whole Middle East. In Iraq, the people were poor and starving. Rich landowners controlled water distribution and taxes were high. People blamed

England and America for their wretchedness. Hordes of refugees swarmed to the two main cities of Baghdad and Basrah to eke out an existence in dirty shanty towns. So there was a revolution there in the summer of 1958. The young King Faisal, the royal family, and many able leaders were brutally killed. General Abdul Karim Kassem came to power with the help of Communists. We listened to BBC radio news and got some information from our mission in Iraq. We heard that life was unsafe; there was no personal security and everyone was under suspicion. An electrician who had been rewiring the small Christian church in Basrah was arrested and publicly hanged with twelve others. People who were able to fled to Kuwait to stay with relatives.

In June 1961, Kuwait state was given sovereignty and full independence by Great Britain, its former protector. In July, Kassem claimed Kuwait as part of Iraq and prepared to invade. Kuwait had a very small army, as the Arabs did not care much for military service. Much of the Kuwaiti force consisted of Iraqis. Kuwait appealed to England for help, and the British airlifted thousands of men to Kuwait from Kenya in three days. They immediately began digging trenches along the border in the 110–120 degree heat. Some of the British soldiers came to Kuwait and called on us. We were glad to give them hospitality, help them to cool off, and give them a bath. In the end the Iraqi threat fizzled out without a fight.

Relations between Kuwait and Iraq were never without suspicion. That is why Kuwait never dug a canal to bring Iraq's abundant water to the desert town: she never could trust her neighbor. Kuwait kept relations stable by frequently giving Iraq large loans of money. Kassem eventually was deposed. We heard he was executed on February 8, 1963. Col. Abdul Salam 'Arif replaced him.

With all the political changes, our mission in Iraq suffered, too. A union of several churches had taken responsibility for most of the missions in Iraq. The girls' high school in Baghdad was closed by the new government, and our hospital and compound in Amara were ordered to be closed. A soldier was posted at the hospital gate to prevent patients from entering. Dr. and Mrs. Heusinkveld and Dr. and Mrs. Nykerk were ordered to leave but allowed a few days to take out hospital and home furnishings.

Later, the government set a day in court to decide how much they would pay for the valuable Amara property. Basrah Mission sent a lawyer to Amara on that day to represent its interests. The lawyer was stopped along the way and held by police so he could not be present. The court decided that since the case was not contested the government should pay only a trivial, token amount. Within the next year our two schools in Basrah were also closed. The missionaries were allowed to take out only their personal possessions.

Kuwait's Shaikh Abdullah Mubarak set himself up to be the strongman of the Gulf. He built a grand palace on a small desert hill south of Kuwait, with a wall that enclosed an area about the size of a city block. The palace boasted an impressive gate, guards, and an avenue of trees leading up to the door. Mubarak invited 250 guests, mostly expatriates, for dinner and a tour of the long, high-ceilinged halls and reception room (furnished by an English firm). A cinema had walls of rose satin tapestry with pillars entwined with gold rose branches. We all sat down on gold chairs at one long table and dined on roast lamb and rice with all the appropriate table settings. Of course, no Arab woman graced the meal. I visited his wife, who was a simple, retiring young woman. The Shaikh had dismissed his Bedouin wife and gave her little girl to the resident wife.

The British Agency gave a lovely garden party to celebrate the Queen's birthday and invited all the foreign community as well as Arabs. Col. De Gaury was the agent, which amounted to being Britain's ambassador to Kuwait. He was not married and specialized in interests that were a scandal to the Arabs.

The American consulate was given land by the sea on the east side of Kuwait. The American diplomatic staff consisted of two consuls and two vice consuls. Some of them were very friendly and attended our church. Bill Brewer married Alice Van Ess, daughter of the missionaries in Basrah. Jim Akins and Bill Stolzfus later advanced to full ambassadorships in Arabia. They were very able men and not fully appreciated by our State Department.

Sometimes when I was out on medical or social calls, the wives of the wealthy Kuwaiti men showed me the modern furnishings of their new homes. One of them had a complete Christian Dior wardrobe which her husband had bought. The wives of the shaikhs had gorgeous jewelry. One had a complete set encrusted with about a thousand diamonds. Another wife had an emerald set which I had seen priced at $60,000.00.

Every year in June a northwest wind blew for forty days. The heat was more bearable, but the wind brought dust storms which lasted for days. We could hardly see the buildings next door. It was impossible to keep the hospital and houses clean. Once, out in the desert, we watched a dust storm approach on the horizon like a tidal wave rolling toward us.

The city allowed us to use piped water from the new distillation plant, so I decided to make a garden and planted some trees and daisies. Some agriculturalists studied the soil of Kuwait and said it completely lacked any organic material. So I cast about in my mind as to where I could get some. We had two or three placentas to dispose of every day, so I told my houseboy to make a trench and bury them in my garden. That fertilizer was very effective. The daisies grew over my head.

But then came a cloud of locusts. When they came in late afternoon they settled down for the night. We could hear them munching away as they ate every green thing but never touched the oleanders. How did their tiny brains know they were poison? The Bedouin, as well as John the Baptist, welcomed locusts for food. They brought some into the hospital boiled and showed me how to remove the legs, wings, and head. The rest was an egg case which tasted a bit like caviar.

The Qabazards were a Persian family, immigrants to Kuwait. There were six brothers who might have become laborers in poor days, as the Arabs despised those kind of people. But they had ability and ambition, so with the new wealth, they advanced in business. Mohammad was especially astute. He opened a marine equipment shop, was appointed harbormaster of Kuwait, and became a member of the new parliament. He went back to Shiraz to marry a beautiful and gracious wife, Mumtaz. They had five sons and a daughter, all of whom were my patients at various times.

Mohammad and Mumtaz were very friendly. Once they invited us to bring our staff of thirty to a party in their new house and garden. He told us he had three tankers of sweet water brought every day to keep it green. After a lavish Persian dinner, where the table groaned with the delicious spread of all kinds of food,

Mohammad showed us his color movie of their trip around the world in ninety days. It took four hours, but it was worth it. It started with Europe and risqué night club scenes in Paris. He told us how he called on the harbormaster of New York, who took him for a helicopter ride over the harbor and around the Statue of Liberty, shown in his pictures. Then he drove up Fifth Avenue. He was fascinated by the sight of women's faces, which were never seen in his country. So on the film we watched the girls walking down the street, suddenly noticing that they were being photographed, and looking embarrassed. Mumtaz's face was nowhere to be seen. It would have shocked the Kuwaiti men to see it. The show went on and chronicled their trip across the U.S.A. and Japan, Hong Kong, Australia, India, and Pakistan. They were very good pictures. He must have had a good camera, and he knew how to use it.

Colonel Dickson had lived most of his life in the Middle East as a Political Agent of the British government. He had lived in Kuwait for years. He was required to retire at 55, so the oil company employed him as a liaison officer between them and the ruler. He spoke Arabic like a native. He and Violet, his wife, were very hospitable, so we were frequent guests, and they always attended church. He would frequently read from the two books he was writing when we came for tea. He was picturesque, a typical English colonial character and a fascinating storyteller. We suspected he embroidered the tales to make them more thrilling. He had been failing with circulatory problems and died on June 13, 1959, a great loss to Kuwait. Vi asked the government if she could continue living in the seafront house, so she continues there to this day—a grand old dame of the British Empire.

Shaikh Fehed, the black half brother of the ruler, was in charge of the Public Works Department. He thought he had the right to demand any amount of money for his department at any time, so he ran into trouble with the Treasury. Feelings ran high but things were working themselves out. So he and Bederea went off in the yacht to cool off and visit Bahrain and Saudi Arabia. While resting after lunch, he suddenly died. Bederea had his body flown back to Kuwait. He was buried in a barren cemetery beside what is now the new Meridian Hotel. Shaikh Fehed Street was named in his honor.

Mohammad Qabazard told me that the parliament recommended by the British didn't last very long and was given up because of the disgraceful infighting it seemed to encourage. Kuwait went back to traditional Arab government by a ruler or amir and his ministers.

A NEW VIEW OF ISLAM

In July 1959, I had the privilege to study religion in Jerusalem under the auspices of the Middle East Christian Council. It was a thrilling month and Jerusalem was cool, at 3,400 feet elevation. About fifty scholars and missionaries assembled from Europe, India, Pakistan, and the Middle East. Many of us were lodged at St. George's Close, adjoining the Anglican cathedral, where we had pleasant rooms around a sunny, flowered courtyard.

Our outstanding lecturer was Canon Kenneth Cragg. He was a tall, slim, blond Englishman with a courteous humble attitude who took extreme care to be very precise and correct in his speech. To know him was to love him. He had been the Anglican chaplain at the Jerusalem cathedral from 1939 to 1947 and lectured in philosophy at the American University in Beirut. He took his Doctorate in Philosophy at Oxford, then devoted his proficiency to profound study of Arabic and Islam. Dr. Cragg wrote many books on the subject, the most famous being *The Call of the Minaret*. Later he was appointed Bishop of the Anglican cathedral in Cairo, Egypt.

Cragg's revolutionary approach to Islam was that it rejects Christ for God's sake. Islam has sincere, deep convictions about Allah as the sole and only God, repudiating Christ as God in order that God may be magnified. Granting that anything that finite man can say about an infinite god must be a paradox, Kenneth wrestled with the key terms of Islam, as: Allah, the One God; *rasool*, the Messenger of God; *shirk*, the greatest sin in Islam; worshiping anything except the One God; seeking forgiveness; and many other topics. He plumbed the depths of meaning and feeling in Islam and then interpreted these concepts in the light of our Christian faith, bringing out new meanings in both faiths. Dr. Cragg showed us that the greatness of the Trinity is brought out in God's love. The greatness of God is that there is no one like Him.

I had to concentrate to follow Kenneth's ideas as I had no training in philosophy, but my faith was stirred to the depths and illuminated by his analysis of the profundity of the Christian-Muslim encounter.

Every day, Professor Burton Thurston lectured on the awesome meanings of the great key words of Christianity—Son of man, Son of God, and Word of God.

Dr. Daud Rahbar, professor of Muslim literature at Ankara University, came and talked with us for a day. He had won his doctorate in England on his thesis, "The God of the Qur'an is a Just God," and had published it as a book. He had been an ardent Muslim. Under Kenneth Cragg's hospitable influence at a previous course, Daud read the Gospels for the first time. He became a Christian in the space of one night. It was awesome to listen to him tell how his loyalty swerved as he felt the violent animosity of Islam. We gasped at his courage. Later, he decided he could not continue in his position in the Muslim world and emigrated to the U.S.A. with his family.

We also studied with Katharine Kenyon, who talked to us about her excavations and archaeology in Jericho and Jerusalem; Dr. W. A. Bijlefeld of the University of Utrecht, who lectured on European Islamic studies; and Mrs. Vester, who told us some of the history of her family, which had lived in Jerusalem for a generation. Her father wrote the hymn "It Is Well with My Soul" after most of his family died on the ship coming over.

In 1959 Jerusalem was a divided city, with a wide, barren area of no-man's land where gunners kept a fatal eye for anyone trying to cross without permission. Nonetheless, in the afternoons, we walked around Arab Jerusalem and took pictures. We bought tennis shoes and flashlights to walk through Hezekiah's tunnel. The water was not deeper than our knees. It took about a half hour to transverse it. We marveled at the engineering feat of cutting a tunnel through rock in 700 B.C. The tunnel had been forgotten and unknown for centuries until some Arab boys discovered it, with the ancient inscription by Hezekiah.

Of course I patronized the library and bookshop. I was introduced to the book *The City of Wrong*, by Kamel Hussein. Hussein, an Egyptian, wrote a story of the events leading up to the crucifixion. Being a Muslim, he stopped short of the Christian outcome, as the crucifixion is denied in the Qur'an. Of course, Hussein wrote in Arabic, but Kenneth Cragg translated his interesting work into English. So I bought both the Arabic and English versions. How can a mind come so close to the event and reject it?

One afternoon, we went for a picnic at the Dead Sea, stopping at the Good Samaritan Inn and swimming in the salty Dead Sea at evening.

Sunday afternoon, Kenneth led us on a devotional walk from Bethany to the Mount of Olives. Another Sunday evening, he led us on a walk from Gethsemane, where we read over the story of Christ's passion and crucifixion under the ancient olive trees. We meditated there in the moonlight. Then we walked across Kidron Valley and up into the old city to Saint Mark's Church.

This was the apex of all my vacations, and I remember every part of it clearly, with thanks to Kenneth Cragg.

9. Changes in the Mission Field, 1958

BACK TO THE MISSION

Our new house had three bedrooms with baths and generous downstairs common rooms. There were usually two or three people living with me. We had a cook, Francis, from Goa, India, which was settled by the Portuguese, who converted the people to Roman Catholicism. He occupied one of the rooms behind the house. The other back rooms were a kitchen and a room for the houseboy. The houseboy, Abdulla, came from the southern coast of Arabia. I offered Francis a larger salary if he would do the housework, too, but he disdainfully refused, saying he could not possibly do the work of a sweeper. Then, suddenly, he declared he had to go back to Bombay. When I pointed out that his contract was not yet fulfilled, he told me quite a tale. Some Indian woman servant in the neighborhood had come and visited him in his room, and as a result she became pregnant. He was delighted and informed me that he had to go back and ask his sons for permission to marry her. So he left me, but the marriage did not go through. When she met his sons, she changed her mind. I tried to make do with Abdulla, but he didn't know how to shop or cook, and I had to get up early every morning to get him out of bed and start making our breakfast.

The government gave us a window air-conditioner for downstairs, and the Kew Gardens Church on Long Island, New York gave me one for my bedroom. Gradually we each had one in our bedrooms, so living was quite comfortable.

Daisy Hoogeveen, who came out to teach school, lived with me while in evangelistic work. Everything she did was done strenuously. She had furious dates with some of the young Arab men. This led to criticism and Daisy left the mission. Alice from Bahrain lived with me. As she was a native Christian from Bahrain, she was making tapes for the Christian radio broadcasts from Beirut. The young Arab men called her a running dog for the West.

In October 1959, we had a full mission meeting in Bahrain with the Kuwait, Bahrain, and Oman stations. The Iraq stations had formed a united mission of Iraq but were prevented from coming by government troubles. The Muscat plane was delayed by engine trouble. So we settled down to a long session. It was fun to get together, but the humidity in the low-lying islands made us itch and feel that everything was too much work. The drinking water from the artesian wells tasted like dilute magnesium sulfate.

There was a lot of tedious business, especially for the accounting committee. All accounts had to be gone over twice for accuracy and suitability, counting receipts in pounds, rupees, and dinars. It was perfected frustration, a gruesome tangle of new labor laws, legal and political involvements, strikes and pressure from employees, not to mention moral obligation. Who should pay pensions for household servants? How should the car fund be replenished? What is a fluorescent table bought for eleven rupees? You mayn't transfer funds from one special account to another! If you have to borrow some funds, don't let it show! We on the accounting committee went around in a dizzy fog for three full days of sessions, three times a day.

Each department of each station read its written annual report aloud. Some curious statements came up. Wells Thoms expressed gratitude for the American nurses. "I always liked nurses, but I never had any before to like." Muscat hospitals gave a hundred blood transfusions, but all the blood came from expatriates. The Bahrain hospital described some staff travel as unberthed, and gave poor food to the sick. Parents whose kids went to the school in Kodaikanal, India, were asked to send golf balls, as they cost too much in India due to customs. We heard that Dr. Sarah Hosmon, an independent missionary, neglected to ask official permission to go to a village. She was arrested and put in a men's prison for three days. Nothing stopped her. She had an amputated leg but got around everywhere she wanted. Dr. Heusinkveld was seen entering a hareem. Scandalized neighbors were heard to remark, "Never mind—he's not a man, he's a doctor." We sent out a desperate appeal for new career missionaries with the descriptive prayer made for the Jackson sisters "as self-sacrificing people."

The home office sent out a couple of speakers who underscored the gap in thinking between missionaries in the field and the Board and the churches in the States. They seemed to want us to exercise triage over our clinic patients: have better patients and not so many of them. We wondered whether the Board read our reports. It seemed that the policy makers in the U.S.A. didn't want to do anything and just hoped that the local governments would put us out of business. Their theme seemed to be, "Missionaries of the world unite, you have nothing to lose but your hospitals."

We *had* made some visible progress in Bahrain. The people of Bahrain and other friends contributed enough money to rebuild most of the Bahrain hospital. The Board sent out a young builder to take charge. A Palestinian family living in Bahrain accepted the position of living with and supervising the mission orphanage of twelve children. We had high hopes that that would solve the difficult situation. A couple of years later, we found it did not work. The orphanage was a continuing problem. Some of the girls married and were divorced and came back to the orphanage with more homeless orphans. (It is customary for a divorced woman to return to her father's house.) Some of the boys emigrated to the U.S.A. Others, trying to live where they were despised bastards, turned viciously against the mission.

The increase in the number of outsiders living in Kuwait created a dilemma for our mission. Many of the emigrees were of the Christian minority groups in the Middle East. Their spiritual lives were at a low ebb, and they pursued a deliberate policy of not witnessing to the Muslims, whom they considered beyond redemption.

The supreme and controlling aim of the mission was to make the Lord Jesus Christ known to the people of Arabia as the divine savior. Our primary goal was to evangelize the Muslim people of the area and persuade them to become Christians.

But what place should local congregations take in witnessing to the Muslim? Should we concentrate considerable resources on those congregations, encouraging spiritual rebirth so that they in turn might proclaim the evangel to the Muslim? Could we give financial assistance in the initial stages without impairing their self-reliance? Or should the mission concentrate on direct evangelism among Muslims, hoping that a convert church would bring new life to the older congregations and break through their self-centered defensive complexes?

For a practicing Christian living in an official Muslim culture, there was always the strain of deep underlying opposition to our presence. We encountered particular resistance to carrying on any prominent work with a missionary intention. One tactless word could bring down ferociously adverse official pressure that could mean expulsion not only of myself but also of the entire mission. So it was easier to keep silent and hope that the effect of our lives and work would do the job. This did not seem successful in the short run, but the eventual result would be in the hands of God and depended on our faith. Of course, we had to admit that we certainly weren't perfect.

One young Lebanese evangelist came to Kuwait on his own, bravely walking around the shops and selling Bibles. He was arrested and threatened with prison if he didn't leave on the next plane. I heard about him and drove down and picked him up to give him a place to stay the night. He was ashen and so stiff with fear that he could hardly talk. I wondered if the authorities would so terrorize a person if they did not fear his message.

Under the guidance of the Rev. Garrett and Everdene De Jong, the church grew with all these expatriate Christians. Young men taught the Sunday School classes. The hospital ambulance made two trips every Sunday to collect the children. The Christmas programs drew large crowds, women held a monthly prayer meeting, a committee called on others, and a Christian library of English and Arabic books was built up. Rev. and Mrs. MacNeill joined our staff and tried the experiment of living off the compound. They rented an apartment in a new housing district with the idea of forming a church in their home. The various congregations broke up as their numbers increased. They found it difficult to form a united Christian church.

When Jesus' seventy disciples returned after their mission, the writer gave a scanty report of what they did. I should be equally modest. But for the record of what so many contributed, I am setting it down.

By January 1960, the men's and women's hospitals were combined. Mrs. Dorothy Scudder and Haider (mentioned above) carried the main management load with 130 employees. The government had made new laws about employees, so we had many midnight sessions to solve the problems of assigning salaries by classification, hours of work, vacations, housing of foreign workers, separation benefits, travel, and sick leave for local, Indian, and other Middle East personnel. We really needed international business experts, because if anything could go wrong, it did. The more modern men's hospital now had a kitchen and furnished meals for all inpatients. It also boasted a laboratory, X-ray, central supply, drug storeroom, laundry with modern machinery, sterilizing equipment, and two well-equipped operating rooms with an anesthesia machine. We were making a profit financially, but the mission decided the excess money must go to support medical work in Bahrain and Oman, where they couldn't meet expenses. This was a little unfair, as our expensive equipment was always wearing out. All employees and their families, including ex-employees, were treated free, and we did a lot of charity work. The usual clinic charge to see the doctor and get treatment was about two dollars.

The women's work leaned heavily on south Indian Christian trained help. We had two Indian lady doctors, ten Indian nurses who were also midwives, and sixteen local women, which included Sikhs, Lebanese, Syrian, and various other nationalities. Sitt Sara of the ancient Chaldean church of northern Iraq made a good Bible woman, so she received a small salary. There were six men cleaners who also carried meal trays, and one man clerk. Both hospitals ran clinics twice a day, six days a week, and cared for emergencies at all hours. We had many guests who came to see the hospital and foreign visitors who stayed at our homes.

In one month I had three white maternity cases, an American, a German, and an English lady. The last of these had waited seven years for this baby, so it was highly valued, and when the delivery did not progress, we decided on a Caesarian section. To my consternation, the baby had a harelip and complete cleft palate. The mother was inconsolable, but I assured her they could do a successful operation to repair it. Hilda Staal came from Basrah to deliver her sixth child, a healthy boy. She decided six was enough, so the next day I tied off her tubes.

A brother brought his sister to me. She was a high school girl, about fifteen, with an air of quiet despair. The brother told me she was pregnant and offered to pay anything to relieve her, as he was certain the other brothers would kill her. I asked why she couldn't marry the man. The brother said that was impossible, as he didn't belong to the family and they would never accept him. "Couldn't the girl visit someone out of Kuwait?" I asked. "No," he shook his head. "My sister has never been out of Kuwait and we have no such relatives."

I offered to help with the delivery and keep it secret, but he shook his head and they departed. I never heard what happened and felt deep regret and some guilt for not helping.

FRESH RECRUITS

Some Dutch missionaries returning from Indonesia visited us, telling of the marvelous changes there—of Muslim converts forming Christian churches. Our church couldn't seem to find the new personnel we were needing in Arabia, so we considered recruiting from the Netherlands. The summer of 1961 saw me flying off to Holland.

First, I stopped in Geneva to call at the offices of the World Church Council to ask whether they could help. They couldn't, but I toured Geneva and saw the church where John Calvin preached. At a meeting, some black ministers from South Africa told their story.

My mother joined me in Holland. We found the Van Dees, who had worked in Kuwait. They helped us find a pleasant summer hotel and took us for drives on the dykes.

I found ways of getting around on the local trains and called at the office of the general secretary for missions of the Reformed Church. He had been a missionary in Indonesia and was very helpful. He gave me the names of several women doctors, one of them his young niece, Dorothea Van der Horst.

The first contact I made was with an Indonesian girl. She had emigrated to Holland when the Dutch surrendered Indonesia, intending to practice medicine in a Christian atmosphere. She was quite unhappy about her choice. She explained the Dutch people did not accept her socially, and she was lonely. She did not think she was well enough to try a career in Kuwait.

I met with Dorothea Van der Horst and talked over our offer of work in Kuwait. She had just finished her training and was searching for a post. She seemed the right person and wanted to work in a mission, so I was very happy. After thinking it over she agreed to arrive in Kuwait in January of 1962.

I had a dream of building up a hostel home for girls in Kuwait; something like a YWCA where girls could be independent, work in our hospital, and live in a Christian atmosphere. I had read of a deaconess home in Germany and thought I'd like to observe how it worked. I wrote to ask if I could come and was invited. I had to figure out trains to the small village of Bielefeld and arrive at evening. Sister Lily Scholten met me and gave me a room. She had been educated in England, so we could converse easily.

The next day, she escorted me through the building and hospital and introduced me to some of the English-speaking administration staff. They welcomed me cordially because, they said, since the war they had few guests—perhaps because Germany was so despised. They said that during the war they actually knew almost nothing of what the government was doing. The hospital was especially for retarded and mentally defective children. They seemed to be loved and cared for. The doctor showed me how one hydrocephalic child with an enormous head responded to attention. He told me that during the war the government had ordered them to turn over all such children. They refused, running into some danger.

At noon, I sat with the eighty sisters in the refectory. They wore dark blue dresses and white caps and ate in silence. One of them read the daily news aloud and then read from a book. When I was about to go to bed, a dozen of the young sisters came to my door and sang lovely German songs. They were very sweet. The next day I took the train to Oberamergau to see the Passion Play and then flew back to Kuwait.

Dr. Dorothea Van der Horst arrived in Kuwait in January 1962 on a local contract, to live with me. We sat in the clinic where I tried to teach her Arabic but soon found myself picking up her accent and saying, "How do zay shink we can live sheep here?" She was not as ready to accept my ways as the Indian doctors were. I found that the Dutch attitude to politics, Communism, religion, and medicine differed from ours. It even seemed that the Dutch had invented obstetrics.

In 1961, I had the opportunity to read the report of Saba

George Shiber, Ph.D., a town planner employed to study Kuwait. He had the opportunity to see Kuwait from a different point of view than I. He said that old and new Kuwait is perhaps the most unusual city in the history of the world. Everything needed, even sand, had to be imported, and yet the standard of living vies with the highest in the world. He regarded the Kuwaiti character as singularly honest and broadminded. To quote some of his sentences:

"What city of 260,000 people has over 30,000 employees? What city has carpets covering every square inch of government floor space? What city has an astronomical budget that is not known with certitude? The proportion of tangible results produced to the amount of money expended is little and the few results produced are so unproductive that the more thoughtful authorities have begun to be alarmed by the non-productive expenditures and future of Kuwait." He admitted that the sight of lost opportunities were driving him to a nervous breakdown. One of the troubles Dr. Shiber admitted was that the ordinary citizen cannot deal with the government even in trivial matters without pull, bribery, or total physical exhaustion. The Arab world is in the throes of unparalled challenge in physical and social development. As long as disorderliness, lethargy, and inefficiency reign supreme in Arab governments it is vain to hope for progress.

I wanted to drive our new Pontiac up to Basrah to introduce Dorothea and Nurse Bhagyamma. But what a complicated pleasure expedition it turned out to be! The Basrah mission said they would get a permit to bring the car into Iraq and would deposit it at Safwan, the border police station. To get visas for an Indian, a Hollander, and an American took a month. We were leaving on Friday, the Muslim Sabbath. I had forgotten to get permits for us to leave Kuwait, so Haider had to hunt the official's house on Thursday evening. On Friday morning, I suddenly found we had to have a permit to take the car out of Kuwait. Haider again had to hunt for the official, who of course had gone calling on his relatives. Finally we started at 1 P.M. on the 130-mile trip. But first we had to get some Iraqi money.

The engineers had just discovered a vast underground expanse of sweet water near the northern border of Kuwait. They were letting it flow freely to find out how much water there was. Dorothea said it was like riding the dykes in Holland. At Safwan, the police were still at lunch, so we waited an hour. The Iraqi police looked poverty-stricken with torn, dirty uniforms. The office was dirty with broken chairs. They searched through their books and files but could find no permit, so they said they would have to send a policeman with us. He took us along dusty, rough back roads. By the time we arrived everybody had gone, so we had to leave the car with them.

But arriving at the mission was worth it. The mission had a wonderful dinner and room prepared for us. The next day, they took us on a picnic in bellums up the Shatt el Arab (the combined Tigris and Euphrates rivers) to a cottage built by our Shaikh Abdullah Mubarak for a new Iraqi wife. She wasn't at home. The guard was a friend of the Gosselinks, so he showed us the grand furniture and marble halls. When we were ready to drive back, the police still had not found our permit, but since the car had been in the police station, they said they could count it as not having entered Iraq. When we returned to Kuwait, we were scolded by the officials for not having a permit to bring the car back to Kuwait! But what's a mere scolding under those circumstances?

Shaikha Bederea invited Dorothea and me to a luncheon at her new palace on the seashore at Salamiyah. It had a large, round stained-glass window featuring a fantastic sapphire seascape with a pearl diver. The halls, walls, floors, and tables were of variously colored marble. The dressing room was enclosed with pink mirrors. Tapestry drapes portrayed Aesop's fables. Shirley Stephens and a friend had arrived for a return visit. Shaikha Bederea surprised me by saying that she thought religion should be one's personal relation to God.

When Shirley was the guest of the aristocracy, she drove their car with the royal insignia of crossed flags. We received instant attention; no police may stop these cars and no one may pass them. Along the way, we saw the total wreck of one of the mammoth tankers which deliver water. Inquiring, we learned that its driver sighted some gazelles and chased them across the desert. The tanker turned completely upside down.

The mission eventually decided that Muscat station needed Dorothea more than I did. I was relieved, for we were developing conflicting views on many things. At a farewell dinner for her, I invited Shaikha Bederea and Ali, who was thirteen. His sisters were in schools in Lebanon. Dorothea did well professionally in

Muscat but resigned before her contract finished because the station members didn't approve of her social activities.

World-famous guests visited Kuwait and called on the mission too; we saw various British surgeons and a British lawyer trained in Paris who was rewriting Kuwaiti law for a Muslim state. He explained how the Muslim theologians had rationalized the Qur'anic verse that gives permission for a man to marry up to four wives. The verse says, "If you fear that you will not do justice then (marry) only one." The modern conclusion is that a man should marry only one wife.

We heard that some of the young foreign-educated Kuwaiti women were refusing to wear the veil and abba when they became teachers. The rule was softened to requiring only an abba, but even so, some declared they would not teach in traditional dress.

THE SIXTIES IN KUWAIT

For the Christmas season of 1960, I took over the holiday decoration of the parish hall and church. We put a lot of time into preparing for the growing numbers of Christmas programs and people. I was thrilled when Sultan Ajeel sent me a dozen red roses fresh from Holland.

Christmas Day began with a dismaying wind. The first callers were the hospital staff. Fatima sailed in with her abba billowing in the wind (though her veil stayed perfectly in place!). On one arm she carried her last baby, and a toddler clung to her dress. In her other hand she clasped an upright, artificial tree decorated with a huge star and a dozen glass balls bobbing in the breeze. She was sure she had brought just what I wanted. Other callers brought gifts of a large sheep and a small goat. I had to lock them in the kitchen behind the house. It made a bit of a mess, and the goat cried all night. But the five Heusinkvelds were living with me for a couple of weeks, so the meat came in handy. The wind turned into a heavy dust storm which coated all our holiday decorations most inappropriately.

Nineteen hundred and sixty-one was a crowded year. Dr. Dorothea Van der Horst arrived in January and helped for six months. The Indian physicians worked at various times. Dr. Mary Mathen wanted to do more surgery, so she left for more training in England. Dr. Lilly was useful, but she was having her own babies. Dr. George was competent and sweet. She was unwilling to go out on night calls, as she didn't know Arabic and was a single girl.

The demands of medicine were also great. One night a wealthy and aristocratic family sent for a doctor. The whole family evidently had drunk some contaminated milk and were in the various throes of food poisoning. They were too nauseated to swallow. Protocol demanded an injection, so I settled on an injection of penicillin for all ten and then had to do the same for all the servants and driver and several neighbors. I figured it was a self-limiting illness. They gratefully gave me a large fee.

The new government hospitals were attracting ever-larger crowds, but at the mission we still had more to do than was good. There were two or three doctors to see the smorgasbord of diseases—we saw everything possible in pediatrics: asthma, diabetes, epilepsy, pulmonary, cardiac, respiratory, gastrointestinal, skin, and gynecology, all mixed up with accidents and emergencies.

I had hoped for a day off during the Muslim holiday, but in came a very black woman in labor. She had six children, with the last one a Caesarian section. I didn't dare let her labor pains proceed for fear of a ruptured uterus. Her hemoglobin was only 50 percent of normal, we had no blood, and all the local staff was off for the holiday. Dr. Mathen and I decided on a section and Swamidoss gave some anesthesia. He had just returned from a course in Philadelphia. We had just delivered a lively little girl when Swamidoss said the mother's blood pressure was falling. We decided to remove the whole uterus to prevent any more bleeding. It worked surprisingly well. The woman made a rapid return to health.

Distressed by losing three burned children, I found an article in a British medical magazine recommending a modified Eusol solution of boric acid and chlorine. I tried it. It kept the surface clean and with some grafting, cured two children. The men's hospital was also successful with burns and cared for a man 60 percent burned for a year until he recovered.

Then there was the Bedouin mother hanging over her dying child singing a desert lullaby as he drifted away—a tragedy too deep for tears. I found myself getting inured to pain just to get the patients off the work list. I violated my own rules at times.

One of the wealthy families had a spastic daughter they were anxious to help. After some correspondence with the Christian

Medical Association, a specialist came from the University of Pennsylvania. He was a partial cripple himself. He recommended treatment for the girl in Philadelphia and offered to take her mother into his own home. When she returned with an electric wheelchair, all of us marveled.

Babies with tetanus were treated with the new tranquilizers, which saved some. Mortality was usually 75 percent in those cases. At the men's hospital we were helping with an appendectomy on a young Indian merchant. He suddenly died. My letter home that day ended with, "I don't have any joys and these are my sorrows."

Some people in the government said the mission hospital would soon wither away. The Board of Health, which were mostly Egyptians, tried to help it wither. They made rules that hospitals had to have specialists in many departments and a registered pharmacist. They didn't enforce the rule, fortunately for us. We did attempt to train and employ more specialists, however. Dr. Nawgiri, the Indian doctor at our men's hospital, went to London to study eye surgery, and Dr. Mary Mathen went there to earn a higher certificate in obstetrics. I heard that two Kuwaiti girls started to study medicine in London.

But we also cooperated with the government hospital on many cases. Once we had a very serious case of ruptured ectopic pregnancy. The government hospital generously gave me three units of blood, so we saved her. Another time, I had to take three abandoned babies to the government hospital as directed.

In June 1961, the Kuwaiti state was pronounced independent of Great Britain. There were demonstrations and decorations. Men went around with guns and bandoliers. Our hospital guard wanted a gun, too, but we thought it was safer for him not to have one. The government was offering courses on shooting. A parliament was organized. In late June, Abdul Kassem of Iraq declared that Kuwait belonged to Iraq and would be peacefully annexed. He announced that our Shaikh Abdullah al Salim al Sabah would be the governor with a salary of 75 dinars—about a secretary's pay. The British flew in troops from Kenya at the government's request. They dug in out in the desert about a hundred miles north of Kuwait City. We had to change all our money, checkbooks, stamps, and accounts from rupees to dinars. On top of all the political upheaval, it was hot. As I said to one of my patients, I felt like a wet rag in a bucket of water. Everything felt like too much trouble that summer.

But just when things were at their worst, my vacation came due. I flew to Jerusalem with my cousin Madeline, who had been working at the orphanage in Bahrain. After a lovely stay, we flew on to Beirut to shop and sightsee. My Kuwaiti friend, Shaikha Bederea, invited us to stay with her at her new mountaintop marble palace.

One day, we drove down to another villa on the seafront with the whole family, ten servants, and food for all. We wandered around the site to find some archaeologists digging up a grand Phoenician house with mosaic floors. They were carefully brushing earth from some skeletons in what must have been the ancient family cemetery. It was wonderful to realize that 2,800 years ago, another family loved the same gorgeous location.

Back in Kuwait, I got back to work. I was making hospital rounds one afternoon when I came upon a family that had been admitted with what was thought to be skin eruption from penicillin given the day before. A suspicion stirred some memory as I felt the vesicles and found they were in the deep layer of the skin. It was smallpox in two children. But I could see the marks of vaccination on their arms. The family had just returned from a visit to relatives in Iran. They had mild cases, but it was evident that vaccination had not been a complete protection. We immediately vaccinated everybody in the hospital.

Dr. Mylrea had told me of the epidemic of smallpox in 1930, when over three to four thousand children died and filled up the cemeteries. Some vaccine was brought by ship. Dr. Esther Barny sat in a stall in the sook to vaccinate. The demonstration was effective, and the Kuwaitis accepted the procedure ever after. Whenever we could get vaccine, the mothers and babies crowded the clinic.

At this time one of our helpers was Natasha Anastasia, a White Russian refugee who had fled Russia when the Communists took power. She, her daughter, and little grandson had drifted down to Kuwait through Iran. The nursery and baby care were her domain for several years. Her neat white hair, bright blue eyes and bustling figure belied her age of seventy-eight years. She spoke a mixture of various languages. She and her daughter lived in one of the small houses back of the mission compound. Sad to say their place was loud with quarrels, but I liked her anyway. One Saturday evening, crossing the road beside the hospital, she was struck by a lorry and instantly killed. Sunday afternoon we took Natasha's remains out to the Christian cemetery, a walled, barren spot in the desert. Don led a sad farewell service. We heard that the truck driver had to pay a large sum by which the daughter profited.

But it might not have been the driver's fault. Kuwait was changing and the driving was fierce. The *New York Times* of September 15, 1963, stated that Kuwait was leading the world in increase of car owners and accidents. Statistics show that 52,224 vehicles were owned by 321,000 people, with 732 accidents in one month!

Change was happening in other areas of Kuwaiti life. Before independence, the Kuwaiti government had hired many British specialists to guide its development. By the end of 1961, the Arabs decided they could do better without the British, so 165 of them left. And in 1962 the American consulate became an embassy, befitting Kuwait's advanced status.

Despite all the economic and political changes, the clinic work stayed pretty much the same. Whenever I thought I'd have a day off, in would come an emergency maternity case. There was this thirty-seven-year-old primipara. I had done several tubal insufflations for her, and wonder of wonders, she achieved a pregnancy. When her labor did not progress, Dr. Mathen and I decided on a Caesarian section. The reward was a lovely boy. I always did the low section incision, which I had learned in Chicago. And then there was a difficult breech case—successful, but my hands ached for several days.

One Sunday I had invited the doctors for lunch, but Dr. Mathen called me for another section. The husband had set down his wife in the middle of the night and gone off. We had to wait for him, as the wife could not give permission for surgery. The woman had had six babies. Her abdomen was like a sack. We had a terrible time trying to find enough firm tissue to hold sutures. I always sutured the tubes on such cases. I didn't want to do her again. Then I rushed home and opened cans and packages of the new stuff from the supermarket. Did you ever eat boiled ginkgo nuts? The Indian nurses didn't seem to care much for our food.

They would invite me to their warm, rich, voluptuous curry dinners. The delicious, exciting rich stews had all the mystery of the Orient. I set myself to learn how to combine those glorious spices whose fragrances twined and twisted into what seemed like the soul of nature.

Christians in Muslim society had very real problems finding marriage partners. Farida, one of our Christian helpers, had assisted me most efficiently in the women's hospital for many years, but she needed to marry. Her problem was solved when she met George Ghoryafi, a Lebanese Maronite who had joined our church. They had a grand wedding on a terribly hot July day. The temperature soared to 118 degrees.

We all helped to get the flowers revived and decorate the church. Farida wore a white lace dress and veil with rather drooping flowers. The last-minute preparations were done at my house—next to the church.

The church itself was absolutely jammed with three hundred guests of many religions and nationalities. Outside, a large overflow crowd of Arab neighbors and friends complicated the occasion. The groom had arranged a catered reception in the parish hall with a refrigerated truck for soft drinks. The six-tiered wedding cake was cut by a waiter bathed in sweat which steadily dripped off his nose. The reception was over in forty-five minutes—no one could stand the heat inside any longer.

We were all worn out by the end of that day! Farida and George continued to live happily in Kuwait. They had a boy and a girl in a marriage that worked out well.

Some time afterwards, one Sunday morning at the Arabic service, a tall man wearing full, stately Arab robes walked down the aisle and sat in one of the front seats. I did not see his face, as it was hidden in his head scarf. A deep-felt throb stirred my heart and sudden tears came as I felt how wonderful if an Arab found Christ. The man turned out to be Farida's handsome brother, Saeed Shemmas. He had been appointed Kuwait's minister plenipotentiary to the U.N. in New York. He and his wife Basima took four servants along with them and launched his career as an ambassador.

For the summer of 1962 we were able to count on our two Indian doctors for the women's work, so I could go on a vacation to Africa. I visited many of the new friends I had made at the

Near East medical conference and our mission conference earlier that year. Though I visited many missions and saw the sights of Aden, Ethiopia, the Sudan, Kenya, and Uganda, I still considered myself fortunate to have been assigned to Kuwait. I studied Arabic for a whole month that summer at Chemlan in the lovely mountains above Beirut. My Arabic never did get to be very good, but I tried. Then I flew back to Kuwait.

By spring 1963 I was living with three other women in my house. We had fired the cook and so did all our own shopping and cooking, even though we were each busy with mission work—at the hospital, teaching, writing, and preparing programs for broadcast from Africa.

I really needed a wife to help with housekeeping. Our house had three bedrooms, each with a bathroom, and if necessary a guest could sleep in the study. Sometimes we had up to six stray guests or odd missionaries. When my mother spent the winter with me, she insisted I put in hot water heaters, which seemed a terrific luxury to me. I was thankful for running water. We had a tank on the roof which the government tankers came around and filled daily from the water distillation plant.

We eventually hired Hasan, a young houseboy from Yemen, to keep the house clean. He slept in the room behind the house. Except for being unable to get up for our breakfast, he was thoughtful and ingenious in making our lives more convenient. I had a kerosene heater in my bedroom with a kettle to warm water in the morning. One morning after heating the kettle, I found I had been heating a kettleful of kerosene. He had thoughtfully filled the kettle with kerosene in case the stove ran out at night. Somehow Providence saved me from a fiery end.

Weather did curious things. On April 28, at 6 A.M., the sky was a brilliant orange. By 7 A.M. it was black as night and the air was dense with dust. There had been no rain that winter. By 9 it was clear, but there were tragic consequences. Five German businessmen were being driven by an Arab driver. The Arabs feel an inferiority complex about driving slow, so he concentrated on speed and hit a truck. They all died.

My brother sent me a birthday card in March of 1963, "Sixty years, Wow!" So I decided to kill the fatted calf and invite the gang to a royal dinner at one of the new hotels. Fourteen of us gathered at a flower-bedecked table in the grand dining room. The maitre d'hotel and I had plotted a jubilee. We started with hors d'oeuvres—real caviar, angels on horseback, artichoke canapes, foie gras, tabbouleh, baba ghannooj, Grecian olives, and anchovies. Next was the fish course of sautéed prawn with hummus bi'tahina sauce, and then the gastronomic climax: real Chateaubriand with stuffed tomatoes. The finishing touch was English Trifle. It was a dream. I never felt able to afford the like again.

At Easter, so many congregations used the church that the Syrian Orthodox of south India had to start the series of services at 2 A.M. Their Easter services carried on for three hours. At 5, we had sunrise service on the flat roof of the men's hospital, with breakfast for all at 6 in the parish hall. The Arabic service was at 9, the English at 11, and the Armenians were at noon. Other congregations kept the music going all afternoon. On Easter, as on all our great days, the mission dined together. That year, Fred and Louise Willey sent us a hot, roasted, stuffed twenty-pound turkey. Twenty-three of us sat down to enjoy it.

The clinics seemed to get wilder and wilder. Patients kicked at the door. Callers brought all their children and told them to play in the halls. They brought food and threw garbage out of the windows. The helpers screamed and fought and told me what wasn't their work. I never was good at discipline. I'd come home and declare, "I have fought with the beasts at Ephesus."

I was supposed to have a night off that Easter. Dr. Al Pennings was on duty, but he called me over at 7 to help with surgery for an acute abdomen. At 10:30, I figured I was due some sleep but Al called again: "Would you please come and help with an obstetrical case?" It was one of the most awful catastrophes of all maternity cases. I had never seen one before but had heard of it. This case was a mother of five, unconscious, with no obvious blood pressure and a rigid, wooden, silent uterus. It is called abruptio placentae, in which the placenta separates from the uterus, the uterus goes into a tetanic spasm, and the internal bleeding affects the mother's entire blood supply so that it won't clot. The woman bled relentlessly from every needle prick. Al said he couldn't help because of his back, but he would give a unit of his own blood. I begged the men of the family for blood. They don't like to give, as they think it will diminish their sexual powers, but two of the men gave blood. Then the staff, who were all sleeping soundly in houses in the neighborhood, had to be called. We had no telephones and had to send servants to call them. Dr. Mary George came to help, then the lab men appeared to match the blood. Finally, the anesthetist and operating room staff came. Things were ready by 1 A.M. I decided that the only way to prevent more blood loss was to remove the entire uterus. Of course the baby was dead, and this was the easiest possible operation. After four units of blood, the woman revived, though her hemoglobin was still only 45 percent of normal. She didn't lose any more blood and eventually recovered. We should have been exhausted, but strange to say we were enjoying ourselves. It seems the rush of adrenaline brought on by a crisis produces an exultation of one's spirit.

One night Lew and Dotty Scudder had dinner guests, so Dr. Scudder called me to help Dr. Varkey with a case in the men's hospital. I was certain the man had intestinal obstruction which needed immediate surgery. Dr. Varkey was new and just out of training, and I knew I was no surgeon. We sent word to Lew, but he said, "Just go ahead." I couldn't let Dr. Varkey see my timidity. He probably didn't want me to think that he lacked courage, either. So we scrubbed up and got the anesthetist to go to work. We plunged in resolutely and went down to the depths to search and destroy the enemy. We roamed around the cavity. There was no volvulus, intussusception, mass, or strangulation. But the bowel seemed to be stuck up at the top of the abdomen. Finally I pushed the panic button and sent word to Lew that he'd have to come. He came and scrubbed up. He did a little sweating, too, and then found it was a rare condition. The man had a hole in his diaphragm. The omentum and part of the large bowel had herniated into the opening. Fortunately it was not strangulated, so we hauled it out, put it back in its proper place, and sutured the hole shut. It was just like the way Mom used to darn the holes in our stockings. Of course in this process we had to open the man from stem to stern. It took from eight to midnight. The patient was just fine the next morning.

In the women's hospital, there were sometimes two Indian lady doctors, and sometimes none. The doctors came and went, with marriage, children, overseas study, vacation, and resignation (due to higher salaries at the government hospitals). But the crowds still came. One day we counted 135 women and children in the morning clinic and 75 in the afternoon. Emergency appendix cases turned up, which we did with the men in their operating room. On my day off or on Sunday, some baby case would turn up needing help. I remember my small brother once saying, "We've been to the piddle-haas and I'm such a tire." I felt that way, too.

A German firm had sent us a large supply of thalidomide tablets with glowing testimonies of its efficacy in treating morning sickness in pregnancy. Out of loyalty to my American training, I waited before adopting the drug to see if our professional magazines confirmed its utility. While I was gone on my vacation the news broke about thalidomide's tragic effect on young fetuses. How thankful I was that I had not distributed any! I dumped the lot down the drain. Strangely, years later when I was treating leprosy patients in Oman, I heard that the drug was effective in certain stages of leprosy. I tried to get some then, twelve years after the tragedy, but it was not available.

The mission hospitals in Kuwait continued to do well. Income from the two hospitals for the year ending September 1, 1963, was very good—almost 180,000 Kuwaiti dinars, which amounted to $350,884. It was all paid out to salaries, staff housing, pension fund, travel from India for staff, drugs, and local expenses. We did a lot of charity cases for staff and their relatives and friends, but the most of our charity work was for needy cases. We cared for one burn victim, Jameel, for three years. Dr. Scudder had one dramatic charity case of bleeding from a gastric ulcer. After a partial gastrectomy and twenty-seven units of blood, the man recovered. Another charity case came in with abdominal obstruction and enormous bowel distention. Lew had to puncture the bowel to close the abdomen. After 10 million units of penicillin, this patient also recovered. We were fortunate to be able to treat such needy and deserving cases with the resources at hand.

Marriages were part of our job, too. In Muslim society, marriage is crucial to women for their personal fulfillment; it is also a girl's sole hope of establishing future involvement with the larger community. But a satisfactory marriage is not always easy to achieve. For example, I always wondered about the house in the elite center of Kuwait where six unmarried Arab sisters lived with their widowed mother. The sisters were past the age when most Kuwaiti girls would have already been married. They were intelligent and longed for contact with the outside world, so they often invited us to tea or a meal.

Their mother had a manner so dignified that her least whim seemed a moral judgment. She rigorously enforced all the modes of modesty upheld by Kuwait's grand ladies. So the girls seldom went out of the house and could observe the outside world only from the flat rooftop. They had no brother, so shopping was done by neighboring servants.

The girls were attractive, but the family was black. The word in Arabic for the black people meant slaves. But these girls were daughters of a nobleman. Though children of the concubine, the girls were regarded as part of the noble family.

Their father had been a man of note, who achieved distinction as a sea captain of those famous Kuwaiti sailing vessels that plied the seas to India and Zanzibar. The girls enshrined his memory. They kept his framed picture, massive wooden desk, and nautical instruments dusted and polished as he left them. He had no wife but was always faithful to his black lady, with whom he had these six daughters.

It seemed that long ago, perhaps before the father's death, a marriage had been arranged for the oldest daughter with her aristocratic cousin on the father's side of the family. The two had never seen each other, as was considered proper. Anticipating the wedding, the whole household was thrilled. For months the house, furniture, rugs, embroideries, and new clothes demanded their entire attention, making ready for the big day. Gold jewelry was rented from the shops. Legal papers were signed. The house was festooned with strings of tiny lights.

On the great day, Lateefa was tense with excitement and forebodings. The wedding party consisted of the many women guests served with soft drinks and cake and splashed with rose water. A pot full of frankincense smoking over glowing charcoal was passed around for each woman to hold under her cloak, filling her robes with exotic perfume. Coffee spiced with cardamom seed was served in tiny cups. All this time the bride sat alone in the bridal chamber until the women guests left and the bridegroom arrived with some men of his family. After his party had been served, the bridegroom was escorted to the bride's room. He entered, gazed at her dark complexion, turned around, and walked out of the room and the house forever. He left Lateefa to bitter grief. The sisters were so shocked that in their loyalty to their sister they resolved that none of them would ever marry. So they lived—resigned, gentle, proud virgins from that day.

But weddings, when they went right, could be fantastic! One day we received engraved invitations to an evening wedding in a wealthy family. Dressed in our best, we arrived at the gate to find a swarm of a hundred black-dressed women who had not been invited. The advantage of a veil is that you can do things you wouldn't do if you were known. The servants had to pull us into the courtyard, brilliant with strings of colored fairy lights strung like a net over the whole court. The ground was covered with priceless carpets. In the center of almost three thousand women sat the modern girls on chairs. They had shed the black covers for spectacular Paris model dresses of brocade and gold-embroidered sari clothes encrusted with pearls and jewels. They wore strings of real pearls, diamond-studded necklaces, bracelets, and rings. Some of the girls were really beautiful, but some were developing a weight problem. The bride was enthroned on a divan on a dais, wearing a white satin gown embroidered with pearls, her train so long it completely covered the divan. A diamond coronet crowned her flowing black hair. With grave dignity, she sat alone waiting for the bridegroom but surrounded by the cherubs of the household, the little girls with lovely white dresses and the boys in white tailored suits in a stage setting of fresh white flowers. The bridegroom tarried for hours so everyone could see everybody else. A black women's orchestra beat the drums with chords of the lute in the usual Arab tempo. Finally the bridegroom and some of his men friends arrived, the drums beat a terrific din, as he came up and kissed the bride and sat down beside her. Then everyone was invited to serve themselves at the sumptuously laden tables of food. Lemonade and Pepsis were brought around by the servants.

Today many of the new brides want houses of their own instead of living with the in-laws. There are thousands of new houses in exotic architecture, three stories with dashing colored verandas, screens, pillars, and window shades in green, pink, lavender, and aqua shades, but all surrounded by walls and gates of fancy ironwork. The old pattern of life is departing and the new one is a vision of splendor.

Marriage continued to hold a prominent place in women's

lives, even as Kuwait's increasing wealth put a new twist in the old practices and ways of making alliances. In the new Kuwait, segregated girls' schools flourished—both primary and secondary—with thousands of Egyptian teachers. Buses transported the girls, who began to discard their face veils but not their black abbas. Some fathers showed their disapproval by beating their daughters.

At the close of the year, the school invited women only to a program. The girls didn't want to perform, as they surmised they would be studied by the older women as future brides for their sons. The program was excellent, concluding with an act from the crusades when Saladin sent his private physician to heal King Richard.

Some American and foreign girls married to Kuwaitis came to the hospital for delivery. I tried to get acquainted, but they rejected any advance except for professional care. I wondered why. Some Arab men, discussing foreign wives, concluded that American girls were the best, because they didn't demand gold jewelry and expected to share everything they had.

Barbara attended our English church services while her grandmother from Texas visited her. She didn't come back again after her grandmother went back home. The grandmother wrote and asked Garry to try and see the girl, because the family had received no letters. Garry did see her, finally. The girl said she had written and had given her letters to her husband to post.

I was asked to make a house call on an American wife. She had the vomiting of pregnancy and was very lonely, living by herself and unable to get out. She was a graduate of the University of Michigan with an R.N. degree. I urged her to come and work with us, but she had to ask her husband and he refused.

Practicing good medicine requires good thinking, and that takes time. The temptation was to jump at a conclusion and not bother with the questions necessary to get a history. When there were many patients I yielded, because the answer I usually got to my questions was that what had happened was the will of God. If my questions were intimate or sensitive, the women resented them, feeling that I as a foreigner would be critical of their way of life. It was necessary to be secretive when living in a hareem with several other women. Truth had to be concealed, and even chil-

drcn had to be taught to lie. Lying wasn't considered a very serious sin. The attitude was, if you are a doctor why do you have
to ask questions.

Dr. Mary Thomas, who had worked with me, returned from
her vacation in India with a new husband chosen by her parents.
He worked for the government and demanded that she work for
it, too. So I was alone again until we could find new doctors in
India, which took a lot of time.

Every day had its new crisis. A Lebanese brought his elderly
mother with a chronic trouble and asked for a special room and
food, for which he would pay. He never returned. Finally I
heard of some relatives so took her in my car and deposited her
with them.

Early one morning, parents brought in an exsanguinated child.
He had been circumcised by a local barber and bled all night. We
had no blood, so he died in a few minutes. The government then
forbade barbers to operate.

The new Board of Health sent us an order that any unmarried
women coming to us for delivery must be reported. I had been
keeping such cases secret because sometimes the relatives killed
such girls.

January of 1964 began with an ominous foreshadowing of coming disasters. Its foretaste was an icy dust storm, followed by a
frost. Icicles hung from our outside faucets, car radiators froze,
and the Prosopis trees dropped their leaves. The government had
planted miles of these along the new paved roads. Once that January, driving, I was shocked when some rude little boys shouted,
"Look at the old woman driving a car." My life had been blos-
soming with honors, but frost was coming.

Ramadan fasting began, so the hospital work slackened. We
called on Arab friends who had special open house in the evenings. I began the tedious packing of some household things preparing for my furlough in the summer.

MY BROTHER, PAUL BRUINS

My brother, Dr. Paul Bruins, Ph.D. in chemical engineering,
was coming for a visit. Many invitations crowded the schedule. He
arrived by Air Liban the night before the great Muslim holiday—

the first day of celebrating after the month of fasting. I roused him at 5 A.M. and whisked him off with the men of the mission to make the formal calls on the royal family and other important houses. It was an extraordinary spectacle which I as a woman could not view. Our mission group consisted of Drs. Lewis Scudder and Gerald Nykerk, the Rev. De Jong and Rev. Lyle Vander Werff, with Paul. Hundreds of men in their dignified best clothes thronged the streets around the new gorgeous palaces ringed with uniformed soldiers. The social procedure was for the visitors to either shake hands or kiss the shoulders of the shaikhs and other hosts, murmuring, *Idakum Mubarak* ("may your holiday be blessed"). Servants with shiny brass coffee urns served a couple of teaspoons of bitter, hot coffee in the tiny cups, and smoking incense pots were passed. Paul told me they visited about fifty houses of royalty and multimillionaires, where the same ceremony was performed. The following day, we women called on the women of the royal houses in strict rank order. Paul was thrilled with the whole thing. I remember how I had thought, years ago, that missionaries went to poor people. How green was my folly! Paul noted how everywhere the mission personnel were received with affection.

My friends offered to show Paul the sights. Fred Willey spent a morning taking him around the oil fields, which were twenty-five miles south of Kuwait. Ten wells had been drilled before the war and now there were over four hundred, partly supervised by Fred. They were producing 2 million barrels a day at $1.75 paid per barrel. As Kuwait received 50 percent as its royalty, its income was $175,000,000 per day. The wells produced at various levels between 3,000 and 10,000 feet deep under tremendous pressure of 400 to 800 pounds per square inch and sometimes up to 4,000 pounds. Each well was controlled by special devices at the top and also by a slurry of mud containing barium with high specific gravity. The natural gas dissolved in the crude oil was piped off and burned. This was wasteful, but some was being used for the city electric plant and water distilling plant. Fred showed Paul how they slid the drilling towers across the desert to new sites. A large amount of salt came up with the oil, so a processing plant was constructed to remove the salt. As the fields were on high ground, the oil ran down by force of gravity to tanks and tankers at the two jetties. Up to ten ocean-going tankers filled constantly.

Another day, Paul saw the seawater distillation plant—the largest in the world. It began operating in 1957 and had been added to four times. Its capacity was about 6 million gallons per day. Paul, a chemical engineering professor, was fascinated by the process. The water produced was so pure they had to add brackish water to make it taste good. Large tank trucks with pumps delivered the water to houses which had roof tank reservoirs.

Paul marveled at the furious pace of construction in the new Kuwait. Hundreds of new office and government structures and thousands of elaborate, exotic new houses were in progress. The workers were expatriates from Iran, India, Palestine, Lebanon, and Egypt who came on work permits without families and had to leave when their permits ran out. Illegal immigrants were arrested and imprisoned or expelled. The government was building many low-cost houses for their poorer citizens.

Our hospital buildings surprised Paul, as they were so open, with winds blowing through the corridors. The complete informality of comings and goings was quite novel. A Dutch mother delivered, which I let him watch.

All too soon, Paul's visit was over. When he left, he said to me, "You have turned out lots better than I thought you would when we were growing up." I waved good-bye as he flew off to Palestine, where I had arranged for him to stay at St. George's Close by the Anglican cathedral. After seeing the Arab side of Jerusalem, he crossed the no-man's land strip and entered Israel for lectures and conferences, after which he went to Europe. He wrote that he concluded our life was very happy. I enjoyed that week very much, too.

TIMES OF SORROW

Paul's visit must have been the grand finale, for after it came our sorrows. The next week Fred Willey, our friend at KOC, died in a car accident. We mourned his loss as a firm Christian friend. Louise sadly packed up their family belongings and went back to America. Then Dr. Jerry Nykerk, who shared the work at the men's hospital, was taken by a coronary infarction. His wife Rose stayed on as mission secretary and treasurer. We also had to bid farewell to the De Jongs, who retired.

Dr. Alfred Pennings accepted the challenge of running the Kuwait medical work for the last 3½ months of 1964. The tragic loss of Dr. Nykerk, the illness of Dr. Scudder with the absence of Mrs. Scudder as hospital administrator, and my absence on furlough, plunged the work into a crisis. There was a large staff geared to a large volume of surgery, with no surgeon until Dr. Ommen came from India in the middle of November. Haider Al-Khalifa, who had been sent to Tanta, Egypt, for a course in hospital administration, had to be recalled to assist with the men's work, while the two Indian lady doctors ran the women's medical work.

We felt the economic effects of the government's health care initiatives. Our large number of charity cases continued, but higher-paying patients went elsewhere for care. At the same time, the government issued complex new rules for hospitals. Surgery must be done by internationally qualified surgeons. All nurses and nurses' aids had to be registered. We were hard-pressed and frustrated, but the staff were cooperative and understanding. Mrs. Vander Aarde supervised the operating rooms, Miss Sluiter gave generous time to the nursing care, and the Rev. Vander Aarde provided personal attention to inpatients. Arab friends cheered Dr. Pennings by many expressions of confidence and appreciation. Dr. K. Bebb came from home to conduct surgery. But the X-ray tube blew out, the new laundry equipment needed adjustment, and there were legal problems to settle. We thought we owned the seafront, but the government said no. Various details of property had to be adjusted.

As usual, the summer ended with an epidemic of diarrhea, vomiting, and fever among the babies. For gastroenteritis, the clinic helpers bandaged the baby on a circumcision board and ran normal saline subcutaneously into the thighs. In desperate cases, I tried blood transfusions. The mothers were able to contribute the small amount of blood needed and usually matched. Often I couldn't get the blood in the tiny soft veins. My solution was to run the blood intra-abdominally, as I knew the peritoneum could absorb whole blood cells. It worked, but later I was grateful to a girl intern at home who taught me how to do a cut-down on tiny veins.

One father brought scrawny Adnan, a six-month-old whose mother had died, and asked that we take care of him. We kept him several months and were happy that under the Indian nurses' loving, tender care and with good food, he blossomed.

When trouble came, as it always did, I learned I had to face it quickly and move with speed, even though the speed was often thoughtless and sometimes damaging. Many women came bleeding profusely from spontaneous incomplete abortions. I decided the best treatment was a quick uterine curettage to remove the remaining fetal tissues, which usually stopped the bleeding.

That summer of 1964, when I was alone, I did a curettage on an older woman who had a history of bleeding. I accidentally ruptured the uterus. I felt heartsick, tried a laparotomy without benefit, and she died. A cloud hung over my furlough, as the family sued for malpractice. Dr. Pennings hired a Lebanese lawyer to defend the mission. As soon as the Scudders got back, I hurriedly began packing up my household to leave on furlough, so I didn't get a chance to talk over the situation with them.

I was greatly distressed and seriously considered whether or not I should return to Kuwait. But I decided to go back and face the case since it was an accident.

The case was taken up in the Kuwaiti court, and I was summoned to appear. The Rev. Robert Vander Aarde sat with me. We were allowed to sit in seats, but the rest of the accused, who were prisoners, were put behind bars and a chicken wire fence. It was the first time I had ever been in court. A veiled Arab woman came in to present her case, complaining loudly and bitterly. The prisoners snarled about having to go to the bathroom. The judge listened to my tale in a separate room. He later pronounced me guilty but dismissed the case without penalty. It was a shattering blow to my self-confidence and a lasting grief. Whether for that reason or some other, the mission decided to transfer me to Bahrain on my return. It was the end of my career in Kuwait, but Bahrain opened another door.

FURLOUGH, 1964 – 1965

I had been working so hard for so long that I scarcely had time for anything, much less time to update my medical training. After a visit with my brother Paul and his family on Long Island, I decided I must study. I knew I needed refresher courses in medicine and Arabic.

Through the kind help of a physician of the Christian Medical Association, I was introduced to the superintendent of St. Joseph's Hospital in Ann Arbor, Michigan. She gave me a room on the obstetrical floor and circulated a letter to all the departments asking them to admit me to their clinical lectures and rounds. I was particularly grateful for the instruction in care of sick children and burns—blood chemistry, nursing care, and skin grafting. I marveled at the progress that had been made since my days in medical school and got completely lost in lectures on the new understanding of kidney physiology. My Arabic course was equally valuable. It was with great regret that I left after six months to make a speaking tour for my church. I found out what troubles there are in driving on snow and ice—which I never had to contend with in Kuwait!

While I was home on furlough our New York office informed me that I was to be transferred to the mission hospital in Bahrain. I was disappointed, but since the Kuwait work was in good hands, I felt I should be willing to terminate my career there.

Humility is a Christian virtue, so I must decrease if the work was to increase. So I accepted my age and my transfer and began to anticipate an interesting new situation in Bahrain. I packed up my furniture in Kuwait, shipped it off to my new station, and settled down in the upper flat of a Bahrain mission house.

10. Bahrain

Bahrain is a small, flat island shaikhdom in the Arabian Gulf, about thirty by fifteen miles in size, twenty miles from the Saudi coast, and a little farther from the peninsula country of Qatar. In 1965 when I arrived, its population was about a quarter-million people of mixed Middle Eastern origin. It had a wide-ranging merchant fleet with many trading activities, which made it open to new ideas. The winters were pleasant, but the summers were very steamy and uncomfortable, like a sweat-dripping, humid blanket until October.

Oil was discovered in Bahrain in 1931 before it was found anywhere else in the Gulf. Bahrain used its head start constructively to build a modern state, developing gradually and comfortably into a fairly well-educated and prosperous little country. The oil had played out by 1965. A large plant distilling oil piped from Saudi Arabia and an aluminum plant were the main industries when I began my stay there.

Bahrain boasted many freshwater springs and artesian wells, some of them under the sea, so the island had many date gardens and trees made the place attractive. Because sweet water had always been so plentiful, Bahrain had a great prehistoric civilization about 2,000 or 3,000 years B.C. It was mentioned in the cuneiform tiles found in the archaeological dig in ancient Ur. Bahrain had been an important center in the trade between the civilizations of Mesopotamia and Mohenjo-dara in northern India. The largest prehistoric cemetery in the world, consisting of 100,000 small, round, gravel hillocks, extended over a ten-mile area. Most were small, but some were eighty feet high and one hundred feet in diameter. The Portuguese had conquered Bahrain in 1521 and held it until 1602. They left an immense fort on the northern shore which was still in a fairly good state of preservation. Other times the Persians, Turks, and Arabs ruled.

Despite oppressive humidity, Bahrain had golden days and balmy nights, perfumed with jasmine and melodious with the nightingale and hoopoe. We were never far from the aquamarine sea. The breezes carried a slightly acrid, tarry smell of crude oil from the refinery. We had running water from the artesian wells. It was too bitter to use for tea, but we could buy distilled water for drinking. The sewerage system worked, even though the ground water level was high, so we had flush toilets. There was plenty of electric power, which made life much more comfortable. We had ceiling fans in every room, later air-conditioners, refrigerators, and good lighting. Even the telephones worked, and cable and wireless kept us in touch with the rest of the world. Bottled natural gas was delivered, so cooking was convenient. There were small supermarkets where the world's foods were available. For special treats, we could go to the restaurants, which improved every year. Local specialties were zamboses, mosombies, and mahalabis.

The streets in the old part of the city were narrow, with houses of bare, white plaster and almost windowless walls. Many still had the picturesque wind-towers with graceful arched balconies. Some of them had the grand double wooden doors with carved portals and brass studs. I had a paralyzed woman patient whose husband was poor but ingenious. He made a wind-tower out of oil cans and burlap to keep her comfortable.

The shopping area kept its ancient atmosphere of narrow streets, some shaded by a roof. The shops were mostly small one-man affairs but displayed goods from all over the world. Later, some larger shops appeared, and high-rise banks and large government buildings were constructed.

The mosques had tall minarets with ample courtyards and were well-attended. Prayer call was given through a loudspeaker. There were many new housing areas with modern, beautiful houses and gardens. Newly paved wide roads ran through the city and out to the villages, beaches, the shaikh's palace, and the experimental garden. Cars, and furious driving, increased. Cinemas were popular. Some people had TVs, which showed films from Saudi Arabia dubbed in Arabic. It was fun to hear cowboys and Indians talking Arabic.

The British had maintained a Political Agent in Bahrain for a long time. James Belgrave had been adviser to the rulers for many years. He was a wise and congenial man, in the right spot at the right time. For a long time Iran claimed that Bahrain belonged to her but finally gave up her claim in 1969. The British maintained an RAF station and army and navy positions but declared they would leave in 1972. Men from these groups often joined us at church and helped us with many jobs. Some even took the mission girls away as wives. British clubs entertained by putting on plays, music, and cinemas.

The population was increasing, so the government built a new housing district south of Manama, to be called "Isa Town" after the ruler. Arabs could obtain a house there at low rent, and after twenty years would own it. Isa Town was carefully planned with all the modern conveniences: clinics, schools, mosques, and shopping areas.

The ruler owned many fine horses, which he allowed anyone to ride. We heard they even had air-conditioned stables. On Friday afternoons, Shaikh Isa would appear at an open course where anyone could gather and watch horse and camel races. I don't think there was any betting.

The oil company had leased an area of the beach where Shaikh Isa had a rest house. We were invited to use it, too, and had many jolly picnics and swimming.

Bahrain's population was about half Shiite Iranian and half Arabs of the orthodox or Sunni sect. The strong antagonism between the two sects came to a head yearly at the Moharam memorial. Then the Shiites mourn the death of the Prophet Mohammad's family, Ali, Husan, and Husain, who were killed in battle between the two groups. Reading and reciting of the saga goes on for a week beforehand in special places of worship. Then the faithful march in the street with much melancholy music and wailing. On the great day, the men march in a slow procession with mournful, slow music. The men beat their bare backs with scourges until the blood flows. A white horse would carry an image of the slain bodies of the saints. Feeling was so intense that foreigners like us were advised not to appear on the street or to take pictures.

Shaikh Isa's wise government kept the land quiet, but in 1968, there were demonstrations over the Israeli situation with crowds shouting for Jamal Abd el Nasser. They burned a couple of cars and smashed some bicycles in front of our house. The police quieted the situation and the crowd ran away. There was a deep feeling of resentment against the U.S.A.

MISSION IN BAHRAIN

Samuel Zwemer and James Cantine of the Arabian Mission first arrived in Bahrain in 1890. They visited the main city, Moharrek, and toured the villages on donkeyback. The next year Samuel Zwemer rented a room and a small, dark shop to sell Bibles, Testaments, and other books in Arabic. He gave what medical treatment he could. Abscesses, ulcers, and aching teeth were the main ailments, but malaria and cholera were rampant all over the Gulf.

All kinds of people frequented the bookshop, but a storm of anger burst when a local religious judge forbade the selling of books and the town crier warned people not to buy Christian books. The denunciation provided free advertisement for the small shop and its sales increased.

An American friend gave $6,000 to buy land and build a hospital. It was very difficult to buy land, but finally the ruler permitted it. With a great deal of trouble, a hospital was built and opened in 1902.

By the time I arrived in 1965, the original hospital had passed its usefulness and had been torn down and rebuilt. This rebuilding was financed by the Church at home, with very generous contributions from the ruler of Bahrain and local merchants.

His highess Shaikh Isa bin Sulman Al Khalifa was the wise, cheerful ruler, who became Shaikh of Bahrain in 1962. Because Bahrain's oil was already running out, he set his sights on developing all kinds of business and made foreigners welcome. Shaikh Isa was a great friend of the mission, giving us his political support and contributing generously to all our building projects, even to our new church building. Guests were always welcome to call on him at his palace and were usually invited to dine at his bountiful table.

At the Bahrain mission hospital, we had five physicians and a staff of about a hundred local and Indian personnel. Our patients and hospital finances were much like the situation in Kuwait. The government's medical services were free to all, but people liked to have the choice of going to the mission hospitals. Private practitioners also flourished.

Our mission compound included lodging for the Indian nurses and some married staff, two houses, a bookstore, a church, and a school for about a hundred local girls. The buildings were locally constructed of coral rock, cement, and whitewash. Another walled compound about a block away from the hospital enclosed apartments for single women, houses for evangelistic workers, a tennis court, a small chapel, and an orphanage house. My cousin, Madeline Holmes, lived there with ten or so orphans in her charge.

My colleagues were a happy breed and were my family in Bahrain. Twenty or more of us assembled every month to discuss and resolve our problems, usually amiably. I worked most closely with Dr. Don Bosch, our surgeon; Dr. Corine Overkamp, a recent graduate of my own medical college; Dr. A. Koshy, an Indian surgeon; and Jeannette Veldman, R.N., our able and efficient nursing superintendent. Dr. Overkamp wanted to specialize in internal medicine, so we divided the women's work between us, and I took most of the obstetrics and gynecology.

CASES

Our mornings began with an English-language devotional service with the Christian staff in the prayer room. We then made rounds on inpatients and had a short song, talk, and prayer in Arabic with any of the local staff who wanted to attend.

Our morning and afternoon clinics encompassed everything in the medical books: pediatrics, women's diseases, dermatology, orthopedics, ophthalmology, nose and throat, dentistry, and even some things not found in the books. We took turns being on call at night when anything could happen. The Indian nurses were also midwives and could take care of normal deliveries. One night the nurse called me by phone and said a woman had come in and suddenly precipitated a three-month fetus. What should she do? I suggested that she put it back inside, as it was too small.

One surprising case was Miriam Yusuf, 19 years old, who came in at 6 P.M. with abdominal pain and some vaginal bleeding. There was a large mass in the fornix which was buzzing like a hive of bees. I'd never felt anything like it. I admitted her. Next morning, finding her pregnancy test was positive and hemoglobin only 50 percent of normal, we gave her four units of blood (one from me). Dr. Koshy and I operated. We found a huge tumor attached to nearly all her internal organs so diagnosed an inoperable carcinoma and let her go home to die. To my surprise six months later she came back to see me looking quite well. The tumor was still there but smaller. She had gone to the government hospital where they diagnosed a chorio-carcinoma and were curing her with methotrexate. I was only *practicing* medicine, and still learning.

One of my inpatients was a young woman with tubercular meningitis. I was sure she could be helped in the hospital with Streptomycin and Isoniazid. But when she had spells of stupor, the family insisted on taking her home. They believed that abnormal mental states were caused by evil spirits. Their treatment was to have a religious teacher read the Qur'an over her. I implored, "Bring the mullah to the hospital. He can sit here all day and read." But they felt we didn't have the right atmosphere and took her home, where she later died.

"Please stay in the hospital," I asked a woman with blood pressure of 260/110. "I can't, I have four little children at home."

The Arab lady from Saudi Arabia weighed 233 pounds, but weeping, said she couldn't diet.

I began to see men patients in the afternoon clinics. One wanted to speak English and told me, "I've got a prospect and the doctors say I need oppression."

Many of the healthy-looking men complained of "weakness." In my innocence of the male scx, it took me a little time to figure out that trouble. One of the men complained of a feeling of heat and burning and asked if I didn't have something to cool him. "The prostitutes are so expensive. I can't afford them." So I gave him an injection of female sex hormone and some stilbestrol tablets.

The family of a woman with throat cancer kept her at home as long as they could stand the smell and then brought her to the hospital. I had been hardened to most terrible sights, but this head with its open cavern shook me.

A British lady delivered her normal-looking baby girl at night. The nurses told me the baby later had blue spells. One of our visiting surgeons gave me a hint. "Look for a tracheal-esophageal fistula" (in which the two tubes end in a blind pouch). That

proved to be the correct diagnosis. Four surgeons and an anesthetist came over from the government hospital and repaired the
congenital defect before the baby was twenty-four hours old. A
year later, the grateful mother sent me her picture.

Our patients began to expect the most modern care. One man,
examining his X-ray plate, complained, "Why is this only black
and white? Don't you have them in technicolor now?"

A man asked me to come to his home to help his mother who
was very constipated, so I took an enema can, which gave good
results. The man was so grateful, he gave me a Persian carpet.
The patients were most grateful for even slight attention. I was
the undeserving recipient of gold rings, pearl bracelets, and many
other gifts.

For my six-week vacation in the summer of 1966, I flew to Istanbul and spent some time exploring Turkey. At first I splurged
by staying at the Hilton (I had just received some extra funds).
But my Dutch thriftiness couldn't enjoy the expenditure, so I
moved over to the YWCA.

I visited the grand mosques, Santa Sophia, Topkapi Palace,
and other historic sites; took a ship to Turkish cities along the
Black Sea; and toured ancient sites at Ephesus, Pergamon, and
Asklepeion, which was a center for healing about 300 B.C. Tem-
ples of Aesculapius and Dionysos indicated that medicine and
religion were combined in those days. The great physician Galen
was born here in 131 A.D.

Philosophers, clergy, and leaders came to Asklepcion for rest
and healing. A circular rest stop was lined with testimonials of
healing, written in Greek. Another round building consisted of
many small rooms, thought to be consulting rooms. The patient
slept alone in a room. If a snake touched him during the night,
he would be cured. I took a picture of the caduceus, the staff entwined with serpents that symbolizes medicine to this day, carved
on a plinth two thousand years ago there at Asklepeion.

My vacation concluded with a stop in Athens, from which I
returned to my duties in Bahrain. Many of the problems I had
encountered in the women's practice in Kuwait were reenacted in
Bahrain. Once again I was faced with difficult decisions concern-
ing unwanted pregnancies. The government of Bahrain started a
course in nursing for the local girls and asked me to teach the
Obstetrics and Gynecology course. I tried to do it in Arabic and

English. One of the girls came asking me to do an abortion for her. She told the problems of living in a polygamous family where half brothers and sisters live intimately in the same room. She said she couldn't help what happened. I felt I couldn't help her. Somehow she managed to start the process and came back to me in labor and delivered five-month twins which were not alive.

Many young women were employed by the wealthy Bahrain families as household servants. Most came from the Seychelles Islands, which were Roman Catholic, overpopulated, and poor. The girls were desperate enough to be willing to do anything. They attended the Sacred Heart Church, where crowds of local men offered their attention. Many of the girls came to us with their problems. One had fever and was hemorrhaging. I did a curettage and packed the uterus, but the bleeding would not stop. The blood just wouldn't clot. I strenuously repacked as tightly as possible, but the bleeding still did not stop. To my grief, she died in a few hours.

One woman came in with extreme paroxysms of tetanus after a home delivery. I had lost too many of those cases, so I promptly took her over to the government hospital. They saved her life by doing a prompt tracheotomy and kept her on a respirator with a nurse beside her twenty-four hours a day. After a month, she recovered.

A girl and her mother from an aristocratic family came to my office. They had been progressive, let the girl take an office job, and I found she was pregnant. I couldn't help her but advised her to tell her mother. In spite of her tears and protesting, I told her mother. The woman solved the problem by taking her daughter to Beirut, where anything conceivable was available.

Muscat doctors sent me a young girl, accompanied by her family. She had jaundice and liver disease. She was a sweet child. I did everything I could think of, but she kept slipping in and out of coma depending on how much penicillin I gave and finally died.

There was a case of an Indian woman with progressive muscular atrophy of both arms. The government doctors diagnosed amyotrophic lateral sclerosis and said they could do nothing. She insisted that some cases just like hers were being cured in India. The doctors restudied the case and finally found she had leprosy, which could be treated.

Madeline (not her name) was the daughter of a Palestinian

family who lost their home to the Israelis. She had been in a girls' boarding school and wanted more education. She applied to the Bahrain nursing school. On her first physical examination, it was found she actually had male sex glands and immature genitalia. Girls in the Middle East never undress, so she was shocked and couldn't consider a sex change. The male glands were removed, but the government school refused to take her. She came to us. We took her and found she was a very likeable, intelligent, and energetic helper. She seemed happy. Some years later she told me she had dates with a young doctor and had fallen in love with him. But she said, "I can't bear to tell him my history." So she remained single.

The government hospital had some excellent physicians and specialists. Most were British or Indian. Dr. Ali Fakharoo, a Bahraini, had specialized in cardiology in Boston. He was most generous with his consultations. We were invited to attend valuable teaching clinics at the Sulmaniyah Hospital. I subscribed to taped medical lectures from the U.S.A. so kept up some education in the rapidly changing science of medicine. We had a chance to treat some newly discovered diseases and use progressive techniques. Dr. Corine found some thalassemia and I spotted sickle-cell anemia, both congenital blood diseases. The burn cases were the greatest problems. One little girl was saved using the Eusol dressings and skin grafting, but she developed heavy keloids. The laboratory found African trypanosomes in a blood smear, but the patient refused treatment.

We followed the unusual case of the little girl with epidermolysis bullosa, a congenital skin disease that ulcerates unless meticulous daily care is provided. The British nurse at the government hospital practically adopted her and finally took her to live at her home in England. It was impossible for the girl to live with her own family in Bahrain.

I admitted an American worker who came off a ship. He had a history of sudden acute cardiac pain. Dr. Corine took care of him but could never find any proof of disease. It seems that it is possible to fake the illness if one knows the symptoms well enough. He took me out to dinner. After T-bone steaks, he declared he didn't have enough money to pay the bill and managed to charge the shipping line. After the ship left, the fellow recovered.

Since alcohol was forbidden by Islam, we saw only occasional cases of drunkenness. There was drug abuse, though. One mission cook smoked enough hashish to make him incompetent, and we had to let him go.

We started a prenatal clinic at the small village of Dair. The town was on the shore of the brilliant blue-green sea studded with the white sails of fishing boats. An astonishingly prolific freshwater spring poured out right beside the shore and watered the date grove. One of the evangelistic couples went with me and talked with the village people.

Mary Hammand, a black teacher from the Presbyterian mission in Egypt, had to leave when war came. She came to help in our school and joined our upstairs household of Anne Lisa Jensen and me. Bill and Mae Dekker, who lived downstairs, invited us to eat breakfast with them daily. Jeannette Veldman inherited the mission cook, Qassim, and generously invited all of us single people to eat noon dinners with her. When J. V. retired Rose Nykerk carried on the tradition. We enjoyed the happy companionship of congenial friends sharing our burdens and our jokes over daily sessions of home cooked food, tasty fish, succulent prawns, curry, dates, and homemade bread.

The cook Qassim always brought his little son Hassan to help him work. Hassan played with the mission children and unconsciously became a Christian. He grew up and was employed at the airport as a mechanic. He was an attractive personality but surprised us all when he asked Judy Zeitema to marry him. He first became a legal Christian by baptism at a Sunday morning service, which is the critical step out of Islam. Judy accepted him and they went home for the wedding. Hassan took courses in airplane engineering. They intended to come back to live in Bahrain, but it didn't work out. They had children and lived happily ever after in the U.S.A.

THE CLOSING OF KUWAIT'S MEDICAL MISSION, MARCH 1967

The conception of missions by "those whose minds were lighted by wisdom from on high" in the U.S.A. was changing. The book, *The Bridges of God* by Donald McGavran of Fuller Seminary advocated that the Church should undertake its main mission efforts in places where people were ready to receive the Gospel and churches could be organized. The chief aim should be church growth. Places where there was little response should receive only nominal maintenance.

Dissenters protested that where the battle is fiercest and the opposition strongest is just where the stoutest warriors should be sent. But the advanced thinkers on our Reformed Church Board were asking, "Why should the Church support a hospital for a state which is oil-rich and is providing medical care for its people by bringing trained staff from all the world?"

I wrote a letter trying to explain our situation, but the Board wrote they would not publish it, as they were sending out a committee to study their position. The group of five that was selected included the Board secretary, a physician of the Church, a secular specialist in hospital planning, and others. We protested that our Arabian missionaries should also be included, so they added Dr. Donald Bosch. They wrote, "Missionaries, who are emotionally involved in the local situation, are unable to make objective decisions." The Board felt that mission methods should be planned in the U.S.A.

This special committee, which arrived in February 1967, was to decide if mission medical work was essential in Kuwait. The evangelistic aspect was not to be considered. Their decision was a foregone conclusion—the Kuwait mission hospital was deemed not medically necessary, and it was decided that the mission should be closed within the month.

We were stunned. Was it possible that our daring undertaking, establishing a beachhead in a fanatical center of Islam, could be obliterated suddenly by persons not even involved in the work? The Arabian Mission had also lost its three stations in Iraq recently. Was the impossible dream of missions in Arabia to fade altogether?

The decision was made so suddenly and by such a small group that there wasn't time to write and inform our supporters at home. The mission as a whole had no opportunity to discuss, vote, or decide about the matter.

I knew there had been a history of friction between the men in evangelism and those in medicine. The medical workers were so obviously popular and the others so ignored that resentment could not be avoided. After Jerry Nykerk died, the new physicians and specialists who came were not committed to the mission approach. The clergymen—Garret De Jong, Jacob Holler, and Leonard Kalkward—felt the medical work was too prominent. Arab Christians from Lebanon and Palestine felt that mission work was not their duty or vocation. So there was no group to oppose the closing of the hospital.

John Buteyn, the mission secretary, planned to make the official closing of the hospital a spectacular event. He invited me to attend, so I flew to Kuwait from Bahrain. I could do nothing but weep. The Scudders and I suffered the agony of it together. The staff we loved, who now lost their positions, were bewildered. The hospital was my child. I was witnessing its dying gasp. And it was my Church that was killing it. It was a grief too heavy to bear. There was to be a reception in the women's hospital so that my friends could come to say good-bye. Very few came. Our Arab friends did not approve of the closing. One of the government leaders took Dr. Scudder aside and told him that if this were a matter of not having enough money, he would personally help.

The American embassy gave a large reception with speeches in appreciation of the medical work. The Scudders were given a medal sent by President Johnson. I went off alone to a quiet corner, weeping, unwilling that my tear-stained face should be seen. The official program was held in the women's hospital, with representatives of the government and chief men present. TV cameras and speeches let all Kuwait know that the mission hospital was finished. Kuwait was now able to take care of all its medical needs by itself. I could not bear to stay. I had to get out and weep bitterly alone.

So, a great dream and the fifty-seven-year effort of many devoted people were ended. Perhaps it was inevitable, but it was unnecessarily abrupt. We lost contact with many friends among the Kuwaitis. The Arabs considered the hospital to be the mission itself. They came to the conclusion that Christianity was inferior to the wealth and power of the world. The Church failed to take the great opportunity to use the position it had achieved over the years to display Christ's healing power in a new way.

I wrote a letter to some of the leaders in our church at home. They wrote back that John Buteyn had their complete confidence and approval. They sternly criticized my views. They claimed the mission work would still go on in the bookshop. The Church would carry on with Board support. There were now thousands of Christian expatriates in Kuwait who would be Christian witnesses, they claimed.

The Kuwaiti government took over the mission property and buildings, which they used as offices. They very generously paid the Reformed Church of America $2,400,000.00. The Church used it mostly for expenses in the American church. The Kuwaitis have allowed the church building and homes of the two pastors, with various other buildings, to be used for Christian worship and service up to this day.

My distress was deep. For months my heart was filled with turmoil, misery, and bitterness. In the daytime I was busy and I could forget, but I wept at night.

Next, John Buteyn came to Bahrain with the idea of closing the hospital there. Shaikh Isa sent his personal representative to the State Department in Washington asking information as to who really supported the mission and hospital. When he found out, he informed John that the hospital had his personal support, and he wanted it to continue in Bahrain. Shaikh Isa made it clear that closing the hospital would cost the mission his friendship. So the medical work continued in Bahrain.

The situation in Oman was quite different. At that time, there was no other medical care for most of the Omanis, so the Board did not consider closing the hospitals in Oman.

And life did go on. The Indian and local staff from the Kuwait hospital quickly found positions in the government system. Some emigrated to America. Dr. Scudder was appointed staff physician at the military hospital, and Dorothy Scudder joined him there as nursing superintendent.

I was deeply disappointed in my church. Some of us agreed that the men in power made a mistake in closing the work the way they did. We had lacked people with vision who could communicate our concerns to the Board. People at home did not realize what a stern opponent Islam is. There were other options, but none were studied. The government of Kuwait was willing for our work to continue. The hospital earned enough to pay its own expenses, except for the missionaries' salaries, and sometimes made a profit. Dorothy Scudder was a wonderful manager and was not properly appreciated. Still, Christians have failed the Church many times, yet it is the Church which must carry on the Gospel.

Here is a translation of a letter in Arabic written to the American church after the closing of the Kuwait mission hospital. It was sent by Amina, daughter of Sayyid Amr, wife of Mohammad Akeel:

> Ladies and Gentlemen,
>
> It is with deep sorrow to express my feelings at the closing of the American Mission Hospital and the departure of the medical staff plus other members of the hospital staff.
>
> It is difficult to put in words the appreciation that I have felt for the work that each one of the staff did, and the noble services rendered to the people of this country who were supposed to be hosts to these people during the past 54 years, like Dr. Mylrea, Dr. Scudder, Dr. Nykerk, Haleema, Miriam, and Wasmeya [Arabic names for Dr. Calverley, Miss Van Pelt, and Dr. Mary B. Allison]. They gave all their time and effort for humanitarian services to the people of Kuwait, during a time when Kuwait had no medical facilities, transport, or any other modern facilities.
>
> These people not only ran the clinic but made calls at homes at any time and they received hundreds of patients each day. They treated them with love and without malice or prejudice. They performed their services with sincerity, faithfulness, and love. They took pride in the work they did. They helped in every way no matter what the cost was, without making it known as to how they helped (without blowing their horn) and through this they made many friends in Kuwait who still remember and talk about them.
>
> With this, I close this letter repeating my thanks and appreciation, and I pray God to reward all for the work they have so diligently done for the people of Kuwait, and I assure them that though they are away, they are still in our hearts and minds and we have good memories of their love and work.
>
> (Signed) Amina bint Mohammad Sayyid Amr

INTERLUDE IN OMAN, 1968

The closings and changes in the mission hospitals affected us all. Fewer and fewer people were interested in the career, which seemed to be in its waning days. By June 1968, Oman station was so short of doctors that they had to ask for help. When Dr. Alice van der Zwaag left Oman on vacation, Dr. Wells Thoms asked me to come for ten days to give them a hand. We had two women doctors in Bahrain at that time, so I could be spared.

My plane stopped at Qatar, Sharjah, Abu Dhabi, and Dubai. In Dubai they were feverishly building a great new airport, but still used an old courtyard crowded with black-draped women and children, all fanning themselves and drinking Pepsis.

Our plane came down between bare, black mountains to Oman, where Midge and Jay Kapenga met me. Since it was Saturday, they took me for a picnic and swim on the glorious sandy beach north of the cities where the mountains kept it private.

Sunday brought a series of religious services, some in the town of Mutrah and some in Muscat, its twin city three miles away by mountain road. The first meeting was a Sunday School class for the twenty-five leprosy patients cared for by the mission. They had a separate lot where they had small rooms and cooked their food. Tubercular patients had yet another building and space. We sat with the patients on mats under a shady tree. It was surprising how cheerful they seemed in spite of missing fingers, ulcerated feet, and blindness. The Omani Christians had an Arabic worship service. Then Anne De Young, the mission nurse, gave a talk about Christ to any hospital patients who wanted to listen. In the evening, we had an English service in the little chapel attended by British political officers and oil company personnel.

Muscat and Mutrah are humid seaside towns, each set in a bowl of bare, rocky mountains that cuts off any breeze and radiates the heat so that the nights are even hotter than the days. Most summers, the local people flee and spend the hot days on the coastal plain called the Batina, where good dates grow. But this particular summer, what with the new roads and lorries, people streamed back to town bringing their sick. There were at least a hundred inpatients—not counting the families who settled down to take care of them. Those that camped under the scrawny trees we called the "Under Tree Ward."

In Oman, people had to live on the local products. That meant mostly fish and dates, but they were the best in the world. The cook had to get down early to the seashore to buy sea salmon, carrupa, and red snapper. The fishermen brought in the large hammerhead sharks, too. A special treat was smoked fish. The

Rev. Dykstra, now retired, had planned and built a special chimney in the kitchen for smoking fish. The cook used excelsior to produce fragrant smoke. So between smoked fish, curry and rice, limes, and tiny, tasty bananas, we enjoyed really good meals.

My patients in Oman had every disease known to us! My first group of inpatients was typical. There were two cases of tetanus and several of meningitis; two children had nephosis with swollen bodies; one boy of twelve had heart disease; a mastoid case; pneumonia; diarrhea; fevers of malaria and unknown origin; terrible anemias; terrible teeth; leg ulcers; abscesses; osteomyelitis; starving babies; all kinds of eye disease; and one woman with a vesicular-vaginal fistula that had been leaking urine and smelling foul for years.

One afternoon, I sat with Dr. Wells Thoms treating the leprosy patients. I never saw more concentrated human misery in my life. The lepers were discarded by their families, blind, syphilitic, tubercular, with leprosy and starvation all in one person. Now there are good and effective drugs to treat leprosy. The Worldwide Leprosy Association helped to care for these people financially.

There was no end to new problems in medicine, even in Oman. Some Lebanese presented with tapeworm. They were fond of a dish of raw ground meat. I had to retreat to my books to figure out a treatment. I found that the worm's head is the all-important item. The worm fastens itself firmly just beyond the stomach sphincter in the first part of the duodenum. The drug Oleoesina Aspidii has to be applied in full strength to this head to make it release its grip. To do this, the patient has to swallow a long, narrow stomach tube with a metallic weighted tip. This tube slowly works its way past the sphincter. You check its position by X-ray, and if it seems correct, a generous dose of the drug is forced down through the tube onto the worm's head. After a short time a big draught of magnesium sulfate washes the worm out. Finding the head in the resulting mess proves the cure. It was usually a very satisfying treatment.

Dr. Wells Thoms treated a most tragic case one night. An elderly village man brought in his dying bride, who was about ten years old. She had been bleeding from a torn perineum for a couple of days. He refused to give blood until Wells shamed him with reproaches. But it was too late. Wells censured the parents of the child for marrying her off so young. They protested, "But he promised he wouldn't take her until she was older!"

The second Saturday I was in Oman, Wells and Beth Thoms took me on a picnic to Cemetery Cove. We hired a local skiff with men to row us down the mountainous coast. We read the names of the missionaries who had given their lives in Oman. Bishop French, buried there, was British. He came in 1900 and died of heat stroke after only a few months. George Stone had been an enthusiastic young man who came out in 1898 and died after a year, of fever. Wells' father, Dr. Sharon Thoms, started medical work in 1909 and died from a fall in 1913. Now, our colleague Dr. Heusinkveld lies there, too.

We went swimming in the clear blue sea between the rocky ledges. It was thrilling. The sandy floor was covered with sea plants. We had snorkels and could watch the lovely fish with dramatic colors and exotic patterns—all playing around and not afraid of us. That evening we followed the road back past the ancient Portuguese fort that served as the sultan's prison. Several hundred political prisoners lived out their days there.

Wells was working on an ancient Arabic manuscript with one of the well-educated Arabs. It was written in 1335 by an Arab physician in Damascus. Judging by the evidence in the manuscript, this medieval doctor, Dr. Ibn Nefccsi, had almost figured out the major and minor circulation of the blood. But Harvey got the credit for the discovery in the West when he published his article in 1628. It is fairly certain that Arabic manuscripts were available in Padua, Italy, where Harvey studied medicine, so we may have to give credit to the Arabs for the momentous discovery. About 1350, the best physicians in the world were Arabs.

My last Sunday in Oman started with a bang and never let up. I was sleeping on the flat roof of the mission's two-story house. It was wonderful to watch the stars, the Milky Way, and an occasional shooting star. Hospital staff called me by a rope and a string of bells at 5 A.M.

The first case was an unconscious child with a hemoglobin of 23 percent and a large liver and spleen. We had some blood given by men on a British ship, but before I could do the cut-down, he died. "This is the will of God," said the broken-hearted father, consoling himself with the only solution he knew.

The next case was an eight-year-old child with fever and convulsions. I did a lumbar puncture, but it was clear. I didn't realize it then, but these cases are usually from the malignant falciparum malaria endemic in Oman. Complicated with the anemia of malaria and malnutrition, the result is a quick death.

The next case was a young woman burned in the explosion of her kerosene pressure cooking stove. Cotton dresses and head veils burn quickly; she was about 75 percent burned. I started fluids, gave her some blood, and put her in our air-conditioned room. The relatives liked the AC room so wanted to sit beside her. The nurses did the dressing. Another woman who had come for eye surgery suddenly shot to a fever of 106, so I put her in the AC room, too.

In the afternoon, two car accident cases came in, but they weren't very serious. But the next one appalled me. A young woman had delivered her premature baby in the village and then went into a toxic hepatitis with jaundice and coma. Such cases were described in our medical books in a footnote, as they don't see them anymore in America. They have many of them in Oman. All of them die. The family were so desperate that they gave blood. Intravenous glucose did not help. I heard she died the next day, after I left. The burned girl died, too. When I heard the news, I felt I was in the slough of despair.

The next case cheered me a bit. I did a curettage for a bleeding miscarriage and she was cured. At 11 P.M., the nurse at the Muscat hospital called to say she was sending over a maternity case that required a Caesarian section. Dr. Dass, the Indian doctor, and I performed it together. It was a perfect success, so the strenuous day ended well.

The Muscat hospital took all the normal maternity cases. They performed 1,500 deliveries in six months with a staff of one Indian doctor, the mission nurse, and several Indian nurses who were also midwives.

The situation in Oman was incredible. The ruler Sultan Saeed bin Taimur was getting some money from the oil which had just been discovered there. It wasn't much, so he felt he couldn't start government medical care. He refused to befriend or even recognize Dr. Thoms because Wells helped and was friendly to some of the village chiefs who the Sultan considered to be his enemies.

Sultan Saeed really worked at his job of ruling. Everything had to have his formal written permission and his answer to most requests was, "No." The mission had to ask to bring in needed staff or visitors, so we couldn't improve the care. Even travel into the interior was forbidden. He wrote out the exact specifications of clothes for women. Women were not allowed to drive cars, which was a nuisance to us, because our men had to stop their work to drive women between the two hospitals. Wells said that the sultan was starting some clinics in some mountain villages. There was one boys' school in the twin cities. Permission was not given to go abroad for study. Men were allowed to leave the country for work, but their women were never allowed to leave Oman. The mission had a small school for girls. The sultan lived in his palace far off beyond the desert in a beautiful, fertile oasis on the southern seafront—Salala. He kept his only son Qaboos, who had been educated in England, under house arrest.

Wells was turning gray after his forty years of service in Oman, but he still walked briskly and spoke with assurance. When he came around with a cheery and optimistic word, it lifted the strain and stress of seeing so much human misery. We knew him for God's saint.

The next day, Monday, my permit to stay expired. Just before I left, a little boy was brought in with his intestines protruding from a jagged intestinal wound. He said he was paddling his little homemade boat of oil cans when a swordfish jumped out of the water and stabbed him. Yet another boy, about twelve years old, was rowing his small boat in the bay when the prow of a big ship rammed him. He had broken bones and huge loss of blood. There was no blood for him, but I heard afterward that he recovered.

It had been an exhausting stay, but it was obvious that the work in Oman needed trained and committed medical personnel. After describing my experience in Oman to a friend at home, I wrote:

> The Board in New York are writing letters that I am supposed to retire next year when I will be 65 because that's a mission rule. I wonder what is the matter with their heads in the face of such situations here.

Maybe because I was Dutch and stubborn, I decided I was staying no matter what the Board said.

When I got back from Oman, the mission community in Bahrain had been encouraged by the addition of Danish missionaries. The Danish Church had been working at Aden, which they had to abandon when the British withdrew and the Communists took over.

We gained two evangelistic couples. Their talented bookshop manager opened a shop beside the hospital and soon had it financially secure and stocked with a variety of beautiful books. The bookstore filled a real need for the growing numbers of educated young Arabs and expatriates.

I had the pleasure of living and working with Anne Lisa Jensen, a young Danish nurse. Her first morning at the hospital, she set out with a bucket of hot, soapy water to scrub the bottoms of our baby bassinets. We kept the tops where the babies lay nice and clean but just didn't look below. The Indian nurses watched with amazement to see a graduate nurse doing sweepers' work.

The arrival of new missionaries from the United States also brought changes, at times not so pleasant to accept. The New York office had sent out two young physicians, with their families, to study Arabic and help with surgery. We began to feel a generation gap as the two newcomers loudly criticized our mission's work. They even voiced disapproval of the church building plans, which had gone through years of careful planning, hard bargaining, and discussion with the Board before finally being granted. One of our evangelists, who had fought devotedly for the project, exploded in wrath at the newcomers' lack of appreciation.

Then one of the doctors lit into me at a hospital staff meeting. He severely criticized me for giving the nurse midwives authority to deliver some maternity cases, and neglect grossly deformed newborns. He condemned my medical ethics and accused me of malpractice. I was shocked and deeply hurt by his sudden attack. The other physicians I had worked with understood the dilemmas we faced in dealing with large numbers of primitive people. The new generation of doctors came from an America where great changes in medical thinking were taking place. I had to realize I was getting out of date.

This young surgeon took charge of surgical cases. He, too,

made tragic decisions. He finally decided that mission work did not suit his talents and went home. The other young surgeon continued with us. We gradually came to understand each other, and I learned a lot from him. He continued his commitment to our work when he transferred to Ethiopia.

The dissension among our mission community in Bahrain was only symptomatic of the stresses being felt at all levels of the mission effort. In February 1965, the World Council of Churches had held a convention at Tubingen, West Germany, to discuss the Church's involvement in medical work. The conferees concluded that the Church should not be saddled with the heavy medical burden of running hospitals if other resources were available. The Church and hospital should work together to obey Christ's commandment, "Go heal." Modern medicine needs the Church to treat the whole person by healing souls of sin, fear, and hatred. There must needs be continual education and dialogue between healers, beginning with prayers for the sick by the hospital chaplain.

The Reformed Church of America, which sponsored our mission in Arabia, concluded that the role of its mission stations needed serious review. As local governments assumed responsibility for medical care, our hospitals might become redundant. Thus, we needed to face the possibility that they would be closed, or phased out by limiting their activity to providing specialized medical services or to training paramedical and administrative staff which would enhance local medical capabilities.

In March 1968, Bahrain entertained the entire mission of a hundred souls, including children. The New York office sent out high-powered speakers to wrestle with the big questions. Why does Communism have such power to sway people, while the Church, with the power of God, seems so ineffective? Is baptism advisable for Muslim converts when it cuts them out of their community? Does God move in secular history?

It seemed to me that we are most effective missionaries to Muslims when they are absolutely certain we are not trying to convert them. People who can't stand the situation at home become missionaries. If they are misfits there, they go home to become Board secretaries!

I could not agree with the thinking of church leaders at home that mission institutions such as schools and hospitals were now superfluous, had passed the time of their fruitfulness, or had been failures in evangelism. I believed that now was the time to redouble our efforts. The situation in the 1960s was no different than the challenge that Islam had always posed to Christianity. Islam is Christianity's direct competitor and has always resisted Christianity no matter what method was tried. Islam has spread over the entire globe and enjoys a prestigious 1,400-year history.

Moreover, Islam's basic premise is that Christianity is not truth. It despises Middle Eastern Christian groups as inferiors and losers; thus they lack prestige and power and refuse to do mission work among Muslims, as they are met with persecution and massacres.

Muslim culture invests Islam with political and social power; in turn Islam gives the Arab Muslim a security that is so positive, proud, and self-sufficient that he sees no need of change. And Islamic nations now have the riches to spread Islam effectively.

Therefore, mission work among Muslims requires the strongest kind of advocacy—not retreat and retrenchment. Anthropologists state that social change of any magnitude at all cannot be made by individuals. Transformation is accomplished by groups.

To advocate a change in worldview, as mission does, requires the strongest kind of witness. It requires a community of persons with prestige, recognized as Christian, who have the ability to work and live with each other and with people of other faiths. Missionaries must also demonstrate skill in secular life in order to make Christ visible, intelligible, and desirable. Such a group needs to be large enough to allow for changes in personnel, family emergencies, drop-outs, short-termers, vacations, and furloughs. Most of the group needs to be committed to a mission career. The personnel need to be highly trained in language, theology, and sociology. They need to be practical and flexible enough to adjust comfortably to another culture.

I believe the institutions of mission school and hospital provide the best setting for this kind of community. Our schools and hospitals are historically and presently acceptable to the people and governments of our stations in the Gulf. They should be strengthened. No other kind of approach is now acceptable.

Some examples of individual approach were tried in Kuwait while I was there, but they failed. Here are a few examples:

Paul, an Indian mechanic, worked for the oil company. He would invite other employees to his tent evenings to talk about Christ. The oil company quickly found an excuse to send him back to India.

An earnest Lebanese evangelist came to Kuwait and walked around the bazaar offering Gospels. He was promptly arrested by the police and compelled to leave.

An Australian nurse got a job in the government hospital and talked with her patients about Christ. The hospital discharged her even though she was a good nurse.

The pace of change in Arabia now is rapid. Such change begets change. A culture which is changing rapidly tends to believe in change. The Arabs are confronting the serious moral problems of the present age and are looking for solutions. It may be the first time that they will seriously consider the Christian message. Radio will not be sufficient. The message needs face-to-face personal encounters to spread effectively. Even so, it was still hard to sense progress in our goals.

In Bahrain, my endeavors in evangelism were limited to taking the morning prayers in English or Arabic in the hospital. I bought Christian books from the bookshop and offered them to patients who could read. One was the mullah of the mosque next door to the hospital. He took several. When he left I asked him if he wanted to give them back. He said, "No, I'm taking them home for the family to read."

Several Christian families had lived in Bahrain a long time. They were business people, descendants of the ancient Assyrian or Nestorian Church of northern Iraq. Some were Roman Catholic. Some attended our church and wanted Christian education for their children. But they felt that mission was not their work and took no part in witnessing to their faith. They did not associate socially with Muslims.

God only knows how many people were influenced by the mission. Ray Weiss told of a group of young men who gathered to read the Gospel and pray but kept it secret. They felt they couldn't join the despised local Christian group.

Ray also told that when he was visiting a tubercular patient in the government hospital, he saw another patient reading the Gospel. He asked him how he happened to have a copy. The man replied that he had picked up some tracts in the mission hospital that explained how to send away for a correspondence course in Christianity. He had sent for it and was studying it.

Um Miriam had become a Christian thirty years before I arrived. She was an Iranian widow who came with three little children, two of whom were sight-impaired. Um Miriam took care of the orphaned babies to earn a living and became a Christian after hearing the Word. So her three children grew up Christian and received treatment in our hospital.

Yusuf received a fair education in Bahrain and became our hospital manager, with local business on the side. He married a Palestinian school teacher in our mission school. They had three children who were Christians. They flourished with the oil riches that came to the Gulf.

The ten or twelve children in the orphanage suffered under the stigma of being illegitimate. Some of the girls became Christians, but the boys either emigrated to the U.S.A. or turned bitterly against the mission. Some of the girls married men who came from outside. When their marriages fell apart, they came back to the mission house with children, so we had to raise second-generation orphans. It was the custom in Arab society that when a girl is divorced, she can return to her father's house.

But these converts were all from the fringes of society, despised by the Muslims and sometimes an embarrassment to the mission.

But despite all my feelings to the contrary, the work of the Arabian Mission was changing. The Board sent out Kenneth Warren, a businessman, to modernize the mission and try to get the mission out of running institutions. A local school board was formed, consisting of a local woman as principal, some missionaries, concerned local Christians, and an Arab businessman, Jamal Arayad. I was asked to be its secretary. The idea was to put local people in charge of the institutions. When one of the local women was made principal, it caused hostility and jealousy. We had to deliberate in long and heated discussions at board meetings. The school was to be enlarged and to add junior high grades. A new building would be built. The local people felt that no Muslim pupil should sit in a class where Bible was taught unless the parents requested it in writing. Some parents did request it. The government sent a Muslim woman teacher of Islam.

The Church sent out some short-term teachers to teach English. The other teachers came from Palestine or were local women. Islam was taught to all the students, 98 percent of whom were Muslim.

So eventually our problems were worked out and the school became an unqualified success. By 1970, the population of Bahrain was about 200,000, 56 percent of which was under twenty years of age. The government schools had 48,000 students in separate boys' and girls' schools. Our mission school had 355 students and was the only coeducational school. Classes ran from kindergarten up to junior high. Both Arabic and English were used. The school occupied two lines of rooms with a large open court on the mission grounds. Most of the students paid tuition of about $25 per month, but some were charity cases. The school had a good reputation, with more applicants than could be admitted. Fancy trying to choose 60 kindergartners out of 175 applicants!

Then, of course, there was the question of the hospital itself. Our hospital was a complicated institution with its hundred employees. Ken Warren recommended that it gradually become a locally supported organization with a local board. The Reformed Church would send medical personnel. Even so, the Church cut back on medical staff, and it was difficult to provide the usual assistance when the hospital confronted normal staff shortages due to illness or furlough.

Finances were usually favorable, as the patients paid fees, although one out of every ten cases we treated was a charity case. Shaikh Isa gave us a generous monetary gift every year, and many local merchants also contributed. Ali Yateem donated a large air-conditioning unit for the clinic. Foreign firms made contracts for us to treat their staff. So we usually managed, though when hospital staff members had to go home unexpectedly, the hospital suffered.

The hospital board wanted us to try new ventures. So I went out to one of the villages to run a prenatal and postnatal clinic one day a week, hoping to entice more delivery cases to come to our hospital. A nurse and sometimes an evangelist went with me.

Bill Dekker set up a public address system in the hospital to broadcast prayer and talks to all the patients' rooms. They could turn it off if they didn't want it.

The clinic, as usual, was divided into a men's and women's side with two or three doctors for each. The clinic was open twice a day most days. Later we added an evening clinic. Each of us took turns being on night call. Many of the women spoke only Irani, so we each had to have a translator. Patients came from all over the Middle East, Yemen, Aden, Oman, Palestine, Egypt, Baluchistan, Somaliland; there were native Jews, as well as Europeans, Chinese, Japanese, and Indians.

Dr. C. Ambalavanar was a tall, gracious physician from Sri Lanka. Her husband was the bishop of the Tamil Christian group. I admired her calm wisdom and asked how she could stand to be separated from her people. She explained that she had two sons and wanted a better education for them than could be obtained in Sri Lanka so came where she could get a better income.

Baba, a local Iranian, had worked in our laboratory for seventeen years. He was about forty years old. He was always cheery and helpful, but he was very thin, smoked cigarettes, and had extremely high blood pressure for which he refused treatment. Inevitably, tragedy struck. I was called over to his home one day, only to find him unconscious. Some neighbors helped to put him in my car and take him to the hospital. He drifted in and out of consciousness for a couple of days and died. When they were about to bury him, his wife, who had been left with six little children, gave a farewell message: "Remember to say to the angel of death, Islam is my religion, Mohammad is my prophet, and Ali is my Imam." Women did not go to the cemetery, but the men of the mission went. The cemetery next to the mission was about a square mile of barren soil with only crude rocks to mark the graves. I watched the sad procession with real grief from our rooftop.

Another time, a woman with leprosy from Saudi refused treatment which would take a long time, because she had five little children at home and she did not want to be away from them. But then there was the case of the woman with a large draining ulcer who cured herself at home. She described how she used to pack it with a mixture of dates and spices daily.

I acquired a decidedly realistic view of my capacities, sitting in the clinic and trying to solve the dilemmas that kept popping up. "But who hath despised the day of small things?" (Zech. 4:10). I'd shamelessly order penicillin for any fevers. I'd ask, "Did you

get any benefit from the medicine?" The answer invariably was,
"In shah Allah" (if God wills). "What happened to your preg-
nancy?" I would ask. The patient said, "God didn't treat me well.
I aborted with convulsions when I was visiting in Qatar."

VACATION IN KUWAIT, 1968

For my six-week vacation in 1968, my housemate Anne Lisa
and I flew to Kuwait and stayed with Dr. and Mrs. Scudder.
Dorothy Scudder was nursing superintendent in the government
military hospital. When she started she found that orderlies had
to wear military uniforms and heavy combat boots. If they met an
officer, they had to set their bedpans or equipment on the floor
and salute. She vowed to change that quickly. Lew Scudder said
the cooks had amoebiasis, so everybody caught it and just had to
get used to it. They still had a hard time getting sufficient supplies of drugs, even aspirin.

In contrast, my old friends Mohammad and Mumtaz Qabazard
invited us to a sumptuous dinner at the new ten-story Hilton
Hotel. The display at the cold buffet was a work of art, a lavish
dream, thirty dishes of fanciful shapes. I wasn't used to this luxury and filled my plate too full. There were also numerous en-
trees, nonalcoholic wine, and desserts. Mohammad just smiled at
my bewilderment.

Kuwait's new wealth and the passage of time had brought many
changes for my friends and associates. Sultan Ajeel, my black
friend and merchant, gave us a tea so we could meet his white
wife from Damascus and his six children.

We called at the home of Melicko, my old cook. He had sold
his property for over a million and built a new three-story house.
Now he was in Spain for eye surgery.

Haider and Ma'sooma also had a new house. They had beds
in rows like a dormitory for their thirteen children.

For our flight from Kuwait to Iran, we had to have two passports, because our regular one had Bahrain stamped in it as a
sovereign state and Iran still laid claim to Bahrain.

In Shiraz, two Australian nurses at the Anglican mission hospital invited us to stay with them. They were about to leave, as
they couldn't work with the Armenian doctor whom the mission
put in charge. The new philosophy was that natives must be given
more authority.

Lisa and I flew on to Isfahan and Tehran, and later Tabriz, visiting our friends in the mission communities there.

BAHRAIN, 1970

By 1970, I had been working in Bahrain five years and was over sixty-five years old. That was the age at which we were supposed to retire, but I had not yet done so—because I didn't want to, and because I thought the place needed me. I had no definite plans but was considering joining the Southern Baptist Church's hospital in Jibla, North Yemen. They required another baptism, but I didn't object to that.

I did object to the men in the New York mission office setting an arbitrary age limit at which a missionary must retire. They were appointed by the Church to be in authority, and they had to make the decisions. But their goal was supposed to be to keep the missions going. When there is a person that is available, healthy, willing, and experienced for a position and there is no one else to fill the place, I think arbitrary rules about age should be set aside. After all, missionaries are really sent by Christ (not by the Church), and He said, "Follow me." The Bible doesn't mention retiring from the service of God. Mission was my answer to the question, "What doth the Lord require of me?"

Still, I had no choice but to accept the Church's limits. I packed up my furniture and possessions, the usual task whenever you go home. I hired a firm to pack everything in wooden boxes, ready to ship out if I did not return to the Gulf. The mission let me store the boxes in an empty storeroom. My friends gave fond farewell parties. The Board had announced that this really was my retirement, so I decided to have some adventures on my way home and planned a few excursions in Europe.

First I stopped off in Lebanon to visit old friends and then proceeded to Stuttgart, Germany. I took a leisurely bus tour of Spain and Portugal and flew on from there to Paris and London. I registered for a term at Selly Oak College in Birmingham, which was the British School of Missions. My fellow students came from all over the mission world: Egypt, Korea, Germany, and Namibia, to name but a few. We attended a conference given by liberal theologian John Hicks, who interpreted Christianity as a mere expression of Western culture, rather than the Truth. I didn't like Mr. Hicks. Another time we were taken to visit an

Indian neighborhood where some 40,000 Muslims, Sikhs, and Hindus who had been expelled from East Africa had settled. The English people had mostly moved away, and the old Anglican church had let part of its building for a mosque and social center for the new Muslim residents.

At Christmas, I flew to Copenhagen to visit Anne Lisa Jensen, our nurse in Bahrain. Then my term at Selly Oak College was up, and I made my way to the London airport to fly home to New York.

BACK TO THE U.S.A.

I flew the Atlantic and was met in New York by my brother Paul, who took me to his home on Long Island. Paul gave me the sad news that my stepmother had died while I was traveling in Europe. I had feelings of guilt for not spending more time with her, as she was the only mother I had ever known. She had been a good mother and a generous person, intelligent and sociable. In her last six years she had Alzheimer's disease and lived quietly at a good nursing home in Rochester. My brother Richard had found the place for her; as he lived near, he had attended faithfully to her needs. One night she quietly stopped breathing. She was nearly ninety-six years old. The family buried her next to my father in Milwaukee.

My brother's home in Douglaston, Long Island, was a large three-story house in an aristocratic neighborhood. It was set on a peninsula which extended out along the north shore into Long Island Sound. While I was visiting that time, a snowstorm transformed the place into fairyland, icing every branch of the trees and bushes with white.

When I was in New York, I called on the men at the headquarters of our Reformed Church on Riverside Avenue. John Buteyn informed me what my pension would be. I didn't receive the full pension, because my years of being married, working in private practice in Englewood, New Jersey, and serving in Dahanu Road with the Church of the Brethren didn't count as service in the Arabian Mission. That didn't worry me, since I had inherited some family money. But I did feel that I was no longer of any interest to the men in charge of the Church, now that I was officially retired.

Later, I had a chance to read over the Minutes of the Mission

Executive Committee written after I was retired. They gave me a flattering send-off:

Mary Allison arrived in Kuwait in 1934 and soon thereafter, came the first rains of the season, which resulted in her being named Wusmeeya, and symbolizing the showers of blessings God gave to the women of Kuwait, Bahrain, and Muscat through the medium of His servant, Dr. Mary Allison.

Except for the interim of a few years, Mary has been in regular and active service in the Arabian mission and distinguished herself by selfless service. Her constant good humor brightened many a moment. Her readiness to face new ideas was an example to all of us that we should not become rigid or static. Her continuing enthusiasm in the study of Arabic reminded us that study of Arabic should never cease. Her professional reading regularly unearthed new "pearls" and encouraged her colleagues to maintain their own professional nourishment.

As she leaves us for retirement we pray for all happiness and many blessings in a new exciting chapter in the life of Dr. Mary Allison.

My aunt, Ellen Bruins, lived in Ft. Myers, Florida. She had written and invited me to visit her, so I flew out there. She had married my physician uncle Dick after his first wife died and was about my age. So as we got better acquainted, we found we had a lot in common. She had inherited a large, pleasant house and grounds, full of grapefruit and mango trees. Ellen took me on many trips, but I didn't see anyplace interesting enough for my retirement home. I also visited Julie O'Kelly, my Uncle Dick's adopted daughter. She didn't fit my generation's pattern; she had married three husbands and had a son by each one. But she was an energetic personality and had been elected Woman of the Year.

Some of our Florida churches invited me to come and talk about the Arabian Mission, so I took the bus to speak in Miami and a couple of other places. I wasn't a very inspiring speaker, but I felt it was important to make the effort to tell the Arabian Mission story for my colleagues who had given their lives there and couldn't talk now.

After the month with Aunt Ellen, I set out on a Greyhound bus pass to see the Southern states, where I had never been. I had quite a number of friends and relatives in the South, so I could plan to get off the bus at convenient places and visit people.

I made my way through Florida, Alabama, Arkansas, and Texas before I got that fateful message from the Mission Board.

I had left my itinerary with the Board, so I was not too surprised when John Buteyn called me. He told me that Dr. Donald Bosch in Oman was asking me to come and help. The new Sultan of Oman, Qaboos, wanted to run free hospitals for his people and would pay all our expenses. With the increased workload, Don desperately needed more staff. Unfortunately, by then I had decided I wanted to work with the Southern Baptists in Yemen, so I said no to John. But that night I dreamt about the work in Arabia and changed my mind. I called John by phone the next day and told him I would go to Oman. He said, "Come back to New York as soon as possible."

So I did—but not before completing my itinerary. I flew to Arizona to visit the Gosselinks and De Jongs, who had retired in Tucson. The last stop on my long trip through the States was at Redlands, California, where I wanted to visit Cunera Van Emerick. We had been together at Central College in Iowa. She had become a debate professor and had retired at Plymouth Village in Redlands. We had continued a correspondence over the years. I spent a few days with her and after seeing the place, I liked it, too. So I registered for an eventual place. Then I hurried back to Paul's home in New York, packed my suitcase, and flew off for more adventures in Arabia.

So much for retirement!

THE WAY BACK: BAHRAIN'S NEW CHURCH

I'm sure my face glowed with radiance when I arrived back in Bahrain on my way to Oman. I felt ecstatically happy. Was it the thrill and glory of witnessing again for our Lord in another culture and language? Or was it that the mission and hospital staff felt like my true family, and the place had become my home? I decided to stay a week in Bahrain before flying to Oman, to help with the dedication of the new church building.

Even though the mission field was contracting and the Mission Board had been closing its hospitals in the Gulf, there was still hope for our work, symbolized by the opening of the new sanctuary of the National Evangelical Church of Bahrain on June 3, 1971.

The honored presence at this ceremony was the Ruler of Bahrain, His Highness Shaikh Isa bin Sulman Al Khalifa, who spoke these words of welcome:

Ladies and gentlemen. It gave us great pleasure to be invited to open this church this afternoon. The reason is simple. We, our government and our people, are aware that the American Mission has done much work in Bahrain for many years to the advantage of the people, irrespective of race or religion. This has always been appreciated, but it is not often that we have such a good chance to say so in public.

The medical services which you provide, and all the additional services which you give, are fine examples of generosity and good works, qualities for which you are well known throughout our islands. The book shop which you run is also to the educational advantage of our people.

In Bahrain today we try to foster the spirit of tolerance, education and progress, and this we hope, explains the reason why we are so pleased to be here to express our appreciation of what you have done in the past, what you are doing now and what we hope you will continue to do.

It is therefore with great pleasure that we are able formally to open this beautiful new church. We hope that freedom of worship will always exist and different religions will continue to flourish side by side in Bahrain.

This was followed by the reading from scripture of Second Chronicles—the story of Solomon dedicating the temple at Jerusalem. The reading in English from the second chapter of Ephesians was of Christ uniting in one those who are strangers and foreigners, making them fellow citizens at peace and members of the household of God, Jesus Christ being the chief cornerstone. There were greetings from representatives of the Middle East Council of Churches and of the churches of Kuwait and Muscat. Glad greetings were read from many who had worked and prayed for the building but who could not be present. The whole process had taken eight years, with principal funding from the local community and generous gifts from friends in the U.S. and from Shaikh Isa.

We were glad Shaikh Isa was willing to dedicate the new church building. As he was a Muslim, we felt he should not be subjected to possible embarrassment by being seated facing the cross in the sanctuary. The problem was solved by seating him

and his attendants in the rear with their backs to the cross.

His Highness Shaikh Isa bin Sulman Al Khalifa, K.C.M.G., became ruler of the independent island state of Bahrain when his father died in 1942 and was thirty-seven in 1971 at the time of the church dedication. Hollywood's sheiks are dashing, romantic figures. In the real world, some shaikhs wore a scowl and an air of preoccupation—but Shaikh Isa wasn't that kind. He was short and stocky and always manifested the calm dignity of a born ruler. He had a pleasant, intelligent expression, with luminous black eyes, brown skin, a manly moustache, and short beard. He usually dressed simply in the Arab men's white gown, cut like a shirt and collar but hung long to the ankle. Over it he wore a tan cloak with a gold braided border. He wore sandals, which he discarded when he entered the church. A white headcloth framed his face and was crowned with two thin black ropes. *Shaikh* means simply "old man" in Arabic and *Isa* is the Muslim name for Jesus.

He had an attractive family with one wife—a gracious lady whom I met when we called at Muslim holidays. She always kept in the background and did not appear when the shaikh gave dinners. There was one daughter and a son, the heir apparent, who was partly educated in England.

The ruler's chief hobby was raising aristocratic horses. People who liked to ride were invited to use them. It was said that they had air-conditioned stables. On Friday afternoons, Shaikh Isa presided over races of horses and camels on a desert circuit. He sat on a raised platform with comfortable arm chairs with some of his friends. There was no betting. It was all in fun and anyone could come and watch.

His broadmindedness and generosity were evident to us. As the Muslim ruler of a Muslim state he gave generously to support the mission hospital work. When he heard that the building of our new Protestant church had a large debt, he quietly gave a large sum from his personal income. When the secretary of our church intended to close the hospital, Shaikh Isa told him that if it were closed, the mission would lose his friendship. His government also allowed Anglican and Roman Catholic groups to have churches and schools, which is most unusual in a Muslim state.

Under Shaikh Isa's rule, Bahrain's government was stable and reliable, and its people were loyal and peaceful. Very intelligent and capable men were given important positions and the power to govern well. Schools and medical facilities were provided. Some foreign influences did disturb the prosperous state, but alert and vigilant intelligence services promptly suppressed violence.

The day following the church dedication, Shaikh Isa invited the mission and all its guests to a banquet at his desert palace. We were received graciously and treated to a feast of rice pilaf, roast lamb, and a variety of spiced vegetables—all served at a table exquisitely set, in Western style, for forty guests. The shaikh, at the head of the table, ate sparingly, but we enjoyed everything to its fullest.

When our host arose, we all followed suit, returning to the reception room where the ruler's secretary surprised us with gifts—gold Omega watches for the men and pearl rings for the ladies. Somehow, since my name had been written as Dr. Allison, it was assumed I was a man, and so I received a gold watch.

The appearance of hot, bitter cardamom coffee in tiny cups signaled the end of the banquet. We expressed deep thanks to our host and departed.

11. Oman

I was also honored with an invitation to a special Muslim function. The invitation came from my medical colleague, Dr. Adeeba, who had been such a congenial partner during my stint at the Mutrah hospital in Oman. Dr. Adeeba came from a Muslim community in Hyderabad state, India, where Muslims were a minority and took care to preserve all their religious customs.

Dr. Adeeba was holding a reception to celebrate her four-year-old daughter's study of the Qur'an. This was taught in Arabic, a language not used in her home, and the child was expected to recite a few verses for the assembled guests—a crowd of about eighty, mostly Indian, and dressed in business suits and gorgeous silk saris. The little girl was seated on the stage, dressed in a red Punjabi outfit with much gold jewelry and pearls. She wore jasmine in her dark hair. A very dignified elderly mullah sat down beside her and began to chant the opening verses of the *Bismillah*, the Muslim formal prayer. She squirmed, so it took her father and mother on either side to get her to repeat the words.

After the ceremony, we sat down at long tables to a spicy curry dinner with different kinds of rice, spiced meat, and all the side servings of coconut, bananas, chutney, salads, and popadoms—crisp, thin crackers made of pea-flour. Beside the tasty Indian dinners, our American food is tasteless.

In this way, I began my stay in Oman, which was to be my home for the next four years.

HISTORICAL BACKGROUND OF OMAN

Oman is the thousand-mile stretch of land at the southeast toe of the boot that is Arabia. It has the world's longest range of volcanic mountains—one hundred miles—although most of its land is desert. The mountains are high enough to catch monsoon rains, making agriculture possible in terraced mountains and valleys. Bare mountain crags extend down to the sea at the Straits of Hormuz and encircle picturesque harbors. Muscat, the capital city, has been called "the comic opera port" by the British, because its spectacular cliffs rise sheer above the water and are crowned on either side by ancient Portuguese forts. "Every prospect pleases," but living in Muscat and its sister port of Mutrah is misery in the summer. The air is humid and the bare mountains cut off any breezes. The nights often are hotter than the day, as the mountains radiate the heat. The cities are stark, with no trees, gardens, or green, yet they have charming old architecture. The old sultan, Saeed bin Taimur, preferred to live in his palace in the green, fertile oasis of Dhofar on the southern coast of Arabia.

Oman was an independent country, but it was protected by the British. The British Consul General, Major F. C. L. Chauncey, was a friend and adviser to the sultan. Sultan Saeed had only one son, Qaboos, whom he sent to the British military academy at Sandhurst, England, for his education. Prince Qaboos came back wanting to modernize the country, but his father refused to change and kept his son under house arrest for many years. Sultan Saeed absolutely resisted change. He allowed only three small schools for boys in the whole country. He refused to allow the mission to bring in more staff. Tourists were not allowed.

Change finally came when the Communists took over Aden and the half of the southern coast of Arabia called Haudhramaut. The Communists persuaded the mountain people above Dhofar that their ruler was cheating them. A serious rebellion supplied with Soviet weapons was succeeding. The British, waking up to the danger and seeing that the old sultan was totally opposed to satisfying his people, incited some of the leading men to demand his resignation. They confronted him in his palace. The sultan retreated into his armory, seized a gun, but accidentally shot himself in his foot. He agreed to resign. The British had a plane ready beside the palace. Without giving him time to change his mind they whisked him and some of his women off to Bahrain and later to London, where he lived in retirement. Young Qaboos was proclaimed sultan in July 1970. In this story, I only knew what the British declared to be true.

The people went wild with joy and burst into music and folk dances, which had long been forbidden. They informed Qaboos that they wanted the income from oil (discovered in 1967) to be used as it had been in other Gulf states—to build schools for boys and girls, free hospitals, electricity, roads to mountain villages, and modern improvements. And they wanted this all done immediately.

Oman's oil, discovered out in the desert, had come in on a small scale not comparable to the fabulous wells further north. Much of the oil income had to be used to fight the war with the Communists. There was practically no other income.

The mission, wanting to help, offered to run its two hospitals for the government. The mission would continue to be in charge, but all treatment and drugs would be free. The government would pay all running expenses, with the increase needed for staff and building. The sultan's government gladly accepted the offer. The mission agreed to try the arrangement for three years. I had been sent to Oman to help with the enormous increase in patient load which followed this agreement between the young Sultan Qaboos and the mission.

The medical ministry to the people of Oman had begun with the arrival of the Reverend and Mrs. James Cantine in Muscat in 1899, supported by the Reformed Church in America. The work grew rapidly and in 1909 a medical couple, the Drs. Thoms, arrived in Mutrah. They reported seeing more than 10,000 patients in their first year of service.

Tragically, Dr. Thoms, Sr., was killed in an accident in 1913. The Mutrah hospital functioned only intermittently, depending on the availability of other physicians from mission hospitals in Iraq, Kuwait, and Bahrain.

The Muscat clinic kept functioning fairly steadily, however, and grew into a women's hospital in 1931. The Mutrah Mission Hospital was constructed in 1933 with funds from the Reformed Church. Gifts from the Church and from the International Leprosy Mission facilitated the construction in 1948 of special treatment units for the chronic leprosy and tuberculosis which so afflicted Oman. As in other Gulf missions, the Church provided trained medical personnel, while nursing and support staff were hired locally among the Omanis, expatriate Indians, and Pakistanis.

Before the reign of His Majesty Sultan Qaboos bin Sa'id in July 1970, the hospitals fell under the direction of a Board of Managers selected from the local community. The all-volunteer board set hospital policy until Sultan Qaboos established a national Ministry of Health. The Ministry undertook an agreement with the mission to fund the mission's hospitals through 1973, and when the agreement expired, the Reformed Church deeded its properties to the government without compensation. In return, the mission retained one house and a small chapel. The mission's medical personnel were seconded to Oman's Ministry of Health and continued their work under the Ministry's auspices.

THE MUTRAH HOSPITAL

I took up my position at the Mutrah Hospital amid incredible hustle and bustle.

With the agreement that the hospital would provide free medical care for the population of about 750,000 (no census had ever been made), the hospital was inundated by an overwhelming throng of the sick, their number swelled even further by the merely curious.

The hospital stood on the one paved road, which wandered from the seafront through the town. Other roads were no more than footpaths cutting between datestick houses and cement buildings, through the dirt, stones, and dust. Bare mountains ringing the town cut off any breezes. It was hot, hot, hot.

At the hospital, the government provided water piped from the mountains, so we didn't have to use our windmill. The cesspits were a horrendous problem. They had to be dug out and the contents carried away every week by laborers willing to do such loathsome work.

The hospital itself was like a busy shopping district, with crowds coming and going constantly. Women in their gaily colored layers of scarves and clothing added a touch of brightness. The men made a striking picture in their long, whitish gowns. In their belts, they wore the traditional short curved blade thrust into a silver scabbard. Men from the interior strode haughtily through the halls carrying long guns and wearing belts bristling with bullets.

That day when I arrived, I stowed my belongings in the apartment above the storeroom, put on a white uniform, and walked

over to the plain, gray, cement hospital building to the tune of
"Onward Christian Soldiers."

Dr. Doorenbos blithely turned over his inpatients to me before leaving on his vacation, saying, "You can find them easily. My charts have a red patch on the corner." I trusted that all his patients would be in the final stages of convalescence and entered the hospital through the milling crowds at the door.

The male nurses were busy with a man dying from an appalling cancer of the face. He had just been brought in. Every time I returned from a furlough in the U.S., our mission hospitals shocked me. Hospitals at home were quiet, orderly, and immaculately clean. Here, everything was confusion, noise, and disorder, with callers, family members, babies, and children sitting on the floor talking, fanning, and eating. The bedding was messy, and piles of blankets were shoved under the beds with an occasional bowl of leftover food. The toilets smelled. After the first couple of days, I knew I would get used to it and feel it was all quite human, sociable, and natural.

But for now I studied the rows of about a hundred inpatient charts, bewildered by the simple problem of finding the patients. Rooms one, two, three, etc., were quite clear, and BQ meant the Bedouin quarters. I asked one of the Indian nurses, who was a vision in her neat white sari, to help me make rounds. Most of the charts were classified under various capitals. H meant the patients put in beds lining the halls outside the rooms because the rooms were filled. K meant the small rooms that had been built for kitchens for the families before the hospital fed the patients. G meant the old garage which had room for two patients. DDO meant Dr. Doorenbos' office. Since he was on vacation, it could be used for a hospital room. NSA and NSB were two treatment rooms—Nurse's Stations A and B. NL was a little space near the laboratory. US was under the stairs, where a cot could be squeezed. "What is UT, then?" I asked, bewildered. Sister Indira showed me. It meant "under the tree" ward. There were two scrawny mesquite trees between the two wings of rooms. Cots had been set out under them, suiting some Bedouin families very well. They could hang blankets from the branches for privacy and drape any excess clothing there, too. The nurses hung bottles of fluids for intravenous medication—even blood if we had any—to run down from the branches. While we were making rounds that day, loud wailing broke out from the family of a young woman who had suddenly died. She evidently had had malaria and extremely low hemoglobin. None of the men would give blood, so she died.

My days at the hospital soon began to fall into a routine, although the cases were as unpredictable as ever.

THE MUTRAH MORNING CLINIC

The morning clinic began at 7 A.M., five days a week. By that time the crowd was formidable—350 to 500 men, women, and children. Women who had never learned to queue were in danger of injuring each other. Nurse Anne's solution was a sort of cattle run of cement blocks and iron pipes, to enforce some order in the line. Each woman presented her previously numbered card. If she was a new patient, she obtained a new number at the clerk's window. The clerk found her record and the ones for her children and gave them to her to hold until she could see the doctor. Two men and two women physicians tried to cope with the crowd.

A young local man unlocked the door and admitted four or five women at a time, each with a baby and two or three toddlers. They sat on a bench. The women chatted, the children screamed, the ceiling fan hummed, the air-conditioner roared, the helpers yelled, and the doctor shouted, too. Two of us women physicians sat in the small, dark room lit by an electric bulb, separated by a curtain. Each of us had a local woman helper to translate, because a large percentage of the population was Baluchi-speaking.

The Arab women wore black abbas over their heads. They covered their faces with a thick black mask that had eyeholes and a stick inside, extending from the forehead to the tip of the nose to facilitate breathing. The Baluchi women did not cover their faces but wore colored scarves tightly wound around their heads and chins. I couldn't help admiring the women for their determination and courage. Their men shouted at them like inferiors, but they snapped back haughty answers in wrath. These women were not meekly resigned. A policeman stood by to keep order, but even he was afraid of the women.

Many women from the villages had never seen a chair and wondered how it was used. They stared at the foreign doctor whose face was bare and tried to decide whether this person was male or female.

"What is your name?" the doctor asked.

The language bewildered the woman and she answered with a "Huh?"

Every sentence must be repeated.

"What is your name?"

"It's written on my card."

"What's the matter with you?"

"I'm sick."

"Where does it hurt you?"

"All over."

"How long has it hurt you?"

"Oh, a long time."

(I have to hurry. There are so many waiting outside. If the patient doesn't look very ill, I try to dismiss her with, "I'll give you some pills.")

"I don't want any pills. I want an injection."

"What's the matter with your little boy?"

"I want to have him X-rayed."

"Why do you want him X-rayed?"

"He hasn't any brains."

"What's the matter with the baby?"

"He's not well. He doesn't suck anymore."

The problem is obvious. The shrunken limbs, hollow face, and burning fever indicate chronic malnutrition or malaria. The black eyes gaze deeply. The quiet ones were the most serious, because they couldn't even cry anymore.

"Lulua, what's the matter with you?" I inquire.

"From my childhood, I died often," answered the sad-looking girl. I was puzzled and protested, "But you didn't die, you are alive." With the help of my local interpreter and relatives, we figured out that she had epilepsy. I decided it wouldn't be safe to give medicine to take back to her village. My helper supplied the theology, "It is from God."

"Fatima, how many babies have you had?"

"Ten, but only two are living. I haven't had any more for two years. Can you help me to get pregnant again?" Sadly, I said that I didn't have any medicine for that trouble. The sweet face tied up in scarves sighed and said the usual Muslim expression, "The praise be to God."

I looked at Sara, to whom I had given twelve tablets the day before, telling her to take one pill three times a day. She replied, "I took them all right away. I wanted to get well fast."

Aysha came in with her card asking for medicine for herself. She had a little boy with her who had inflamed eyes, so I asked her, "Shall I make a card for him and write for some medicine for his sore eyes?" She answered, "No, don't bother. He's not mine. He's an orphan."

I came to the bedside of the patient under the tree whom I was treating for edema. She had been a very old lady and was rolled up thoroughly in her blanket like a cocoon. "Did Saroor pass urine today?" I asked the relative with her. She gave me a confused answer, so I started to uncover the patient's face. I was startled by a man's face with a full beard instead of a little lady. The nurses had changed the patients.

One woman was brought in with coma and a fever of 108. Guessing that it was cerebral malaria, I treated her with intravenous quinine dissolved in a liter of saline. To my surprise, she pulled through, but her thinking and words were confused. The village people are certain that the patient was possessed with evil spirits and needed a religious reading of the Qur'an by a mullah. So they insisted on taking her home, and as the Indians say, "We lost her sight."

A family from a village brought a beautiful young girl who had been bitten by a snake. She had been bleeding from the bite in her toe for a couple of days. I couldn't stop it. She was pale as a sheet and we had no blood. She had just been married, and her frantic young husband gave his blood. I tried desperately to start the transfusion running by cutting down on the vein, but it was too late. She died. The family broke into bitter weeping. I never forget the tragedies I have been a part of. They will always be as vivid as if they were just happening.

One day, the helpers informed me that an Arab man had come to the hospital asking especially to see me. I cleared the clinic room of women so he could come in. After some pleasantries, he said with great earnestness, "I have come to you with a question that has concerned me greatly. I trust that you are one who can give me the right answer." I answered that I would try. With an air of confidence in my wisdom, he asked, "What is the right number of children to have?" Of course I was flattered, but humbly told him that only the man and wife could decide what they thought right, and must leave it to God to grant their wishes.

The morning clinic was a daily grind. It wasn't professional or medically ethical to see so many patients with only a few minutes for each. But the government was opening more clinics and hospitals, so it was only a temporary situation.

I usually did not allow men to come in with the women patients because of the crowding and the fact that their society did not permit men and women to be in one room. The policemen were the most obnoxious, as they were in a hurry and wanted to use their position of authority to demand attention ahead of the other patients who had been patiently waiting all morning. Once, two policemen abruptly entered the clinic with an air of official urgency. I was angered and was getting ready to summarily order them out when to my surprise Sultan Qaboos and his bodyguard came in the door. I was chagrined and stood up to greet him. The sultan saluted me and graciously expressed his thanks for my assistance in the country's health care emergency.

Despite the government's good intentions, it seemed to me that all the free treatment began to spoil the people. One woman who had been successfully treated for tuberculosis complained loudly when she was discharged from the hospital. I asked Musa, our helper, what the trouble was. He said, "She thinks the government should give a new outfit of clothes, too!" But this was not a common occurrence.

We really did work very hard with the clinic and our hospital patients. In one day's diary, I listed my current inpatients:

1. middle aged woman with cancer of the stomach
2. young girl with anemia Hgb2 Gms. Large spleen—malaria
3. Arab woman with large fibroid and gastro enteritis
4. Small boy—Erythema—Multiformed—not improving
5. Prolapsed uterus
6. Woman large neck glands, Tuberculosis? Hodgekins?
7. Premature, weight 2 lbs 15 oz.
8. Young woman—bleeding vaginal 6 mo. Preg test positive Vesicular Mole Hysterectomy
9. Small boy anemia, gastro enteritis—spleen to pubis— Malaria
10. Little girl with epistaxis—anemia

11. Woman with nephritis and nephrosis edema
12. Diabetic—gangrene of foot, tumor in uterus—her son gave blood.
13. Baby with edema 18 months—nephrosis

I rarely knew for sure if my diagnosis was right—I just put down my impression and treated as best I could until something could be more certain.

We followed the local customs in Arabia. Everybody started work at dawn and quit at noon. Because of the extreme heat at noon, the whole population had lunch and then slept for two or three hours. All shops closed and the streets were as empty as at midnight.

At the time of the afternoon prayers, when the sun had run three-fourths of its course, everybody got up and went to work again. Work lasted until sunset—the time of the evening prayers. It was a sensible and satisfying arrangement.

Some afternoons, I was on duty to see emergency and stray cases. Otherwise, I'd study my inpatients. I'd follow the orderly procedure taught in medical college; chief complaint, history of the illness, history by systems, past history, family history, and then do the complete physical examination. There's an awful lot to a human body. I skimmed over it, excusing myself because of the inconvenient low beds, noise, and crowd, aside from the fact that the language and concepts of the patients were so different from my own.

One afternoon I examined a wealthy town woman who complained she couldn't sleep. With our crushing patient load, I had gotten to the point that if the patient did not have a fever over 103 or convulsions, I would ask her to come back the next day. So after a superficial exam I told this woman that there was nothing wrong with her. Of course, no good doctor should ever say that. Her husband, who seemed to be an important person, became quite irritated with me and declared he was going to report me to the authorities. He evidently went to Dr. Bosch about it. Don said, "You'd better write out an apology, because he will cause us trouble." So I did and was careful never to tell anybody there was nothing the matter, no matter how tough our caseload was.

Anyway, there were certainly enough instances of genuinely

puzzling medical problems that presented themselves to us every day, with serious consequences.

One night when I was on duty, I admitted three unconscious women, all with temperatures of 106. One with a fever of unknown origin died the next day. One was about five months pregnant and jaundiced—we had many such cases. The other doctors and I tried everything, but without exception they all died. I think it was due to liver damage from endemic malaria. I gave this particular one a massive dose of intravenous cortisone and a million units of penicillin every hour. It did no good and she died. We tried giving blood if we had it, but it didn't help either.

A young woman was brought from a village with fever. She lay on a cot in one of the tiny old kitchens. Her family filled up the rest of the space. Again, what was the diagnosis? The laboratory indicated typhoid, but she could possibly have had two diseases. I started her on treatment for typhoid fever. It seemed to help but she suddenly expired. I felt a horrible sense of failure. It could have been an internal hemorrhage or a rupture of the bowel. I will never know what happened.

A sixteen-year-old girl came in with swollen, hot, painful joints of hands and feet, ill for one month. She was post partum two years and had a temperature of 101. No cough, could not sleep. My notes say, "Admit for study"; nothing more.

The doctors make grand rounds together once each week on our difficult and interesting cases. I particularly appreciated suggestions made by Dr. Harvey Doorenbos on these occasions, because he had more recent and advanced training than I. He was a member of the American College of Surgery and performed five or six operations almost every morning. In Bahrain he had helped me by suggesting a diagnosis which saved an English baby's life. The nurses kept repeating that the baby was having blue spells, which I could not explain. Harvey suggested that it might be a tracheal esophageal fistula (a hole between the breathing and digestive passages which kept air from reaching the baby's lungs). The diagnosis was proved by X-ray, and in an urgent, delicate, and dangerous procedure, surgeons saved the child.

Sometimes Harvey and I disagreed in a professional sense. Once I was treating a case of typhoid fever, proven with a Widal test. The patient's 105 fever continued for days after she had received enough chloroamphenical for a cure. Medical books I consulted recommended cortisone for a couple of days. I tried it, to dramatic effect, and reported the success at our next physician's meeting. Harvey began to berate me, saying, "Don't you know how dangerous it is to use cortisone?" I got out the book and he pulled in his horns.

Another time I had a case of a young boy whose body was as hard as wood. I consulted my books and diagnosed it as scleredema—a rare disease of generalized brawny edema. It is benign and resolves in six to eighteen months, and there is no treatment. When I reported this, Harvey said, "There isn't any such disease." Again I got out the book, so he backed down.

I certainly had my share of mistakes and sins of omission, but I felt somewhat relieved, because I saw the other doctors make their sad mistakes also. I realized that we are only human.

MALARIA

Our death statistics were appalling. The people had chronic malaria and anemia. Hemoglobin concentration was often only 20 to 30 percent of normal. Fever was the predominant symptom—sometimes 108 or even 109. A sufferer from fever and sweats in Baghdad about 800 A.D. left these lines. He described the fever as a maiden:

> She comes to my couch at eventide
> I offer her my silken cushions and my linen sheets
> She refuses them all and spends the night in my bones.
> When she leaves me, she washes me with her tears.
> I await her coming nightly, but not with joy.

Many of our deaths were young people. I couldn't estimate the average life span, but it must have been very short. We couldn't learn from the deaths, as postmortems were not permitted in the local customs. Our laboratory was able to do only simple tests. We had no blood bank. To compound the problem, the men usually refused to give blood for a woman, who was regarded as an inferior being. Whenever an American ship came into port, we went out and asked for donations. The crews were most generous and gave twenty units once, which we used up quickly.

Sick babies were the saddest cases. It seemed we had a dying baby every day. The mothers had begun to use plastic feeding bottles and powdered milk. The mothers guessed at the proportions of milk powder to any available water and filled the bottle full. It lay on the floor in the hot weather and soon was contaminated. The babies commonly developed diarrhea. When heat combined with the first bout of Oman's endemic malaria, the results were tragic.

I had little experience treating malaria before I came to Oman. In Kuwait, there was no sweet water for mosquitoes to breed in. Bahrain had long ago cleaned up its standing water. But Oman had water for irrigation, breeding plenty of mosquitoes to transmit the malignant variety of malaria called falciparum. Treatment and eradication were complicated because each country had a different malarial disease pattern, as well as a different dialect of Arabic. A technician from the World Health Organization came to do research on the problem. He sat outside my office and took a blood smear from each patient who came through. He found that a large percentage of them had circulating parasites, even though they had no fever. So there must be some immunity that enabled people to live with the disease.

Diagnosis of malaria was often complicated by the presence of other serious diseases. I remember in particular the case of Zuwaina, an emaciated young girl who was brought in from a village. She had already had fever for a month, which rose regularly every afternoon to 103, and fell each night to 97. What was it? Malaria? Typhoid? Military TBC? They all cause the same fever, enlarged spleen, anemia, weakness, and lack of appetite. The X-ray didn't tell me anything. Our lab man couldn't find any parasites in my patient's blood. Nothing I saw was typical of the disease as described in the medical books. What should I do? The girl was desperately sick. I thought to myself, "Doctor, you've *got* to do something!"

I decided to make a therapeutic diagnosis, that is, give the treatment for one disease and hope it hits the bull's-eye. This is not good medicine, but I was in a corner. So I wrote a five-day prescription for chloroamphenical, the typhoid fever drug. But that exasperating fever shot up every day. And every day on my round I looked into Zuwaina's sad eyes and saw her wasting form. I decided I must try something else. So I wrote orders to give the drug chloroquine for malaria, for three days as is usually prescribed. Still that aggravating fever went on, as inexorably as the waves on the seashore. *I* couldn't stand the torment.

On our weekly grand rounds, I brought Dr. Doorenbos and our two Indian physicians in to see Zuwaina. I presented the case to them and asked for suggestions. Harvey asked with a thoughtful air, "Have you considered Kala Azar?"

I answered, "That's a disease of East Asia."

"We'd better consider it," he replied. "There are plenty of sand flies here."

So I went home to hit the books. Sure enough, the disease was also found in the Middle East and Africa. I'd heard of it at medical school, but there had been such a colossal amount to learn that I had excused myself from studying such a foreign disease. I had just dismissed it from consideration.

Kala Azar was transmitted by sand flies, delicate midge-like flies that live near water. There were plenty of them in the villages, and they bit. The abominable microorganism called Leishmanasis enters the body and hides in the spleen and bone marrow. The resulting fever may run for two years, and without treatment 75 percent of the afflicted will die. To make a conclusive diagnosis, bone marrow must be obtained with a special needle. This aspirated tissue must then be spread on a slide and stained, so that a trained technician can identify the typical organism. We had no one who could do this kind of test.

Even though I had no way to confirm the diagnosis of Kala Azar, I started Zuwaina on daily doses of Neostibiosan, available from our stores. The drug contained antimony, a poison, and must be given in dilute intravenous form beginning with small doses. The fever knew it had met its match. Slowly but surely it backed down and gave up—to my intense satisfaction and relief. In time Zuwaina went home, cured.

CHOLERA

Another specter of medicine in Oman was cholera. Its onset could be dramatic, as my own experience proved. On this particular morning I made rounds on my inpatients after 7 A.M. prayers, as usual. The Indian nurse presented charts to me; I looked at the fever records, noted perfectly obvious signs, and waited for her to tell me anything that needed fixing. Then the Indian doctor and I began our clinic. With one or two hundred crowding women and children to be seen, we could only allow about five minutes for each, and we saw them on a first-come, first-serve basis, as we had no one outside the door to sort out urgent cases to be seen more quickly. My attitude was, "I don't know if I can help you, but at least I'll listen to your chief complaint, look you in the eye, and give you some drug which I hope will help."

With such a hurried practice, I wasn't at all sure I was giving the right treatment, but to please the patients, I always wrote out a prescription for some drug, lest nature should seem to have healed without the physician's aid. Since malaria seemed to be endemic, there was always chloroquine to fall back on, or aspirin. I'd pray, "Dear God, please help the sick. Grant that what I'm doing is right. I don't know what else to do."

That morning was no different from any other, but when Merzook, the doorman, opened the door in the middle of the morning for the next batch of patients, a tall woman staggered in and collapsed without warning. Watery, profuse, odorless stool soaked her clothes and the floor. I'd heard there was cholera in some villages, and this was it. These cases lose up to twenty liters of their body fluids, which must be replaced quickly or they die.

I loved to have something dramatic to do and rushed out to call for the rolling stretcher. The helpers lifted the limp, cold figure with her withered, gray face and put her on the cart. We rolled her over to the inpatient nurses. I asked them if we still had those old wooden beds with a hole in the middle for runoff. I ordered twelve liters of normal saline to be run intravenously to replace fluid, because these cases vomit. The men helpers had such good technique getting a needle in veins that I didn't want to try it myself.

The woman's family and friends hovered around the bed, wringing their hands, and getting in the way. When they saw all the fluid running in, they protested, "Don't give her so much. It will make the diarrhea worse." I left the case to the staff. They ran in the fluids at full speed. When I came back to see her at noon, she was beginning to look better. She recovered and went home cured.

There aren't any drugs to treat cholera. It is caught by drinking contaminated well water, so a whole village will catch the disease at once. Without treatment, 50 percent of the cases die. No drugs help, and though we gave injections of killed cholera bacteria, it is doubtful that it prevents the disease. Our own safety depended on drinking boiled water. Helping to cure even one case gave me a happy feeling, although I tried to keep a safe emotional distance from my patients. It seemed necessary to do this in order to be able to think and act effectively on their behalf. I cared most of all for the successful results of my treatments.

LEPROSY

One of my principal assignments in Oman was to treat the lepers, because the Indian doctors did not like that chore. Our mission hospital had become committed to this important work through the efforts of Dr. Wells Thoms, who served in Oman with his wife Beth for thirty-one years, from 1939 to 1970. Their influence had so colored the atmosphere that we felt embraced by Wells' winning spirit.

Dr. Thoms had cared so deeply about the many cases of leprosy that he founded a leprosarium. He persuaded the sultan to contribute land adjoining the Mutrah hospital, and the International Leprosy Association contributed money for an open-air building.

When I arrived in 1971, there were about twenty-five men of various ages living in the open air hospital for lepers. Most of the patients were in the sad advanced stages of their disease because they had delayed coming for treatment. They had the disfigured faces and ulcerated hands and feet. I didn't know how to treat leprosy. Dr. Thoms had taught Musa, a local Christian nurse, how to give the effective sulfa drug DDS. I had to learn from him how to treat leprosy.

Leprosy is now called Hansen's disease to avoid the social stigma attached to the word leper. Dr. Hansen was the first to isolate and identify the leprosy bacillus in a leprosarium in Bergen, Norway, in 1873, although there was no treatment until sulfones were found effective in 1941. The physical disfiguration associated with leprosy is due to the fact that this is primarily a nerve disease. The resulting loss of sensation causes multiple injuries. Victims may live for years as social outcasts, because leprosy is feared as contagious and the leper's appearance is so revolting.

However, the disease is not as contagious as is popularly supposed. When one person in a family has it, only about 5 percent of the rest of the family contracts it. The diagnosis is difficult, as there are several varieties of leprosy and the patient can have the disease as long as twenty years before it becomes manifest.

I relied on the experience of our Omani nurse, Musa, who cared for the leprosy patients. Musa was very short—only about five feet tall—but his loud, deep masculine voice made up for his slight stature. He had lived and worked with Dr. Thoms since childhood, and the quality of his speech made us feel as though Wells were still with us. Musa spoke Arabic as a second language, being a native Baluchi. He did not read or write but knew enough English to read medical orders and drugs. The patients respected his dignified presence.

Musa became a Christian, though his wife did not. With real Christian spirit he accepted the most menial and despised position of treating the two most feared departments. He dressed the filthy, ulcerated feet of the lepers and insisted on keeping their rooms and bedding cleaned with no fear of contamination for himself.

I'm sure Musa realized I knew very little about leprosy, but he insisted that I sit at the desk while he stood beside me and gravely suggested the appropriate and traditional dose of pills of the DDS drug for each patient, and I wrote them on their records while he handed them out. He addressed me with great dignity as a superior being. So I came to rely on his judgment and often asked, "Musa, what should we do about this case?" I studied the subject in the books available, but they didn't give much practical help. Musa and I sat to treat these patients two afternoons a week. A few patients lived in their own homes with families.

The men used to do their own cooking, but later the government provided a hospital cook. Each man had an Indian aluminum tiffen canister with three compartments. Three times a day, two men would hang them on a long rod and carry the hot food to each patient. The compartments always had rice, stewed meat with vegetables, and a dessert.

Social pressures still interfered with the treatment of our patients, even in 1971.

Once, a village shaikh sent us a solemn woman, five months pregnant, with her two children. She had a deep ulcer of the foot and had had no treatment. Her skin test was what the lab called "four plus," meaning her blood was swarming with the leper bacillus. We gave a large single room to this woman and her children and started her treatment. The children received preventive care.

Living alone in a place with all men, whose faces and deformities were as ugly as figures in a Hieronymous Bosch painting, she was depressed and lonely. She couldn't stand it. In a month, she left and went back to her village, where there was no treatment for her disease.

In another incident, we treated two boys for over six months, past the point where they would have been contagious. I asked the principal of the nearby school whether the boys could attend. He refused definitely.

Even personnel assigned to our hospital were sometimes afraid of our leprosy patients. At one point I had a new leprosy patient who had been a gardener. He was willing to stay for treatment but sat disconsolately on his bed day after day with nothing to do. I decided he needed some physiotherapy so assigned him the job of sweeping around the compound and paid him a small wage myself. I discovered long ago that it is better not to ask for permission when you want something done.

But soon after the patient began his duties, Mr. Farcy, our government-appointed Omani administrator, came stalking into my office. He was frowning and exclaimed, "I saw that new man sweeping in front of my office this morning. I don't like his looks. It gives a bad impression."

I suddenly realized that he had never worked in a hospital before and hadn't seen many really sick folk. I answered as gently as I could. "I don't like his looks, either. That's the way sick people look. The hospital is here for sick people—not for us."

Mr. Farcy stormed, "I don't want him around."

"Couldn't you just try not to look at him for the short time he sweeps the place?"

"No, I won't have it."

Before the current discussion, I had already begun to feel tensions with Mr. Farcy as to who was in charge at the hospital. I also sensed that as a Muslim Mr. Farcy resented our religion, and felt frustrated in his determination to convert our pragmatic management style into modern hospital administrative methods. So as it now was obvious that a state of hostilities was arising, I decided to back down. He, as an Omani, would be increasing and I must decrease, so I assured Mr. Farcy I would change the patient's work.

After four years, the mission gave the hospital to the government. The mission offered to care for the leprosy patients and continue to treat them. The government planned to provide shelter and food for all such patients in the land but did not promise medical treatment. All the patients decided to accept the government's offer and left the mission medical service. Musa was offered a high salary and fringe benefits in the government medical service. He built himself a large house, his wife produced twin boys, and he left the Christian church.

TAZIAH FOR DR. WELLS THOMS, OCTOBER 1971

Dr. Wells Thoms and his wife, Beth Scudder Thoms, devoted thirty-one years to medical work in Oman, from 1939 to 1970. Wells' parents were also medical missionaries in Arabia, arriving in Bahrain in 1899. Though both his parents died tragically in the field, Wells decided he would carry on his father's career there, "where the ranks are thinnest and the battle hottest." Three of Wells' own four children also became doctors, and two returned to Oman for short periods to help their father.

Dr. Thoms was an extraordinary man with a cheerful, attractive countenance. His hobby was gardening, as the scrawny trees and bushes around his home attested. They survived under his care, even with scant and brackish water.

Wells loved the open country and made many visits to the desert and mountain villages—even up to Jebel Akhthar, the green mountain, with its eerie beauty. He made friends of the fierce and fickle Arabs who lived beyond the frontiers of the ruler, Sultan Sa'id. This offended the sultan, who considered them his enemies. From that time he refused to receive or speak to Wells—not even on his retirement.

Wells died of cancer soon after his retirement in October 1971. The mission commemorated Wells in the following words:

> Everyone who knew Dr. Wells Thoms was immeasurably enriched by the experience. His patients, sensing his big heart and his concern, felt firm confidence in Wells' care, a confidence enhanced by the feeling that his particular problem was the center of Wells' life.
>
> There are, perhaps, three factors which effectively characterized this great man.

First, there was his boundless energy. No one in his right mind ever tried to follow Wells' physical footsteps through the course of a day. But more than his boundless energy was his abounding spirit, fueled by a supreme faith and dependence upon God's power in Jesus Christ. For Wells, "To live was Christ," and this spirit characterized his entire personality.

Second, there was his unlimited love for people. From prince to pauper he loved them all—dirty or clean, educated or illiterate, saint or sinner—all were the recipients of his affection, to them not only the door of his home but also the door of his heart was open.

Third, there was his ability to see in every individual a person beloved. Wells never gave up on anyone, because fundamentally he knew that God doesn't give up on anyone. This quality made Wells overlook people's faults and accept them as they were.

When Wells died in America, we held a service for him in accordance with the local custom. The Arabs bury their dead the same day if possible. Sorrow draws the community together, so they have evolved a satisfying ceremony called a *taziah*, or "comforting." The bereaved sit in their room on floor mats. Neighbors, relatives, and friends come in silently and sit with them for hours or days. Sometimes there is loud weeping, but often the grief is too deep for tears. The comforters leave with a kindly caress.

The mission held a taziah for Wells in the small chapel beside the hospital. Word was sent to the bazaar. Many came and sat with us. We grieved but had the firm comfort that we shall all be together again in the presence of Christ in pure joy. Our evangelistic men read from the Psalms and prayed at intervals. In the evening a stream of Arab, Indian, British, and Dutch friends came to call, expressing their affection and appreciation for Dr. Wells Thoms.

The next day, Awaad, one of the young helpers of the hospital, requested a meeting to tell what Dr. Thoms had meant to the staff. He wanted to hold the meeting on the tennis court and offered to take charge. We thought it a grateful response and set out mats and chairs. About two hundred came, mostly men. Awaad delivered a long, passionate speech mentioning Dr. Thoms. He used such an exuberant flow of words (for which Arabic is justly famous) that we could not understand what he said. Then he introduced a girl who threw back her veil and spoke with vehemence. It was most extraordinary.

Afterward, we asked some of the audience for the meaning of the words. They seemed embarrassed. Awaad had complained that the government disparaged Dr. Thoms. He evidently gave a political tirade against the government. We were appalled.

A couple of days later, there was further evidence of the content of Awaad's speech. Early one morning, around 6 A.M., a crowd of scowling men in an angry mood swarmed the area in front of the hospital. They had no guns but invaded our property and picked up wood used for construction. They strutted around with a menacing air. The affair seemed well organized. The men attacked some buses parked along the road that were used to transport workers, smashed windows, and began to set fires.

We watched with fear and astonishment. The new government and sultan were doing so much for the people and seemed so popular. The group complained that the government was providing houses and privileges for foreigners and the oil company and not doing the same for the local people. Police soon appeared and threw tear gas bombs and shot off some guns. One man was wounded and brought into the hospital, where he died. The gas blew into our houses, too, and burned our eyes.

When the attackers fled, there was an ominous calm. The staff was afraid to go home. Some Christians had come over from Muscat and didn't dare to travel the single mountain road to go home. The hospital had no cook, so we "did the necessary," as the Indians say. The police drove around and announced a curfew. Only women were allowed on the streets, to draw water from the town wells.

Police came and arrested Awaad with some others, even some girls. The affair ended as abruptly as it began. We surmised that agents working from Aden, then under Communist control, were secretly influencing young people in the towns. One of the mission's Arab girls started to work in a government office called the Research Department. She told us they were making dossiers on all the people in the country.

Later there was a trial, and Awaad was sentenced to life imprisonment in the dungeon of the old Portuguese fort which crowned the rocky cliffs of Muscat harbor. We never saw him again. Anne called on Awaad's mother. She was distressed, not knowing where he got his rebellious ideas. It was said that he was accused of receiving guns and ammunition at our hospital at night and distributing them.

The police arrested fifty terrorists in all and found a large armament dump of all kinds of weapons made in Communist China. A ship loaded with guns got away. Fifteen of the prisoners were executed and the rest given prison sentences of five to fifteen years. Even the girls who cooperated were given prison sentences.

By mid-1972, a vicious war was being waged between the Omani army—with British assistance—and Aden's Communists. The battleground was just five hundred miles from Muscat. The British press reported at the time that Omani children were being conscripted and trained in Yemen by the rebel Popular Front for the Liberation of the Occupied Arab Gulf States.

DIVERSIONS, 1972

I spent my summer vacation in 1972 attending the Islamic Conference in Dhour-el-Shweir, Lebanon, a Christian mountain retreat. In all we were twenty-nine conferees and ten visitors, from Europe and all over the Middle East, and representing a variety of Christian denominations.

Once again, Bishop Kenneth Cragg led the conference. He claimed that if Islam followed its own teaching logically and reverently, it would be led to Christ. Strangely, the Near East churches seemed to reject this thinking.

From our studies of Islam, I was learning that a main difference between Islam and Christianity lies in varying concepts regarding God's character. In Islam, God is omnipotent and cares naught for man. His forgiveness and punishment are arbitrary. Sin is always punished; if it has no punishment, it is not sin. For God to simply forgive sin, as Christians believe, makes him an unjust judge. This is a problem for Muslims when considering Christianity.

In Christianity love manifests the power of God, not His weakness. God's perfect justice does make punishment necessary. The only hope for the Christian is that the perfect Man and perfect God, Jesus Christ, took the punishment on Himself. This Islam denies.

Aside from this theological difference, Islam is principally a religion of works. Merit is gained by following exactly the rules laid down in the Qur'an and books of the Shar'ia, or law of Islam.

After the conference, my friends and I took rooms in beautiful, exciting Beirut. One evening we were invited to the home of Dr. Bruin, a professor at the American University of Beirut. Professor Bruin taught mathematics and astronomy and was quite interested in learning how Muslims set the date for Ramadan, the month of fasting. Someone had to actually see the new moon and report it for the festival to start. This was done because the moon is God's authentic sign, as opposed to reckoning by the calendar which is the work of man. Professor Bruin asked his students about this procedure. They told him the moon sighting was announced from the airport. Well, he asked, who tells the airport? The students investigated and discovered the man who informed the radio at the airport. Where did he get *his* information? They found he called a friend who worked at the American University astronomy department. Dr. Bruin knew the man, who was a clerk, and asked him about it. The clerk said, "You put it in the daily reports when the new moon is due, so I call the airport and tell them." Without knowing it Professor Bruin was announcing the time for the Muslim religious holiday!

I had many adventures before returning to Oman. With friends I took a bus trip to see historical sites in Lebanon and Syria. We visited Biblos, Tripoli, Homs, Damascus, and the ruins of the desert city Palmyra, returning to Beirut through the fertile, green Baaka Valley. I also accompanied a couple to Cyprus for a short trip. It was a short flight, but what a different atmosphere! Beirut had shops full of customers and goods from all over the world, everybody was rushing around and apparently having a wonderful time. Cyprus was as quiet as an old people's home. In Nicosia, there was a U.N. soldier with a gun stationed every two blocks to keep the Greeks and Turks from massacring each other. This had been going on for ten years. They couldn't make peace and they didn't dare to fight.

Archbishop Macharios III swished into the lobby of our hotel with his retinue, his black silk robe flaring, his high, black, straight hat giving him imposing stature, his bishop's staff topped with a gold emblem, and a large pectoral cross making a terrific impression. How these despots do dramatize themselves. I heard later that he wore thick soles and high heels to give him height.

I feel it's a catastrophe for the religious leader to be head of government.

One evening back in pre–civil war Beirut, we went to see *My Fair Lady* at the cinema. We just happened to sit down behind two young ladies, daughters of my old friends Shaika Bederea and Shaikh Fehed of the Kuwaiti royal family. I was delighted to see them again, for I had known them almost since they were born. The girls seemed more American than Arab, because they had lived so long with their teacher, Shirley Stephens, in Philadelphia. Now they were finishing their college work and planning their careers. I had not seen them for many years, as I was in Bahrain and Oman, so I was fascinated to hear of the changes in their lives. One girl told me she was going to write her book on Kuwait, exclaiming, "So many other people are writing books about Kuwait and they get it all wrong!" The older sister, Lulua, had majored in languages. She was given the position of supervising the foreign language programs for Kuwait Radio. Then one of the men relatives in the royal family who didn't like her cut her out of the job. None of the American-educated girls was marrying the Kuwaiti cousins, as they would have in the old days.

I was reminded again just how much change had come to the lives of women in the Gulf when we met later with representatives of the Ford Foundation who were interested in assisting Oman. They were proposing sociological studies of Omani villages and asked our advice. At the party we met three lovely young Arab girls who were earning their doctorates in anthropology and sociology. They were Muslim girls from Aden, Saudi, and Beirut. It really was a surprise to talk with Arab girls who were our educational equals. They planned to come to Oman later that year and live in some villages to do research, but I never met them again.

To complete my vacation, I decided to see Jibla in Yemen, because I had considered joining the Southern Baptist mission hospital there before I was invited to Oman. The Beirut travel office routed me through Aden, where I should be able to take a small plane to Taiz in North Yemen. A friend met me at the Aden airport and invited me to stay with her. She filled me in on the local situation.

The Communists had taken southern Arabia and Aden, and their oppressive presence could be felt in the air. The economy was collapsing; everyone wanted to leave. Salaries were taxed outrageously; nearly all shops and apartments were nationalized; school girls were required to take bayonet practice. Tourists and foreigners were subject to close questioning. Indian government workers had been denied permission to leave the country, and their passports had been confiscated.

The mission school and bookstore were only barely operating under a new series of repressive regulations and requirements. No one but the missionaries attended the church anymore. Prayer call from the mosque went on for hours—it was horrible—and small boys read the Qur'an in screams.

The small plane I had planned to catch from Aden to Taiz had been crowded, with all the unrest. The border between the People's Republic of South Yemen and North Yemen was closed. So I had to buy a ticket back to Jidda in Saudi Arabia. The airport was crowded with everybody silently tense in dread of not getting away from this sickening place. The scowling official examined my papers minutely but let me get on the plane. A tall, black Ethiopian man was stopped and ordered out. He had a desperate look of apprehension when he was not allowed to leave on that plane.

Even with this change in plans, I still wasn't able to get to Taiz by air. After a four-day layover in Jidda, a new Turkish friend, Lale, and I finally got a small plane to Hodeideh and from there took a taxi fifty miles up the mountain to Taiz. From there Lale's father offered to drive me up to Jibla on his rounds as a U.N. agricultural expert.

The road to Jibla was spectacular. We drove over lush, green valleys with terraced fields where tall millet grew over my head. Picturesque villages crowned the hills, where the stone houses and whitewashed mosques with towering minarets looked quite romantic. The Southern Baptist mission at Jibla stood on the side of a beautiful hill, with green grass, trees, and a prefab hospital and houses. The doctors and nurses there were quite hospitable and friendly to me—maybe they hoped I would come and work with them as I once planned.

The Arab city of Jibla was like a fairy tale picture—stone houses on the top of a hill, four or five stories high, each one rising higher than the others. Windows in their upper stories had plaster arches. A couple of minarets boasted artistic stone decorations. Streets were more like stairs, paved with crude stones. It rained every day, so there was plenty of mud, too. Two small streams, alive with waterfalls, wound under stone bridges; naked little boys swam there. Some new houses were built of green and pink rock which had been dressed.

The other women missionaries and I walked down the muddy hill of the mission and up the stony street to visit some of their friends. I took some pictures. Coming back, some of the townspeople called out, "Who is the new lady with you?" One of my hosts answered, "She's a lady doctor who maybe will come and work with us." They answered, "We want a young doctor, not an old one." I didn't notice I was looking so old.

Jibla is a very conservative city that has had very little contact with the outside world, so its citizens are friendly but suspicious.

One night, I happened to walk out and saw the magnificent, starry sky. It was stupendous. The sky was full of lights. At 6,000 feet elevation the air was dry and clear, and there were no lights of the city or oil flares. It was such a brilliant scene that I still remember the thrill I felt.

At last the time came to go home. I took a ride to the coast with a kat-chewing driver. Kat is a green plant which is mildly stimulating or psychoactive. Many people waste their early afternoon hours chewing kat. My driver had a bunch beside him on the front seat. I tried chewing some but just got a bitter taste. Probably the other effect takes longer.

The next day I caught a small Yemeni plane for Jidda, where I again faced the myriad rules and officials of Saudi Arabia. Without a proper document for exit or entry, I had to run all over Jidda fulfilling visa requirements before I could catch my plane to Bahrain and thence to Oman.

TRAVELS IN OMAN, OCTOBER AND NOVEMBER 1972

At the end of the month of fasting the Muslims celebrate for five days, so our medical work was light. We took a couple of days, too, for a holiday. Saeed Nasr, an elderly, dignified leprosy patient whose disease was arrested by long treatment, invited us to visit his mountain village. He lived in his own house with his wife and family back of the mission. He had read the Gospels when he came for treatment, became a Christian, was baptized, and even preached the sermons at the Arabic services. He had a tall, spare figure, deep-set eyes, and a wizened, lined, intelligent face. He wore the typical Omani headdress called the kummah, and spectacles when he read. The kummah was shaped like an upside-down pan, made of white, fine cotton, embroidered with pierced fine stitching—beautiful work which took months of stitching by women. Saeed wore the simple long, white dress of all Arabian men, and sandals.

Eight of us took the Land Rover, packing our bedding rolls, toothbrushes, food, and water. We traveled north up the coastal plain called the Batina, which extends more than a hundred miles and is five to ten miles wide between the mountains and the sea. Quite surprisingly there is an abundance of fresh water, with wells right beside the salty sea. About one-third of Oman's population lives on this coast. They have lush, green, cool gardens with date palms, fruit trees, limes, guavas, mangoes, bananas, and melons. It was a delight to see the shaded concrete tanks and flowers and hear the bird calls.

We passed the inlet, Kurum, where we used to go swimming and where now the oil company has its relaxation park. We drove the dusty car track to the town of Seeb, site of the sultan's palace and the new international airport. Then we passed the sleepy adobe towns of Birka and Masana, whose beaches were bloody from the animals killed for the feast that concludes Ramadan.

After driving sixty miles along the coast, we turned west toward the mountains called the Jebel Akhthar, or green mountains, because they have rocks with that hue. It is the longest range of volcanic mountains in the world—two hundred miles. Its highest peak is 10,194 feet. The range has plentiful, terraced gardens and good crops because it catches the summer monsoon rains. The water filters through the porous rocks and comes out in springs and wells in the fertile valleys.

We drove thirty miles further west to the town of Rostaq, which has a picturesque old fort very strongly built of stone and adobe. We walked through it to see the well of fresh water in a court, the dungeons, six-foot-thick walls, and then climbed up into the tower. At its top was a long brass cannon lying on the floor with Spanish words stamped on it. We also visited the hospital which the government was building.

We turned into the mountains on a road which was only a trail in a dry wadi full of huge boulders ten to twenty feet long. Our car sort of hopped from one stone to another. Then the trail passed between narrow, steep walls several hundred feet high. These crevices could be deadly, as sometimes a rush of water from some distant storm would burst down and wash everything away. In one place, water gushed out of a spring with oleanders, bushes, and flowers, so we stopped, to find it was warm water. The silence there was profound, with only a camel munching some leaves and goats running among the bushes. Some walls had petroglyphs of animals.

It took two hours to get through the canyon before it widened out into Wadi Sakhtan, where Saeed's native village lay. The women welcomed us as if we were a part of the family. Their adobe house had only two rooms. The large one was their living room, dining room, or bedroom, as need required. There were reed mats and an old carpet on the floor, two windows, and the door. We sat on the floor and ate the lunch we brought. You don't realize what a great invention tables and chairs are until you sit on the floor and do all your work sitting on the floor. The other room was a small kitchen.

We walked around the town, which consisted of about a dozen houses. We saw the flowing irrigation ditch and learned how to use the bathroom facilities. There was an enclosed area for females which was conveniently near the irrigation ditch. You could even take a bath in it. The males have a similar place, but a little better—it had a shelter of branches.

Our hostesses had killed the fatted calf or goat and had cooked it over one primus pressure stove on the floor. It was served with rice.

We divided the room—males on one side and females on the other—and slept on the floor. Our hostesses must have been up all night, as they wakened us with the holiday dish of hot millet porridge and a bowl of spiced goat's buttermilk. It was the great day of the holiday, and the neighbors came to greet us soon after sunrise.

The women were dressed in their best, with bright dresses and wide, colorful pantaloons. They tightly wound two scarves around their heads and necks. Then two yards of printed cloth called the *lahaf* was worn over their heads like a cape. If they went out of their hometown they wore the traditional mask of thick, black cloth, with neat holes for the eyes and a stick sewed inside it to form a beak from the forehead to the nose.

The men dressed up, too, in their fresh white tunics and caps, carrying a gun, belts studded with bullets, and the traditional short curved blade in front of their waists. The men all went to the small mosque. Don Bosch and Paul went with them. The women don't go to the mosque. I heard that Saeed read the Qur'an. I didn't ask him how he reasoned out his theology. Perhaps he couldn't explain it, either.

Afterward we sat eating the festal meal, and Saeed took off his cap, showing his bald head. Don said some Americans wore a second head and dared me to take off my wig, which I did. Saeed's face shifted into an expression of unbelieving astonishment. His mouth fell open, his eyes widened, and he sat as rigid as a statue. We all laughed uproariously, but Saeed took a long time to recover.

Don and I treated the sick, for we had brought our medicine bag with us. It was so sad to see the sick babies. Most of them had malaria, diarrhea, and sore eyes. No doctor came to their town, and they had no way of traveling for medical treatment.

We made our return trip uneventfully and were glad to get back to tables and chairs. But that was not the end of our field trips. When the weather cooled a bit at the end of November, some of us drove off in the Land Rover to see the oasis of Samayle. Many Bedouin had taken up residence outside it. This meant finding a low desert tree, some big cartons, and oil cans, weaving them in the branches and lo, you have shelter. With a blanket, a primus burner, and a couple of pots, you have a home. Some families had brought their sick members to the hospital and managed in this way.

The scenery was barren, but even so, the topography of hills and mountains was dramatic. Every now and then we came to a small village with houses of mud brick. Ancient mud fortresses crowned some hills. The road was stone, washboard, and dust, but we made 120 miles in three hours. Samayle is a group of villages said to have a population of 10,000, located at the foothills of the mountains where water pours out in astonishing streams. Irrigation canals keep the place green and lovely with many trees— mostly date, but there were mangoes, guavas, and citrus, too.

We ate lunch at the new government hospital with the Indian nurses who had invited us. The people there had no experience of medical care and insisted on coming in at any time. The Pakistani doctor would close the door of his house at night and refuse to answer calls, but the nurse, whose room was in the hospital, had to see all visitors at all times.

The shaikh's wife had just had a baby and he came to call. I sat down to chat. I said, "I hope your Arab children will get an education and run the hospitals themselves." He frowned and said, "That will take too long. We'll send out our dates and you can send us doctors and nurses." He seemed to think that was a fair deal.

On Thanksgiving Day the whole mission had a picnic on the sandy beach surrounded by mountains. It was a heavenly spot. We swam, snorkeled, ate, and gave thanks.

KUWAIT REVISITED

As my career drew to a close, I found myself going back to see the places and people that had been so important to me in my early years. I was invited to Kuwait for a week at Easter 1973. It was almost ten years since I had left the hospital there to work in Bahrain. My plane flew over the brown desert state, now crisscrossed with wide, straight, paved highways, new neighborhoods with modern streets and buildings, industrial plants, oil collection centers, and desert palaces surrounded by walled gardens. The oil jetties extended out into the blue water of the Gulf, and many large tankers stood beside them, testament to Kuwait's oil prosperity.

Suddenly, forgotten memories stabbed me in a rush of immense sadness for a life that was no more. Was it I myself who had lived those intense, strenuous years, or was it a story I'd read of some other person? Had I really served the Lord? Why had there been so many deviations and unfulfilled opportunities? Why did I make so many wrong decisions? What had happened to all the others with whom I lived so closely?

Do other people feel this way when they look back on their lives? I don't hear them talking about it if they do.

The mission compound on the seafront looked outwardly much the same as before. A broad corniche with heavy traffic had been built. The two hospitals looked empty and silent. It hurt deeply to see them forlorn, as once they were built in such high hope, and for many years were so crowded and noisy with life.

At the back of the compound the church buildings—sanctuary, parish hall, and pastor's houses—were still in use, by permission of the government. Kuwait had gratefully given two and a quarter million dollars to our church for the property. This was a free gift, as no firm or foreign organization could own property in Kuwait. Sixteen congregations of expatriates used the buildings, for there were thousands of Christian workers from all over the world. The services were for Armenian and Greek Orthodox; Indian Christians speaking Urdu, Tamil, Telegu, and Malayalam; and sects from Egypt and Lebanon speaking Arabic. The large Roman Catholic group had a separate church a block away from our compound.

The Rev. Wayne and Gloria Antworth were living in the two-story evangelist's house, where I was their guest. The house where we single women had lived was now occupied by the Rev. Yusuf Abd en Nur and his family, who served the Arabic-speaking group. Dr. Lewis and Dorothy Scudder still lived in the house atop the hill where they had always been. Both worked at the Kuwait military hospital, he as staff physician and she as nursing superintendent. The nurses' home was used as a nursery school for children of English-speaking families.

Dr. Scudder looked tired and old, but Dotty still stayed busy. She had a gardener who kept the place beautiful with many colorful flower beds. Their trees had grown tall and green. Dotty and I spent most of Saturday picking and arranging twenty-two bouquets of flowers for Easter. The sunrise service was held on the hill, with almost three hundred attending. Afterward, we all went down to the space around the church, where a breakfast of eggs and hot cross buns was provided.

The mission had employed several Christian Arab families, originally from Turkey. We had hoped that since they were Kuwaiti citizens, they and their children would carry on the mission tradition. That seemed not to be the case. They had acquired position and wealth as Kuwait grew. But the deceitfulness of riches brought enmity and materialism.

I was invited to dinner by Amal (not her name), the youngest sister of one family, who had worked with me many years giving out drugs. She had no formal education but learned to read and write Arabic and English by herself. Amal told me she had been fortunate to marry a Christian Lebanese who came to work when Kuwait expanded. Thereby, she lost her Kuwaiti citizenship, because by that time Christians were not allowed to become citizens. She had a happy home and two lovely children. Their family was loyal and faithful to the Arabic church.

Several of the young Arab women who had been little girl patients of mine invited me to their grand new homes. Beautiful Ayisha (not her name), a daughter of a most aristocratic family, came for me in style, driving her own shiny Cadillac. She made no pretense of wearing any veil or abba and was dressed in a tailored suit that probably came from Paris. Her marriage to the son of another stately Kuwaiti family had seemed like an ideal romance—at first. They would never have met in Kuwait, where women are secluded and marriages are arranged, but both of them were sent to segregated schools in England. At some social event there they met and fell in love. They married with full family approval even though they had chosen each other.

Even that happy story did not prevent a distressing divorce. Ayisha took me up to her luxurious eighth-floor apartment overlooking the Gulf. Her whole life was bound up in her only child, a ten-year-old son. He arrived home from the American school and talked enthusiastically, in American idioms. He showed us his drawings and paintings. Ayisha said, "I intend to put him in Harvard when he's old enough." She evidently was lonely and tense. There could be no social life for her, as custom did not allow women to attend social functions outside the family. "My problem is how to manage my money. I don't know anything about finances. I don't know whom to trust. I need to manage my life by myself." Evidently, even great wealth did not bring satisfaction.

She had a gorgeous apartment and had gone personally to London to choose the furniture. She was especially proud of a twelve-foot-long Tudor table of one solid piece of oak. One entire wall was a vivid painting of a happy, bright, Egyptian wedding procession with flowers, birds, trees, and gardens. The bridal party was resplendent in rich mantles and embroidered cloaks, decked with golden jewelry and flashing gems.

I said to her, "Ayisha, you have become so much like us. Are you willing to talk over what Jesus Christ means?" But she changed the subject.

The lady Wusmeya Shashabad (not her name) invited me to a meal with her prominent family. She managed her car capably in the mad traffic. Her ancestors long ago came from Persia, yet she declared intensely, "Even if your family are here four hundred years, the Arabs refuse to call you a Kuwaiti." At home, her mother, who had been my friend as well as my patient, embraced me heartily. Her mother had come over for a visit and sat at the table as we talked over what had happened while we had been separated. Her many sons had gone to American universities and one had brought back an American bride. The girl had adjusted well to Arab family life.

Wusmeya's mother, Shaha, had long been the second wife, but now that the first wife and the husband had died, Shaha ruled the family. She proudly related how she arranged a noble bride for one of her sons through family connections in Iran. The girl was from the prestigious Bahtiara tribe.

They told me of a daughter whose husband had suddenly died not too long before. The young widow was now having intense pain from a slipped disk in her back and wanted to fly to California for surgery. The family felt they couldn't break with the old custom that a new widow must remain in the house four months. Custom was still inseparable from religion. So Bulua had to wait in great pain before she could get relief.

Shaha told how she had been ill and had been cured after prayer on one of her four pilgrimages to Mecca.

Shaha came over later for a more private visit with Dorothy Scudder and me. She had a fund of witty, humorous stories and gossip about the prominent families. She spent a couple of hours laughing with us, telling how other families were coping with the changes. It was partly innocent gossip, but as the old joke goes, what else can you do with it?

The Scudders and I visited Abbas' large new house in the new suburbs. It had a tiled courtyard and a wall around the house. We sat down in the large family room to talk with Munera. She was Abbas' one and only wife and mother to his eighteen children, of whom fifteen survived. Only three were boys. The family was a close unit, sufficient to itself, and visited only with close relatives. Twelve bright and healthy daughters attended the public schools and were preparing to be teachers. But one son had caught a glimpse of a neighboring girl and decided to marry her against his parents' wishes. They regarded her family as beneath theirs and forbade him to ever return to the family circle. The girls were more submissive and agreed to marry the men arranged for them. One girl wanted to study medicine.

Mohammad Qabazard and Mumtaz had built a grand mansion in the new suburbs. He brought masons from Isfahan to decorate the exterior with copies of tiles from the famous Persian mosques, and surrounded it with a Persian garden. They invited us to a delicious dinner. Most of their five sons were attending universities in the U.S., but Ismahan, the youngest girl, was still at home. The furniture was the best obtainable from England; there were priceless Persian carpets, and oil paintings. Mohammad had built one typical Persian room where the ceiling and walls were decorated like the shah's palace. Stained-glass windows were set in plaster, mats and cushions stood around the walls, and the ceiling design was a copy of a carpet. He told us how he and Mumtaz had traveled around the world. He took a picture of us in the gorgeous room with a wide-angle lens.

Dorothy Scudder and I drove over to the old walled Christian cemetery, now in the Al-Ghanum General Motors complex. It was no longer used and was unkempt and dirty. Dr. Mylrea's headstone, and others, had been piled against the walls. Dr. Gerald Nykerk's grave was in the new Christian cemetery out in the desert. The cemetery reflected the large expatriate population. Roman Catholic graves were laid out on one side, the Protestants on the other. Now Dr. Scudder lies there, too.

Dr. and Mrs. Adolph had worked with us in the hospital for many years—he as physician and she as head nurse. They invited me to a delicious curry dinner. After our hospital closed, he decided to go into private practice but found it very frustrating. The rules of medical practice forbade doctors to store or dispense any drugs in their offices. All drugs had to be purchased at the drug stores, which often did not carry complete stock and were very inconvenient for the patients. The biggest problem was what to do in emergencies if drugs were not easily accessible.

Sharifa (not her name) was a teenager when I first knew her. She never was a beauty, but she had a strong, dominant personality. Sharifa gloried in being the daughter of a prominent Turkish gentleman who had emigrated to Kuwait. She had survived several marriages, had five sets of twins and at least fifteen children in all. Several sons and three daughters with all their children lived together in one large three-story house in a new suburb. Now Sharifa was the mother superior and controlled her household with a raucous, bellowing voice. Actually she was a loving, affectionate person. Her esteem was gratifying to me but embarrassing when she praised me loudly and heartily for the medical help I gave.

Sharifa also invited me to a dinner. I arrived to find her in the reception room, sitting on the floor surrounded by her great tribe of daughters, grandchildren, and one son who had studied in the U.S.A. The TV was squawking, but Sharifa's voice surged above it, and she welcomed me vigorously with a kiss and sang my praise to her entire family.

The extended-family lifestyle of the Arabs was warm and cozy. Each one had his or her place. The men came and went, and the children attended schools, but there was always a group of women at home. They took care of the babies, small children, and numerous servant women.

For dinner that day, twelve of us sat down on chairs at a broad table loaded with a vast array of delicious dishes. Afterward, we gathered again on the cushions and Sharifa told of the accomplishments of her numerous family. She generously pressed gifts on me—a gorgeous robe of black chiffon embroidered with gold thread and gold sequins. This garment is to be draped over a dress and gracefully fall from the head to the floor. She also gave me a brass coffee pot, the symbol of Arab hospitality. Sharifa's son drove me back to the mission, expressing his appreciation of his mother as he drove. He seemed so friendly to me because his mother rated me so highly, I think.

Dorothy Scudder and I drove out to the American embassy, where Bill and Janet Stolzfus were in charge. Bill came from the family who had started the mission and university in Beirut. They had been very friendly and always attended the English church services; Janet had some of her babies in our hospital. Now Janet was much concerned with security. They always left the compound at irregular times and took irregular routes. They would accept invitations from the Arabs but did not attend any functions, as it was not considered safe.

I also had lunch with the Egyptian minister and his family, who were living in my old house. He was much concerned about his children. He had put them in the Roman Catholic school, but it was forbidden to teach Christianity there. The local condemnation of any Christian service was a heavy pressure. Every now and then the church would receive an order to vacate the mission property. The order would be rescinded through influential friends, but we all knew that eventually the church would have to find a new location.

It had been a nostalgic but happy visit back to my old home.

Later in 1973, I had the opportunity to attend the International Leprosy Conference in Bergen, Norway, and to stop over in Europe with many friends from my years in the Gulf. In December, I again traveled—to Salalah, Oman, this time. The mountain people nearby were fighting the Omani government, and the British had established a large encampment. There was also a contingent of Iranian soldiers to help the young Sultan Qaboos. The war was demanding most of Oman's oil income, which was sad, because Oman did not have much oil.

I got in some rounds at the hospital in Salalah and a walk along the seafront and past the bare outer walls of the old sultan's favorite palace. It was here that he held his own son under house arrest for many years.

I returned to Muscat in a plane of the Sultan's air force, flown by British pilots—just in time for Christmas at the mission. It was an exciting season, starting with the church rummage sale held by the mission and the embassy and oil company wives. One of the new women came wearing such brief clothes that the others said to me, "You ought to advise her how the local people disapprove." So I did. She muttered, "Stiff old missionary."

Other than the rummage sale, we put up a real tree from Cyprus in the church, held a special dinner for the twenty-five leprosy patients, and threw a party for fifty Arab Christians and their families. We also practiced music—"Night of Miracles"—but Don Bosch asked me not to sing, because I put the others off key! Nonetheless, the British embassy invited all of us to come sing Christmas carols and attend their traditional midnight service on Christmas Eve.

Dr. Harvey and Margaret Doorenbos invited us to a holiday turkey dinner. Their two sons Dirk and Keith were home from Kodaikanal school in India. Harvey was now Chief Medical Officer for our hospital, as Dr. Donald Bosch had been asked by the government to take charge of their new surgical hospital in the new town of Ruwi.

In the midst of all the fun, a young Peace Corps volunteer had a serious motorcycle accident and was brought for Harvey's care. The boy had a compound fracture of the femur, a ruptured spleen, cracked ribs, and a bleeding stomach ulcer. The other Peace Corps members lined up to give blood. They couldn't eat the hospital food, so we helped by feeding them ourselves. He finally recovered.

MY LAST YEAR

In January, the Muslim feast of the pilgrimage to Mecca came due. The staff were entitled to take off six days, so we had to scramble to keep the hospital running, although there were fewer patients.

One of our local staff members, a Christian, was caught by one of the Indian nurses giving himself an injection of Demerol with Hyalase. We felt we had to discharge him. It was the first case of drug abuse in our staff. Somehow we didn't succeed in imprinting a Christian character in converts.

A group of religious leaders from Saudi Arabia came to inspect our hospital, now subsidized by the government. They disapproved of the beautiful Persian wall tiles inscribed with the words of Christ. Dr. Bosch had gone to Iran to have them made and had put them up with great care. The mullahs demanded that they be removed, so we had to. They also criticized the wall hanging with Christian tracts in Arabic.

For me, 1974 began with the realization that it would be my final year of active medical work. Would I have any mission afterward? I'd enjoyed every other place where I lived and always found interesting work, so I didn't worry much. I looked forward to living in Plymouth Village in Redlands, California. I had visited my college friend, Cunera Van Emerick, there in June 1971 and registered my name for one of the new apartments in a ground-level four-plex house. Cunera had died suddenly, but I had met other friendly people there. There was a church of our Reformed denomination near. My brother had paid the building cost from my inherited funds. So I anticipated a new adventure and trusted there would be a mission, too. The Lord had given me good health, so I was determined to enjoy my last year in the mission.

Returning from a beach party one afternoon, the police stopped our car, saying there was a big fire in Mutrah. Sure enough, a huge, black cloud was billowing up between the hills. As soon as we could we drove in to see the desolate scene. A large area of datestick homes across the street from our hospital was flat. There were only smoking black ashes and the smell of charred embers. About eighty families had rushed out and were squatting, disconsolate, in the mission grounds. Some had grabbed sleeping mats, clothes, odd pots, and pans. Others were sitting silent and anxious on a few tin trunks. No one was burned, but they were suddenly bereft of their meager treasures, their shelter, and privacy. Our first thought was, what can we do? Nurse Mary Sanggaard of the Danish mission suggested, "Let's give them our cold water." They stretched on the ground to sleep. I don't know how they managed the toilet problem. As the mountains were near, they probably had one area for men and another for women.

The next day, the government sent lorries with tents and set them up in the mission ground. They sent food, too, which our hospital cook prepared. After three days the government took all the people away, saying they would be given a place in the new city. The burned area was outside the ruined old city wall. None of the people owned the land legally. The area was needed for growing businesses, banks, and government buildings. It was possible that the fire was sabotage, but fire was common in an area of datestick huts.

British visitors told us of the progress Oman was making. New oil wells had been found. The national income had increased to $100 million per year. Even so, the defense department was buying a fleet of twelve Jaguar fighter planes at $9 million each and had to borrow the whole next year's income. The American consulate rated Oman as one of the most expensive places for expatriates in the world. Of course, we didn't live in the expatriate style. We shopped at the new supermarkets, but we did our own cooking. The rebellion of the mountain tribes instigated by the Communists of Aden was finally cooling. Some thousand Pakistanis were imported to work in the oasis of Salalah on the southern coast. They got very small pay and no medical treatment.

The government had opened ten new hospitals in villages but found staffing them difficult. All the staff had to come from foreign countries, because there were so few trained Omani medical personnel. The man in charge of the state's medical work, Dr. Asim Jamali, was Omani but Russian-educated. Many other high posts were filled by British and Indian expatriates.

It seemed that all of a sudden many Lebanese and Palestinians came to Oman to open modern shops and delightful restaurants. Then just as suddenly we heard they were arrested and ordered to leave because they didn't have the proper work permits.

Sultan Qaboos donated some new land for churches in the new city, Ruwi, that the government was building just beyond Mutrah. Half the property would go to Catholics, the other half to Protestants, and the donation included a small cemetery where foreigners had been buried. The sultan was friendly because he appreciated living in the home of an Anglican priest while he was studying in England. He invited the minister and his wife to be his guests and built them a house on the seafront in Oman.

At the ground-breaking ceremony for the new church, the mission people helped dig the first spadefuls. So I hoped that the medical and church work would go on after I had left.

That last year in Oman, a nice, lonesome British agent about to retire flattered me with his attentions. But marriage had long been unattractive to me, so I bade him farewell.

Things were already changing, even before I left. Nineteen hundred and seventy-four was an easier year at the hospital. Our clinics got smaller as the new government hospitals took on some of the medical burden. We began to have a little free time, for once; and new roads had been built to the interior, so we could more easily take the Land Rover to see the villages.

Oman's mountains are high—6,000 to 10,000 feet—enough to catch the monsoon rains, which are absorbed in the porous volcanic rock. The mountains are said to be 30 million years old. The water comes out in wells and springs. The Persians who controlled Oman in the first centuries A.D. conveyed the abundant water by channels from the springs to places where there was enough level soil to raise crops. Sometimes these channels ran in underground canals along the foot of the mountain. They had ingenious inverted siphons at places, where the canals might be washed away by sudden gushes of rainwater. Many of the channels, called *falajes* in Arabic, ran underground for as much as twenty miles. Every hundred feet an open pit to the channel allowed inspection of the water flow. It must have taken great skill to dig the canals by hand and adjust them so the flow of water would be exactly correct and last for two thousand years. The system is still in use today.

Once in Nizwa a man showed me how today's Omanis divide the water flowing in the canals. They had a tall, upright stone with lines drawn in the ground around it like lines of a sundial. They regulated the flow by the shadow so each man's garden received an equal share. He said that at night they go by the stars.

Once we traveled north on the coastal plain, past many green gardens and towns watered by wells. A hundred miles north we came to the town of Sohar. In the tenth century, Sohar was a great city with many fine buildings. A large mosque built at the time of Mohammad still stands.

Another time, the historical society made a trip to Sur, a city two hundred miles south of Muscat. We drove to the ruins of the city Qalhat, which still has traces of former grandeur. No archaeologists have worked on it, so the ground is full of small treasures which were picked up by some of the visitors. It was described in the Middle Ages as being one of the most beautiful cities in the world. Some buildings are still standing.

In the eighth century, eight hundred years before Columbus, sailors from these ports sailed to Canton, China, and returned. Abu Ubayda was the first captain of these voyages. The seashore along these ports still has broken bits of the blue and white Chinese pottery the seagoing traders used to carry.

In the flat surfaces of the rocky mountains we saw many places where the ancients had pecked out pictures called petroglyphs. The pictures were stick men, animals, and letters of some old language. Other places, there were large dome-like graves said to be four thousand years old.

The archaeologists had found evidence of ancient copper mines. The present government was anxious to develop any area of income in case the oil decreased, so they employed an American mining firm to study the prospect. Paul Bosch, the son of our Dr. Bosch, had studied geology and was one of the group. They found enough evidence to begin mining in a small way.

Archaeologists think there must have been much more water in Arabia thirty thousand years ago, because they find traces of ancient man at that time. One time on a later visit to the province of Dhofar on the southern coast of Arabia, I was visiting the Staals. We drove up to the mountains north of the green oasis. We came to a ridge above a depression that looked as if it might have been a lake. On the highest ridge, we found thousands of chipped flint tools, evidence of fireplaces, and mounds of stones which looked like graves to my untutored eyes. The area was also littered with black stones which looked like they had been blown from a volcano.

We also came to some frankincense trees. The branches, when broken, ooze a resin that forms sweet incense. Herodotus wrote that not less than two and a half tons of frankincense were burned every year in a single temple of Baal at Babylon. Frankincense grows only in Dhofar and Somaliland. I read somewhere that the Catholic Church now uses an artificial incense rather than natural frankincense.

RETURN TO DAHANU ROAD

For my six-weeks vacation that year, I went to Kashmir, India, with Anne De Young. We rented a houseboat and took full advantage of local sightseeing, with side trips by bus, car, and on horseback to some of the places I had seen when I lived in India.

On the way back to Oman, Anne and I stopped over in Bombay—for longer than we had planned, because of a two-week airplane strike.

Bombay had changed from my memories of thirty-five years before, when I lived there for several months. Now there seemed to be a hundred new high rise buildings. Beggars still filled the streets at all hours, attached themselves to any tourist, and stuck like glue until one paid them off from embarrassment.

We took the sightseeing trips. Crawford Market, the large covered trading market, still looked the same. Small retail salespeople sold everything: flowers, fruits, vegetables, meat, fish, novelties of all sorts, and caged birds. We wandered through the crowded streets and tried the restaurants.

One day I suggested that we take the BBCI railroad up to Dahanu Road, where I had worked with the mission hospital. The trip took only two hours. Then, what a thrill it was to walk the short distance to the hospital! The house where Nurse Hazel Messer and I lived still stood, and the hospital looked the way it used to. Inside, we asked what had happened to Dr. Peter Paul and how we could find him. A young man came up and introduced himself as Steven, Dr. Peter's son. He would take us to his father's house.

Dr. Peter had retired, so he and Shantbai had found a small house at the edge of the town. What a thrill to meet again and find that we were still the same spirits. Shantbai said, "Don't you remember Steven? You delivered him when you were here." We sat down to talk about the old days, since we had not corresponded. We recalled our cholera cases, strenuous surgeries, all the tragedies, and the death of Tarak from malaria. Why did it give me such a heart pain to remember those days? Would I want to live them over again? I don't remember that I was particularly happy then. But I remembered the joy of friendly companionship, of feeling I had a responsible, serious duty to carry out. I felt some success and some regrets, too.

Dr. Peter's humble little home had only the absolutely necessary furniture. Dr. Peter was short and rather round now. Some arthritis made him stiff, and Shantbai limped from an old fracture of the hip. They wanted to talk of their children. One son had become a doctor, Steven worked in the hospital, and a daughter had gone to live in New Jersey. The government had taken over the hospital. The church was still there and fairly well-attended. Hazel Messer, the nurse, had married and settled in Ohio. We recalled the Parsee friends and their gardens.

They generously shared their scanty noon meal of rice and dhal. He said they received a small pension from the Church in America. It hurt me to think how very small it must be. Dr. Peter accompanied us back to get the evening train. It was packed, standing room only—all I could find for a seat was a tin trunk tied with hard ropes.

In Bombay, a visiting mission doctor from the provinces shared our rooms. He told us that he had witnessed an epidemic of smallpox in which at least 50,000 Indians had died. The government sent vaccine and vaccinators, all free, but the operators couldn't resist asking a rupee from each. The people couldn't see the need for vaccination, feared the wrath of the gods, and were not willing to pay. So the plague spread and killed many. It must have been the world's last epidemic of smallpox, for I read later that there was not a single case of it again in the whole world.

CHOLERA EPIDEMIC

Anne and I arrived back in Oman to find a cholera epidemic had struck. I was on duty because it was Friday, when the Muslim staff want the day off. I admitted ten patients with the water diarrhea characteristic of cholera. One was a man fasting because it was Ramadan. He had gone out fishing. He got sick, managed to reach the shore, and was brought to us. He died before we could start fluids. Another old man living in a shack on the seafront reached a telephone and called us for an ambulance, because the taxi driver refused to take the messy case. Our ambulance was out of order as usual, so Jim Dunham went to find him. We succeeded in curing him. Can you imagine what a thrill it was to save lives all day?

The government asked us to vaccinate the entire population of the two cities and provided vaccine. Radio directed the people to come. So we set up tables and equipment in the mission yard for the crowds. The last figure of vaccinations I heard was 12,000. Then we lost count.

The daily clinics were very demanding on my return, because the other doctors then took their vacations. One wife, whose husband had been away for almost a year, came in four months pregnant. Another woman from an Omani island was brought in by her brothers. She was a widow, and eight months pregnant. In these cases, and in cases of young unmarried women unfortunate enough to get pregnant, it is said that within the family the men's duty is to kill the woman. I felt guilty not to prevent this fate by performing an abortion. And in these cases, I must admit, I passed responsibility over to the doctor at the Muscat hospital. I never heard how she solved the problem.

I did only one operation of that sort, but that was different. A psychiatrist stated that an elderly American woman could not go through with a pregnancy, then in the early stages. I still feel guilty about that.

The saddest case I remember from this period was an Indian girl, brought over to be the wife of a young Omani. Local custom ruled that men give quite generous dowries for their brides. Some who couldn't afford dowries sent to India, where fathers were willing to sell their daughters. One young bride brought to Oman this way was so unhappy with her life that she poured kerosene over herself and lit a match. She was completely burned except for her face. I saw her when they brought her in and ordered them to take her to the new military hospital. She died in three days. The young husband was shocked. The girl had been begging him to send her back to India, but he refused. She didn't know, of course, that there was an Indian ambassador in the town who could have helped her. She didn't know the language and had no one to talk with, so she preferred death to such a life.

TURNOVER

Finally, the day came that the mission turned over the hospital, with all its equipment, and its management, to the government of Oman. To commemorate the occasion, I wrote a history of the mission's medical work in Oman for all the new people and expatriates who knew nothing about its background. The Mission Board liked it well enough to print it in their monthly report.

One perfect Sunday at the end of January 1975, I began to feel sorry to consider leaving Oman. So I decided to enjoy the seafront alone, walking and thinking. There was no one else on the sandy shore north of Mutrah that day. A brisk, cool wind blew the clouds, and the sea was a gorgeous, deep blue with waves and white caps at low tide. The sand was full of beautiful shells and purple sand dollars. A large flock of gulls held a convention aloft, watching me. The agile sandpipers darted about, busy getting lunch. To the west ran the graceful sand dunes and on the horizon, the mountain range drew curved lines. I walked for hours but never felt lonely. It always seemed there was someone with me. It was all so natural—all except the men and machines building the new grand seaside hotels for tourists who would come to enjoy the sight in years to come.

The Danish nurse, Mary Sanggaard, and I kept on cooking and eating in Anne De Young's apartment. Anne came back from her hospital in Sur to tell us of the changes there. My days were filled with clinics and inpatients, as always. Evenings were taken up with dinner parties where we who were about to resign our authority could meet those from abroad who would now guide the state.

There was a general feeling of progress and cheer—everything was improving. Smiles, bustling hurry, new cars, and machines enhanced the feeling that everything was getting better and better. Suddenly color television appeared, with viewing boxes placed by the government in various places about town. Crowds of men gathered around each evening to gape at the color programs. Unfortunately, it was mostly cartoons and Wild West films. We heard that the whole array of TV equipment had been flown in from abroad.

We often went for walks through the shopping area down to the seashore, where there had always been a dirt road. The water's edge had been the town dump, dirty and smelly. Suddenly an artistic two-way, paved corniche appeared, with a walk for pedestrians. Just as suddenly, the bay was full of engines, machine ships, cranes, and men busy building Port Qaboos, which was to have six berths for ocean vessels. The roaring, blasting, explosions, and grinding went on unceasingly. The shore was covered for acres with concrete structures like knees, with three legs that would interlock for the new jetties. All at once the old picturesque bay was gone, and a modern harbor appeared in its place. This was too wonderful for me. I didn't like it at all. But I was getting out of date.

Human error appeared, too. One morning the sea was covered with a black, oily scum which invaded every lovely cove and left a black line on every enclosing rocky mountain. Some engineer in charge of the pipes running oil to the tankers at sea had forgotten to turn off the faucet.

In the sister city of Muscat, the whole old area of small shops was razed to make room for a new royal palace on the seafront. There were three buildings with pillared walls made to look like date palms. The flat roof for helicopter landings had a decorated border of blocks, each with a floral brass design. The town took on the air of a capital city of leisure, power, and aristocracy. Abruptly a grand, white mosque and minaret with large, arched windows arose beside the palace. When lit at night the window decorations and chandeliers looked like fairy lace.

In the countryside and the smaller villages, there were dramatic changes, too. On the way to Sohar, a hundred miles north of Mutrah, I encountered a British agriculturalist appointed by the government. The government was concerned about the amount of water that the local farmers were now using. Their wells were turning salty. They were using gasoline pumps instead of the old manual methods. No records had been kept of how much water was available in the past, so there was no way to know how fast the depletion was really occurring.

In another location, Oman had constructed a new international airport; and in Sohar, the medieval port city, a new hospital had been created and staffed by the government. The Peace Corps volunteers there criticized our holding Christian church services in a Muslim country. Strangely, it seemed that the rest of the world did not agree with my way of thinking.

The first two months of 1975 I worked in the hospital clinic with the usual procedure—treatment comes first, you make the diagnosis later, if ever. I asked a small school girl one day, "What are you going to be when you grow up? A teacher?" Her luminous black eyes rose admiringly as she answered, "No, I want to be a doctor."

The Book of Ecclesiastes says, "To everything there is a season and a time for every purpose under the heaven." I decided that it was time for me to change my ministry. The government now took over the complete management of the hospital. A new Indian lady physician was assigned to the Arrahma hospital, so I felt free for other interests.

My call to ministry, I felt, was from God to follow Christ. He was willing to live humbly for most of His life, so I felt it worthwhile to do some ordinary jobs as well as the exalted one of a medical doctor, and it was well with my soul.

In Mutrah, the mission retained the small chapel and one two-story house with a garden. The other people who helped us were leaving. Les and Joyce Kelly, who retired from Aramco, came to help us with maintenance for two years and now moved out of their apartment. Les said his friends in Saudi ignored them after he joined our side. Mary Sanggaard was moving to Bahrain to work in our hospital there. The Bosches and Anne De Young had moved their belongings to their new places. Three houses and two storerooms were full of mission furniture and equipment, so I set out to empty the rooms, sort the stuff, and send it where we could use it. It is one of the prosaic mission chores, but it took me a whole month.

One day Mary Sanggaard and I took a walk over the old mountain trail from Ruwi, which the Omanis used before there was a road between Muscat and Mutrah. It had long been used by men with donkeys to haul loads and had steep steps which were crumbling but well-marked. Rains had filled the pools, and some green plants bordered the water; so it was picturesque. That day we heard some singing and were surprised to come around a spur and see a group of about twenty Arab men who apparently had just come up to enjoy themselves with their music. Funny, I never thought of them doing such a thing.

Another day, I drove the car out to a little village ten miles away off the main road. I'd always been so confined to the hospital that I never had time to sit down with women who weren't sick and just visit. So I spent the whole morning sitting down beside a house and talking with some women. It was such a pleasure that I wished I could have done more of it.

John Buteyn, the Arabian Mission secretary, and four American ministers came for a visit to study the new situation in Oman. We provided entertainment, food, and transport for them and then had three evenings of station meetings when we all talked until late.

In the future, Muscat mission property would consist of the compound with its two-story house and large open area, the old chapel, the school building with a mission apartment upstairs, and our cemetery.

The main mission area would be located in the new town of Ruwi, with a bookshop and the new church building. The mission would supervise the building of auxiliary rooms for the church and the building of a house for the minister. Five congregations of expatriates would use the building. Our church would send out a short-term clergyman for the English services. Our two nurses would work, at their mission salary, for the government's new village hospitals.

The Omani Christian families, whose men had been nurses in our Mutrah hospital, stopped coming to church. The men had been advanced to administrative positions in the government hospital with greatly increased salaries. The social pressure to desist from Christianity was too difficult for these families to oppose. One day I went over to Hajer's house and sat down on the floor in her courtyard to talk about the church. She straightened up and with a hostile air said, "You missionaries don't know what it is to stay and live here. You come for a while and then pack up and go back to your country where life is easy." She struck home with me—it hurt. Could I follow Christ if I had to stand alone and confront an antagonistic society? I wasn't too sure I could.

I screwed up my courage and made a farewell call on the men in charge of the Ministry of Health. I went to their offices in their impressive new building. They were surprised to learn that I had worked the four years in Oman without a salary and expressed kind words of appreciation for my service. (Actually, I lived economically on about $150 per month.) The health officials talked about the difficulties they faced in the development of medicine for Oman. When I suggested that they ask Jesus Christ to help them, they responded with a surprised silence.

Just before I left Oman, one of the British women interviewed me for an article in Bahrain's English newspaper. "It's Forty Years of Gulf Medicine for Dr. Mary," the headline read. I also had my last birthday party, inviting all of us single mission girls to an evening dinner at a Lebanese garden restaurant. For the occasion, I made placecards with a cartoon showing a sad-looking caterpillar saying, "I'm just an old caterpillar after all. All the talk of butterflies will *never* come true."

After a round of farewell parties, I packed my belongings for the trip home. The Omani government paid my airfare to Redlands, California, where I planned to retire, but my ticket allowed many stops. So I made one last trip to Bahrain; Amman, Jordan; and to various cities in Europe.

In Bahrain, which felt like home, the station made me welcome with invitations to dinners, teas, and garden parties. Our hospital was the only one of the mission to keep running, because the ruler, Shaikh Isa, so strongly expressed his desire to keep it when John Buteyn came out from New York intending to close all the mission hospitals. I felt that the U.S. church office, consisting mostly of clergymen, was antagonistic to mission medical work. Perhaps they felt they lacked control over physicians. Yet Christ sent His disciples out with the command to heal the sick as well as to preach the Gospel. When direct evangelism is impossible, as in Muslim countries, medical work has traditionally been an acceptable contact. The Arabian Mission abandoned its mandate to engage Islam directly. From that time on, its main occupation would be to minister to the expatriate population.

At last I boarded the flight which took me away from Arabia.

After so many fond reunions with friends and colleagues in Bahrain, it broke my heart to say good-bye.

On the final flight from London to New York, I happened to sit beside an Arab whom I had known in Kuwait. He was most kind and said, "We Kuwaitis are grateful for what you did for us, but more than anything else we appreciate the fact that you came and lived with us."

Statistics and Hospital Data

ANNUAL REPORTS OF THE KUWAIT WOMEN'S HOSPITAL
TO THE MISSION BOARD IN NEW YORK

1937

Clinic patients	31,879	Inpatients	118
Vaccinations	1,103	Maternity cases	37
Teeth extracted	280	Surgery	328
Outcalls	220		

1938

Clinic patients	31,672	Baby cases	37
Inpatients	103	Surgery	96
House calls	146		

1939

Clinic patients	33,149	Baby cases	40
Inpatients	188	Surgery	212
House calls	347		

(New hospital—gift of the Bacenstos family—34 beds)

1940

Clinic patients	30,042	Baby cases	53
Inpatients	251	Surgery	158
House calls	224		

(Dr. Ruth Crouse was in charge of the women's medical work from 1941 to 1945 while I was away in India and America. I haven't any of her records.)

1947

Clinic patients	26,825	Eye surgery	142
Inpatients	465	General surgery	181
Baby cases	120		

1948

Clinic patients	21,000	Baby cases	110
Inpatients	432	Eye surgery	75
House calls	55	General surgery	100

1949

Clinic patients	19,000	Eye surgery	55
Inpatients	430	Minor surgery	95
Baby cases	140	Major surgery	24

1952

Clinic patients	32,282	Obstetrics	105
Inpatients	515	Surgery	172

1953

Clinic patients	25,500	Baby cases	194
Inpatients	756	Eye surgery	56
House calls	125	General surgery	154

1955

Clinic patients	27,584	Eye surgery	59
Inpatients	1,196	Minor surgery	279
House calls	131	Major surgery	54
Baby cases	305		

1959

Clinic patients	40,830	Obstetrics	398
Inpatients	1,581	Calls	160

(Surgery done at men's OR) *See Men's Hospital statistics*

1960

Clinic patients	43,852	Obstetrics	456
Inpatients	1,786	Surgery	1,710
Outcalls	118	(major and minor)	

1961

Clinic patients	36,308	Obstetrics	504
Inpatients	1,848	Surgery	2,084
Outcalls	135	(major and minor)	

KUWAIT MEN'S HOSPITAL, 1960

Outpatients	71,333	Outcalls	381
Inpatients	1,381		

KUWAIT MEN'S HOSPITAL, 1961

Outpatients	62,888	Outcalls	308
Inpatients	1,130		

AMERICAN MISSION HOSPITAL—KUWAIT

STATISTICS: SEPTEMBER 15, 1961—AUGUST 31, 1962

Men's Hospital

New cases (outpatients)	20,530	Inpatient hospital days	11,632
Old cases (outpatients)	42,263	Outcalls	283
Inpatients	1,403		

Women's Hospital

New cases (outpatients)	18,821	X-rays	6,789
Old cases (outpatients)	25,197	Fluoroscopies	257
Inpatients	2,231	Plaster casts	75
Inpatient hospital days	9,057	Electrocardiograms	173
Outcalls	95	BMR	16

Obstetrical Record

Normal deliveries	552	D&C's of incomplete	
Forceps	67	miscarriages	2
Breech	10	Premature	3
Twins	2	Total	646
Caesarian	10		

OR Record Combined

(Surgical record for both men's and women's hospitals)

Appendectomy	70	Skin graft	7
Caesarian section	10	Gastric resection	5
Herniorrhaphy	111	Miscellaneous major	86
Oophorectomy	5	Total major	294

Cauterizations	99	Hemorrhoidectomy	126
Circumcisions	386	Incision and Drainage	377
Cysts	46	Suturing	100
D&C	201	Tonsillectomy	83
D&C with T.I.	37	Miscellaneous Minor	133
T.I. (tubal insufflation)	95	Total minor	1,707
Fistulectomy	24		

Eye operations—total	121
Total surgical procedures	2,122

STATISTICS FOR KUWAIT MISSION HOSPITALS, 1964

Men's outpatients	44,427	Men inpatients	1,268
Women's outpatients	27,183	Women inpatients	2,482

X-ray exams	9,150	Obstetrical deliveries	691
Minor surgery	1,551	Dilatation and curettage	147
Major surgery	251		

BAHRAIN ATTENDANCE RECORDS FOR ELEVEN MONTHS OF 1969

Total outpatients	30,094	Inpatient charity cases	90
Total inpatients	1,683	Deaths	18
Outpatient charity cases	2,263	Newborns	272

OMAN: AMERICAN MISSION HOSPITALS—STATISTICS, JUNE 1 TO DEC. 31, 1971

MUTRAH GENERAL HOSPITAL

Total outpatients seen	111,330		
Total inpatients	3,629		
General surgery	426	Intercostal drainage	3
Genitourinary	1,309	Eye surgery	1,192
Orthopedic	86	Cataract (123)	
Gynecology	112	X-ray	4,796
Vesico-vaginal		Laboratory tests, total	20,680
fistula repair	(8)	Leprosy hospital	
Plastic	84	average daily census	27
ENT	59	Tuberculosis hospital	
Arterial reconstruction	1	total admissions	166

MUSCAT OBSTETRICAL HOSPITAL, ASSAADA

Total number of inpatients	4,693	CS	82
Total deliveries	4,005	(performed at Mutrah hospital)	
D & C	184		

MUTRAH, OMAN: HOSPITAL STATISTICS, 1973

2 U.S.A. physicians   4 Indian physicians

Admissions, general hospital
Medical (including pediatrics)   1,788
Surgical (including pediatrics)   1,187

Total admissions   2,975

Average daily census 75
Hospital bed capacity 77
Total deaths in hospital 265
Leprosy hospital new
 admissions 11
Average daily census 19
Tuberculosis hospital
 new admissions 123
Average daily census 235
Total outpatients 101,606

Average number of
 pts./day 330
Total operations in
 operating theater 1,370
6 months (July–Dec.)
 total operations in
 emergency room 830
Total circumcisions
 (done by Qumber) 1,104
C-sections (Doorenbos) 96
Ruptured uterus 3

MUSCAT, OMAN: ASSAADA HOSPITAL STATISTICS, 1973

Total admissions 5,764
Total number of deliveries
 in the hospital 5,077
Average daily census 47
Hospital bed capacity 44
Total outpatients 83,698